Negotiation Excellence

Successful Deal Making

Negotiation
Excellence
Successful Deal Making

Editor

Michael Benoliel
Singapore Management University, Singapore

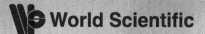
NEW JERSEY · LONDON · SINGAPORE · BEIJING · SHANGHAI · HONG KONG · TAIPEI · CHENNAI

Published by

World Scientific Publishing Co. Pte. Ltd.

5 Toh Tuck Link, Singapore 596224

USA office: 27 Warren Street, Suite 401-402, Hackensack, NJ 07601

UK office: 57 Shelton Street, Covent Garden, London WC2H 9HE

British Library Cataloguing-in-Publication Data
A catalogue record for this book is available from the British Library.

NEGOTIATION EXCELLENCE
Successful Deal Making

ISBN-13 978-981-4343-16-9
ISBN-10 981-4343-16-1

Typeset by Stallion Press
Email: enquiries@stallionpress.com

Printed in Singapore by World Scientific Printers.

To Talia Benoliel,
my daughter

Contents

Acknowledgements

A book like this cannot be put together without the cooperation and support of many. First on my list of people to thank has to be the authors who have presented the most important foundations in the field of negotiation. Their contributions will undoubtedly be appreciated by the readers.

This book will not be possible also without the support of my colleagues at the Lee Kong Chian School of Business. In particular, I would like to thank Adel Dimian, Don Ferrin, Gary Greguras, Gregor Halff, Thomas Menkhoff, Layne Paddock, and David Wagner. I wish also to acknowledge Howard Thomas, Dean, Francis Koh, Associate Dean, Sharon Tan, Director of Advancement and Kirpal Singh, Director of the Wee Kim Wee Center for supporting the launch of the book at the Singapore Management University.

Many thanks are due also to the wonderful staff at World Scientific Publishing: Dr. Lim Tai Wei, Acquisition Editor for encouraging me to edit the book; Ms. Alisha Nguyen, my most patient and talented Book Editor; Senior Marketing Executive Ms. Lee Hooi Yean, for her special interest in the book; and Artist Jimmy Low for designing the attractive book cover. Special thanks also to our independent editor, Ms. Amrit Kaur for editing the works of several authors.

Finally, I wish thank all my family members for their support and encouragement.

Michael Benoliel

About the Contributors

Christopher K. Adair is a doctoral student in Industrial-Organizational Psychology at DePaul University in Chicago. His research interests include work-team composition, personality, and workplace motivation. He received his B.A. in Psychology from Saint Louis University and his M.A. in Industrial-Organizational Psychology from DePaul University.

Wendi L. Adair (Ph.D., Northwestern University) is Associate Professor of Organizational Psychology at the University of Waterloo (Ontario, Canada). Her research on cross-cultural negotiation has examined how communication norms, negotiator schemas, strategy sequences, and nonverbal behavior impact negotiation outcome. She also studies conflict, communication, and emergent culture in multicultural teams.

Ariel C. Avgar is an Assistant Professor at the School of Labor and Employment Relations at the University of Illinois. He is also the assistant director for research at the Cornell University Scheinman Institute on Conflict Resolution. Dr. Avgar's research focuses on conflict and conflict resolution in organizations. His current research examines the relationship between work restructuring, conflict and conflict management in healthcare organizations.

William P. Bottom is the Wood Distinguished Professor at Olin Business School of Washington University where he studies bargaining, negotiation and group decision making. His research, supported by grants from the Russell Sage Foundation and the National Science Foundation, has appeared in such journals as *Organization Science* and the *Journal of Conflict Resolution*.

Graham Brown (Ph.D., University of British Columbia) is currently an Assistant Professor in the Faculty of Management at the University of British Columbia. Graham's primary research area is territoriality with a specific focus on employee's claiming of territories in organizations and how people mark and defend these territories vis-à-vis their coworkers. His most recent work explores how employees react when a coworker or supervisor infringes on their territory, and shows that people respond in a variety of ways from directly confronting the infringer to avoiding working with, or even sabotaging, the infringer or their work. Graham's research on territoriality has been published in a wide range of outlets including the *Academy of Management Review*, *Organization Science*, and *Organizational Behavior and Human Decision Processes*. Currently, Graham is applying territoriality to a variety of essential organizational issues including leadership succession and transition, change, and creativity.

Nancy R. Buchan (Ph.D., Wharton School) is Associate Professor of International Business at the University of South Carolina. Her research focuses on the factors such as social identity and globalization that influence the development of trust and cooperation in cross-cultural relationships. She also studies cross-cultural communication and social interaction styles in negotiation.

Sabine Chai (M.A., San Diego State University, 2005) is Assistant Professor of Communication at Western Kentucky University. Her research interests include the influence of power differences on negotiation processes, intercultural negotiation, and negotiation goals. She is currently working on her dissertation and expects to obtain her Ph.D. from the University of Maryland in 2011.

Xiao-Ping Chen (Ph.D, University of Illinois) is Professor of Management in the Foster School of Business at University of Washington. She is also Editor-in-Chief for *Organizational Behavior and Human Decision Processes*. Her research interests include cross-cultural studies of cooperation and competition, social interaction and communication style, leadership, organizational citizenship behavior, and Chinese guanxi.

Roy Chua is an Assistant Professor in the Organizational Behavior unit at the Harvard Business School. His research draws on human psychology to understand social processes in business organizations. Roy also has a keen interest in Chinese organizational behavior and management processes, and more broadly in multiculturalism and cross-cultural interactions in the workplace.

Patrice Cottet is an Associate Professor at the University of Reims (France) and co-founder of "The Emporium". His research interests and teaching areas are negotiation, industrial marketing, consumer behavior, shopping behavior, communication (resistance to advertising), and methodology.

Helena Desivilya Syna is an Associate Professor of Social and Organizational Psychology. She serves as department head of sociology and anthropology at the Max Stern Academic College of Emek Yezreel. She conducts research on conflict management in organizations and communities and partnerships building, publishing her work in conflict and organization-related journals.

Kurt T. Dirks is the Bank of America Professor of Managerial Leadership at the Olin Business School at Washington University in St. Louis. His research is in the field of organizational behavior, and focuses on issues related to leadership and teams. He is best known for his research on the determinants, barriers, and outcomes of trust within organizations.

Noam Ebner is an Assistant Professor at the Werner Institute at Creighton University's School of Law, where he chairs the online graduate program in Negotiation and Dispute Resolution. Previously, he has taught negotiation and conflict resolution at universities in Israel, Turkey and Costa Rica, and directed a commercial mediation center in Jerusalem. He received his LL.M from Hebrew

University. In addition to online negotiation, his writing focuses on negotiation pedagogy and the role of trust in negotiation.

Donald L. Ferrin is an Associate Professor of Organizational Behavior at the Lee Kong Chian School of Business, Singapore Management University. His research focuses on many different aspects of trust in the workplace, including the nature of trust, determinants of trust and trust formation processes, benefits and functions of trust, trust networks within organizations, and trust repair after a violation.

Gregor Halff is an Associate Professor of Corporate Communication Practice at Singapore Management University, Honorary Professor at ISM, Germany, and Visiting Professor at National Taiwan University of Science and Technology. Before joining academia, Gregor was managing partner at Publicis, the world's third largest advertising and PR group. He also co-founded Publicis Consultants|Deutschland, an agency providing communication consulting to numerous blue-chip corporations across the globe.

Guido Hertel holds a chair position in Organizational Psychology at the University of Münster, Germany. His current research interests include process gains in teams, electronic human resource management, demographic changes, and conflict management in organizations. His work is published in many international journals, such as *Journal of Personality and Social Psychology, Journal of Occupational and Organizational Psychology, Human Resource Management Review*, and *Journal of Vocational Behavior*. Guido Hertel works also as consultant for organizations.

Joachim Hüffmeier did his undergraduate studies in Psychology and Philosophy at the University of Münster, Germany. He received his Ph.D. in Social Psychology from the University of Trier, Germany, in 2008. Since 2008, he is a lecturer at the Department of Organizational Psychology at the University of

Münster. He does lab and field research on three broad topics: negotiation processes within and between teams, process gains in teams, and processes that foster and inhibit the transfer of scientific findings to the public domain.

Sujin Jang is a Doctoral Candidate in the Joint Organizational Behavior and Social Psychology Program at Harvard University. Her research focuses on how people make sense of social situations, and the dynamics that arise when people from different backgrounds come together to collectively work on a task.

Dejun Tony Kong is a doctoral student of Organizational Behavior at the Olin Business School, Washington University in St. Louis. His research is in the field of organizational behavior, and focuses on negotiation, judgment and decision making, emotions, and cultures. He is especially interested in how emotions, cultures, and social contexts influence negotiators' judgment and decision making.

Laura J. Kray is the Warren E. & Carol Spieker Professor of Leadership at the Walter A. Haas School of Business, University of California at Berkeley. Kray earned her doctorate in social psychology and she applies this lens to her work on gender and negotiations, counterfactual thinking, and decision making. In 2008, her work on gender and negotiations was recognized with the "Most Influential Paper" award from the *Conflict Management Division of the Academy of Management.*

Eun Kyung Lee is a doctoral student at the School of Labor and Employment Relations, University of Illinois. Her research focuses on conflict, conflict management, and the role of leadership in developing social networks within a team. Her current research projects include empirical studies of the effects of leadership behaviors on team conflict management.

Min Li is a faculty member at the Carlson School of Management at the University of Minnesota. She received her Ph.D. degree in Management from the Fuqua School of Business, Duke University. Her current research focuses on cross-cultural management with an emphasis on cross-cultural negotiation, knowledge management in groups and teams, employee diversity network, and ethics in negotiation.

Meina Liu (Ph.D., Purdue University, 2006) is Assistant Professor of Communication at the University of Maryland, College Park, where she specializes in intercultural communication, organizational communication, and negotiation and conflict management. Her current research focuses on the cognitive and emotional processes involved in dyadic negotiations, as well as culture's influence on these processes.

Ababacar Mbengue is a Professor at the University of Reims (France) and at Reims Management School. Co-founder of "The Emporium", a research center in negotiation, his research interests and teaching areas are negotiation, strategic management, consumer behavior, knowledge management and methodology. He was a Professor at ESSEC, in France, and a Visiting Professor at Wharton (Snider Entrepreneurial Center) and University of Orel (Russia).

Alexandra A. Mislin is an Assistant Professor at American University's Kogod Business School. Her research interests focus on how social factors in negotiations interrelate to influence negotiated agreements, contract implementation, and post-negotiation behavior. Her work has appeared in *Administrative Science Quarterly* and *Organizational Behavior and Human Decision Processes*.

Shira Mor graduated from Columbia University with a B.A in psychology and sociology (magna cum laude) and is currently a Ph.D. candidate in Management at Columbia Business School. Mor researches the intersection of cultural psychology, organizational behavior, and conflict resolution.

Jayanth Narayanan is an Assistant Professor in Management and Organization at the NUS Business School. Jayanth got his Ph.D. from the London Business School in Organizational Behavior. His research focuses on understanding the physiological basis of workplace behaviors. His research uses a combination of laboratory and field research to examine these questions. He has recently embarked on a research program to understand how mindfulness can be beneficial at the workplace.

E. Layne Paddock is an Assistant Professor of Organizational Behavior at the Lee Kong Chian School of Business, Singapore Management University. Her research focuses on conflict and emotion, often focusing on the role that gender plays in intra-individual and inter-individual situations related to work and home domains.

Kelvin Pang is an Instructor in the department of Management & Organization at the National University of Singapore Business School. He received his Ph.D. in Management and Organizations from the National University of Singapore Business School at the National University of Singapore. Kelvin's research and teaching interests are in the area of negotiations, leadership and ethics in organizations.

Smrithi Prasad is a second year Ph.D. student in the Department of Management and Organization at the National University of Singapore Business School. Her research interests include understanding the physiological correlates of social processes in business settings, disrespect in the workplace and work engagement of mature workers.

Jill M. Purdy is an Associate Professor of Management at the Milgard School of Business at the University of Washington, Tacoma, where she also serves as Academic Director of the Center for Leadership and Social Responsibility. Her research interests include business-government-society negotiations and collaborative processes. Jill's research has appeared in such journals as the *Academy of Management Journal, International Journal of Conflict Management,* and *Public Administration Quarterly.* She currently serves on the editorial board of *Negotiation and Conflict Management Research.*

Julie Sadler is an Assistant Professor in the Department of Labor Studies and Employment Relations at Pennsylvania State University. She received her Master's in Industrial and Labor Relations and Ph.D. from Cornell University. From 2006-2008, she was a faculty member in the Leadership Program in the School of Urban Affairs and Public Policy at the University of Delaware. For the past decade, she has been conducting research on industrial relations and leadership development within the health care and education sectors.

Daniel L. Shapiro is Founder and Director of the Harvard International Negotiation Program. He is on the faculty at the Program on Negotiation at Harvard Law School and in the Psychology Department at Harvard Medical School/McLean Hospital. He has contributed to a wide array of scholarly journals and practical books, including the bestselling *Beyond Reason: Using Emotions as You Negotiate* (with Roger Fisher). He chairs the World Economic Forum's Global Agenda Council on Conflict Prevention.

Joël Sohier is an Associate Professor at the University of Reims (France) and co-founder of "The Emporium". His research interests and teaching areas are negotiation, industrial marketing, consumer behavior, supply chain management, and methodology.

Alice F. Stuhlmacher is a Professor of Psychology and director of the Ph.D. program in Industrial-Organizational Psychology at DePaul University in Chicago. Her research interests include negotiation, personality, workplace safety, and decision making particularly as related to gender and technology. She received her Ph.D. in I-O Psychology from Purdue University.

Alexandra Suppes is a social psychologist doing post-doctoral training in the Division of Medical Ethics at Weill Cornell Medical School. Suppes researches the influence of everyday language use in both professional and personal contexts that include business negotiation and medical decision making.

Brosh M. Teucher is a Visiting Assistant Professor of Management and Organizations at the Kellogg School of Management, Northwestern University. His research focuses on the impact of national culture and individual factors on negotiation and dispute resolution processes and outcomes. He also studies the impact of organizational culture on stock prices. He teaches negotiations at the Kellogg MBA program. He received his Ph.D. in Business Administration from the University of Washington, Seattle WA.

Cynthia S. Wang is an Assistant Professor in the department of Management & Organization at the National University of Singapore Business School. She received her Ph.D. in Management and Organizations from the Kellogg School of Management at Northwestern University. Cynthia's research and teaching interests are in the area of negotiations, ethical decision-making, and diversity in organizations.

Stephen E. Weiss is an Associate Professor at the Schulich School of Business at York University (Canada) and Visiting Professor at HEC School of Management (France). He specializes in international business negotiation. An award-winning instructor, he has worked with business and government professionals and students worldwide for over 20 years.

Introduction: Adding Value through Negotiation

Michael Benoliel

When a fine sword first comes out of a mold, it cannot cut or pierce until it is sharpened. When a fine mirror first comes out of a mold, it cannot reflect clearly until it is grounded and polished.

Thomas Cleary

When a fine negotiator first comes out of a mold, he cannot create value until he is developed.

It was in 1716 that French diplomat, Francois de Callieres wrote the worlds' first book on negotiation, *On the Manners of Negotiating with Princes.* It was in this book that he famously observed that the fate of the greatest states depends almost entirely on the good or bad conduct of their negotiators. It appears that his comments have stood the test of time, for even in today's increasingly competitive global economy, the fate of an organization depends largely on the skill and conduct of its negotiators.

To appreciate the critical role of skilled negotiators, one has to look no further than at the dismal record of mergers and acquisitions, especially recent high-profile deals. Acquirers have wiped more value off their market capitalization through failures in due diligence during the negotiation process than through lapses in any other part of the deal (Aiello and Watkins, 2000). For example, despite the grand promises of the "transformative" mega merger between AOL (America on Line) and Time Warner, "some $200 billion in shareholder value had vanished" (Munk, 2004: xiii). Similarly, the $5.8 billion acquisition of Rubbermaid by Newell was described by *BusinessWeek* as the "merger from hell" as it effectively robbed Newell's shareholders of 50% of their investment, and Rubbermaid shareholders of a further 35% (Harding and Rovit, 2004). After the acquisition, Newell's former CEO admitted that Newell had overpaid. In another transaction, Quaker Oats acquired Snapple for $1.7 billion, which some industry analysts said was as much as $1 billion too much. Twenty eight month later Quaker Oats sold Snapple to Triarc Companies for less than 20% of what it had paid (Eccles, Lanes and Wilson, 1999).

Are these examples outliers? Perhaps not. A study by KPMG International in 1999 looked at shareholder returns on corporate mergers relative to the performance of other companies in the same industry one year after the announcement of the merger. Using this commonly cited standard of success, it "found that 83% of mergers failed to unlock value" (Harding and Rovit, 2004:5).

While there are many reasons why mergers and acquisitions fail to unlock value, an analysis of these factors reveals that the most major mistakes are related to the negotiators' irrational and self-serving behavior. These include: hubris; over optimism; information availability bias; confirmatory bias; escalation of commitment; and "deal fever"— individuals produce many deals because they are evaluated on the basis of the number of the deals done and not on the basis of their intrinsic value.

In a recent survey, two hundred and fifty global executives involved in mergers and acquisitions admitted that there were breakdowns in their due-diligence processes, and half these individuals reported that this resulted in important issues not being detected. Amongst the most common mistakes they reported was a failure to understand that the targeted companies had "perfumed" themselves for sale just before they were acquired (Harding and Rovit, 2004). For example, in the acquisition of

Rubbermaid by Newell, Rubbermaid used a classic time pressure tactic and gave Newell only three weeks to perform its due-diligence. Instead of negotiating a more reasonable time period, Newell accepted the short deadline and expedited the process. It was only much later that Newell discovered that Rubbermaid "perfumed" its balance sheet and inflated its worth before closing the deal by stuffing the distribution channels with heavy promotions and deep discounts.

But not all companies perform as dramatically poorly as AOL and Time Warner, Newell and Rubbermaid or Quaker Oats and Snapple. What distinguishes the more successful firms from the less successful ones is that they have, what I call, a clear and disciplined **negotiation thesis**. They know precisely what value they must get from the deal, how the deal should be designed to create that value, and they focus diligently on negotiating this value. Among the serially successful deal makers are Bain and Company, a top-tier private equity firm; Cinven, a leading European private equity firm; and Nestle, a Swiss conglomerate and textbook acquirer. These companies know how to avoid the traps of deal making and how to create value through superior negotiation capabilities.

If companies like these are a seeming rarity, it is not only because many business enterprises have not fully recognized the value of effective negotiation. The stellar failures can be traced back to the institutions whose purpose it is to train the business executives and future deal makers. Although some better-rated business schools are leading the way by including negotiation courses in their list of core MBA courses, others have yet to follow this lead. However, the majority of future business executives will not hold MBA degrees. Thus, future deal makers should be required to study negotiation and build effective negotiation skills early in their undergraduate programs and professional careers. A well-designed experiential negotiation course or workshop, based on solid principles, practice, reflective analysis, and analogical reasoning (Moran, Bereby-Meyer and Bazerman, 2008), will indeed add value. After all, negotiations are a core business skill for anyone looking to create successful deals.

Given the limited exposure of a majority of current and aspiring negotiators to the study of negotiation and the fact that most negotiators often fail to reach integrative agreements (Thompson, 2005), the purpose of this book is to introduce the readers to key factors involved in an effective negotiation and a successful deal. The book includes 22 chapters covering critical topics such as how to prepare and dynamically plan for negotiations, how to build relationships and establish trust between negotiators, how to negotiate creatively to create mutual value, how to avoid cognitive biases and negotiate rationally, how to use power and persuasion effectively in the pursuit of mutual goals, how to tackle ethical dilemmas appropriately, and how to transact with negotiators on a global basis across multiple cultures.

The following section provides brief descriptions of the chapters in this book.

Chapter One: Planning and Preparing for Effective Negotiation

Comprehensive preparation and continuous planning are perhaps the most important elements of any successful deal. In this chapter, Meina Liu and Sabine Chai provide guidelines for conducting a well-rounded analysis of factors impacting the negotiation. Specifically, they suggest how to identify and analyze the opportunities and constraints impacting the negotiation. These include the issues at the table and each party's position, interests, preferences, goals, and alternatives.

Chapter Two: Setting (and choosing) the Table: The Influence of the Physical Environment in Negotiation

Little is known about the effects of the physical environment on negotiation outcomes. Yet negotiations take place in a variety of environments from coffee shops to boardrooms, each with its own potential to change the nature of the interaction and the final outcome. Graham Brown suggests that an understanding of the physical environment and how it triggers attitudes and shapes outcomes can be key to improving negotiation effectiveness. Be it the temperature of the room, the color of the walls, or the smell of flowers as you enter the space, he reviews the territoriality literature and demonstrates how the physical environment indirectly or directly influences negotiation outcomes.

Chapter Three: Negotiation Approaches: Claiming and Creating Value

How negotiators approach a negotiation has a significant impact on its process and outcomes. Researchers have described negotiation as consisting of two fundamentally different processes: discovering all the value that can be created and dividing it among the negotiators. Jill Purdy discusses the processes of claiming and creating value and addresses the challenge known as the negotiator's dilemma, which occurs when negotiators engage in both cooperative and competitive behaviors during negotiation. She concludes the chapter with an overview of interest-based negotiation, which emphasizes principled rather than positional bargaining.

Chapter Four: Creativity in Negotiations

Joachim Hüffmeier and Guido Hertel examine how creativity contributes to creating novel and more beneficial agreements. They present the value creating strategies that are used by creative negotiators to add value to the deals. These tried-and-tested strategies include log-rolling, exploiting compatible interests, unbundling issues, expanding the resource pie, using contingent contracts, making time trade-offs, and risk-sharing. They also discuss hindrances to creativity and conclude with recommendations of contextual conditions that support creative solutions in difficult negotiation situations.

Chapter Five: Social Capital in Negotiation: Leveraging the Power of Relational Wealth

Negotiation is an arena in which greater attention to social capital can lead to improved interactions, processes and, most importantly, outcomes. Negotiators interested in an additional resource to enhance distributive and/or mutual gains, should consider the social ties that they have with their negotiating counterparts and with individuals and groups outside the specific negotiation arena. In this chapter, Ariel Avgar and Eun Kyung Lee examine how social capital can influence negotiation processes and outcomes. In doing so, they examine social capital benefits and costs and how these can be applied to a negotiation setting. They conclude by highlighting the implications for negotiators and outline ways in which negotiators can be strategic in creating and maintaining social capital.

Chapter Six: Trust Building, Diagnosis, and Repair in the Context of Negotiation

Most, if not all, negotiators would agree that trust is critically important in negotiations. But what is trust? How can trust be built? How can one accurately assess another's trustworthiness? And can trust be repaired after a violation? These questions, Donald Ferrin, Dejun Tony Kong, and Kurt Dirks suggest, are as difficult to answer as they are important for negotiation effectiveness. Fortunately, trust researchers have made significant advances in the last 15 years toward answering these very questions. In this chapter, they summarize the empirical research on trust and discuss how it can be put into practice to effectively diagnose, build, and repair trust in the context of negotiations.

Chapter Seven: Power and Influence in Negotiations

The emphasis in this chapter is on the interplay between power, influence, and negotiation strategies. Min Li and Julie Sadler define power as the potential to influence others and regard influence as power in action. They review power from a broad perspective, provide an overview of the research on various sources of power, integrate different frameworks of power sources, and apply them to negotiation situations. In light of the prevalence of uneven distribution of power, the authors illustrate the effects of power imbalance on the negotiations process and outcomes, and emphasize the importance of assessing one's relative power in negotiations. They conclude the chapter by providing practical advice as to how to effectively tackle various power imbalances, propose a linkage map depicting how certain power sources are more likely to relate to specific influence tactics, and demonstrate how power can be translated effectively into influence in different contexts, specifically national cultures.

Chapter Eight: Power and Influence in Sales Negotiation

While the previous chapter outlines the role of power in negotiations, this chapter hones in on the role of power in sales-related negotiations. A common question asked by both buyers and sellers with low bargaining power is how to negotiate effectively with a sole supplier or a powerful buyer. Ababacar Mbengue, Joël Sohier, and Patrice Cottet review the literature on power imbalances in sales negotiations, identify the sources of imbalance, and provide interesting examples of the dynamics typically observed in industries where power is in the hands of a dominant player (e.g., Microsoft, Wal-Mart, Best Buy, DeBeers). They conclude the chapter with tips on how to negotiate more effectively with dominant sellers or powerful buyers.

Chapter Nine: Negotiation Strategy

Experienced negotiators stress that strategy is critical to reaching a successful deal. But what exactly is a good negotiation strategy? In this chapter, Brosh Teucher asks what a good negotiation strategy entails, summarizes key negotiation strategies, and stresses that good negotiators are not reluctant to shape and reshape their strategies in mid-negotiation.

Chapter Ten: Personality and Negotiation

Alice Stuhlmacher and Christopher Adair provide a brief background on why personality is an important influence on negotiation outcomes, how individual traits relate to aspects of negotiation, and what negotiators should know about their own and other's personality before sitting down at the negotiating table. They provide also an overview of research on relationship-orientations, Machiavellianism, the five-factor model, self monitoring, and self efficacy traits as they apply to the negotiation process. In addition, the authors emphasize the role of the environment in determining which personality traits are emphasized in different situations, and explain the negotiation-related implications of the human tendency to attribute actions to one's personality.

Chapter Eleven: Judgment Bias and Decision Making in Negotiation

William Bottom, Dejun Tony Kong, and Alexandra Mislin take a historical perspective to the study of negotiations, looking specifically at the wonderfully educational role of errors. They focus on negotiator biases as highlighted first by Walter Lippmann from his participation and observation of the failed negotiations of the 1919 Paris Peace Conference. Such biases include those stemming from the availability, anchoring and adjustment, and representativeness heuristics. Also discussed are the related biases of overconfidence and perceptions of integrative potential as well as the role of issue framing on the level of acceptable risk.

Chapter Twelve: The Role of Gender in Negotiation

At the negotiation table, does being male or female matter? This question, Layne Paddock and Laura Kray propose, has important implications, especially if the answer is "yes", as women and men negotiate over larger (e.g., compensation, condominium purchases) issues, as well as everyday issues (e.g., weekly work schedules, children's bedtimes). They examine the idea of gender, identify the answer to whether gender within negotiation matters, and draw on previous empirical and theoretical reviews and more contemporary research to explain why and when gender matters in negotiation. They conclude the chapter with practical advice related to gender in negotiations.

Chapter Thirteen: Physiology in Negotiation

Negotiations are complex social phenomena. Smrithi Prasad and Jayanth Narayanan suggest that negotiators are driven by two fundamental motives: competition and cooperation. Although the mechanisms behind these motives are closely correlated with basic human physiological functions, few studies have examined the physiological factors that affect the behavior of negotiators, the process of negotiation, and its outcomes. However, a handful of studies have examined how physiological systems affect the psychological and social processes that are relevant in a negotiation. In this chapter, they explore the motives of competition and cooperation and the physiological processes underlying them. Specifically, they examine the role of the endocrine system and the nervous system in driving negotiation processes.

Chapter Fourteen: Understanding Negotiation Ethics

The business world has faced a number of moral challenges in recent history. In the face of these events, it has become especially important to understand how to recognize and resolve potential ethical conflicts. In the negotiation context, it is common for parties to believe that their counterparts have acted unethically, just as it is common for negotiators to engage in behaviors without realizing that they may be viewed as unethical by others. In this chapter, Kelvin Pang and Cynthia Wang bring to the fore situations in which ethical considerations are often overlooked, and help illuminate the human tendencies that sometimes lead us to behave unethically. They address how self-interest, norms, fairness biases, collective dilemmas, and cultural stereotypes affect ethical considerations during negotiations and impact negotiation outcomes. They conclude the chapter by presenting strategies for resolving such ethical dilemmas.

Chapter Fifteen: Navigating International Negotiations: A Communications and Social Interaction Style (CSIS) Framework

As important as it is to communicate effectively during negotiations, doing so becomes exponentially more important and complex when negotiators are faced with counterparts from different cultures. Viewing culture as both implicit and unstable, Nancy Buchan, Wendi Adair and Xiao-Ping Chen adopt the communication and social interaction style (CSIS) framework to make sense of the impact of this variable on negotiation interactions. Among other aspects, they examine how individuals from different cultures attend to contextual cues in their environment and use such cues to reason and relate to others during negotiations. The CSIS framework explains why misunderstandings occur in intercultural negotiations, and how to bridge communication gaps in order to achieve a win-win solution for negotiators from different cultures.

Chapter Sixteen: Building Intercultural Trust at the Negotiating Table

Intercultural negotiations are often characterized by a lack of trust. This is not surprising given that building trust is hard within the context of a business relationship and even harder when the person across the table speaks an entirely different language and comes from a different culture than yours. In this chapter, Sujin Jang and Roy Chua examine the challenges of intercultural negotiation, with a focus on the critical role of trust. They discuss what trust is, why it matters, why it is so difficult to establish trust in intercultural negotiations, and offer guidelines for building trust in intercultural negotiations.

Chapter Seventeen: Negotiating the Renault-Nissan Alliance: Insights from Renault's Experience

In this case study, Stephen Weiss describes the negotiations leading up to Renault-Nissan alliance. Many observers doubted that Renault and Nissan would reach an agreement in 1999, let alone develop a solid partnership lauded throughout the auto industry 10 years later for its success and foresight. Using an analytical framework, the author identifies and analyzes the parties' interests, strategic alternatives, preparation and planning for negotiation, negotiation process, and outcomes. Important lessons from this case study include the value of probing beyond parties' surface differences, expanding typical avenues for preparation, conceiving unusual forms of relationships, influencing counterpart's no-deal alternatives, and incorporating long-term effects into the evaluation of an agreement.

Chapter Eighteen: The Arcelor and Mittal Steel Merger Negotiations

A phone call on the night of January 26, 2006 launched this century's largest industrial merger between Arcelor and Mittal Steel. It was during that conversation that Indian multibillionaire Lakshmi Mittal made his unfriendly bid for Mittal's main competitor, Arcelor. In this case study, Gregor Halff describes how the negotiations between the world's two largest steel producers attracted a huge amount of attention from not only the steel industry, but governments, unions, banks, and shareholders as well. The battle for Arcelor became a battle for global public opinion, with each side counting on a media relations team for its defense. This case describes the negotiation process from Arcelor's perspective.

Chapter Nineteen: The Emotional Underbelly of Collaboration: When Politics Collide with Need

How does one go about encouraging collaboration amongst politically divided stakeholders who hold deep suspicion and distrust of one another? In this case study, Daniel Shapiro describes two important key components to improve relations. First, encourage norms of cooperation to override adversarial attitudes. Second, equip stakeholders with the Core Concerns Framework and associated skills to navigate the emotional complexities of political negotiations and decision making. The case, based on Shapiro's consultation for the leadership of a diverse coalitional government, highlights the benefits of the consultation intervention on collaboration between the members of the coalitional government.

Chapter Twenty: The Role of Negotiation in Building Intra-Team and Inter-Team Cooperation

Negotiation is a key mechanism for fostering team cooperation and resolving team conflicts. But effective team negotiation is complex, involving both structural and process aspects such as the management of power-relations, conflicting goals and differing practices, as well as the building of mechanisms for coordinating, communicating, and decision making across large teams. In this chapter, Helena Desivilya-Syna examines the intersection between two social and organizational phenomena: teams and negotiation. She focuses on informal team negotiation, addresses overt and hidden attempts to reach consensus, presents and discusses three cases using conceptual frameworks, and integrates theory and practice of team negotiation.

Chapter Twenty One: The Role of Communication Media in Negotiations

How does negotiating over the phone impact the outcomes relative to face-to-face negotiations? Shira Mor and Alexandra Suppes provide theoretical and practical insights on how negotiators can utilize different forms of media to their advantage. They first explain how communication media differ and in turn, influence negotiation outcomes. They then discuss how relationship building and impression management are facilitated or hindered by the availability of different communication cues. Finally, they summarize research findings on the role of the media in influencing distributive and integrative negotiation outcomes.

Chapter Twenty Two: Negotiation via Email

Increasingly, negotiation interactions are taking place outside of face-to-face meetings as more negotiators use electronic communication channels to conduct business. Negotiation via email has significant impacts on the dynamics between negotiators, their level of trust and cooperation, the type of information they share, and the outcomes. Noam Ebner argues that while theoretical models of negotiation take inter-party communications into account, they do not usually examine the effects of particular communication media. In this chapter, he examines the effects of email communication on relational and transactional elements of negotiation, outlines common pitfalls, and recommends on how to improve the outcomes of email negotiation.

Planning and Preparing for Effective Negotiation

Meina Liu
University of Maryland

Sabine Chai
Western Kentucky University

Negotiations take place in a wide array of forms, whether to resolve a dispute, get a better deal, or find new solutions that neither party could realize on their own. The first, and often the most important, step toward successful negotiation is planning and preparation. According to Thompson (2009), about 80% of negotiators' effort should go toward the preparation stage. However, planning and preparation go beyond what negotiators should do *before* negotiation. Because negotiation is a dynamic communication process where new information, concerns, emotions, and goals may arise, negotiators should also be prepared for dealing with contingencies, as well as factors that may interfere with goal pursuit. The purpose of this chapter, therefore, is to provide guidelines for effective planning and preparation both before and during the negotiation process, including guidelines for assessing the negotiation situation, analyzing the negotiation structure, planning for strategies that facilitate goal attainment, and re-orienting to manage contingencies that may arise during the dynamic, interactive negotiation process.

Negotiation Analysis: Know the Situation, Yourself, and Your Opponent

Negotiation is often defined as three *"I"*s — an *interaction* between two or more *interdependent* parties who perceive *incompatible* goals. Negotiation parties enter the negotiation because they depend on each other to fulfill some needs but also perceive the other party's interests as conflicting with their own. To reach a mutually acceptable agreement negotiation parties have to cooperate with and understand each other. An essential component of effective preparation is to conduct a well-rounded analysis of the bargaining situation, to understand not only one's own positions, interests, priorities, and alternatives, but also those of the counterparts.

Analyze the negotiation context: Opportunities and constraints

Negotiations do not take place in a vacuum. The historical, economical, legal, and socio-cultural contexts all determine the codes of conduct that shape negotiators' perception of what is permitted or not permitted, expected or not expected (Watkins, 2000). A sufficient understanding of the bargaining situation allows the negotiators to identify the rules of the game, resources to draw upon, norms to abide by, as well as constraints to deal with. For example, when Google publically criticized China's internet censorship as violating free speech rights and threatened to pull out of China in January 2010, China not only made no concessions but also denied any talk with Google regarding its threat. After two months, Google discontinued its operation in mainland China, losing the world's largest market of online users. This case has been widely considered a lose-lose negotiation. In July 2010, China renewed Google's operation license when the company stopped automatically redirecting mainland Chinese users to its uncensored Hong Kong page. Below this case is used to illustrate various aspects to consider when analyzing a negotiation situation.

Assess the historical, political, legal, and cultural context in which negotiations take place

Research has shown that the quality of deals negotiators reach is significantly influenced by their bargaining histories (O'Connor, Arnold, and Burris, 2005). Negotiators who reached an impasse in a previous negotiation are more likely to repeat their failures because their prior experiences can influence how negotiators judge their skills, set their goals, and formulate their strategies. When negotiations occur across national boundaries, the diplomatic histories, as well as the power dynamic in international relations, can have a significant impact on the course of the negotiation, including what issues are to be negotiated, what is and is not possible, and even the types of outcomes that may occur. Likewise, differences in the political and legal systems in the host country may entail a completely different set of values and assumptions negotiators have to work with, making communication between parties exponentially more complicated. Corporations conducting business in different countries need to consider all of these issues.

For example, in the controversy between China and Google, a U.S. based company, history cannot but be a quiet guest at the table. The early relationship between China and Western countries (including the U.S.) was marked by a series of unequal treaties that forced China to give up sovereignty in a number of ways in the late 1900s. Considering the cultural context in this case also means understanding that China is a history-conscious nation that values both knowledge of history and learning from it. If foreign entities, such as the U.S. government or U.S. businesses challenge its sovereign rule by asking China to change its policies regarding the internet, the now much stronger Chinese government has to reject and condemn such an attempt. In addition, due to China's political system, internet censorship is prescribed by law. From China's perspective, Google should have given sufficient consideration to this issue prior to establishing a contractual relationship with China. When the issue was brought up in the middle of the contractual operation, it was considered non-negotiable by the Chinese government, hence their denial of any talk concerning this issue.

Assess the purpose of the negotiation: Deal-making or dispute resolution?

In a typical business negotiation, parties come together to attempt to exchange resources, or make a deal. Negotiators use *distributive bargaining* strategies to claim greater value for themselves, whereas they use *integrative bargaining* strategies to expand the pie for both parties. In other situations, negotiations take place to resolve a dispute because a claim has been made by one party and has been rejected by the other party; the two parties' alternatives to a mutual agreement are often linked, or identical. If neither party is willing to revise the original position, they either are deadlocked or go to a third party for intervention. In the Google-China case, business negotiations are embedded in a political context in which China and the U.S., two of the world's biggest countries, have had long-standing value-based disputes concerning human rights. When Google brought up the human rights violation issue, it automatically turned a business transaction into a political dispute, which pushed China away from making any possible concessions, due to their political implications. As a result of insufficient consideration of the surrounding political contexts, Google had to eat its words and suspended its accusation of and resistance against China's censorship. After all, as a for-profit corporate entity, its primary interests are market values, rather than political power.

Assess the nature of the conflict: Are ideologies involved?

Conflicts and disputes may simply involve competition over scarce resources. However, many conflict situations, especially those between members of diverse cultural, ethnic, or social groups, also involve ideologies. As negotiators uphold fundamentally different assumptions, moral standards, and beliefs, the likelihood of reaching an impasse is significantly increased, often accompanied by increased tensions and emotions. Effective planning for such negotiations, therefore, involves an analysis of the relationship between interests and ideologies. Negotiators can manage to find an interest-based resolution by totally ignoring ideological differences, or to find a resolution on both aspects by identifying a common ground in each other's value systems, or when ideological differences are the only issue at table, to work toward not a resolution, but an open dialogue that involves recognizing and appreciating each other's values and beliefs. In the Google-China case, a resolution was temporarily reached by re-focusing on business interests and ignoring ideological differences concerning human rights. In other situations, however, finding an interest-based resolution without openly discussing ideological differences to instill mutual understanding and respect may prove short-lived because it means the problem still exists and is likely to arise again in the future. For example, in a dispute between a conservative Christian employee who condemns homosexuality in a poster inside his office cubicle and a Diversity Manager who is in charge of a diversity campaign featuring pro-gay-rights posters and later fired the Christian employee for insubordination, discussing what constitutes diversity and freedom is as important as finding an interest-based resolution (Kovick and Harvey, 2009).

Assess the temporality of the negotiation: One-shot or long-term?

In a one-shot negotiation, such as bargaining with a street vendor over the price of an antique-like sugar bowl, what happens at the bargaining table has no future ramifications. However, when negotiators come from a common social network, or when they negotiated in the past, or must renegotiate at a future time (e.g., to renew a contract), parties must consider the impact of their relational history on the current negotiation, or the impact of their negotiation on their future work relationship. For a long-term work relationship, what matters during the negotiation goes beyond tangible, quantifiable issues; intangible issues, such as negotiators' reputation, interpersonal trust, face concerns, and relational harmony may be equally, if not more, important. In the Google-China case, although Google pulled itself out of China's market for a while, it did not "burn the bridges" and was able to have its operation license renewed once the company stopped resisting censorship.

Assess external constraints: Is time an issue?

Negotiations are often associated with some time-related costs. Negotiating under time pressure may activate a need for closure (i.e., an epistemic state of wanting a quick solution). Negotiators are more likely to rely on heuristics rather than engage in thoughtful, motivated information processing in their decision-making (De Dreu, 2004). As a result, they may either prematurely end the negotiation with an impasse, or reduce their aspiration level and conform. Assessing time-related constraints, therefore, can help negotiators to guard against such irrational tendencies. In addition, an assessment of time-related costs for both parties may even help negotiators to turn constraints into opportunities: If time puts more constraints on the counterpart than self, negotiators may gain concessions by highlighting the undesirability of a delay in agreement; if delays cause higher costs on one's own part, negotiators may set a deadline for the negotiation. In the Google-China case, Google gave up its original position and conformed to China's internet censorship when its operation license was about to expire.

Assess external constraints: Place

In addition to time constraints, where negotiations take place also matters. Negotiating on one's own territory is typically considered an advantage, as the outside party may experience greater uncertainty and perceive less power. However, negotiating on the opponent's territory may have advantages as well, as the outside party may be better prepared, more alert, less concerned about hospitality and information leakage, and more flexible in "walking away" (Sims, 2005). In the Google-China case, although Google may have experienced greater pressure to conform, it also had greater flexibility in "pulling out" or "coming back". Nevertheless, negotiators also have been advised to find a private neutral territory when possible.

Assess external constraints: Communication channels

With the rapid development of new technologies, negotiations are increasingly conducted in mediated contexts for greater convenience. Negotiators should be mindful of the properties of various communication channels (e.g., telephone, videoconference, email, instant messages) as well as their potential influence on negotiation process and outcomes to make a sound choice. For example, face-to-face negotiations are often deemed necessary if the two parties have not established a prior relationship, because mediated communication may pose barriers (e.g., lack of synchronicity, insufficient audio and/or visual cues) for the two parties to develop rapport and cultivate trust. When communication media have to be used, negotiators should consider strategies that enhance social awareness to counter the effects of barriers.

Analyze the negotiation structure and components

Diagnosis of the negotiation context should be complemented with a careful analysis of the structure of the negotiation, including who are the involved parties, what issues are to be negotiated, what are each party's positions, interests, and preferences for these issues, and what are their best alternatives to a negotiated agreement (BATNA).

Identify the negotiation parties

A party to a negotiation is any person or group pursing distinct goals in the context of a specific negotiation. Who the parties are may be obvious in some negotiations, but is not necessarily so in others (Thompson, 2009). For example, in the Google-China case mentioned above, the obvious parties are Google and the Chinese government. In the course of the conflict, however, a number of other parties were involved, including members of the Chinese and the U.S. public and media, the U.S. Congress, politicians and other public figures in both the U.S. and China, and Google's biggest competitor in China, Baidu. Although most of these parties were not present at the negotiation table, they influenced the negotiation dynamic in various ways. For example, when U.S. Secretary of State Hillary Clinton criticized China's practice of internet censorship and Chinese media responded by criticizing the U.S. for forcing their values on other parts of the world, this exchange clearly goes beyond a conflict between a business and the legislative agencies of its host country.

Influential parties that are nevertheless not present in the actual negotiation are known as the *hidden table* (Friedman, 1992). Identifying these parties in the preparation phase of a negotiation can avoid ugly surprises down the road. Even if the negotiation is expected to be between two parties only, negotiators need to analyze whether there are other parties that may enter the negotiation later on. Each new party will change the dynamics of the negotiation as they bring in their own interests and potentially form coalitions. Mapping out the relationships between multiple parties in terms of their incentives, interests, and power will be very helpful to identify strategies for managing the dynamic multi-party or team negotiation process. In addition, as soon as a party consists of more than one person, it is unlikely to be monolithic (Thompson, 2009). Different sub-groups may have different priorities and preferences, different approaches to conflict resolution, and very importantly, different amounts of say in the final decision. Negotiators need to find out as much as possible about the inner dynamics of the other parties involved because this knowledge will allow them to make educated choices in whom to approach about what issues and at what stage in the negotiation process.

Define the issues

The number of issues each party brings into the negotiation tends to have a strong influence on the strategies negotiators choose. Single-issue negotiations, also referred to as zero-sum, distributive negotiations, generally entail a competitive, win-lose approach (Lewicki, Saunders and Barry, 2006). The underlying assumption is that both parties are seeking to maximize their own share of a fixed amount of resources; as such, negotiation parties' goals are in fundamental conflict with each other. When focusing on a single issue, negotiators tend to come with a clear position and fight for it. Negotiations involving more than one issue are likely to be non-zero-sum, integrative negotiations. When negotiators add multiple issues to a negotiation, or unbundle one single issue into multiple issues, they are more likely to focus on interests (i.e., their needs and concerns), as well as the relative importance of these issues, rather than being deadlocked in a rigid position. As such, negotiators tend to be more cooperative, striving for a win-win outcome based on the assumption that both parties' needs and concerns can be met (Walton and McKersie, 1965). Instead of focusing on claiming value, negotiators tend to explore ways of creating value, or "expanding the pie" in multi-issue, non-zero-sum situations. For example, in a negotiation concerning the purchase of a new car, if both buyer and seller concentrate only on price, one person's gain is the other person's loss. However, if they add other issues, such as repairs, time and form of payment, bonus features, warranties, etc., the pie can be enlarged allowing both parties to maximally fulfill their respective needs without making the other party "lose" (i.e., get less than half of the original size of the pie). Therefore, a careful analysis of the issues one can bring to the negotiation table can open doors for more profitable settlements.

Once all relevant issues are identified, it is important to consider the relationships between those issues (Lewicki *et al.*, 2006). For example, a buyer expecting a pay raise at the end of the year may be able to afford paying a higher price on a car if payment can be deferred until that time. Price and time of payment therefore, are linked. Understanding these linkages is critical for creating package offers. Furthermore, issues need to be prioritized. Knowing the relative importance of various issues on the list allows negotiators to have a clear vision about where there is potential for possible logrolling (i.e., both parties could "win" by trading off issues of differential importance).

Negotiators need to keep in mind, however, that negotiations may not only include tangible issues such as numbers and conditions, but also intangible issues, such as negotiators' identities, worldviews, face concerns, emotions, and the interpersonal relationship between negotiators before or after the negotiation. In dispute situations such intangible may be the focal issues at the negotiation table. For example, in the conflict described above between a devoutly religious employee who was so deeply disturbed by a diversity campaign that he made repeated attempts to post anti-homosexuality posters inside his cubicle, and a Diversity Manager who fired the employee after repeated failures to have him remove those posters, the focal issues concern identity, religious belief, emotion, and the notions of "freedom" and "respect", none of which are tangible. To resolve the dispute effectively, focusing only on negotiation parties' tangible interests (e.g., getting the job back) is no longer sufficient. Negotiations or mediators must prepare strategies for dealing with the emotions that may arise from identity- and value-based discussions, in order to promote mutual understanding, build trust, and produce attitudinal change.

Understand the underlying interests

Identifying issues is about finding out *what* one wants. Identifying interests is about asking oneself *why* one wants those things

(Lewicki *et al.*, 2006). For example, job applicants may have a specific salary in mind, but the reasons for why they need that amount to take a job may differ greatly. Are they paying off a house? Are they helping children through college? Are they saving for retirement? Even for seemingly distributive issues such as salary, identifying the underlying interests can create additional options for integrative negotiation. An employer may, for example, not be able to offer quite the amount the applicant has in mind, but may have loan programs to help with financing the house, separate funds for support with education related expenses, or advantageous retirement packages to offer. Similar to issues, interests can be tangible or intangible. The job applicant above may, for example, ask for a high starting salary in part as an expression of the appreciation of her/his value s/he hopes to get from the company. If the company is able to show that they value the applicant by non-monetary means, s/he may be able to accept a lower starting salary. Finally, interests can not only concern the outcome of a negotiation but also the process. For example, if a company is willing to donate large funds to a non-profit organization because they want to "look good", it would serve both parties' best interests to widely publicize the negotiation process, rather than conducting it behind closed doors.

Consider alternatives

Once issues and interests are well known, negotiators need to set specific parameters for the negotiation, such as the best deal they can hope for (also referred to as the *target or aspiration* point) and the worst deal before they should walk away (also referred to as the *resistance* or *reservation* point). To have a realistic estimate of these parameters, negotiators need to consider their best alternatives to a negotiated agreement (BATNAs). BATNAs are the options a party has if a negotiation fails. For example, if I do not buy House X, what alternatives do I have? Are similarly attractive houses available? Will I rent? Will I be able to stay in my current place? Strong BATNAs decrease one's dependence on the counterpart (Emerson, 1962). The better a negotiator's BATNA, the more negotiation power s/he has and the stronger his/her position in the negotiation. Unfortunately, BATNAs are not always clear. For example, in the example above, I may have seen two equally attractive houses, but I may not know how many others are interested in them and may have already made offers. To realistically judge one's alternatives, negotiators need to carefully research their options as well as assess the probability of those options remaining available. In this example, a buyer's BATNA suffers when the other houses of potential interest are taken by others, but it becomes stronger as more attractive places become available. Therefore, it is important to keep in mind that BATNAs are not static but can change during the negotiation. Understanding the dynamic nature of BATNAs allows negotiators to understand the importance of improving BATNAs.

Create a scoring system and sort out preferences

Once negotiators have a clear understanding of their underlying interests for all the issues they have identified, as well as their BATNAs, it is important to sort out their own preferences. Are some issues more important than others? If they were to give up something, what would they choose? How do they know which offer package is the best? Due to the complexity of many multi-issue negotiations, working out these problems can be a mind-boggling exercise. Negotiation scholars have proposed a viable approach to streamlining the process, that is, to generate scoring systems that assign points to various options of each issue and quantify the offer proposals involving multiple issues (see Raiffa, 1982). Specifically, the values of each issue can be determined by observing preferences between simple hypothetical choices. For example, suppose that you, a job candidate, are entering into negotiations with an HR manager to get an optimal offer package. You are concerned about three factors: salary, vacation, and moving expenses. From your research as well as preliminary discussions you limit the ranges of these factors to, respectively, $60K – $72K, 5 to 25 days, and 60% to 100% coverage. You would of course prefer to get the best of everything, $72K, 25 days and 100% coverage; likewise, the worst deal possible would be to get $60K, 5 days and 60% coverage. To streamline the process, you decide to give the best contract a score of 100 points, and the worst contract, a score of zero points.

Like an exam with 3 questions, you must also decide how much weight you should give to each question and how many points you should give to each partially correct answer. You decide to score each issue in the same way (100 = best, 0 = worst), and to combine the scores with proportional weights that sum to 1. For example, suppose that you give a weight of 0.5 to salary, a weight of 0.3 to vacation, and a weight of 0.2 to moving expenses (see Table 1). A contract that gives you $69K, 15 days, and 80% coverage would then receive: $(75 \times 0.5) + (50 \times 0.3) + (50 \times 0.2) = 62.5$ points. Based on this scoring system, getting the highest salary ($72K = 100 points) and getting the worst for the other two issues (5 days and 60% coverage = 0 points) would be a more desirable contract than the previous one. Such a scoring system does not only allow negotiators to compare multiple package offers to assess tradeoffs and concessions, but also allows negotiators to compare the current negotiation situation with their BATNAs. BATNAs serve to help negotiators decide on their reservation or resistance point, which is the point at which negotiators can walk away from the negotiation, because accepting a settlement that is less profitable than one's BATNA makes no sense.

TABLE 1   Job candidate's benefits

Salary (×0.5)	Vacation (×0.3)	Moving Expense (×0.2) (%)
$72,000 (100 pts)	25 days (100 pts)	100 (100 pts)
$69,000 (75 pts)	20 days (75 pts)	90 (75 pts)
$66,000 (50 pts)	15 days (50 pts)	80 (50 pts)
$63,000 (25 pts)	10 days (25 pts)	70 (25 pts)
$60,000 (0 pt)	5 days (0 pt)	60 (0 pt)

The type of scoring system discussed above allows negotiators to assign an overall numerical value to any contract such that contracts with higher scores are preferred and no uncertainties are involved. Such a system is also called a *value* scoring system. In some situations, however, there is uncertainty as to whether the desirable values can be obtained. For example, if a television station is entering into negotiations with a producer of a television show concerning the licensing fee per episode as well as the number of runs, it is likely that both parties have differing expectations as to the ratings and adverting revenue that can be drawn from the show. Assigning points to different levels of the licensing fee per episode does not necessarily reflect any attitudes toward risk. In this case, a *utility* scoring system is more appropriate. Such a scoring system can not only reflect preferences under certainty, but also use expected utility calculations as guidelines for choices between options with well-specified probabilities, as illustrated in the following example. The overall estimate of net advertising revenue would be: (0.2 × $7M) + (0.5 × $8M) + (0.1 × $9M) + (0.1 × $10M) + (0.1 × $11M) = $8.4M.

Determine the target/aspiration and reservation/resistance points

Knowing BATNAs and creating a scoring system allow negotiators to determine their reservation/resistance points, the points at

TABLE 2   TV station (Buyer)'s expected likelihood of ratings

Ratings	Likelihood (%)	Advertising revenue
2–3	20	$7,000,000
3–4	50	$8,000,000
4–5	10	$9,000,000
5–6	10	$10,000,000
6–7	10	$11,000,000

Note. This example is taken from *Moms.com*, a negotiation exercise published by Northwestern University's Dispute Resolution Research Center.

which negotiators can walk away from the negotiation. Thompson (2009) suggested calculating resistance point as the sum of all options multiplied by their probability. It is important to bear in mind however that not all issues come conveniently in counts and amounts. Establishing a good relationship with the other party, or reaching a settlement by a certain date, for example, may be important but do not naturally have a dollar value attached. Therefore, to make reasonable comparisons possible that include both tangible and intangible issues, we can use the value scoring system described above. For example, a job candidate is interviewing with three companies. Based on thorough research, s/he knows that company A tends to pay new hires in her position $65,000 per year, and give them a three-week vacation per year as well as a new laptop for work purposes. Company B may be willing to offer $67,000, only a two-week vacation, but also a new laptop. Company C may pay as much as $70,000, give two weeks of vacation, as well as a nice large office with all technological equipment including videoconferencing. To make these options comparable, the candidate can assign a common unit of measurement to the vacation days and office equipment. If s/he decides that both the extra week of vacation and the better office equipment would be worth $5000 to her, this will bring the overall value of the three options to the following:

Company 1: $65,000 + $5000 + $0 = $70,000
Company 2: $67,000 + $0 + $0 = $67,000
Company 3: $70,000 + $0 + $5000 = $75,000

This simple comparison shows that company A is actually slightly more attractive than company B in spite of the lower salary due to the value the candidate assigned to the additional vacation time. To determine the reservation point, the candidate also needs to consider how likely she is to get an offer from any of these companies. Suppose that based on her knowledge of the companies, the number and quality of other job candidates, and her impression of her own interviews, she believes that she has a

50% chance of receiving an offer from company A, a 30% chance of receiving one from company B, and only a 20% chance with company C. [Please note: Although it is possible that she will not receive any offer at all, this example assumes that these three companies are all available alternatives. For the purpose of calculating the resistance point, the probabilities of all alternatives should sum to 100%.] Calculations based on the hypothesized propabilities are as follows:

Company A: $\$70,000 \times .50 = \$35,000$
Company B: $\$67,000 \times .30 = \$20,100$
Company C: $\$75,000 \times .20 = \$15,000$

The overall value of all current alternatives is the sum of these three values, $70,100. If the job candidate were to receive an offer from any of the three companies, this number could serve as her resistance point for her overall package including salary, vacation days, and office equipment. Although negotiators need to keep their resistance points in mind to avoid settling for anything below their BATNA, they also need to keep an eye on those BATNAs as they may change in the course of the negotiation. For example, company C may hire somebody else, forcing the candidate to recalculate the resistance point accordingly.

In addition to the resistance point, negotiators also need to set a target or aspiration point, the best deal they can possibly get. Research has consistently shown that negotiators' aspiration points are positively associated with their negotiation outcomes (Zetik and Stuhlmacher, 2002). Based on the goal-setting theory (Locke, 1968), goals promote performance when they are difficult but feasible. An outrageously high opening price may give the impression to the counterpart that the negotiator is not serious about the negotiation; as a result, they may just walk away. On the other hand, if an opening bid is too conservative and gets accepted right away, negotiators may suffer what is called the *winner's curse* (i.e., the tendency to settle quickly on an item and then subsequently feel discomfort about a win that comes too easily; Neale and Bazerman, 1991). Although BATNAs do not help determine aspiration points directly, having a strong BATNA allows negotiators to set higher aspiration points and be more persistent in the bargaining process.

Assess your negotiation style

After analyzing issues, interests, preferences, and alternatives, as well as setting aspiration and reservation points, negotiators should conduct a self-assessment in terms of their attitude toward risks, preferred approach to conflict, and personal negotiation history. Such awareness will help negotiators identify and possibly guide against irrational tendencies during the bargaining process (Thompson, 2009).

All negotiations involve an element of risk in some form. BATNAs may appear and disappear on either side of the negotiation table. The agreements that have been reached may be prematurely terminated for unexpected reasons. Like in the stock market, however, higher risks may also promise higher gains. Whether negotiators focus on risks or opportunities can have a significant influence on their bargaining strategies. Negotiators need to know how much risk they are willing to take and be realistic about the profit that can be achieved with that level of risk. In addition, if negotiating in teams, negotiators need to consider the attitude any of their constituents may have toward risk. Constituents may hope for the best possible outcomes, but may be unwilling to risk losses that can be incurred by using strategies such as threats and ultimatums. If that is the case, negotiators need to negotiate strategy choices a priori with their constituents and make sure to create realistic expectations for the repertoire of strategies they are given.

Negotiators should also consider their social value orientation, or preferred approach to negotiation. Pruitt and Rubin (1986) distinguished five main approaches to conflict: Inaction, yielding, compromising, contending, and problem-solving. The five styles express differences in focus on one's own versus the other party's outcomes. Competitive, or egoistic, negotiators tend to view negotiation as a fixed pie where both parties compete to claim value; they tend to do better in distributive negotiation but may overlook potential for integrative logrolling. On the other hand, cooperative, or pro-social, negotiators are more likely to orient toward win-win outcomes, however, they may also prematurely conclude the negotiation before reaching pareto-optimal outcomes (i.e., agreements where there is no further room for value creation).

Finally, negotiators should consider their personal negotiation history. How much experience do they have? What does that experience tell them? Have they made any mistakes in the past that may influence their behavior in future negotiations? Learning from mistakes can be a valuable source of information, but negotiators also need to keep in mind that each negotiation is different and may involve different risks and opportunities. Similarly, prior successes can be great confidence builders, but negotiators need to be careful not to let this confidence shadow their realistic evaluation of the current situation.

Practice perspective taking

Ideally, negotiators would like to have all the information they need about the other party's positions, interests, preferences, and alternatives, in order to achieve the best outcome possible. Unfortunately, most of that information is not directly accessible. Therefore, negotiators need to gather information about their counterpart before the negotiation in order to make appropriate judgment concerning tradeoffs and concessions.

The process of collecting information about the counterpart and putting oneself in the counterpart's shoes is known as perspective taking. Research has found that perspective taking can decrease negotiators' cognitive biases, such as stereotyping and confirmation bias, and facilitate social coordination (e.g., Galinsky and Moskowitz, 2000). Undoubtedly, understanding the counterpart's interests allows negotiators to overcome the mystical fixed pie assumption and focus on exploring integrative potential. Learning about the counterpart's priorities and preferences allows negotiators to come up with specific strategies for formulating mutually acceptable solutions. Finally, regardless of how big the "pie" can be expanded, most negotiations involve a competitive element of value claiming. Knowing what the other party's alternatives are allows negotiators to estimate what their counterpart's reservation point is so as to maximize their own share of the (expanded) pie.

Once all available information is gathered, negotiators can develop a rough idea of the *zone of potential agreement* (ZOPA). A ZOPA is a range in which each party would be better off reaching an agreement than going with their BATNA. Not all negotiations necessarily have a ZOPA. If the reservation price of the seller is higher than the reservation price of the buyer, no agreement is possible. In this case, negotiators should either seek to change their counterpart's reservation point, or prepare to move on rather than investing too much time and energy in the negotiation in vain. The meaning of ZOPA may differ in distributive and integrative negotiations. As distributive negotiations assume that one party's gain is the other party's loss, ZOPA refers to the spread between the two parties' reservation points. For example, if the seller of a car needs at least $5000 to sell and the buyer will not pay more than $5200, the ZOPA lies between those two values. In integrative negotiations, on the other hand, negotiators cooperate to create additional value, for example, by focusing on common goals and identifying mutually beneficial trade-offs. The ZOPA, therefore, becomes a more open space including all potential packages the parties could agree on. Ideally, negotiators would identify an agreement that utilizes all value created and gets the best possible result for each party. The area of agreements where all created value gets claimed and no party could claim more without hurting the other is called the *pareto efficient frontier* and agreements in that area are called *pareto optimal solutions* (Neale and Bazerman, 1991). The more openly both parties share issues and interests, the more likely they are to be able to work out solutions on the efficient frontier.

Assess the relationship with the other party

The importance of the relationship between the two parties is rarely discussed in detail but can have significant influence on what gets accomplished in a negotiation. For example, the success of the negotiations to end the Cold War between Ronald Reagan and Mikhail Gorbachev is often at least partly attributed to the two men developing a warm relationship. Negotiators need to consider not only the history of their relationship with the other party in general, but also specifically any differences in power or cultural background that could influence the negotiation.

If negotiators or the parties they represent already have a pre-existing relationship, this relationship will create expectations for future encounters. Compared with a counterpart one knows little about, it is much harder for a negotiator to make an ultimatum offer to a friend. Likewise, negotiators are more likely to engage in open and honest exchange of information with a friend than with a stranger. Parties may also expect that if prior negotiations ended with an advantageous settlement for them, future negotiations will do the same, whereas parties who ended up with a less-than-ideal settlement may be particularly wary of the other. Another important aspect of analyzing the relationship is to find out whether there are power differences between negotiating parties. Power can be defined by the dependence each party has on the other (Emerson, 1962). Negotiators who have stronger BATNAs tend to have more power over the other party because of a more favorable interdependent relationship. Parties who are in a less favorable position, however, may use power tactics, such as threats and put-downs, in order to gain an upper hand.

Cultural differences between negotiation parties, if underestimated, can pose barriers to effective negotiation. Members from different cultural backgrounds may have radically different assumptions and norms concerning appropriate, acceptable behavior. For example, negotiators from most Asian and Southern European countries are used to spending significant amounts of time developing a positive relationship before talking about business related issues. Not valuing time spent for such purposes may cause unnecessary confusion and frustration, or lead to agreements that prove short-lived; not planning for this additional time frame can also put negotiators under unnecessary time pressure, which can work to their disadvantage. To avoid culture related problems, negotiators should carefully research any culture related differences in negotiation behavior before the negotiation and plan to navigate these differences successfully.

Conclusion: Planning and Preparation as an Ongoing Process

Although most planning and preparation takes place prior to the negotiation, they should be considered an ongoing process that continues throughout the negotiation. Due to various constraints, negotiators may not be able to gather sufficient information about the other party before the negotiation; even if they think they do, new information may still arise that requires their prompt adjustment and adaptation. In some situations, negotiation parties may change in the middle of the negotiation, new issues may emerge, coalitions may form, BATNAs may improve or deteriorate, relationships may develop, and the overall context of the situation may change as well. Each time something changes or new information becomes available, negotiators need to update their assessments.

In addition, negotiation is often an emotion-laden process. Negotiators may come to the meetings with a rational analysis of possible outcomes. However, many of their aspirations may be thwarted in the encounters with the other party, a precondition for a wide range of emotions to arise. For example, research has shown that angry feelings may cause negotiators to experience increased distrust in the counterpart, and consequently activate

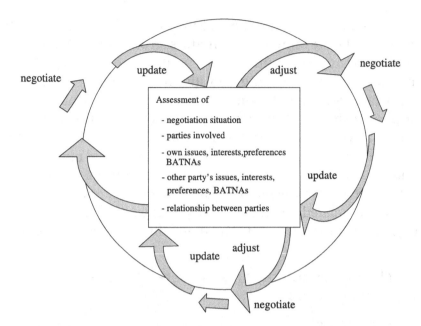

FIGURE 1   Negotiation preparation as an ongoing process

competitively oriented goals, such as wanting a better deal than the counterpart, withdrawing information, attacking the counterpart's face, and wanting to gain power over the other party; likewise, compassionate feelings may cause negotiators to experience more trust, and consequently activate cooperatively oriented goals, such as maximizing joint gains, promoting information exchange, and developing a positive relationship with the counterpart (Liu and Wang, 2010). Understanding how cognitive and emotional factors influence pre-existing goals and planning accordingly will help negotiators develop strategies to counter their effects.

As the above Figure shows, both planning and negotiation are dynamic processes that are constantly (re)defined as interaction unfolds. Planning and preparing inform negotiators' strategic choices; the attitudes, emotions, and behaviors of the counterpart will cause negotiators to revise their pre-existing plans and develop new goals, which will in turn result in behavioral changes. The above guidelines constitute basic, general preparatory work that negotiators should perform prior to the negotiation in order to maximize the potential toward goal achievement. Whether or not such potential can be realized depends substantially on how it is complemented by the effective use of distributive and integrative bargaining tactics during the dynamic, interactive process.

Setting (and Choosing) the Table: The Influence of the Physical Environment in Negotiation

Graham Brown
University of British Columbia

"All social interaction is affected by the physical container in which it occurs" (Bennett and Bennett, 1970: 86)

Helen looked around nervously. Jasmine had asked to meet at a restaurant to discuss the sale of the house. Both were realtors and were discussing the division of commission on the new block of condominiums that were for sale. Helen checked her watch and looked around nervously again. Had she got the address right? This was a dangerous part of town. Outside she could see a group of young men pushing each other around. The restaurant she was in had bars on the door and windows. She wanted to leave. She was just about to call Jasmine to see if she had the correct location when she saw Jasmine enter the restaurant. Jasmine talked causally for while about one of her clients. Helen shifted in her seat and only caught part of what Jasmine was saying. How long was this going to take she thought to herself. Eventually they started talking about the details of the agreement. Jasmine took a firm stand and Helen found herself agreeing with Jasmine's points. Even later, after they had left the restaurant

Helen kicked herself for giving in so easily. What was wrong with her?[1]

Environments influence who we are and what we do. Our behavior is often subtly, and at times nonconsciously, influenced by our surroundings. For instance, where one votes can influence how one votes with the type of building affecting how people vote (e.g., voting in a school influences people to vote for the candidate/party that has a stronger emphasis on education).[2] Physical environments also represent a subset of social rules, conventions, and expectations about certain behavior that trigger certain behavior and/or define the nature of the social interaction. For example, entering into someone's office cues the norm of visitor feelings and behavior.[3] It is not surprising then to think that the environment can have a strong, even if subtle, influence on negotiation behaviors and attitudes towards one's negotiation partner. However, the extent that this affects negotiation is not well known. The purpose of this chapter is to organize what is known, identify opportunities for research, and provide insight to negotiators on how to "set (and even build or choose) the table".

In this chapter I divide the influence of the physical environment on negotiation into 4 categories 1) location; 2) physical structure; 3) physical stimuli; and 4) symbolic artifacts.[4] Within

---

[1] Based on an example in *Negotiating tactics for legal services lawyers* by Michael Meltsner and Philip G. Schrag. September 1973 issue of the Clearinghouse Review [7 CLEARINGHOUSE REV. 259 (Sept. 1973)] — reprinted in 23 Clearinghouse Rev. *858*, 1989–1990.

[2] Berger, J. A., Meredith, M. N., and Wheeler, S. C. Can where people vote influence how they vote? The influence of polling location type on voting behavior. Unpublished paper.

[3] Brown, G. and Baer, M. Lure the tiger from the mountain: Territorial dominance in negotiation. In press. *Organizational Behavior and Human Decision Processes*.

[4] This follows from the framework developed by Tim Davis's (1984) with the addition of location. Davis, Tim R. V. (1984). The influence of the physical environments in offices. *Academy of Management Review*, 9, 271–283.

each of these aspects I review the related studies, which suggest implications of each aspect. Where possible I will talk about the direct effects of the physical environment but often times I will argue for indirect effects based on research that links the physical environment and factors known to impact negotiation including affect and confidence. As such the current chapter draws on much of the work presented in other chapters to show that the physical environment is an important factor in negotiation.

Location

When an employee asks for a favor from a colleague or a raise from his boss it seems commonsensical to approach that person in their office. However, following this strategy may carry with it potentially significant implications for the success of the request: Where we make our request may impact the outcome. For instance, in sports there is a widespread belief in and evidence to support the concept of a "home-field" advantage. The home-field advantage in sports refers to the fact that, across a variety of sports including baseball, basketball, and ice hockey, home teams win a greater percentage of games at home than they do as visitors to other teams' venues.[5] Can this affect negotiation?

Although there are few actual empirical studies on negotiation and location, research in a study of decision making suggests that negotiating on one's turf may provide an advantage. In a study of undergraduate decision making, two researchers found that the outcome of a decision making task will reflect the views of the resident more than the visitor(s), even when the resident has a non dominant personality and the visitor has a dominant personality.[6] In this study the authors had students write down their personal views on a particular issue

---

[5] Gifford, R. (1997). *Environmental psychology*. Boston: Allan & Bacon.
[6] Taylor, R. B. and Lanni, J. C. (1981). Territorial dominance: The influence of the resident advantage in triadic decision making. *Journal of Personality and Social Psychology, 41*, 909–915.

and then meet with two other students to come to a group decision. The authors found that in neutral settings the final decision
reflected the dominant person's view but in situations where
they discussed the issue in one of the student's room, the final
decision reflected the views of the resident, even if the resident
was characterized as having a low dominant personality. A similar effect was observed in a debating situation where the debater
who was viewed as the resident outperformed the debater who
was seen as the visitor.[7] These studies suggest that in competitive
situations and social interactions, being in one's territory provides an advantage, and can even outweigh other, potential,
disadvantages. In one of the only studies that has directly tested
the existence of the home field advantage in negotiation, I, along
with my colleague Markus Baer of Washington University, found
that the home field advantage effect exists not only because of a
resident advantage but also a visitor disadvantage that in part
stems from a decrease in confidence when entering another person's territory.[8] In this study, our residents were students who
were asked to decorate and spend 20 minutes in an office prior to
negotiating with a fellow student. Given the strength of the finding it is not unreasonable to assume that this effect will be even
stronger when someone negotiates in an office that has been
theirs for more than 20 minutes.

Although empirical research is still needed, in practice many
negotiators appear to believe that negotiating on the home-field
is advantageous for the resident, or at least disadvantageous for
the visitor. When asked where they would like to negotiate, most
people tend to choose their own territory — their home turf. A
recent survey revealed that 66% of people feel more "confident"
when negotiating on their own turf and 59% of them believe that
they "perform more effectively" when negotiating on their own

---

[7] Martindale, D. A. (1971). Territorial dominance behavior in dyadic verbal interaction. *Proceedings of the 79th Annual Convention of the American Psychological
Association*, 6, 306–307.
[8] See iii.

turf. In fact, 69% of these participants believe that the person who designates the negotiation site has an advantage in negotiations.[9] History supports this belief with examples that negotiation on one's home turf can be beneficial to the hosting part. For instance, the agreement of the Western allies to meet in Soviet controlled Potsdam after the end of World War II in 1945 allowed Stalin to manipulate the negotiation environment to the Soviet Union's advantage.[10]

Overlooking the importance of location can have disastrous consequences for the outcome of a negotiation. This is powerfully illustrated by the catastrophic nature of the Treaty of Versailles — the principal product of the Paris Peace Conference held by the Allied victors following the end of World War I. In 1919, the Great Powers chose to hold the conference in an embattled city that had only recently been under siege by German forces — a choice that eventually was recognized as a crucial early error.[11] French public opinion and the press acutely impacted the negotiation producing a nervous and altogether ghastly atmosphere, which ultimately contributed to the lose-lose nature of the Treaty of Versailles.[12] These findings underscore the importance of location and are consistent with views of Knapp and Hall (1997) who claimed that "our use of space (our own and others') can affect dramatically our ability to achieve certain desired communication goals" (154).[13]

---

[9] Chu, Y., Strong, W. F., Ma, J., and Greene, W. E. (2005). Silent messages in negotiations: The role of nonverbal communication in cross-cultural business negotiations. *Journal of Organizational Culture, Communications and Conflict, 9,* 113–129.

[10] Mayfield, J., Mayfield, M., Martin, D., and Herbig, P. (1998). How location impacts international business negotiations. *Review of Business, 19,* 21–24.

[11] Bottom, W. P. (2003). Keynes' attack on the Versailles Treaty: An early investigation of the consequences of bounder rationality, framing, and cognitive illusions. *International Negotiation, 8,* 367–402.

[12] Nicolson, Harold. (1933). Peacemaking 1919. London: Constable and Co.

[13] Knapp, M. L. and Hall, J. A. (1997). *Nonverbal Communication in Human Interaction (Fourth Edition).* Austin: Harcourt Brace College Publishers.

Recognizing the importance of site selection in negotiation, today locations are often chosen with the intent not only to isolate the negotiations from the pressure of public opinion but also to achieve a degree of balance between the different parties. Indeed, parties frequently discuss long and hard about where they are to meet before they ever sit down to actually negotiate. Often "neutral" ground is sought out and seems to be useful in facilitating agreements. For example, two ships off the coast of Malta, the Soviet cruise ship SS Maxim Gorkiy and the U.S.S. Belknap, were selected as the location for the Malta Summit between U.S. President Bush and U.S.S.R. Leader Mikhail Gorbachev at the end of the Cold War in 1989. More recently, the Dayton Accord was named so after Bosnia and Herzegovina outlined a peace treaty at the Wright-Patterson Air Force Base near Dayton, Ohio in 1995. Even hundreds of years ago, negotiators were using neutral territory. The Treaty of Tilsit between Napoleon I of France and Czar Alexander I of Russian, for example, was signed on a raft in the middle of the Neman River, a neutral territory. Union representatives also prefer neutral locations, such as hotel meeting rooms as opposed to company headquarters, when conducting contract negotiations, reflecting the belief that the location in which the negotiation is to occur can have a profound impact on the ensuing process and the ultimate outcome of the negotiation.[14]

The location also affects other parts of the negotiation. People are better able to resist pressure to conform when they are on their own territory. When asked to sign a petition that they did not like, people were less likely to conform when they were asked on their own territory.[15] Applied to negotiation, being in one's territory would provide the same benefit to accept a bad deal from

[14] Griffin, T. J. and Daggatt, W. R. (1990). *The global negotiator: Building strong business relationships anywhere in the world.* New York: Harper Business.

[15] Harris, P. B. and McAndrew, F. T. (1986). Territoriality and compliance: The influence of gender and location on willingness to sign petitions. *Journal of Social Psychology, 126,* 657–662.

someone who applies pressure. In parallel, based on my own study described above, it appears that visitors tend to be less pushy, thus providing a dual advantage. Not only does the person who negotiate in their home turf do better because of the advantages accrued form the territory but they also do better because the visitor is less likely to push.

Given this evidence, it seems that it is preferable to negotiate in one's own territory. It provides confidence that helps the negotiator be less influenced. Of course, negotiating in one's territory is not always possible. In fact, it may be the case that it is not always desirable. A neutral site is ideal for negotiations because it can be agreeable and comfortable for both sides and advantageous to neither. In this sense, both parties may feel more comfortable and not feel pressured or at a disadvantage. More research is needed to understand the effect of location of collaborative agreements but given the emphasis on meeting in neutral territories for peace treaties perhaps a neutral site can be preferable depending on the goals. Unfortunately, this also potentially reduces the opportunity to manipulate the other aspects of the physical environment, which can be used to influence the negotiation. In fact, some of the advantages of the location may accrue because of other parts of the physical environment. In the next section, I explore aspects of the physical environment that the negotiator can manipulate.

Physical Structure

The physical structure refers to the architectural design and physical placement of the furniture in the building/room. The manipulation of the physical structure, layout, and the use of the physical environment generally speaking in a negotiation is portrayed by Charlie Chaplin in his famous film, *The Great Dictator*.

> Hitler (played by Chaplin) has invited Mussolini to Germany to decide whether Germany or Italy will invade a neutral country. Hitler's aides arrange for Mussolini to enter Hitler's office by a door at an end of the room far from the Fuhrer's desk. Mussolini

will have to walk a great distance to reach Hitler and, of course, will feel small in the enormous office. The aides also constructed an extremely low chair for Mussolini, so that, when seated, he will have to look up at Hitler. But Mussolini takes Hitler by surprise. He enters by the back door, calmly sits on Hitler's desk, and looks *down* at Hitler. The two dictators then adjourn to a barber shop, where they compete with each other during the negotiations by continually raising their respective barber's chairs to achieve additional height.[16]

The ability to "set the table" is a critical aspect of the negotiation. Setting the table can include deciding "who" is going to be there but again an overlooked aspect of the setting the table is "where" to set the table and "what table to use". Whereas "who" is aptly discussed by Lax and Sebenius in their (2006) book on 3D negotiation,[17] and "where" has been discussed earlier in this chapter, the "what" literally refers to the table itself (and other furniture) that can communicate an important message and influence the negotiation.

The furniture can set the tone and lead to a particular type of negotiation. A very large and formal wooden table and formal chairs create a businesslike atmosphere and tend to be the location for formal talks and deliberations and are generally related to competitive interactions. This furniture supports a "no nonsense" tone for people, and suggests that businesslike transactions are to be carried out within them. In contrast, cheerful, bright-colored rooms, and overstuffed chairs create a significantly more comfortable environment in which parties are more relaxed, and can make people feel comfortable. This may cause parties to let down their guard and relax, creating an affable mood, which may cause participants to act more cooperatively.

Negotiators can structure their territory to make others comfortable or uneasy and to encourage competitive versus

---

[16] See i.

[17] Lax, D. A. and Sebenius, J. K. (2006). *3-D negotiation: Powerful tool to change the game in your most important deals.* Boston, MA: Harvard Business School Press.

cooperative orientations. Seat arrangement has a big influence on whether people are seen as opposites in a battle (facing each other across the table) or working together on a joint problem (sitting side by side). When people are placed face to face around a rectangular table the situation is set for competition. In contrast, side by side seating encourages a cooperative tone. Sitting across a desk from the other person is also seen as more distant and formal, whereas moving to a couch or a round conference table is seen as more approachable and casual. Similarly, if the occupant chooses to seat his or her visitor on a chair lower than his or her own (so that there is no eye-to-eye contact, but the visitor is "looking up at" the occupant), the scene is well set for a competitive negotiation that places the visitor at a significant disadvantage. In contrast, if the office occupant moves out from behind his desk, seating himself in a "conversational grouping" of chairs, maintaining level eye contact, and minimizing the number of status symbols within the office, s/he will help to create an environment that encourages more equal-status communication.[18]

Different seating arrangements and distance from each other also leads to different conversations and can affect views of each other. Interactions at a conference table tend to be initiated across the table rather than side to side and the person seated opposite the speaker is the most likely next speaker. The layout of furniture can also be manipulated to change the physical distance between the negotiators with greater distance leading to greater competition. However, it is important to note that people have different preferences for interpersonal distances. This is also important to consider in negotiations involving people from different cultures. Edward Hall's studies of proxemics showed that this different preference for interpersonal space leads to different conversation patterns and that misunderstanding each culture's preference for interpersonal space can lead to distrust and threaten to break down the relationship. For example,

---

[18] See ix.

Saudi Arabians prefer less space and interact much closer to one another than the typical person from The United States of America. Thus, if an American were negotiating with someone from the Middle East the American might find himself almost nose-to-nose with the person from Saudi Arabia. Attempts to back away to regain social space would be met with pursuit as the person from Saudi Arabia tries to maintain a close distance. The American would come away from the conversation thinking the Saudi Arabian was pushy and aggressive while the Saudi Arabian would think the American was aloof and perhaps hiding something.

Just as manipulations of furniture can be used to set the tone for a negotiation and foster competition, some of the few studies that have looked at negotiation and physical structures suggest that the physical environment can also be used to reduce tensions. For example, putting a physical barrier between negotiators, so that they can hear but not see each other, tends to reduce contending under conditions that ordinarily produce such behavior.[19-21] As a result, win-win agreements are more often found with the barrier in place.

In sum, the physical environment can be structured to support the goals of the negotiator. The smart negotiator structures the room and environment according to what is intended to happen. Conversely, if you find yourself in such a situation — adjust your seat, bring your chair to sit beside the other person, and take control.

[19] Carnevale, P. J. and Isen, A. M. (1986). The influence of positive affect and visual access on the discovery of integrative solutions in bilateral negotiation. *Organizational Behavior and Human Decision Processes, 37*, 1–13.
[20] Carnevale, P. J., Pruitt, D. G. and Seilheimer, S. (1981). Looking and competing: accountability and visual access in integrative bargaining. *J. Pets. Soc. Psychol., 40*,111–120.
[21] Lewis, S. A. and Fry, W. R. (1977). Effects of visual access and orientation on the discovery of integrative bargaining alternatives. *Organizational Behavior and Human Performance, 20*, 75–92.

Physical Stimuli

Another aspect of the environment that can affect a negotiation is the physical stimuli such as noise, smells, and temperature. Many of these stimuli occur and exert affects at the unconscious level but surface to influence social perceptions, decision processes, and behavior. Although the impact of these on negotiation is rarely directly tested, research has been done on the relationship between the physical environment and factors that are known to influence negotiation process and outcome. In this section I look at the specific role of environmental stimuli including music, temperature, and smell by linking them to known factors that affect negotiation processes and outcomes.

Decision making quality. Consumer behaviorists have long noted and studied the influence of physical stimuli on shopping behavior and purchasing. For instance, grocery stores will play slower music when it is not busy to encourage people to take their time and look at products. However, during busy times more up tempo music is played so that people move through the store quickly.[22] How might this play out in negotiation? Can fast music lead to a hurried decision where all the options are not considered or discussed?

Noise can also affect people's judgments. Loud noises have been shown to lead to poorer decisions and less generosity. For example, in a study of initial job offers, people who read an applicant's resume in a room with 53 decibels (normal office sound) offered significantly more money than people who read the resumes in a room with 75 decibels (loud but not uncommon in an office).[23] If the environment where the negotiation takes place

---

[22] Milliman, R. (1982). Using background music to affect the behavior of supermarket shoppers. *Journal of Marketing, 46*(Summer), 86–91.

[23] Sauser, W. I., Jr. Arauz C. G., and Chambers, R. M. (1978). Exploring the relationship between level of office noise and salary recommendations: A preliminary research note. *Journal of Personality and Social Psychology, 32*, 571–577.

is noisy, both parties may be less willing to work towards a solution and we might expect poorer deals and greater rates of impasse.

Ambience through lighting and wall colour can also influence people's attitudes and behavior. For example, McDonalds uses bright reds and yellows in their color scheme. These colors raise anxiety levels and cause people to rush in, consume their food, and rush back out, rather than stay and chat.[24] Dark rooms appear smaller and less spacious than light rooms,[25] which can increase feelings of crowdedness and subsequently lead to irritability, hurried decisions, or cause people to overlook things.

Cognitive performance is also affected by temperature. Both high and moderately warm temperatures can negatively affect performance. For example, performance is not affected for the first 30 minutes in 100 degree Farenheight but at 3 hours it suffers at 87 degrees.[26] Performance on complex tasks also worsens with cold — so, don't turn down the heat too much. If the negotiation is complicated having sub optimal temperature could lead to poor outcomes for both parties. The implication from this is that part of the negotiation preparation should be to dress appropriately for the negotiation. Make sure you have a sweater or jacket that you can remove or put on if the temperature changes.

Affect. Affect is associated with increased cooperativeness among other things. For our purposes here, we are interested in environmental stimuli that have been shown to influence affect. For example, pleasant aromas are associated with people setting higher goals and, in one of the few studies that explored the influence of the

[24] Read, M. A., Sugawara, A. I., and Brandt, J. A. (1999). Impact of space and color in the physical environment on preschool children's cooperative behavior. *Environment and Behavior, 31*, 413–428.

[25] Mandel, D. R., Baron, R. M. and Fisher, J. D. (1980). Room utilization and dimensions of density: Effects of height and view. *Environment and Behavior, 12*, 308–319.

[26] McKormick, E. J. (1976). Human factors in engineering and design. New York: McGraw-Hill.

physical environment in a negotiation, people exposed to pleasant aromas prior to negotiating were more likely to make more concessions in a face to face negotiation and adopt a less confrontational negotiation style.[27] These effects are largely attributable to the increase in positive affect that pleasant aromas have.[28] Other studies that look at the relationship between the physical environment and affect show similar patterns. For example, uplifting music is also associated with increased positive affect and helping behavior.[29] Similarly, ceiling height and wall colour relate to cooperative behavior.[30] Conversely, unpleasant aromas, excessive heat,[31] and irritating noise[32] lead to negative affect.[33]

Aggressiveness. We have often heard about a negotiator turning up the heat in a negotiation. Although rarely is this meant literally, changes in temperature may actually affect a negotiation. People become more aggressive when the temperature starts to exceed 91F.[34] Increases in temperature also lead individuals to report less favorable views of others.[35] As heat increases it

---

[27] Baron, R. A. (1990). Environmentally induced positive affect: Its impact on self-efficacy, task performance, negotiation, and conflict. *Journal of Applied Social Psychology, 20*, 368–384.

[28] *Ibid.*

[29] North, A. C., Tarrant, M., and Hargreaves, D. J. (2004). The effects of music on helping behavior. *Environment and Behavior, 36*(2), 266–275.

[30] See xxiv.

[31] Baron, R. A. (1978). Aggression and heat: The "long hot summer" revisited. In A. Baum, S. Valins, J. E. Singer (Eds.), *Advances in environmental research* (Vol. 1, pp. 57–84). Hillsdale, NJ: Erlbaum.

[32] Nagar, D. and Pandey, J. (1987). Affect and performance on cognitive task as a function of crowding and noise. *Journal of Applied Social Psychology, 17*, 147–157.

[33] Zillmann, D., Baron, R. A., and Tamborini, R. (1981). The social costs of smoking: Effects of tobacco smoke on hostile behavior. *Journal of Applied Social Psychology, 11*, 548–561.

[34] Rule, B. G., Taylor, B., and Dobbs, A. R. (1987). Priming effects of heat on aggressive thoughts. *Social Cognition, 5*, 131–144.

[35] Baron, R. A. (1994). The physical environment of work setting: Effects on task performance, interpersonal relations, and satisfaction. *Res. Organ. Behavior, 16*, 1–46.

primes hostility and this could lead to greater impasse and less willing to build value in a negotiation. These studies suggest that taking breaks and "cooling" off are both psychological and physically important. Other environmental stimuli that increase aggression and which could lead to a breakdown in the negotiation are crowding, poor air quality, and noise.[36]

Symbolic Artifacts

The final category that I will cover in this chapter is symbolic artifacts. These symbols affect the interpretation of the setting and include photographs or artwork on the walls, professional image cues like trophies, degrees, or certificates, or even the presence of carpet in a room. These objects serve as material primes that exert automatic, unconscious, and even unwanted effects on relevant behavioral choices and judgments and can set the context for a particular tone in the negotiation. Even without our awareness, exposure to material primes "help us to define situations, recognize operative situational norms, activate appropriate roles, and interact in ways that are congruent with those norms and roles".[37]

People often use symbols as a strategy for establishing who they are in relation to others in the organization and for creating impressions for themselves and others.[38] People can display signals to make statements to others about how they would like to be perceived.[39] Symbols can also reinforce the home-turf advantage

[36] Berkowitz, L. (1993). *Aggression: Its Causes, Consequences and Control.* New York: McGraw-Hill.

[37] Kay, A. C. Wheeler, S. C., Bargh, J. A., and Rossa, L. (2004). Material priming: The influence of mundane physical objects on situational construal and competitive behavioral choice. *Organizational Behavior and Human Decision Processes, 95,* 83–96.

[38] Brown, B. B. and Werner, C. M. (1985). 'Social cohesiveness, territoriality, and holiday decorations: The influence of cul-de-sacs', *Environment and Behavior, 17,* 539–565.

[39] Goffman, E. (1959). *The presentation of self in everyday life.* New York: Doubleday.

and particular symbols may enhance the occupant's perceived status and power. In an unpublished study of office personalizations and negotiation, some participants reported that they specifically chose and put up certain posters that they thought would make them appear "tough" so that the other party would not take advantage of them.[40]

Studies show that these markings and objects elicit similar impressions from independent observers and are particularly important in novel or ambiguous situations where people do not have a lot of other information to go by.[41] Thus the potential to impact the tone and direction of a negotiation is quite significant. Symbols that are inviting create a significantly more comfortable environment and may make the host appear more friendly and welcoming, setting the stage for both parties to act more cooperatively. For example, the presence of plants and wall decorations produces favorable visitor reactions and attributions from visitors. A framed picture of a happy family can serve as a signal that the occupant is empathetic and warm. In contrast, symbols, like muted colored carpets and curtains create a businesslike atmosphere that signal a competitive orientation. For example, environmental stimuli (e.g., business suits) have been shown to increase the number of competitive decisions expressed.[42] Thus the strategic use of artifacts can be important for setting the tone of the negotiation.

Conclusion

People know that the physical environment affects them and is important in negotiation. In a study including Chinese and British negotiators, 62% of participants reported feeling more

---

[40] Brown, G. Personalizations and negotiation. Unpublished manuscript.

[41] Gosling, S. D., Ko, S. J., Mannarelli, T., and Morris M. E. (2002). A room with a cue: Personality judgments based on offices and bedrooms. *Journal of Personality and Social Psychology, 82,* 379–398.

[42] See xxxviii.

calm when they negotiate in a room with paintings of country-side scenes on the walls. 74% of participants feel "more pleasant" when they sit at a table decorated with flowers, and 60% of the people surveyed stated that they felt more at ease when there are soft drinks on the table when they negotiate. However, these relatively simple features of the environment are often overlooked.

In this chapter I argue that the physical environment can be is akin to other "strategies" and tactics in negotiation and that the physical environment can be manipulated to influence the negotiation process and outcome. Although less is known and much research is needed to establish direct effects, there is ample evidence from other studies to suggest that environment can affect the negotiation. Just as the environment can help one claim value it can also be structured to help create value.

One has to be careful about how one sets up the negotiation room. If you want to avoid confrontation and competition then thought needs to be directed to setting the stage for negotiations free of a competitive orientation and this means getting rid of symbols that might induce competition. Avoiding images that suggest domination and differences in power are important to making the other party comfortable. Choosing a round table, setting chairs only on one side of the table, and even the artwork on the wall can influence the tone and process of the negotiation. People prefer round tables to square tables in negotiations because they believe that a round table eases tension. Round tables make the atmosphere more conducive for discussion. Paintings of countryside scenes on walls and a table decorated with flowers and soft drinks will make negotiators feel calm, more pleasant, and at ease.[43] This physical arrangement will ease tension and make your negotiation partner feel calm, more pleasant, and at ease. The setting will be more conducive for discussion, and you will get more cooperation from them too.

---

[43] See ix.

At the outset I suggested that negotiating on one's territory provides an advantage. Much of this advantage accrues because of the ability to control the environment. One of the keys to successful negotiation is to get comfortable. The physical environment is critical to this. Both the location and the physical setup can affect your comfort level and your ability to concentrate. Any physical, emotional or psychological discomfort could distract you from the task at hand and lead to a poor outcome for you and your negotiation partner. If you go to someone else's location make sure you exert some control. Choose a chair. Move your seat around the table. Being able to adjust the environment may help satisfy our innate need for control that all humans possess.[44] In many cases it may be easy, and perfectly reasonable, to adjust the height of your chair, or even to change locations. Choosing where to sit (even if it means moving a chair, or even deciding whether to sit) may help make a negotiator feel more confident and be the most important move you make.

To conclude I offer a few words of warning. Too many negotiators do not prepare by setting the table appropriately or for the right outcome. Yet, as discussed here, the physical environment including the choice of venue, the layout, and factors in the environment can play a significant role in the negotiation. People who expect to negotiate with a cooperative and ethical other are more likely to cooperate, whereas the expectation to negotiate with a competitive and opportunistic other increases one's willingness to be competitive and tough.[45] You may want to cooperate but if you set up the room the wrong way you might send a signal to the other person that you are competitive. It is

---

[44] Baumeister, R. F. (1998). The self. In D. T. Gilbert, S. T. Fiske, and G. Lindzey (Eds.), Handbook of social psychology (4th ed.; pp. 680–740). New York: McGraw-Hill.

[45] See for example, Paese, P. W., and Gilin, D. A. (2000). When an adversary is caught telling the truth: Reciprocal cooperation versus self-interest in distributive bargaining. *Personality and Social Psychology Bulletin, 26,* 79–90.

critical to pay attention to environmental primes because they can create a viscous cycle. If the environment induces an initial competitive offer, we are likely to reciprocate with a competitive offer, reinforcing the other person's view that we wanted to be competitive. Even if the visitor doesn't consciously notice the symbols their negotiation position and style may be affected. The physical environment communicates sends a message whether you are aware of it or not. An ignorance of or lack of attention to the physical environment may take the negotiation down an unintended path.

Negotiation Approaches: Claiming and Creating Value

Jill M. Purdy
University of Washington

Negotiations occur when parties experience or anticipate interdependence. Negotiators may seek to acquire information or resources from others, resolve a dispute, or explore the possibility of creating something new by working together. During a negotiation, the parties use a variety of behaviors to frame the boundaries of the negotiation, exchange information, construct possible solutions, and advocate for a preferred outcome. While these basic elements of negotiation remain the same across many contexts, the approaches that the parties take to move through the negotiation process may vary significantly. Consider the following example.

Small business owner Chris is looking for warehouse space to lease for his growing business. He plans to adapt the space to his needs by investing in some tenant improvements including electrical and plumbing work. Chris first meets with Stewart, the owner of a warehouse facility. Chris inquires about available space and Stewart names his price for the space. Chris counters with a lower price, and mentions that he'll need to make some improvements to the space to make it fit his needs. Stewart asserts that he'll need more details about the improvements before he will consider renting the space, but that his price is firm. Chris objects, saying that the cost of the space is too high given that he will also need to invest in tenant improvements. The men exchange multiple offers but are unable to reach a price that both find satisfactory.

Chris then meets with Bruce, another warehouse facility owner. Bruce opens the negotiation by asking Chris about his business. Chris describes his growing business and his need to have customized warehouse space available as soon as possible. Bruce mentions that he has plenty of space available to rent, then describes his experience in working with other warehouse tenants to customize their spaces. Chris asks the price of the space and mentions that he is trying to keep costs down because he is concerned about cash flow. Bruce names his price, then offers his assistance to get the necessary permits quickly to complete the electrical and plumbing work. Chris suggests a lower price, reiterating his concerns about not having enough cash in the near term for both the lease and the needed improvements. Chris also mentions that he hopes to need even more warehouse space in 18–24 months and would consider leasing additional space from Bruce. After further discussion, Chris and Bruce agree to a lease that incorporates a price about midway between their initial offers. Both men agree that a three year lease would be appropriate given the investments being made in customizing the space to Chris's needs. Bruce agrees to help expedite the permits for the needed improvements, forgo the first month's rent while improvements are being completed, and defer the second month's rent until the second year of the lease. Chris agrees to lease additional space from Bruce within two years as long as his business achieves an agreed-upon volume of sales.

Chris's negotiations with Stewart and Bruce exemplify two common approaches to negotiation. In the first negotiation, Chris and Stewart sought to satisfy only their own concerns, while in the second negotiation, Chris and Bruce tried to create the most possible value in the deal. Numerous negotiation researchers have identified these contrasting approaches, alternately describing them as competitive and cooperative (Deutsch, 1973), concern for self and concern for other (Pruitt and Rubin, 1986; Ruble and Thomas, 1976), distributive and integrative (Walton and McKersie, 1965), and claiming and creating value (Lax and Sebenius, 1986; Raiffa, 1982). While these four frameworks have different origins and assumptions, each describes negotiation as consisting of two fundamentally different processes: discovering all the value that can be exchanged, and dividing the value among the parties. In this chapter we'll refer to these two approaches respectively as *creating value* and *claiming value*.

As the example above illustrates, some negotiators may emphasize claiming value, or doing what is necessary to claim the reward or the largest piece possible (Lax and Sebenius, 1986). Stewart's interaction with Chris emphasized his own self-interest and focused on how value, in the form of the lease rate, would be divided between them. Other negotiators may emphasize creating value, or find a way for all parties to meet their objectives (Lewicki, Barry and Saunders, 2010), as Bruce's interaction with Chris demonstrates. Bruce sought information that helped him identify additional sources of value that could be negotiated in addition to the lease rate. Bruce offered expertise on tenant improvements and decreased the demands on Chris' short term cash flow in exchange for additional space to be leased by Chris in the future. Although the parties in this example successfully created value, it is important to recognize that claiming value was also needed to reach a deal and finalize the negotiation. Each negotiator established parameters for the value they would provide and the value they would receive, including a mutually agreeable price for the warehouse lease.

Research on negotiation indicates that using a mixture of negotiation approaches is most likely to result in processes and outcomes that are satisfactory to participants (Raiffa, 1982). Some authors argue that claiming and creating value are inextricably intertwined and that attempts to separate the approaches ignore the true nature of negotiation (Lax and Sebenius, 1986). Despite this contention, this chapter begins by considering claiming value and value creation separately, describing the behaviors associated with each and the situations in which each approach is likely to occur. The interconnectedness of the two approaches is then discussed in a section on mixed motive negotiation. A central challenge of negotiation is managing the negotiator's dilemma, a term used to describe the tension between creating and claiming value. The chapter concludes with a discussion of the principled negotiation approach and how its methods can be used to address the negotiator's dilemma and reach satisfactory agreements.

Claiming Value

Negotiation is characterized by interdependence between parties, whether they are individuals, groups, organizations, or nations. Independent parties need not negotiate because they can accomplish their goals without negotiation. A one-way dependency also means action can be taken without negotiating, thus mutual dependence is a fundamental requirement for negotiation. Negotiation occurs when interdependent parties experience a conflict and interact strategically to further their interests (Lax and Sebenius, 1986). Typically negotiation is a voluntary process that people participate in because they believe that joint effort will yield better results than unilateral effort. Negotiation yields value — in the form of resources, priorities, expectations, risk, or time — beyond what the person could achieve without negotiating (Mnookin, Peppet and Tulumello, 2000). Value is often thought of in terms of resources such as money, goods or services, but value also exists in relation to time, amount of risk, or satisfaction. Whether something has value in a negotiation depends on the needs and interests of the negotiators.

Some negotiations are characterized by competitive approaches where the participants believe the outcome will yield a winner and a loser. This approach to negotiation, often called *distributive bargaining*, is evident in some labor negotiations when the focus is on wages, and every dollar gained by one side is a dollar lost by the other side (Walton and McKersie, 1965). The claiming value approach to negotiation frames such situations as competitions where a fixed amount of value is available to be distributed among the parties, and the most powerful negotiators will prevail by gaining the largest share of value. Situations with a fixed amount of value are referred to as *zero-sum, fixed-pie,* or *win-lose* situations because a gain for one party results in a loss for another party. As one party's slice of the pie grows larger, the other party's slice shrinks.

Many negotiations are indeed competitive situations, for example, dividing the company budget among departments, establishing wages in a union contract, or striving to be the team that signs the rising sports star. Zero-sum situations typically have a single dominant issue that involves a scarce or limited resource like money, time, knowledge or talent. Because tradeoffs are impossible in single-issue negotiations, the parties work to claim as large a share of the limited value as possible. However, research indicates that people see situations as distributive in nature even when they are not. The *mythical fixed-pie bias* occurs when people assume that their interests directly conflict with those of others when they actually do not (Bazerman and Neale, 1992). People generalize their understanding of win-lose situations to situations that are not win-lose and then negotiate using the claiming value approach even when it is not appropriate.

Claiming value involves a variety of tactics intended to influence the negotiation proceedings. One tactic is to establish a *reservation price* that represents the minimum value that is acceptable to claim in the negotiation (Raiffa, 1982). Using the pie analogy, the reservation price represents the smallest piece of pie you are willing to accept rather than walking away from the negotiation. Value-claiming negotiators are interested in knowing what this minimum is because in a zero-sum situation, it determines the maximum amount of value available to other participants. Negotiators engaged in claiming value try to discover the reservation points of others so they can push toward their opponent's acceptable minimum, and they try to conceal their own reservation price to prevent others from seeking their maximum possible shares. Many of the behaviors we associate with hard bargaining are value-claiming strategies related to reservation price. For example, consider the situation of purchasing a used car. Buyers may feign lack of interest ("it's not really what I was looking for"), find fault with the vehicle ("these tires don't have a lot of tread"), or even walk away from an acceptable deal in an effort to make the dealer believe their reservation price is lower than it actually is. For their part, sellers will emphasize unique attributes of the vehicle ("you'll have a hard time finding this color somewhere else"), try to create a sense of urgency ("another buyer is coming to look at this car in an hour"), or focus the buyer on monthly payments rather than total price to push buyers beyond their reservation price. Misleading others and withholding information can put negotiators on the edge of an ethical dilemma, but most negotiators accept and expect that some exaggeration and concealment will occur during distributive negotiations (Lewicki, Barry and Saunders, 2010).

Another strategy that value-claiming negotiators may use to influence their counterparts' reservation prices is *anchoring*. Anchoring occurs when the initial offer made by a negotiator becomes a mental reference point against which other possible solutions are judged (Bazerman and Neale, 1992). Numerical anchors can have a powerful effect on people's decision making even when the numbers have little or no relevance to the value of what is being negotiated (Kahneman and Tversky, 2004). Because of this tendency, being the first to make an offer in a negotiation can create an advantage for a negotiator (Galinsky and Mussweiler, 2001). The anchoring strategy is particularly effective when the value of what's being negotiated is unknown or uncertain. For example, if you had planned to offer $50 for a ukulele at a yard sale and the seller asked for $500, you might revise your expectations and change your opening offer to $100. Even if you made your planned opening offer at $50, you might be influenced by the $500 offer as an anchor, and revise your reservation price and expected settlement point upward. Negotiators tend to use opening offers as brackets and work their way toward a midpoint between them (Craver, 2002). The $500 and $50 anchors might lead you to conclude that $275 (midway between the anchors) is a reasonable price for the ukulele, but if the seller had initially offered it for $200, you might instead conclude that $125 was a reasonable price (the average of $50 and $200) because your perceptions are strongly influenced by the other negotiator's initial offer. Anchoring occurs whenever initial offers are exchanged, but it becomes a value claiming strategy when the initial offer is deliberately made extreme to influence the outcome of the negotiation.

While some of the behaviors described above can verge on the unethical, claiming value is a necessary part of negotiation. Even negotiators who engage in creating value must claim value in order to finalize an agreement (Lewicki, Barry and Saunders, 2010). Claiming value need not involve deception or manipulation (Lax and Sebenius, 1986). At its most fundamental, value claiming involves communicating one's preferred outcomes from among the alternatives discussed.

A claiming value approach is appropriate to use in negotiation if you are standing up for your rights, defending a position you believe is correct, or simply trying to win (Thomas and Kilmann, 1977). For example, claiming value might be the best approach when negotiating unpopular courses of action that must be implemented, such as cost-cutting or enforcing policies (Thomas and Kilmann, 1977). Value claiming is also appropriate on vital issues where compromise would be equivalent to losing. For example, biologists participating in a negotiation with a hydro-electric dam company sought to claim value when negotiating about the amount of river water needed to flow freely around the dam to ensure healthy fish populations. The company operating the dam wanted to divert more water into its turbines to generate more hydroelectricity (and higher returns on its investment). If the biologists failed to claim sufficient value, the fish population in the river could be lost entirely, so any concession would eliminate all value for the biologists. The situation required value claiming behavior because the river flow was a fixed resource and the two available options for the water (through the dam or around the dam) were mutually exclusive. Claiming value is a valuable skill for all negotiators to have to address situations such as these.

Creating Value

The second primary approach to negotiation is the creating value approach, which involves efforts to expand the opportunities for exchange among negotiation participants. This approach to negotiation seeks solutions that will satisfy the objectives of all participants. Creating value is often called 'expanding the pie' because of its emphasis on identifying many possible sources of value and creative ways to share and coordinate resources. Creating value is also called *mutual-gain* or *integrative negotiation*, which describes the process of finding a solution that blends the interests of the negotiators together. At its core, the creating value approach is a cooperative one in which parties seek to understand the needs and objectives of others and strive to find alternatives that will meet others' interests as well as their own.

One of the simplest strategies for creating value in a negotiation is expanding the number of negotiable issues. Expanding the number of issues allows negotiators to identify different priorities and make tradeoffs on issues, potentially permitting each negotiator to claim more total value. By incorporating additional aspects of value into their negotiation, participants are not limited to simply exchanging concessions on an issue of fixed value. To add issues and potentially create value in a negotiation, the participants must exchange information about their needs and objectives. This requires asking questions, sharing information about one's own interests, and building trust with the other negotiator(s). Trust is important to value creation as it increases cooperative behavior and information exchange (Butler, 1999).

After multiple issues of potential value have been discovered by the negotiators, they must then seek to combine them to best satisfy the needs of all participants. One effective method of creative value is *logrolling*, or trading off on items that the negotiators prioritize differently. For example, business partners Lena and

Jeff have moved into a new building and are choosing their offices. Both would like large offices with good views of the city. However, the office with the nice city view is small, while the large office has a view limited to the buildings across the street. If Lena cares more about the view and Jeff prioritizes office space, logrolling can help satisfy both parties. Jeff can concede on the view in order to gain the large office, while Lena can concede on office space to gain a good view. Another useful strategy for creating value in a negotiation is the use of contingent contracts. A contingent contract takes advantage of negotiators' different expectations about the future and links outcomes to them. For example, if one negotiator believes that costs will rise rapidly and the other believes that costs will remain fairly steady, they can make an agreement that applies different pricing depending on how much costs actually change. Value creation can also occur by brainstorming and constructing several packages of options. By bundling a group of solutions together, negotiators can evaluate the value of the whole package without bargaining over zero-sum items or revealing their reservation price on individual issues. Rather than debating the merits of a single proposal, negotiators who discuss multiple packages simultaneously can continue creating alternatives without revealing the details of their preferences or committing to a particular solution.

The underlying goal of creating value in a negotiation is creating joint gain. Joint gain occurs when the positions of all negotiators are improved because they have received more value. Negotiators striving to create value are working to move their agreement toward a hypothetical line called the *Pareto frontier*. The Pareto frontier represents the maximum possible value that could be created if the negotiators exchange information fully and think very creatively (Lax and Sebenius, 1986). Negotiators using the creating value approach may search for ways to improve on the initial deal (point X in Figure 1) so that they can get closer to the Pareto frontier (point Y). This involves finding ways to cut costs or increase value for participants without harming any other party. In this example, moving from

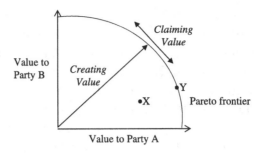

FIGURE 1

agreement X to agreement Y means that both parties receive more value.

The creating value approach is more likely to be used in situations where the parties have a prior positive relationship where trust exists, when the parties wish to develop a long-term relationship, or when parties share a common goal (Lewicki, Barry and Saunders, 2010). Negotiators who have strong communication skills and who understand strategies such as logrolling and contingent contracts may be more comfortable using the creating value approach. Negotiators may fail to create value if they assume a fixed-pie when options for mutual gain actually exist, or if they are accustomed to using the claiming value approach and find it hard to switch.

While creating value can improve outcomes for all negotiators, the creating value approach prompts two dilemmas that negotiators must grapple with: the dilemmas of trust and honesty. The dilemma of trust recognizes that a negotiator must believe the information shared by other parties to work toward mutual gain, but fully trusting others exposes one to possible deceit and manipulation. The dilemma of honesty acknowledges that a negotiator must share information to make her interests known and to generate value, but if she reveals all her requirements and limits she may do no better than her reservation price (Kelley, 1966). Negotiators who take a creating value approach must achieve a balance between complete trust and healthy skepticism, and between full candor and cautious exchange.

Mixed Motive Negotiations

When beginning a negotiation, the participants may not know exactly what issues they will be discussing, whether those issues are zero-sum or integrative in nature, or the relative importance of the issues. As a result, negotiators should approach situations as mixed motive, recognizing that some elements will require creating value and others will require claiming value. Balancing the two approaches is not necessarily an easy task. Both value creating and value claiming are needed to successfully negotiate, but parties face the difficult choice of which approach to choose at any given time.

In Figure 1, note that when the agreement moves from point X to point Y, Party A makes a significant gain (as measured by the horizontal axis) while Party B's improvement is small (as measured by the vertical axis). While additional value has been created and joint gains have occurred, Party A has gained more of the value created than Party B, as represented by movement along the Pareto frontier. This outcome suggests that Party A was more effective at value claiming than Party B, highlighting the importance of using both negotiating approaches well. However, a fundamental tension exists between the cooperative actions required to create value and the competitive actions needed to claim it. This tension is called the *negotiator's dilemma* (Lax and Sebenius, 1986). The behaviors that lead to successful value creation, such as sharing information about preferences, interests, and priorities, may make a negotiator vulnerable when it comes to claiming value. For example, a willingness to make tradeoffs may be perceived as an opportunity to extract unilateral concessions. Similarly, the behaviors that lead to successful value claiming, including concealing information and influencing the other's reservation price, are likely to hinder trust and inhibit creating value. Efforts to claim value through exaggeration or manipulation may make it difficult for negotiators to discover shared interests or new issues that could add value to the negotiation (Lax and Sebenius, 1986).

The negotiator's dilemma suggests that negotiators intent on making a deal must teeter on the knife's edge between appearing too cooperative while creating value and appearing too competitive while claiming value. Some criticism of this perspective has emerged which indicates that real negotiators are unlikely to accept poor deals and will walk away rather than allow the other side to claim the majority of the value (Subramaniam, 2010). Instead, the chances of reaching an agreement decline if the negotiators focus too strongly on claiming value, and the chances of reaching an agreement increase significantly as negotiators create value that improves the outcomes for both sides. This critique suggests that rather than facing a dilemma where creating value and claiming value are equally important approaches, negotiators should favor the creating value approach because the likelihood of the deal increases with the value of the deal (Subraminian, 2010).

Mnookin, Peppet and Tulumello (2000) offer a different perspective on managing the negotiator's dilemma. They suggest that the tension between creating and claiming value can never be resolved, thus the goal should be to support value creation where possible while minimizing the risks of being exploited during value claiming. One means of creating value without making oneself vulnerable is to reduce transaction costs by making negotiation less costly in time or money. For example, negotiators who successfully frame their efforts as mutual problem-solving rather than win-lose bargaining can reduce the time spent on hard-bargaining tactics such as bluffing and haggling. Negotiators also can create value in negotiations by reducing the risk that the parties will deceive each other, and by better aligning future incentives. Negotiators can reduce the risk of deception by offering objective verification of their claims, such as when a car dealer shows the buyer the published value of a vehicle based on actual deals that have occurred over the past year. Individuals and businesses can also use their reputations or offer references to provide assurances of trustworthiness. Finally, offering a guarantee or some future recourse against deception can help the parties create value without increasing the risk of being taken advantage of during value claiming (Mnookin, Peppet and Tulumello, 2000). To maximize their chances of success in mixed motive negotiations, negotiators should prepare by identifying the issues, thinking about all parties' interests, considering possible avenues for value creation, knowing their alternatives should the negotiation fail, and establishing ambitious but realistic aspirations. When at the negotiating table, parties should work to identify each other's interests, resources and capabilities in order to discover the possibilities for creating value and should focus on problem-solving rather than defending their positions (Mnookin, Peppet and Tulumello, 2000).

Another challenge of mixed motive negotiations is that they often involve more than the objective goals of dispassionate people. People approach negotiations with different perspectives about what the purpose of the negotiation should be. These perspectives are oriented around interests, rights and power (Ury, Brett and Goldberg, 1993). For some, negotiation is a problem-solving or deal-making task that is linked to each negotiator's interests. Interests are the desires, needs and concerns that motivate a negotiator's stated position; they define why we want what we want. For other people, negotiation is a determination of who is right. Rights-based negotiation may focus on laws or formal contracts, or it might emphasize social norms, precedents, or beliefs about equity and fairness. Finally, negotiation can be approached as a determination of who is more powerful. In this context, power refers to the ability to get someone to do something he would not otherwise do (Ury, Brett and Goldberg, 1993). Power-based negotiation focuses on evaluating or demonstrating perceived sources of power and testing dependencies.

Understanding which of these perspectives is motivating the other negotiator is very helpful in determining how to plan for a negotiation and what balance to strike between the creating and claiming value approaches. Recognizing these different possible framings of a negotiation is also helpful because negotiations may include elements of all three perspectives, shifting back and forth between them. Interest-based negotiations can be approached using a problem-solving perspective that utilizes the creating and claiming value approaches discussed earlier in this chapter. In contrast, rights- and power-based negotiations are more likely to damage relationships and remain unresolved because they frequently become contests that can carry high transaction costs. Negotiating from an interests-based perspective is less costly than determining who is right, which is less costly than determining who is more powerful (Ury, Brett and Goldberg, 1988). However, if concerns about rights or power are not addressed, negotiators are unlikely to succeed at creating value because their ability to share information or trust others in inhibited by their uncertainty over their rights or power. By recognizing the barriers created by rights and power perspectives, negotiators can attempt to address these uncertainties to help the other party move toward an interest-based approach that is more likely to be fruitful.

Interest Based Negotiation

Understanding others' interests makes it easier for negotiators to identify opportunities to add value to the negotiation, and to create solutions that are likely to be agreeable to others (Fisher, Ury and Patton, 1991). Yet many people believe they must approach situations as either soft or hard negotiators. The soft negotiator wants to avoid conflict and reach an amicable agreement, so he makes concessions to reach an agreement but walks away unhappy. The hard negotiator takes extreme positions and wants to win, but she often provokes an equally hard response that damages relationships and produces no agreement. Fisher, Ury and Patton (1991) propose an alternative approach called principled negotiation that is hard on the problem but soft on the people. It emphasizes interest-based problem solving to create options for mutual gain and using objective criteria as the basis for agreement.

The first principle of interest-based negotiation is to separate the people from the problem. People engage in negotiations to satisfy their own or their company's needs, but they also bring their personal values, emotions, and experiences to the table. A fundamental interest that most people bring to negotiation is a desire to feel successful and effective, but personal attacks, lying, bluffing and manipulation can make negotiators angry, frustrated and fearful. The substance of the negotiation can become entangled with the relationship between negotiators if discussion of a problem is perceived as a personal attack. Separating the people from the problem requires negotiators to focus on the issues at hand, and to think of them as a mutual problem to be solved, while simultaneously respecting and acknowledging people's perceptions and emotions, and striving to communicate well. Building a working relationship with the other side is an important step in building mutual trust that can allow progress on the problem without people getting hurt.

The second principle of interest-based negotiation is to focus on interests, not positions (Fisher, Ury and Patton, 1991). Positions identify what people want, specifically their desired outcomes or solutions, while interests identify the why behind the position, describing people's motivations for choosing a particular solution. Negotiators often begin with positions, as illustrated in the negotiation between Chris and Stewart described earlier in this chapter. Each party presented his desired price for the lease of warehouse space, and when they were unable to achieve a compromise, the negotiation failed. In contrast, the negotiation between Chris and Bruce began with Bruce seeking to understand why Chris was leasing warehouse space. Bruce then shared his interest in leasing available space and described his experience in helping tenants with modifying their spaces. Only then did the two men exchange ideas about pricing.

The exchange between Chris and Bruce revealed three kinds of interests: shared, compatible, and opposing. First, the desire to lease space is a shared interest: Chris would like to lease space and Bruce would like to find a tenant. This shared interest is what initially brought the parties together. Another shared interest emerged later in the negotiation, when both parties found that they preferred a three year lease to satisfy Chris' interest in recouping the investment in tenant improvements and Bruce's interest in maximizing his tenant occupancy rate. The different, yet compatible interests uncovered are Chris' and Bruce's desires for their respective companies to thrive. The men may not be concerned with the success of each other's business, but their interests do not conflict: both businesses can succeed and thrive. Exchanging information about this interest allows the parties to recognize that concluding this deal may result in mutual gains. Another compatible interest is Chris' desire to make tenant improvements to the leased space while managing his cash flow. Bruce is willing to support these interests in exchange for Chris' commitment to leasing additional space, which serves Bruce's interest in securing additional revenues in the future. Only the price of the lease is an opposing interest. Here Bruce would prefer a higher price and Chris would prefer a lower price. If this issue were the only one being negotiated, the parties might quickly move to claiming value, as occurred in Chris' negotiation with Stewart. However, in this case the parties' discovery of shared and compatible interests allowed them to identify multiple issues that expanded the overall value available to be negotiated.

Discovering interests occurs more easily if the negotiation begins with interests rather than positions. One way to do this is for the negotiators to define the problem as they see it rather than immediately focusing on their preferred solutions. Another valuable strategy for uncovering interests is to encourage both parties to be as specific as possible in describing their concerns, and to acknowledge the other side's concerns even if one does not agree with them. By demonstrating understanding, negotiators increase the likelihood of having their own concerns listened to and understood without triggering a defensive response (Fisher, Ury and Patton, 1991). Asking 'why' questions can also be effective at revealing interests.

The third component of principled negotiation is to create options for mutual gain. An initial strategy is to identify additional issues that may have emerged and add them to the bargaining mix to create more value and increase opportunities for tradeoffs. As negotiators begin to focus on solutions and outcomes, they may find it difficult to continue to explore a wide variety of possible solutions without committing to any initially. Brainstorming processes that permit no evaluation of alternatives can be useful for sparking new ideas that may create value. Negotiators should be cautious to avoid negotiating issue by issue rather than evaluating packages that span multiple issues (Fisher, Ury and Patton, 1991).

One effective means of creating options for mutual gain is to address issues based on the three different types of interests identified above. When shared interests exist, finding solutions that satisfy both parties is relatively simple, but negotiators can benefit from investing effort into generating multiple creative options. This effort allows negotiators to practice creative thinking together and to demonstrate their commitment to satisfying the interests of others as well as their own. Interests that are different but compatible present opportunities to use some of the value creation strategies discussed previously that leverage different priorities, such as logrolling. Negotiators who have little concern for an issue can demonstrate good faith and trustworthiness by conceding most or all of the value on an issue that is vitally important to the other negotiator, in exchange for a similar stance on an issue where the priorities are reversed. The importance of negotiating packages rather than individual issues becomes clear with this strategy; the success of logrolling depends upon the ability to exchange value across multiple issues with differing priorities, which is less likely to occur if issues are addressed sequentially. Another useful strategy for negotiators who discover differing priorities is to link them through a contingency clause. This is common in professional sports negotiations, where players want to be assured that they are being paid well for their talent, but teams are concerned that the players will not perform as well as expected. Performance-based incentives allow players to receive their desired level of compensation, but only if they achieve the team's desired level of performance. The last kind of interests, opposing interests, may lead negotiators to identify true zero-sum situations. Occasionally opposing interests lead to creative solutions that expand the pie, however many interest-based negotiations include purely distributive issues that must be addressed by claiming value. If the negotiators have followed the principled negotiation process, their chance of reaching an acceptable compromise on zero-sum issues is greater than if they had begun the negotiation by claiming value.

The final component of the principled negotiation model is using objective criteria to evaluate possible outcomes. If negotiators do not establish unbiased standards for assessing agreements, they must rely on a contest of wills that is a purely distributive process. Rather than relying on manipulation and pressure or vague standards of fairness, negotiators should look for neutral measures that can be used to settle differences. These standards might include precedent, market value, scientific judgment, professional standards, costs, efficiency, what a court might decide or tradition (Fisher, Ury and Patton, 1991). When negotiators agree to standards before evaluating alternatives, concessions are easier to make because they don't represent an act of weakness. Standards themselves may need to be negotiated, but principled negotiators should be open to reasoned persuasion on the merits of different systems of evaluation. The selection of objective standards cannot be accomplished by attempting to negotiate personal values or ideological principles.

The four components of interest-based negotiation can be used in a wide range of contexts, in simple or complex negotiations with two or many parties. The following example provides an illustration of interest-based negotiation according to the principles described above. A colleague named Sandra worked for the United States Department of Defense as a contract negotiator.

She was responsible for negotiating many different kinds of deals, from janitorial contracts for military bases to the procurement of heavy machinery and vehicles. One of the more interesting negotiations Sandra conducted was for the purchase of robotic flight simulators used to train air force pilots. A pilot sits inside the simulator, which looks just like the interior of a fighter jet, and practices flying different scenarios without putting himself or the aircraft at risk. The software is programmed to calculate the responses that a real jet would make in various circumstances, and the robotic simulator moves to simulate the physical feelings the pilot would experience in the jet, such as dips and turns. The simulators are a vital part of ongoing military pilot training.

Because the flight simulator is an exact mock-up of an aircraft that has classified specifications, the U.S. government had entrusted just one company with the information required to design and build simulators. While this was in the best interests of national security, it also meant that the manufacturer had a perfect monopoly on a product it was selling to a customer with deep pockets and a strong need for the product. Sandra thought for a long time about how to approach this negotiation, as it appeared to be a single-issue, distributive negotiation that would focus on claiming value. She decided that her aim in the negotiation was not to get the lowest price, but to focus on getting the greatest possible long-term value from the relationship. It would be in the interests of the U.S. government to have the manufacturer committed to making the best possible simulators, and to do this the company required adequate financial resources and ongoing feedback from pilots. She also recognized that the company was investing significant financial and human resources in developing the flight simulators, and would be concerned with recouping its investment as quickly as possible.

Sandra opened the negotiation by stating her belief that both parties would benefit if the simulators had the highest possible technical performance. She explained that this would support the manufacturer's reputation and assist it in gaining additional contracts, and also allow the U.S. government to support favorable pricing for the deal. The company's representative agreed to this principle and began to discuss pricing, starting with a very high initial price. Sandra responded that this price was something she wanted to discuss, but that she first wanted to focus on the short and long-term aspects of ensuring the simulators had excellent technical performance. For example, Sandra mentioned the need for new software scenarios to be incorporated into the simulator as situations unfolded in the real world. Over the course of the next few hours, the negotiators discussed issues such as how frequently the software would be updated, how the simulators would be serviced and maintained, how initial training on the simulators would be managed, and how feedback from pilots would be shared with and acted upon by the manufacturer. Subsequent discussions included criteria for simulator performance and service as well as methods for evaluation and feedback. When the negotiators again began discussing price, they now had multiple issues to discuss, and they were able to make tradeoffs between the manufacturer's desire for profit in the short run and the government's desire for continuing improvement of the simulators. The final contract included a price lower than the manufacturer's initial offer, but added performance-based incentives that would allow the company to earn more than the value of the initial offer if simulator performance met established criteria over the next several years. The contract marked the start of a successful long-term relationship between the manufacturer and the U.S. government.

Summary

This chapter has explored two main approaches to negotiation: claiming value and creating value. Claiming value is linked to a competing attitude in which one party's loss is another party's gain, and the object is to gain as much as possible. Creating value is based on a cooperative attitude in which the parties exchange information to discover all the sources of value they might negotiate, striving for solutions that create gain for everyone. The maximum possible value in a negotiation is represented by the Pareto frontier. Most negotiations require both creating and claiming value, however each approach requires actions that are incompatible with the other approach. Negotiators experience a tension when trying to use both approaches because their actions in one approach inhibit their effectiveness with the other approach. This tension, called the negotiator's dilemma, can be managed through a variety of strategies that allow negotiators to create as much value as possible without making themselves unduly vulnerable to claiming value behaviors. Interest-based negotiation, or principled negotiation, is introduced as a method for negotiating that assists negotiators in reaching agreements that achieve the best possible outcomes in terms of the substance, the relationship, and the process of negotiation.

Creativity in Negotiations

Joachim Hüffmeier and Guido Hertel
University of Münster

When thinking about the two terms "creativity" and "negotiation", common sense seems to say that those two do not go together well. However, as we will argue below, common sense is not a good counselor in this case. In this chapter, we illustrate that creativity plays a key role in negotiations and that constructive conflict management — such as negotiations — can in fact enhance creativity and innovation. We thereby refer to different taxonomies and theoretical models (Carnevale, 2006; Lax and Sebenius, 1986; Pruitt, 1981; Pruitt and Carnevale, 1993). As a start, we introduce an example from an actual negotiation, which helps us to illustrate the role of creativity.

Opening Example

In the summer of 1997, Dwight Manley represented the basketball player Dennis Rodman in his contract negotiations with the Chicago Bulls. Rodman was not exactly known as a low-maintenance player who was easy to be placed with successful clubs. Rodman preferred to stay with the Bulls, but also demanded a total salary of $10 million for the following season which was one million more than his previous one-year contract had been worth. However, Rodman was also known for being eccentric, erratic, and often irritable and had missed a considerable share of regular season games due to disciplinary problems with his last complete season dating back to 1991.

In the previous season, Rodman had missed about a third of the Bulls' regular season games because of, for instance, a suspension of 11 games for kicking a courtside cameraman in the groin. To make things worse, Rodman's performance had significantly dropped in the play-offs and he had turned 36 earlier in the year, which led doubters to question his remaining ability.

On the other side of the table, Bulls General Manager Jerry Krause was in a not much more comfortable position. He was not willing to spend a significant amount of money for an incalculable player, but allegedly thought of the league's average salary, which was about $2.5 million. Such a rather modest contract would have allowed him to additionally sign another more reliable player, who was (more) likely to play all regular season and play-off games for the Bulls. In previous years, Krause did, however, not succeed in signing a player other than Dennis Rodman to play the power forward position on a championship level. From a pure sports perspective, Rodman was a proven winner, one of the best defensive players in the league, and one of the most dominant rebounders in the history of the game. Not least, he had won two consecutive championships in the two previous years as a centerpiece of the now two-time defending NBA-champion Chicago. His teammate Michael "Air" Jordan — the by then arguably best player in the world — had publicly demanded to re-sign Dennis Rodman for the upcoming season, which had heightened the pressure on Krause as well as the expectations of his coaching staff and the Bulls supporters to keep the nucleus of the successful Bulls team intact.

With the huge difference in ideas about salary, the two parties found themselves near an impasse in the negotiation, and it became increasingly obvious that they needed some *creativity* to come up with a deal that was satisfying both parties' interests (*Chicago Tribune*, September 19, 1997). After a long stalemate, the two parties came together and agreed on a contract. This contract included a rather low base salary and a very refined incentive structure, which rewarded Rodman for each game he took part in.

The wisely negotiated agreement provided the desired outcomes for both parties: Rodman ultimately received about the money he had demanded, and the Chicago Bulls had a dependable power forward that played 80 regular season games for the first time in six years. Together, they won the third consecutive championship in this season.

The role of creativity in negotiations

To better appreciate the role of creativity in negotiations it is helpful to start with a definition of creativity and some basic negotiation terminology. From a scientific perspective, ideas, insights, or solutions are characterized as "creative" when two basic conditions are met (cf. Amabile, 1996; Ogilvie and Simms, 2009). First, the ideas were not previously known and can thus be considered as truly original, new, and unique. Secondly, the ideas must be conducive to solving so-called ill-defined problems, i.e., problems without an apparent optimal solution. In other words, creative ideas, insights, or solutions are appropriate and useful given the context of a problem.

In general, two broad types of negotiation situations are distinguished: In *distributive negotiations*, negotiators "merely" divide existing resources between each other. Mostly, distributive negotiation frameworks involve only one issue such as the price of an item in typical buyer-seller negotiations (e.g., buying a used car). Here, the buyer's *interest* simply is to pay as little as possible, while the seller's interest is to yield a maximum selling price. Accordingly, a gain of one party implies an *equivalent* loss of the other party and *compromise-like agreements* represent the optimal joint outcome.

In *integrative negotiations*, in contrast, it is possible to move beyond mere *compromises* towards *integrative agreements* by creating additional values for the negotiating parties. Typically, integrative negotiation frameworks involve several issues, which the parties value differently depending on their *underlying interests*. It is exactly these differences in valuation that often provide the basis for mutually beneficial agreements. Many conflicts may be perceived as being solely distributive, although most of them possess some integrative potential for mutually satisfying agreements (Raiffa, 1982). At early stages of a conflict, however, it is often not clear whether there is integrative potential and where it might be found. Thus, many negotiations constitute "ill-defined problems", and it needs considerable work to find and/or create effective solutions to these problems.

This is where creativity comes into play: On the one hand, creative ideas may help to transform negotiations that initially seem purely distributive into integrative situations; for instance when negotiators add further issues to the previously distributive negotiation. Imagine, for example, a used car seller who brings in a guarantee certificate which makes it easier for the buyer to make concessions related to the selling price. Here, the seller might have understood that the buyer is not primarily interested in spending as little money as possible but rather to solve her daily commuting problem in a durable and reliable way. On the other hand, creative insights can leverage the integrative potential already inherent in an integrative negotiation framework with several issues. Imagine, for instance, negotiators who capitalize on different valuations of certain issues and subsequently engage in a systematic exchange of concessions on low-versus high-value issues.

In the following section, we will introduce different principles that allow for the creation of common value and ultimately integrative agreements.

Creating value: How creative negotiation strategies allow mutual gains

Creating and claiming value are conventionally differentiated as the two main activities negotiators engage in (Lax and Sebenius, 1986). Although creating and claiming value are deeply intertwined, the specific importance of creating value is obvious because dividing resources in negotiations is much more difficult when the parties previously failed to create additional values. Therefore, we focus on creating value because it is at the core of creativity in negotiations.

Negotiations are a prototypical example of problems without an obvious optimal solution (i.e., "ill-defined" problems) as negotiators usually do not have all information about their counterpart. To effectively create value and thereby establish the optimal solution (a fully integrative agreement), communication and information sharing among negotiators, as well as a spirit of joint problem solving or at least constructive dealing with the conflict are essential. It is equally important for negotiators to temporarily tolerate the conflict inherent in the negotiation and to avoid premature concessions to lessen the tension (De Dreu, Nijstad, and Van Knippenberg, 2008; De Dreu, Weingart, and Kwon, 2000). Without these behaviors, hardly any value creating strategy portrayed in this section is likely to be successfully applied.

As the sheer number of possible creative negotiation strategies is quite substantial, we will focus our description on the strategies we deem most important, prevalent, and best understood (for more comprehensive compilations, see Lax and Sebenius, 1986; Thompson, 2008). Although these strategies rely on different processes to create value, they are rooted in a common principle articulated in formulations such as "value can be created", "the pie is not necessarily fixed and might be extended in various ways", or "value can be gained by utilizing the particular existing interrelations between parties' interests" (Moran, Bereby-Meyer, and Bazerman, 2008; p. 112 and p. 120).

Log-rolling

Imagine a negotiation about purchasing a new car. The issues price, equipment and financing are involved in this negotiation. Before making a decision about any of these issues, the buyer and seller exchange more information about their respective situations and interests. After a while, they notice that the buyer is especially interested in the car's equipment whereas financing is particularly important to the seller. This difference in *priorities between issues* and the resulting insight makes a systematic trade-off possible: The seller can now provide better equipment for the car than he initially intended, and the buyer can reciprocate this concession by accepting less favorable financing terms.

The systematic exchange of concessions on low- versus high-value issues is termed log-rolling (cf. Froman and Cohen, 1970). Log-rolling yields better joint outcomes than mere compromises for each of the issues as both parties achieve what they value most, and only give up on issues they do not value as strongly. Log-rolling is the arguably most investigated and best understood creative strategy to generate joint gains. As illustrated above, it makes use of existing differences in the valuation of the issues in a negotiation. When negotiators engage in log-rolling, they make systematic concessions on one or several issues that they do not value as strongly as their counterpart (low-value issues) and receive concessions on one or more issues they value more strongly than their counterpart (high-value issues) in return. The resulting package deals (i.e., deals involving several issues at a time) lead reliably to better joint outcomes than settlements where the issues are sequentially negotiated.

Although the logic of log-rolling is relatively easy to understand, and although different issue priorities of negotiators are very likely, many negotiators miss the chance to log-roll. They spuriously assume that their counterparts value the issues in the negotiation in exactly the same way as they do it, which results in the conviction that there are no differences in the priorities of the parties. This false belief was termed fixed-pie perception (cf. Thompson and Hastie, 1990). In order to make package deals possible, many negotiators may thus first have to overcome their fixed-pie perception and come up with the idea that negotiators value the issues in the negotiation differently. This change is insofar creative as it may involve a complete restructuring of one's perception of the negotiation situation.

Exploiting compatible interests

Suppose that an applicant and an employer negotiate about the terms of an advertised executive job in early April in New York. Among other issues (e.g., signing bonus, insurance coverage, etc.), the two parties negotiate about the salary, the starting date for the job, and the location of the job. While it is obvious that the job candidate strives for a high salary and the employer prefers to initially offer a more moderate salary level, it is less clear what the parties' interests are concerning the two remaining issues. The job candidate currently lives in New York and will voluntarily terminate his previous appointment by the end of April. Unbeknownst to the employer, he prefers to start his new job not before October, because he would appreciate a longer break to rebound from his very taxing previous job. He would further embrace a change of scenery and for instance like to work in Miami in the future. The employer generally likes the job candidate and would like to hire him. She is well aware that her business tends to lose some speed during summer time when the holiday time starts in the states and overseas. Her problem is that she is not sure how the candidate reacts when being told that he won't be needed before September as the business accelerates again around this time of the year. The employer is also aware that the job candidate spent his whole professional life in New York, but she prefers to hire an executive who is willing to work — at least part time — in her Miami office. In this situation, the potential for joint gains is not to be found in the differences between the two parties, but in their commonalities. For starting date and job location, the two parties have *compatible interests* and thus also identical *preferences within these issues* as they prefer the identical option or outcome related to the issues. If the two parties succeed in exchanging sufficient information, they have a chance to realize these commonalities and thereby to find a mutually satisfying agreement.

In the description above, the identification and utilization of compatible interests for achieving joint gains seems to be rather trivial. However, negotiators often fail to recognize that their own and their counterparts' interests are in fact compatible. Consequentially, they often come to agreements that leave all parties worse off than they could easily have been (Thompson and Hrebec, 1996). The failure to recognize compatible interests can again be ascribed to the negotiators' belief that their own and their counterparts' interests are completely opposed (fixed-pie perception). Additionally, negotiators are often unwilling to share information. For instance, the job candidate may be reluctant to indicate a need for recovery time, or the employer may be hesitant to admit that her business is subject to seasonal fluctuation.

Comparable to log-rolling, exploiting compatible interests may at first not give the impression of involving much creativity. However, to allow for the utilization of compatible interests, negotiators may again have to overcome their fixed-pie perception and come up with the idea that negotiators prefer the same outcomes related to one or several issues in the negotiation. This change of perspective is a creative act as it involves restructuring one's perception of the negotiation situation.

Expanding the resource pie

When we previously explained how a seemingly distributive negotiation can be transformed into an integrative negotiation, we referred to the seller of a used car who suggested a guarantee certificate to satisfy the buyer's interest in a dependable vehicle. Thereby, we already gave an example of expanding the resource pie by adding a new issue to a negotiation. Such a strategy is a frequent advice for negotiators. Different studies empirically support this claim by showing that adding issues to a negotiation is conducive to solving especially difficult negotiations where negotiators seem to be far apart (for example, negotiations with an otherwise negative bargaining zone; Maddux, Mullen, and Galinsky, 2008). More broadly, it was empirically demonstrated that negotiating about more as compared to less issues leads to more integrative agreements (Naquin, 2003).

Unbundling issues

Consider the typical negotiation that evolves when a person is willing to buy a new car. An individual without much experience in such a situation may assume that the whole negotiation is about the selling price. As in many other seller-buyer interactions, negotiations may thus give the impression to be about only one issue. On closer inspection, however, individuals may discover that several issues can be unbundled from such a monolithically appearing issue (i.e., selling price in the car buying example). For instance, these issues can comprise delivery date, given equipment of the car, conditions of financing, or warranty. Once the unbundling is done, the newly emerged negotiation agenda of several issues may well contain potential for log-rolling or the utilization of compatible interests (see above). The buyer may, for example, value the given equipment of the car more strongly than it "hurts" the seller to provide it. The opposite may apply for financing conditions. Here, it may "hurt" the buyer less to agree to the seller's preferred conditions than these conditions may be useful for the seller. Concerning the delivery date, the two parties may even have compatible interests and thus an identical preference. Empirical research supports the general, underlying notion of unbundling an overarching issue in so far as negotiations about more as compared to fewer issues lead to more integrative agreements (Naquin, 2003).

Contingent contracts

Imagine a negotiation in which an aging owner of a company without a natural successor from his family or staff intends to sell his company (cf. Lax and Sebenius, 1986). The company has drawn interest from a potential buyer and the seller generally likes the buyer, but both parties are far apart concerning their ideas about the selling price. When looking into the future of the existing company, the current owner sees continued profit with an already successful business, while the potential buyer sees a changing and very competitive market in which he has to stand his ground. Thus, the potential buyer might rather be convinced that he has to invest heavily into the company to keep it successful. Perhaps surprisingly, the different appraisals of future earnings may be the basis for a mutually satisfying agreement, which could not come about in any other way if not for a contingent contract. Seller and buyer could formulate such a contingent contract, in which they agree both on a relatively low selling price and additional future payments, which are contingent on future earnings. If the company will be as successful as its current owner assumes, he will be paid accordingly. If the market is, however, as difficult as the potential buyer dreads, there won't be as many or no additional payments.

Although recent research has begun to target contingent contracts as a promising integrative negotiation strategy (e.g., Kray, Thompson, and Lind, 2005; Moran *et al.*, 2008), it is not well understood yet under which conditions negotiators see and make use of contingent contracts. Nevertheless, contingent contracts may be an extremely useful tool to pave the way towards integrative agreements especially when the negotiation parties are otherwise far apart. Negotiation practice may here well be one step ahead of empirical research, as our opening example of the contract negotiation between Dennis Rodman and the Chicago Bulls also represents a — cleverly devised — instance of a contingent contract.

Time trade-offs

Suppose that a chief city council planner and a real estate development company negotiate about the development of a residential community project (cf. Moran *et al.*, 2008). One issue in this negotiation revolves around the division of the income from a sports club, which is situated on the respective piece of real estate. As usual, the easiest way would be to reach for middle ground and to split the income from leasing to the sports club — $2 million per year for 3 years — between the two parties. There may, however, be a more creative way of dealing with the parties' interests: As it turns out, the real estate company has high expenses and relatively low income during the first year of the project, and thus will not have to pay any tax on extra incomes. After the first year, the company will most likely have to pay the usual tax, a rate of about 30%, which is the same rate the city would have to pay during the whole project time. Depending on the level of information exchange, the two parties may be able to create value based on the resulting time preferences. A potential time trade-off could, for instance, imply that the company receives the full income during the first year, and 20% of the yearly income during the following two years. In turn, the city might relinquish the income of the first year and receive a bigger share of the income in the remaining two years.

Time trade-offs thus involve an outcome which provides the more needy or impatient party quickly with — usually less — resources, while the less needy party receives more resources or resources over a longer period of time. Although the basic logic of time trade-offs is compelling, time trade-offs are not well understood yet from a research perspective. It is, for instance, not clear how often and why negotiators miss (or use) opportunities for time trade-offs.

Risk sharing schemes

Lax and Sebenius (1986) provide an instructive example of an integrative agreement that is based on differences in risk aversion. In this negotiation, a single, middle-aged, and fairly wealthy accountant and a younger, not so wealthy lawyer and father of several children are about to buy and run a business together. Before getting started, the two have to agree on the terms of their cooperation including their future salaries. While both parties agree that their business has good chances for an early commercial breakthrough, the future business development is still uncertain. Understandably, the accountant is not necessarily as risk averse as the lawyer. An agreement, which takes these differences into account, would allot

a relatively high, fixed salary and a minimum share of potential profits to the more risk-averse lawyer. The accountant, in contrast,
would receive a smaller fixed salary but a much larger share of future
profits. Lax and Sebenius (1986) state that such an agreement optimally satisfies both parties' interests and is thus superior to both,
fixed salaries or substantial contingent payments. Differences in risk
aversion thus can also represent the basis for integrative agreements. Although Lax and Sebenius provide further examples of such
risk sharing schemes, they are not well investigated yet.

Empirical evidence for the influential role of creativity in negotiation

After describing various integrative negotiation strategies that
benefit from creativity, we now summarize available research
insights on creativity in negotiations.

Creativity as a personality trait

The negotiation scholar Terry Kurtzberg demonstrated that high
creativity as personality trait increases joint outcomes in negotiations (Kurtzberg, 1998). While controlling for negotiators'
intelligence, Kurtzberg found that one highly creative negotiator
was already sufficient for discovering and exploiting existing
potential for integrative conflict solutions (i.e., maximizing of
joint outcomes). The creativity of the remaining negotiator had
no further consequences. In a strongly interdependent situation
like negotiations, where negotiators depend on each other's
behaviors and insights, this result is quite plausible as the optimal
solution to a negotiation can well be detected and communicated
by only one negotiator (cf. Thompson, 1991).

Creativity interventions

Different studies confirm that different creativity interventions in
fact have the assumed positive impact on achieving higher joint

outcomes. Negotiators who participated in a short creativity training were found to reach more integrative agreements than negotiators without such a training (Ogilvie and Simms, 2009). Similarly, negotiators who were asked to compare, evaluate, and find a common principle for different value creating strategies (log-rolling and contingent contracts, see above) achieved higher joint outcomes than participants who were asked to focus only on one such strategy (Moran *et al.*, 2008).

Conflict as a precursor of creativity

When imagining a negotiation with its stereotypic features of competing interests and conflicting positions, it is not obvious why and how conflict may even enhance the finding of creative ideas, insights, or solutions. Previous research (Nemeth, Personnaz, Personnaz, and Goncalo, 2004; Postmes, Spears, and Cihangir, 2001) has, however, shown that conflict among group members can in fact lead to more ideas and better solutions. This positive effect seems, however, to be restricted to situations in which group members know that novel and unshared information is required, and that debates, discussions, and even criticism represent the desired behavior. Although the above studies were not conducted in a negotiation context, they are informative as they converge with the notion that conflict can be conducive to creativity and integrative negotiation outcomes if it is handled constructively (Carnevale, 2006; Eisemann, 1978; Schulz-Hardt, Brodbeck, Mojzisch, Kerschreiter, and Frey, 2006).

Challenges and Limits of Creativity in Negotiation

Many empirical negotiation studies have demonstrated numerous challenges that might prevent the unfolding of creativity. Due to restrictions of space, we only portray the most established among those limiting factors. These factors may already have an adverse impact before the negotiation even starts. Anticipating a competitive counterpart or a competitive negotiation may, for instance, directly reduce negotiators' creativity (cf. Carnevale and Probst, 1998). Alternatively, such an anticipation may lead to an untimely reduction of own claims, which is tantamount with premature concessions (Diekmann, Tenbrunsel, and Galinsky, 2003).

Low resistance to concession making is particularly harmful to creative agreements (De Dreu *et al.*, 2000) because negotiators who concede early basically misconceive their situation. They seem inclined to appease their counterpart, and their concessions may in fact succeed in satisfying the other party. However, a negotiator who concedes early often experiences further pressures to concede and, even worse, shorter time to exchange information and ideas about how to find a mutually satisfying agreement without giving up goals and valuable resources. Prematurely conceding negotiators thus prevent the full exploration and exploitation of existing possibilities for mutually satisfying agreements.

Negotiators' social motivation represents another limiting condition of creativity in negotiation. As mentioned above, the conflict which emerges from the negotiation must be handled constructively to successfully create value. Competitively and egoistically motivated negotiators, however, usually exhibit a negative or no regard for their counterparts' outcomes. Thus, when competitively or egoistically motivated negotiators face a similarly motivated counterpart, creative solutions of a conflict are difficult and negotiations often end in impasses (De Dreu *et al.*, 2000). Cooperative orientations of negotiators, on the other hand, facilitate integrative conflict solutions as these persons are more tuned to look for and value mutual benefits. In this respect, it is important to stress that concerns for the other party's outcomes do not have to be genuine to achieve mutually satisfying agreements, and negotiators do not have to be "true altruists" and disregard their own interests. In fact, cooperative concerns are often the best way to maximize individual profits in negotiations when creative solutions offer higher shares for each of the parties than mere concessions.

Crucial preconditions for such benefits of cooperative orientations are the mutual willingness to resolve the conflict constructively and a certain degree of information exchange. Factors restricting the ability or motivation to process this information, such as low cognitive capacity, time pressure, or low epistemic motivation also limit the unfolding of creativity. In most negotiations, the involved persons have to process complex information concerning their own and their counterparts' preferences, priorities and presumed interests in order to identify possibilities for joint gains. Negotiators with restricted processing capacity for complex information normally do not find as high joint outcomes than negotiators with a higher cognitive capacity (Kurtzberg, 1998; Pruitt and Lewis, 1975). Moreover, negotiators who feel pressured by elapsing time do not fully explore available possibilities for joint gains and thus do not find possible ways to create value. Similarly, when negotiators' epistemic motivation is low and they thus do neither seek and generate new information nor process information deeply and deliberately, they also fail to effectively create value and craft integrative agreements (De Dreu, Beersma, Stroebe, and Euwema, 2006).

Finally, a last but crucial limitation to creativity in negotiations is that a small but substantial share of conflicts remains that even a high level of creativity cannot transform into integrative negotiations.

How to be(come) more creative: Creativity techniques

There have been numerous attempts to foster creativity by different techniques. These techniques either focus on the divergent aspect of creativity (i.e., the originality, novelty, or uniqueness of the generated ideas, insights, and solutions), the convergent aspect of creativity (i.e., the appropriateness and usefulness of the generated ideas, insights, and solutions given the context of the problem), or both aspects of creativity.

"Brainstorming" and "Synectics" are two prototypical examples of creativity techniques which center on the divergent aspect of creativity. Invented by the advertising specialist Alex F. Osborn (1953), the brainstorming technique became quickly popular. It involves generating as many ideas as possible without immediate judgments about their quality. Brainstorming was originally designed as group activity and it proved to be more effective in generating new ideas than the instruction to generate only high-quality ideas (i.e., a task with a built-in judgment instance). Remember, however, that conflict in brainstorming groups can lead to more ideas when debating, discussions, and even criticism are the behavior norm in a group (Nemeth *et al.*, 2004). Interestingly, brainstorming in real groups proved, however, to be less effective than brainstorming in so-called "nominal" groups in which an equivalent number of individuals is working alone. This robust disadvantage of brainstorming in groups compared to nominal groups was found even when individuals were under the impression that they were more productive during group work (Paulus, Dzindolet, Poletes, and Camacho, 1993). One of the main reasons for the disadvantage of brainstorming in groups is that group members block each other's productivity (Diehl and Stroebe, 1987).

The synectics technique is based on principles of analogical reasoning, and instructs participants to compare a given problem to other problems they might not usually consider to be related. Transferring the inherent principles and structures can trigger new and unusual ideas. As in brainstorming, judgments about the quality of the generated ideas are not allowed in the first stage of this exercise. To facilitate the creative process, participants are often specifically instructed to apply different types of analogies: For instance, they are asked to compare the topic in question with a topic from another domain, with symbolic images or with self-construed fantasies. While systematic research on the effectiveness of the synectics technique is rare, recent research has shown some promising initial results for related creativity techniques that are also based on analogical reasoning under some conditions (e.g., Kilgour and Koslow, 2009).

"Creative Problem Solving" represents a creativity technique which centers on both the convergent and the divergent aspects of creativity. Being rooted in cognitive psychology (Anderson, 1985), this technique is defined as movement from a perceived need, sense of difficulty or stagnancy to the intuition of possible solutions via the exploration of relevant information and new ideas (cf. Young, 1976). It typically involves five stages: 1) gathering information about the problem that is to be solved, 2) clear formulation of the problem, 3) generating possible solutions to the problem; 4) evaluating the generated solutions, and 5) selling off the preferred solution to others. In numerous studies, the creative problem solving technique has been found to be successful in increasing creativity in school children (Torrance, 1972).

With other samples, the success of creativity techniques may be a more intricate question. A recent study (Kilgour and Koslow, 2009) compared the effect of divergent and convergent creativity techniques on the design of creative advertising in a sample of advertising professionals. Interestingly, this sample consisted of accountant executives who are usually hired because of their decent knowledge about marketing strategies involving client strategy and target markets (i.e., the convergent creativity component). The other part of the sample consisted of creatives who are typically employed because of their ability to come up with original, novel, and unique ideas (i.e., the divergent creativity component). As it turned out, the applied *divergent* creativity technique improved the originality of the accountant executives' advertisement ideas, while the creatives did not benefit. In contrast, the applied *convergent* creativity technique led to an increase in appropriate advertisement ideas among the creatives, while the accountant executives' ideas even got worse through the intervention.

In summary, increasing creativity is not a trivial business. Users of creativity techniques should only adopt such exercises have been tested empirically. Moreover, the study on the advertising specialists suggests that they should also consider the specific abilities and competencies of the involved persons. In negotiations, it may be particularly important to accentuate the constructive handling of the underlying conflict, and at the same time to stress that debates, discussions and arguments represent desired behaviors in order to find mutually satisfying agreements.

Conditions for being creative in negotiations

Realizing conditions that make creative solutions to a negotiation possible starts with its preparation. While preparing, negotiators should make a number of arrangements for the general proceedings of the negotiation that may prove valuable for achieving high-quality outcomes. First, they should clarify with the other negotiation party where, with how many people per party, and with how much time the negotiation should be conducted. Concerning the location for the negotiation, negotiators should prefer a shielded, confidential, and perhaps novel and inspiring site. Such a place may provide the necessary conditions to allow truly creative thinking. Compared to negotiations between individuals, negotiations between teams are typically more successful because the higher number of problem solvers has a greater potential to generate ideas for creating joint gains (Thompson, Peterson, and Brodt, 1996). It is, however, important to keep in mind that negotiating teams usually also come along with greater competitiveness and heightened distrust (Polzer, 1996). The time frame for the negotiation should be arranged generously to allow for a thorough reflection of and discussion about as many possibilities for joint gains as possible.

Prior to the negotiation, negotiators should think thoroughly about their own interests rather than investing too much time to think about the positions they want to take during the negotiation. Once they feel sufficiently confident that they truly know their own interests, negotiators may want to collect as much information as possible about the other negotiation party. This information should also contain reflections about the other party's interests and in which ways these interests may be compatible with and diverge from the own interests. These reflections can also focus on the question how the resource pie may be expanded or modified to satisfy the interests of all involved parties. Moreover, it may be useful for negotiators to arrange a first time period during the negotiation where no decisions are made but goals, general information, and ideas on possible solutions of the conflict can be exchanged. It may be helpful in this period to explicitly establish rules for the interaction between the parties like for example the rule that debates, discussions and a multitude of expressed perspectives are desirable (cf. Nemeth *et al.*, 2004; Postmes *et al.*, 2001) as long as the conflict is handled constructively.

Especially during this early period, negotiators should focus on taking the perspective of the other party (Galinsky, Maddux, Gilin, and White, 2008), on asking questions about the other party's priorities, preferences, and interests and on providing own respective information (Thompson, 1991). Additionally, taking a prosocial stance, even if it is a purely instrumental one, high cognitive effort and positive mood as precursor for high creativity further contribute to creating joint value in negotiations (De Dreu *et al.*, 2006).

Breaks and post-settlement settlements may be two last measures to help negotiators to achieve mutually satisfying agreements. Negotiation parties may profit from breaks when negotiations temporarily get stuck as breaks may help to calm down, regain concentration, and refocus on mutually satisfying solutions for the negotiation. Moreover, negotiation breaks may also allow for incubation (i.e., some latency in which possible solutions to a problem may emerge). When negotiators do not manage to fully exploit the integrative potential of a negotiation, they can arrange a post-negotiation after they agreed on some outcome in the regular negotiation. Post-settlement settlements that result from those post-negotiations may be more integrative than the original settlement, as negotiators have already secured a satisfying result and are now freed from the respective pressure (Raiffa, 1985). Without this pressure and the danger of worsening one's outcomes more integrative outcomes may become possible.

Summary

In this chapter, we outlined why, how, and when creativity might help to generate joint gains in negotiations. Although a considerable share of the derived recommendations are already backed up by sound empirical research, many questions are still open and await further research. We hope that this chapter not only helps negotiators to create more innovative and beneficial solutions in negotiations, but also triggers more interest of scholars and students in this fascinating research field.

Social Capital in Negotiation: Leveraging the Power of Relational Wealth

Ariel C. Avgar
School of Labor and Employment Relations,
University of Illinois at Urbana Champaign

Eun Kyung Lee
School of Labor and Employment Relations,
University of Illinois at Urbana Champaign

Introduction

Negotiation is, at its core, a *relational* process intended to resolve or address underlying conflicts between at least two parties. As such, individuals and organizations seeking to enhance negotiation gains must pay careful attention to their relational ties, or their social capital, with negotiating counterparts and with other parties. Negotiations bring together individuals and groups to engage and communicate about how to allocate or use specific, and often scarce, resources (Pruit, 1983). These social underpinnings of the negotiation processes mean that negotiators' relational ties and networks of connections, strong or weak, in and outside the negotiation context, are likely to influence the ways in which they communicate, exchange information, and interact, and the subsequent resolution achieved (Benoliel and Cashdan, 2005; Bazerman *et al.*, 2000). The access to resources generated by social ties, or the *social capital* possessed by the parties, jointly and separately, is likely to influence both the process itself and the outcomes associated with a given negotiation. *Whom negotiators know* and *how well they know their negotiation counterparts* is likely to significantly influence the process and substance of the negotiation at hand.

Take for example, internet giant Google's approach to negotiating content agreements for the video website, YouTube. In seeking to maintain YouTube's dominance, Google has sought to negotiate content arrangements with a number of key players, like the BBC and other large entertainment studios with whom they accrued relational wealth or social capital. For example, when Google CEO, Eric Schmidt, recently began negotiating with BBC director Mark Thomson about the possibility of hosting BBC content on YouTube, the pre-existing relationships between the two organizations seemed to play a central role. The decision to negotiate with BBC was likely influenced by the fact that the two organizations had been collaborating since early 2007 when official BBC clips were first posted to YouTube (Ferguson, 2009). Google and the BBC were seeking, among other things, to leverage the power of the relational ties in a negotiation context. Similarly, Google has also sought to enhance its negotiation position by hiring Netflix executive, Robert Kyncl, to oversee content partnerships with Hollywood studios (Hachman, 2010). By doing so, Google was, in essence, investing not just in Kyncl's human capital, but in the social capital he brought to the company, in general, and to the negotiating table in particular. Google is not alone in understanding the power of social capital for negotiation. In this chapter, we will address some of the key dimensions associated with the establishment and use of social capital in the negotiation context.

Social capital represents the value inherent to relationships (Coleman, 1988). Social capital can be thought of as the benefits that can be realized as a function of a specific relationship or set of relationships (Woolcock and Narayan, 2000). Simply put, individuals with a broader array of relational networks and ties have greater access to the wealth captured by these relationships. These benefits can be realized by individuals, organizations, communities and nations (Leana and Van-Buren, 1999). At the micro level, social capital can be leveraged to improve individual achievement and development (Burt, 1992, 1997). At the macro level, social capital has been shown to play a key role in the strength and vibrancy of communities and nations (Putnam, 1993). Thriving communities, according to this argument, are, in part, the product of social capital prosperity (Jacobs, 1965; Wilson, 1997). Due to its documented potential, individuals, organizations, and communities are often engaged in activities intended to enhance their social capital stocks. Increasingly, organizations and individuals are aware of the power vested in social relations and are seeking to enhance ownership of this valuable resource.

Negotiation is an arena in which greater attention to social capital can lead to improved interactions, processes and, most importantly, outcomes. Negotiators interested in an additional resource, should consider the social ties that they have with their negotiating counterparts and with individuals and groups outside the specific negotiation arena. How can negotiating parties realize joint and separate social capital benefits? How might negotiating parties leverage their social capital with negotiating counterparts and with others in order to produce the most beneficial outcome? This chapter examines how social capital can influence negotiation processes and outcomes.

The excitement over social capital stems, among other things, from the theoretical propositions and growing empirical evidence that it can affect a host of important relational dynamics. Social capital has been linked, conceptually and empirically, to greater information sharing and knowledge transfer between its joint owners, increased innovation and greater level of power and influence (Adler and Kwon, 2002). These benefits are central to the negotiation process and its outcomes. Thus, the negotiation arena is clearly one of the areas where a solid understanding of social capital can lead to enhanced individual and/or collective gains.

Although the research regarding the relationship between social capital and negotiation is still in its infancy, there are a number of key linkages that can be made building on the established negotiation and social capital literatures. In order to do so, the chapter will introduce the concept of social capital, review its key attributes, and discuss its implications for negotiations. To be clear, while the relationships between negotiators is one very important source of social capital, this chapter focuses on relational wealth accumulated jointly (between negotiators) and separately (outside the negotiation). Unlike other forms of wealth, social capital is very abstract. We cannot hold this asset and we surly cannot calculate the precise amount of capital that has accumulated in our relational reserves as a function of relationship and ties. Nevertheless, in thinking about how a negotiators' relationships can enhance individual and joint gains, this chapter will discuss social capital using language that is similar to the way one might discuss a physical tangible asset. The purpose is to introduce readers to the mindset of thinking about social capital in more concrete, practical and operational ways.

Defining Social Capital

The power of social capital as an asset that can create value, distinguishable from traditional forms of capital, has sparked the imaginations of practitioners and academics for at least the past four decades. If our relational ties can yield returns beyond those stemming from financial or human capital, then a better understanding of what this capital is can shed light on a host of societal, organizational and individual phenomena. Furthermore, if one's relational ties are a resource that can be translated into individual, group, or community advantages, it is important to understand how it is created and the specific types of returns that can be yielded for investment in this social currency.

Since its inception, this concept has been used in countless different settings and has steadily gained popularity across different disciplines including sociology, management, industrial relations, and political science (Portes, 1998). The French sociologist, Pierre Bourdieu, was one of the first scholars to offer a systematic analysis of what social capital was and was not. According to Bourdieu, social capital is "the aggregate of the actual or potential resources which are linked to the possession of a durable network of more or less institutionalized relationships of mutual acquaintance or recognition" (Bourdieu, 1985:248). Coleman, also a social capital pioneer, defines social capital as the resource that "inheres in the structure of relations between actors and among actors" (Coleman, 1988:98).

Different types of social capital and relational ties

Since social capital is built on and stems from networks of relationships, different types of connections have important implications for the accumulation of relational wealth. Two important nuances are central for the purposes of this chapter. First, social capital scholars have distinguished between strong and weak relational ties (Granovetter, 1973). Both types of ties can provide benefits, yet these will differ as a function of the nature of the relationship. For example, despite the common notion that the stronger the relationship the greater the relational benefits, weak ties (i.e., distant and infrequent relationships) are a powerful social resource that provides access to novel information by bridging social actors who otherwise would not be connected (Granovetter, 1973). Embedded or strong ties have also been linked to a variety of benefits such as greater access to private information and problem solving capacity (Uzzi, 2005). In analyzing one's negotiation social capital, it is important to assess the extent to which ties that can be leveraged for the purpose of enhancing negotiation processes and outcomes are strong and embedded or weak and arms length.

A second central distinction is between bonding and bridging forms of social capital. Bonding social capital represents the relational wealth contained within a group, organization, or community. Bridging social capital represents the relationships and ties outside each of these social settings. As with strong and weak ties, the nature of the relationship drives, in many ways, the resources contained in a given relationship or network of relationships. For the purposes of this chapter, we refer to bonding social capital as the resources embedded in the relationships between the negotiating parties. Bridging social capital refers to the resources accessible through relationships that negotiators have with parties outside the negotiation itself.

Outlining the Benefits and Costs of Social Capital: Implications for Negotiators

The benefits of social capital: Implications for negotiators

Why did Google seek to negotiate with partners with whom it already had estabilshed social capital stocks? What are the actual benefits attributed to the possession of different types of social capital? How do these translate into the negotiation realm? Many of the ways in which social capital is translated into gains are of importance to negotiation processes and outcomes. Adler and Kwon (2002) maintain that the effects of social capital "flow from the *information, influence,* and *solidarity* it makes available to the actors" that possess it (p. 23; *italics* added). In other words, the benefits realized from the possession of social capital are a function of the access this relational resource provides to central knowledge, power and influence, or social support.

Each of the categories of social capital channels (information, influence and solidarity) can be linked to specific advantages in general (Adler and Kwon, 2002), and for the negotiation context in particular. For example, social capital has been shown to influence the likelihood of inter-organizational collaborations. Research has indicated that the level of social capital possessed by firms is a predictor of the extent to which cooperation and strategic alliances are formed. Furthermore, social capital also appears to be more central to the formation of alliances when market conditions are more uncertain (Chung, Singh and Lee, 2000). Negotiation, which is, fundamentally, an effort on the part of at least two parties to seek cooperative, as opposed to competitive, resolution to a disagreement or dispute, may benefit in similar ways. The same mechanisms that have linked greater levels of social capital to alliance formation in conditions of uncertainty may also increase the likelihood of negotiator cooperative stance when lacking sufficient information and certainty. Social capital can promote an integrative, as opposed to distributive, negotiation dynamic. Strong and bonding social capital, or the relational wealth between the negotiating parties, can enhance the negotiation process by increasing the likelihood of a collaborative and integrative mode of interaction, thereby affecting process.

Access to information

Individuals and organizations can access a greater wealth of knowledge when they have the greater stocks of social capital, which can, in turn, lead to greater innovation. One of the ways in which social capital translates into benefits through access to information and knowledge, is through the exposure of otherwise untapped opportunities. Burt (1997) states, "managers with more social capital get higher returns to their human capital because they are positioned to identify and develop more rewarding opportunities". As noted above, different types of ties provide access to different types of information (Uzzi and Lancaster, 2003). Thus, the nature of the relationship through which social capital is derived will affect the nature of the knowledge or information that is facilitated. Social capital can be especially useful to its owners by providing access to private information, or information that is not available through public records and sources (Uzzi and Lancaster, 2003). Furthermore, the information made available through greater levels of social capital can also play a role in reducing individual or organizational uncertainties.

One of the most important processes in negotiation is information sharing (Bazerman *et al.*, 2000). If social capital improves the information sharing process, it is likely to improve negotiated outcomes. Ties, strong and weak, may provide negotiators with invaluable and previously unavailable information or unexplored opportunities. These can be used in order to either maximize separate and/or mutual gains. This benefit is especially important for the negotiating party with inferior access to information. For example, in salary negotiations, the employer often has an information advantage *vis-à-vis* the job candidate. Nevertheless, information provided through social ties in and outside the organization, (e.g., connections to previous job candidate or other individuals employed in the organization), he or she can attain increased salary negotiation outcomes (Seidel, Polzer and Stewart, 2000).

New and private information that can affect the negotiation process can be derived from the negotiators' bonding and bridging social capital. When social capital is jointly owned by the negotiating parties, it is expected that it will increase the likelihood of an integrative bargaining approach. Negotiators' social capital with others outside the negotiation will likely enhance access to important information. Nevertheless, this information could be used in an effort to either enhance mutual or distributive gains. Take for example a salary negotiation scenario again. The employing organization has information on the minimum salary levels that past job candidates were willing to accept and job candidates' preferences regarding benefits. The job candidate, on the other hand, may have social capital access to information regarding salary and benefit standards in other organizations and what is usually offered in comparable positions. In this case, the negotiating parties are relying on bridging social capital and not the resources attained from their embedded relationship. Thus, they can choose either to share their private information and increase joint collaborative outcomes, or to use the information to push for the outcome that best achieves their distributive gains. On the other hand, if the organization and job candidate have preexisting bonding social capital due to an embedded relationship (i.e., friend or family member), they are more likely to exchange information between the parties, which can enhance the likelihood that they will reach a negotiated outcome that is mutually beneficial.

Thus, social capital can be leveraged in the service of integrative mutual gains negotiation processes, or as a means of enhancing one's position in a distributive-centered process. The key here is that social capital stocks are created and used actively and intentionally by its owners. It is up to the negotiators to decide whether access to the mutual gains potential inherent to social capital and the resources it makes available to the parties is something that they intend to explore and utilize. In addition, the reduction of uncertainty associated with greater access to information, makes social capital an especially powerful resource in the negotiation process, where negotiators are constantly in search of ways to increase certainty. Like the informational benefits of social capital, reduction of uncertainty can assist the negotiating parties in enhancing mutual gains when it is bonding social capital that is being leveraged, or in advancing separate interests when using bridging or external social capital.

Increased innovation

Social capital has been shown to be an important factor influencing both incremental and radical innovation (Subramniam and Youndt, 2005). Much of the success of a negotiation can rest on the abilities of the parties to think creatively and innovate in the face of potential impasse. In the negotiation realm, this is often referred to as problem solving. Existing social capital research suggests that higher levels of social capital can enhance parties' abilities to engage in creative innovative thinking about the issues that they are attempting to address. Here too, in order for social capital to promote this positive negotiation function, its owners or the negotiators must leverage their relationships within and outside the negotiation context. To the extent that negotiators leverage their relationships, with each other and with others outside the negotiating relationship, they will probably have an easier time thinking outside the box and arriving at integrative solutions.

Power

Social capital can also enhance its owners' power and influence (Coleman, 1990). Since social capital is created on the basis of mutual obligations and norms of reciprocity, its owners have the ability to leverage these obligations in order to pursue specific goals and objectives and advance a given agenda. Power and influence also play a central role in negotiation (Neale and Northcraft, 1991). Since power can be used as a tool through which parties advance their own interests, this social capital benefit could facilitate greater distributive, as opposed to integrative, gains. Negotiators can benefit from the power and influence dividends of social capital in a number of ways. First, with regards to bonding social capital, negotiators can make use of this resource in order to influence counterparts to make certain concessions or to pursue certain mutual gains. Second, negotiators can leverage bridging or external social capital in order to improve their bargaining position and enhance distributive gains.

Solidarity

Finally, social capital has also been linked to greater levels of solidarity (Adler and Kwon, 2000). The social norms associated with social capital increase the likelihood of network members to comply with informal rules and customs (Coleman, 1988). Thus for example, groups with greater social capital have been shown to resolve conflict more quickly (Nelson, 1989). The degree to which negotiating parties are affiliated with each other and have a sense of solidarity can play an important role in determining outcomes. Negotiating parties who are strongly connected within a group are likely to put each other's interests or common interests before their own. The solidarity benefits of social capital are therefore likely to be associated with a greater focus on integrative negotiation elements.

The costs of social capital: Implications for negotiators

Investment of resources

Clearly, social capital has the potential to enhance outcomes for its owners, but can this resource also have negative implications for negotiators? First, like any form of capital, the benefits associated with social capital require inputs and investments. A utilitarian approach to social capital might make the claim that social capital is only beneficial to its owners in situations where its usefulness as a resource outweighs the costs associated with maintaining the relationships and networks that contain it. In this sense, negotiators that spend a disproportionate amount of time cultivating relationships, yet do not activate this resource in ways that could enhance mutual or distributive gains, may not be "capitalizing" on their social capital investment from a purely cost-benefit standpoint.

The constraints of mutual obligations

Maintaining social capital is not just a matter of investing time and energy, but also requires that individuals and groups adhere to norms of reciprocity and mutual obligations (Coleman, 1990). This dimension of social capital can have a number of very important benefits, especially in promoting a collaborative negotiations setting, yet they can also come at a cost. Specifically, adhering to established norms of reciprocity and obligations can hinder the pursuit of conflicting goals and objectives. Thus, social capital may require suboptimal individual or group outcomes where there is a need to forgo promising opportunities that conflict with or are misaligned with the relational norms associated with a given stock of social capital.

In the negotiation realm, this cost could be associated with both bonding and bridging social capital. Negotiators with a high level of bonding social capital with their counterparts may find it difficult to pursue certain strategies that conflict with the associated norms of reciprocity. In fact, in highly relational settings, negotiators appear to accommodate their negotiating counterpart, thereby sacrificing economic benefits (Curhan *et al.*, 2008). It is often the mutual obligations that explain social capital's ability to increase a collaborative negotiation dynamic. Nevertheless, there may instances where this benefit is outweighed by the cost it entails for negotiators seeking to maximize certain individual gains. Bridging social capital can also negatively affect negotiations where negotiators are compelled to pursue certain strategies that may be inconsistent with individual or mutual gains due to the need to adhere to norms of reciprocity and preexisting obligations with individuals or groups outside the negotiation setting.

A recent example that illustrates the effects of a company's external social capital on the negotiation process with another party is the discussion between Japan Airlines (JAL) and Delta about cooperating as part of one airline alliance. In the airline sector, it is common for different companies to belong to one of the existing global airline alliances and take advantage of partnerships within the same alliance by coordinating frequent flyer miles, integrating flights. In 2009, JAL, a member of OneWorld, entered talks with Delta who is a member of rival alliance, SkyTeam. One might expect this negotiation to be dictated by the strategic objectives and considerations of the two negotiating firms, JAL and Delta. However, since JAL is a valuable member of the OneWorld alliance with an important role in providing access to Asia, American Airlines together with other members of OneWorld took a very proactive stance in this negotiation by providing joint financial assistance, consulting services to support JAL and prevent the company from leaving their OneWorld alliance to join the Delta-led SkyTeam. It is, of course, an open question as to whether a move to SkyTeam might have been in JAL's best long-term interest, but it is clear that the decision not to join forces with Delta was made based on considerations related to social capital outside the two party negotiation. In fact, the media covering this negotiation portrayed this as more of a battle between American Airlines and Delta over JAL rather than a negotiation between Delta and JAL (Kwok, 2009).

Restricted information

Some scholars maintain that alongside the aforementioned informational benefits associated with social capital; this resource can also constrain or restrict access to certain information and knowledge. For example, the bonds that allow for the creation of social capital might act to restrict access or attention to other types of information and perspectives. Put differently, the solidarity associated with social capital, which often viewed as a positive, can also lead to a reduction in creativity and innovation. From a negotiation standpoint, excessive reliance on the social capital generated through a limited number of ties and networks may limit the perspectives and information considered by negotiators jointly or separately.

What is clear from these examples of possible social capital costs, is that as with any asset, its owners must engage in an ongoing assessment of costs and benefits and of the manner in which they are being used. As will be discussed below, negotiators should spend their social capital in ways that are strategically aligned with their overarching goals and objectives. In doing so, it is likely that specific social capital benefits can be maximized and its costs minimized.

The Creation and Maintenance of Social Capital: Implications for Negotiators

On October 24th in 2006, a new five-year collective bargaining agreement between Major League Baseball (MLB) owners and

TABLE 1   Social capital benefits and costs: Implications for negotiators

	Types of Social Capital	
	Bonding capital	Bridging capital
Benefits: General	• *Information-sharing* • *Power and influence* • *Solidarity and mutual trust*	• *can reduce uncertainty* • *can increase innovative capability*
Benefits: Implications for Negotiators	• Maximizing distributive and/or integrative gains through increased access to information • Increased bargaining power • Increases problem solving capacity	• *can provide new information and enhance problem solving potential* • *can create innovative solutions* • *can increase foundation for distributive bargaining*
	• *can create cooperative dynamic* • *can increase foundation for integrative bargaining*	
Costs: General	• *Investments necessary to cultivate and maintain relationships can be costly* • *Adherence to established norms of reciprocity and obligation*	• *may restrict access to external information and perspectives* • *may create obligations that are not mutually beneficial (internal)*
		• *may create obligation that is not beneficial to distributive and/or integrative bargaining (external)*
Costs: Implications for Negotiators	• *Need for an ongoing assessment of benefits and costs* • *Loss of economic benefits due to obligations that are not mutually beneficial*	• *may hinder creativity and innovation* • *may cause negotiators to pursue certain strategies that are not consistent with individual gains*
		• *may cause negotiators to pursue certain strategies that are not consistent with individual/mutual gains*

players was announced. Both parties — commissioner Bud Selig and players union chief, Don Fehr, agreed that this time the approach to bargaining was pragmatic, the negotiation was smooth, and the relationship between the two sides has never been better. "There was a shared desire to get this done by about the time of the World Series", Fehr said. Selig added "These negotiations were emblematic of the new spirit of cooperation and trust that now exists between the clubs and the players". (Bodley, 2006). Many factors are likely to have contributed to this spirit of cooperation, but another way to understand the relationship between these negotiating parties and the outcomes they had achieved is through a social capital lens. The league and the union, according to this approach, were able to establish and maintain social capital that could be leveraged during negotiation. In what follows we discuss some of the ways in which negotiating parties can establish and maintain social capital.

Building a negotiation social capital infrastructure

Coleman (1988) states "[A]ll social relations and social structures facilitate some form of social capital; actors establish relations purposefully and continue them when they continue to provide benefits. **"Certain kinds of social structure, however, are especially important in facilitating some forms of social capital"** (emphasis added). Thus, Coleman underscores two additional central dimensions of social capital. First, the formation of social capital is, to a large extent, viewed as a purposeful act that is designed by the actors involved. This implies that actors themselves form specific structures and "rules of engagement" in order to facilitate the creation of social capital. Second, not all structures are created equally in terms of their ability to establish social capital. In other words, actors seeking to capitalize on the resources embedded in the social interactions between their members, will attempt to design suitable organizational structures, policies and work arrangements.

What are the considerations employed by negotiation actors in the establishment of structures and policies intended to increase the available social capital? Social capital and network scholars have outlined a number of important structural dimensions. As noted above, one of the key structural decisions negotiators need to make about their social capital stocks is whether to invest in strong or weak ties. For example, in some situations the amount of energy required for negotiators to maintain a useful network of strong ties is too great to allow for necessary mobilization of resources (Granovetter, 1973; 1375). The type of structural ties necessary for individuals that negotiate on a regular basis will differ from the needs of occasional or one shot negotiators. In other words, negotiators seeking to enable the creation of social capital to be used in the bargaining process will face a decision regarding the emphasis placed on weak or strong ties between organizational members.

A second structural consideration relates to the relative emphasis negotiators place on bridging and/or bonding ties. Research has demonstrated that the geography of the ties leading to social capital is, to a large extent, a matter of context and constraints. Thus, the social capital generated by these different types of ties yields qualitatively distinct outcomes (Coleman, 1988). Bonding social capital, or the resources embedded in the relationship between the negotiators, is likely to increase integrative negotiation dynamics. Bridging social capital on the other hand could strengthen either distributive or integrative bargaining dynamics. Thus, in developing a portfolio of negotiation related social capital, negotiators should consider their overall strategic posture and the expected strategies of their counterparts. Where there is the objective and expectation of engaging in cooperative integrative negotiations, a heavier reliance on bonding social capital is more appropriate.

Social capital is the product of specific structures of relationships and these should stem from the negotiators' strategic goals and objectives. What is clear from this discussion is that creating the appropriate social capital infrastructure between a set of negotiating actors requires a series of decisions, which take into account the type of social capital desired and the structural configuration necessary for fostering it (Coleman, 1988). In other words, social capital creation is a process that actors can manage. In our context, this implies that negotiators can manage and facilitate the creation of social capital among and between the different parties.

The joint ownership and interdependency of negotiators' social capital

As discussed above, the development of social capital rests on the creation of the necessary infrastructure, the vehicle through which members can interact, communicate and exchange information. While the literature recognizes the centrality of this structural dimension, it is also recognized as insufficient on its own. Social capital, by its very essence, must include an interpersonal and relational dimension (Nahapiet and Ghoshal, 1998). The relational social capital dimension can be seen as the breathing of life into the vessel created through the structural dimension discussed.

The relational dimension of social capital has a number of important implications for how this resource is created and maintained. First and foremost, unlike other assets, social capital is, by definition, jointly owned and calls for a foundation of trust and cooperation in order to be used. Social capital scholars have focused on two important definitional elements. First, social capital is seen as a function of actual relationships, which contain the potential value inherent to this currency. Thus, relationships serve both as the vehicle through which social capital is created and the very apparatus through which the value is captured and leveraged. Second, the quality of the relationships themselves is also an important predictor of how much capital the relationship contained.

The value created through relationships is not simply a matter of *whom we know,* but also a matter of *how well we know them.*

Thus, central to Bourdieu's definition is the notion that, unlike other forms of capital, social capital is not solely owned by the individual (for a similar argument see Coleman, 1988). Social capital stems from and resides in the relational space linking individuals and groups. Bourdieu (1985) refers to the resources generated through social networks as "the collectively owned capital". As such, there is no one actor who has exclusive ownership of this capital.

In addition to being jointly owned, social capital entails an inherent interdependence between the owners of this capital. Burt (1992) states that "social capital is a quality created between people" as opposed to other forms of capital, such as human capital. Since any attempt to make use of this social currency requires the active or passive agreement of all of the parties involved, each one is extremely dependent on the other (Coleman, 1990). Thus, the original capital owners are, for the most part, required to work together if they are to make use of the resources inherent to their relationship.

This social capital dimension has a number of important implications for negotiators. First, negotiators seeking to leverage the power of the relationship that they have (inside and outside the negotiation context), cannot do so unilaterally. Accessing the information, influence, and a problem solving resources made available through social capital is not automatic. Negotiators interested in spending their bonding social capital can only do so in conjunction with the other negotiating party. Even where negotiators have a relational ties that can be harnessed as social capital, they must rely on the goodwill of their negotiating counterpart.

What this means is that the likelihood of being able to benefit from social capital declines as the adversarial nature of negotiations increases. Negotiators interested in enhancing joint outcomes through bonding social capital need to consider issues related to timing and the overall negotiations climate. Waiting until impasse is reached before seeking to use jointly held social capital is, therefore, a mistake. Put differently, although social capital has the potential to dramatically influence negotiation, what happens throughout this process also influences availability and levels of this resource. Social capital and negotiation, therefore, have a reciprocal and reinforcing relationship.

Second, the fact that social capital is jointly owned and used implies that it is, itself, a negotiated asset. Thus, negotiators seeking to use bonding social capital will need to negotiate it. On the one hand, adding to the list of issues that negotiators need to engage the other side over could hinder the process. If negotiators cannot agree on how to put their relational ties to use in order to attain more information and increase integrative dynamics, this may exacerbate other disagreements. On the other hand, figuring out how to spend social capital stocks in an effort to enhance joint gains could provide the parties with a foundation on which to approach the central issues at the heart of the negotiation.

A third negotiation implication has to do with bridging social capital. As noted, in addition to the benefits associated with relationships with the other negotiating parties, negotiators can employ their ties with individuals and groups outside the negotiation. Nevertheless, here too, using this resource is not automatic and requires the cooperation of joint owners. Thus, negotiators seeking to maximize the benefits of their ties in relation to a specific negotiation should do so in a planned and purposeful manner. Put differently, negotiators should approach the use of bridging social capital strategically while, anticipating, which of their ties they may need to access.

Maintaining shared values and norms with negotiating counterpart

Social capital also involves a cognitive, or cultural, dimension, which rests on a "shared representation, interpretation and system of meaning" (Nahapiet and Ghoshal, 1998; 244). Social capital researchers have emphasized the importance of attaining this cognitive alignment in developing social capital (Nahapiet and Ghoshal, 1998). In order for individuals and groups to make use of the benefits inherent to their relationships, they must have some common language and a shared basis for engagement. The establishment of shared representation and meaning does not develop naturally and actors must foster it. One way in which cognitive alignment can be reached and sustained is through the establishment of formal and informal rules of engagement. Negotiators interested in enhancing their bonding social capital should improve their ability to maintain shared norms and interpretation with counterparts.

Negotiation often involves the creation of shared models of interaction that are established between the parties (Bazerman *et al.*, 2000). In fact, negotiation research has shown that where negotiating parties share the same norms of interaction, they are less likely to reach an impasse. Thus, in developing this dimension of social capital, negotiators are also creating a foundation for shared models of engagement, which can be beneficial to the process and outcomes associated with their negotiations. As seen in the MLB illustration above, a good example of the establishment of shared norms and interpretation is in the collective bargaining arena. In collective bargaining, labor and management representatives come together to negotiate the terms and conditions that will govern their relationship until the next round of bargaining. Although these bargaining rounds can be extremely adversarial in nature, in most cases the parties have a set foundation regarding the modes of engagement and interaction that can, if the parties choose, be leveraged in order to create and use relational wealth. This means that negotiators that are interested in enhancing bonding social capital stocks should engage in a process of establishing agreed upon norms and rules of engagement. Clearly, the establishment of these shared norms and modes of interaction are beneficial for the negotiation process itself. Negotiators that frequently engage the same counterparts are in an advantageous position in terms of their ability to create and foster social capital.

TABLE 2 Creating and maintaining social capital: Implications for negotiators

	Structural dimension	Relational dimension	Cognitive and cultural dimension
Key Characteristics	• Design and Structure of Relationships	• Trust and Obligation • Quality of Relationships • Joint Ownership	• Common Language and Shared Values • Norms of Interaction
Implications for Negotiators	• Social capital is shaped by negotiators • Negotiators should invest in different types of social ties (strong or weak) • Negotiators should consider the relative emphasis on bonding or bridging ties • Negotiators should adopt strategic approach to the creation and maintenance of social capital	• Negotiators need the other party's consent to use social capital (internal and external) • Negotiators should consider timing and negotiation climate before leveraging social capital for the enhancement of distributive or integrative gains • Negotiators should assess how past interactions between parties can affect the use of social capital • Negotiators should be aware of the effect that their negotiation has on the future availability of social capital	• Negotiators should establish agreed upon norms and rules of engagement to enhance social capital stocks • Negotiators should make planned and strategically aligned social capital investments

Conclusions

Social capital is a unique asset that has the potential to affect negotiation processes and outcomes. Like other tools that negotiators have in their "toolbox", this resource can, when employed strategically, assist the parties in achieving their goals and objectives. In this chapter, we focused on identifying the benefits of social capital, arguing that social capital can be translated into various advantages (information, influence, and solidarity) that are important to negotiation processes. Nevertheless, social capital can also have negative effects on negotiators and their ability to purse their interests. Furthermore, different types of social capital (bonding or bridging) are likely to influence different benefits and costs.

As is emphasized throughout the chapter, the manner in which social capital is used is up to the negotiators and will have implications for the effect this resource will have on the process and outcomes. Thus for example, information derived through social ties and networks can be used to improve negotiators' bargaining position, thereby enhancing distributive gains. Alternatively social capital can promote a collaborative approach, thereby enhancing mutual gains. Negotiators have to decide whether to use social capital to enhance mutual or distributive gains.

Negotiators' active and strategic use of social capital is even more critical in the process of crafting and conserving social capital stocks. Negotiators interested in taking advantage of social ties and networks to enhance negotiation outcomes must be strategic about handling joint ownership, an inherent element of social capital, as well as designing and structuring negotiation-related social capital. In this context, it is important to note that negotiation may actually influence the creation and usage of negotiators' social capital itself since the stocks of social capital owned by individuals can increase or decrease as a result of positive or negative relational experiences. Moreover, the use of social capital is influenced by past interactions. Thus, the manner in which the parties leverage their relationship in one round of negotiations will have significant effects on the willingness of one or both parties to use social ties as a resource in the following rounds. Recognizing and incorporating a social capital perspective to negotiation should help negotiators create and maintain optimal configurations of social ties that can be put to use in order to attain desired outcomes.

Trust Building, Diagnosis, and Repair in the Context of Negotiation

Donald L. Ferrin
Lee Kong Chian School of Business
Singapore Management University

Dejun Tony Kong
Olin Business School,
Washington University in St. Louis

Kurt T. Dirks
Olin Business School,
Washington University in St. Louis

Hong Kong Disneyland, a joint venture between the Walt Disney Company and the Hong Kong government, was conceived during the Asian financial crisis as a strategy for making Hong Kong a major tourist destination and providing Disney with a foothold into the potentially lucrative China market. Unfortunately, the park has steadily lost money since opening in September 2005. The Hong Kong Disneyland is the smallest of Disney's theme parks worldwide, having only four "lands". Many visitors complain that it is too small, with too few attractions to attract them for a second visit. In fact, Hong Kong Disneyland reflects Disney's new strategy of opening parks in phases, rather than trying to build an extensive park all at once as was done in Paris and Florida.

---

[1] We would like to thank Amit Arvind Batavia for his generous research assistance.

Despite the obvious joint interest in expanding the park, and sufficient open land for doing so, in March 2009 negotiations for a US$500 million construction of three additional "lands" broke down due to the Hong Kong Government's reluctance to invest further in Disney. Disney responded with a statement that it was laying off employees in Hong Kong after failing to reach an agreement with the Hong Kong government to fund the much-needed expansion. According to Disney, "the uncertainty of the outcome requires us to immediately suspend all creative and design work on the project". Thirty Hong Kong-based Disney "Imagineers" would lose their jobs, leaving a skeleton team of ten behind. The breakdown in negotiations led the press and industry experts to speculate that Hong Kong Disneyland might be the first Disneyland to close its doors (Balfour and Einhorn, 2009; Bradsher, 2005; Fan, 2006).

In this example, we see two highly respected entities — the Walt Disney Corporation and the Hong Kong Government — who are highly dependent on each other, but who are on the verge of a relationship breakdown due to trust, more specifically a failure to trust. But to say this is a "trust problem" glosses over several nuances that are important for understanding the foundations of trust, how relationships can be built, how trust can develop and be managed, and how trust can dramatically influence the processes and outcomes of negotiation. Most negotiators realise that trust is critically important in negotiations. However, most negotiators do not fully understand what trust is, how it forms, and how it actually influences negotiations. In this chapter, we will attempt to address those issues.

What is Trust and How is it Manifested in Negotiations?

Researchers have made tremendous strides in the last 15 years toward understanding the nature, determinants, role and consequences of trust. In the organizational sciences, trust is generally recognized as a willingness to make oneself vulnerable to another party despite uncertainty about his or her intentions and future actions (Rousseau *et al.*, 1998). And, as Rousseau *et al.* note, trust is only relevant in the presence of risk and interdependence.

This definition of trust, with its emphasis on vulnerability, risk, and interdependence, implies that trust is not just relevant in negotiations, it *permeates* the negotiation experience. In the Hong Kong Disneyland negotiation, neither the Hong Kong government nor the Walt Disney Company can unilaterally decide and implement a plan to expand the park or otherwise address the business concerns in a constructive way. Instead, the two parties' fates are intertwined; they are highly inter-dependent. What risks do they face? Negotiators are known to face three types of negotiation-specific risks: the strategic risk of sharing information during bargaining, BATNA risk that they may agree to a settlement inferior to their BATNA or reject a settlement superior to their BATNA, and contractual risk that the other party may renege on a negotiated agreement (Bottom, 1998). Additionally, both parties face business risk — that their existing business investment and their future business prospects — may be damaged by an impasse or a bad deal. Finally, interdependence and risks combine to create vulner-ability in terms of the potential financial losses as mentioned above, and also reputation loss for Disney as a successful park operator and the Hong Kong government as a steward of public investments.

While this example illustrates the manifestation of trust in a highly publicized negotiation between two large entities, one a corporation and the other a government, the concepts apply equally to trust between two individuals, two groups, or even two countries: Where interdependence and opportunities for coopera-tion and exploitation exist, vulnerability and risk will almost always be present, and trust provides a means through which parties can move forward despite the risks. Therefore, to the extent trust can be built and/or used as a foundation for cooperation in such situations, trust can positively influence processes and out-comes within a negotiation. For instance, as Dirks and Ferrin (2001) noted, researchers have long recognized that trust between negotiators facilitates integrative processes (Schurr and Ozanne, 1985) and inhibits distributive processes (Kimmel *et al.*, 1980; Schurr and Ozanne, 1985). The trust developed via negotiation is also likely to carry over to other settings and tasks in which negotiation partners might interact over time. Recently, in a two-stage game, Campagna, Bottom, Kong, and Mislin (2010) found that in an employment negotiation, the employer's strategic anger worsened the job candidate's perception of the employer's trustworthiness. This decreasing perception of the employer's trustworthiness undermined the job candidate's trust in a subsequent investment game in which the job candidate's trust could actually make both parties better off.

Because trust is so important in negotiations, and because parties often negotiate with others repeatedly, whether over weeks or years or decades, trust is also a frequently-desired outcome of negotiation, as it provides a foundation for future negotiation success with that partner. Thus, trust can be seen as a determinant, and also a consequence, of negotiation processes and outcomes. It is probably most useful to think of negotiation processes and outcomes, and trust, as linked in a virtuous cycle: Positive negotiation processes and outcomes increase trust, which in turn generate even more positive processes and outcomes. Of course, the same dynamics can result in a vicious cycle, where negative processes or outcomes can damage trust, and damaged trust can impair future negotiation processes and outcomes.

Of course, it should not be forgotten that trust can also be misplaced, i.e., placed in a party who is in fact not worthy of trust, which can lead to exploitation. One particularly infamous example occurred in the late 1930s when Adolf Hitler convinced Neville Chamberlain to persuade the Czechs not to mobilize their army but instead to negotiate with Hitler. After his meeting with Hitler, Chamberlain wrote to his sister, "... in spite of the hardness and ruthlessness I thought I saw in his face, I got the impression that here was a man who could be relied upon when he had given his word..." (Jervis, 1970).

What Makes a Negotiation Party Trustworthy?

Researchers have identified three primary foundations of trust: Perceptions of a party's ability, integrity, and benevolence (Mayer, Davis, and Schoorman, 1995). To the extent one believes another party has ability, integrity, and benevolence, one will be more likely to trust that party, whether it is an individual, a group, an organization, or even a nation.

Ability

In the context of negotiation, "perceived ability" refers to two distinct but critically important factors: professional/technical/industry competence, and negotiation competence. First, is one's counterpart perceived to have the professional and/or technical skills, abilities, resources, and judgment to fulfill the agreement you have negotiated with him/her? And does he/or she have the requisite industry knowledge, for example about industry norms, standard terms and conditions, the regulatory regime, the logistics and support networks, etc.? Importantly, ability is not only an individual characteristic, but also an organizational characteristic. When one thinks of the industry leaders across various sectors — Intel in the microprocessor technology, Coke in the soft drinks industry, Procter & Gamble in the consumer goods industry, Singapore Airlines in air travel, Goldman Sachs in investment banking, McKinsey in consulting, Wal-Mart in mass retailing, and so on, these are companies that have a reputation for being able to competently meet customer/client expectations with leading edge business strategies and technology. They are perceived to have organization-level ability.

Second, what is the level of the counterpart's negotiation abilities? Negotiation competencies include a wide range of skills and abilities including the ability to communicate effectively, leverage resources, frame situations, form coalitions, take others' perspectives, and gather information (Shell, 2006). This raises an interesting question: Is it preferable to negotiate 'against' an experienced negotiator, or an inexperienced one? The answer is surprising: Although one might guess that it is preferable to nego- tiate with an inexperienced negotiator because of the opportunity to outmaneuver him/her, experienced and talented negotiators often prefer to negotiate with an experienced and talented nego- tiator, rather than an inexperienced or untalented one, because this provides a better opportunity of arriving at a creative and wise agreement that can provide lasting benefits to both parties (Benoliel, 2010).

Although negotiation ability is typically considered to be an individual skill, it can also be an organizational competence. Organizations that aspire to make negotiation an organizational competence tend to do one or more of the following: (a) create an internal negotiation structure, for example by standardizing their negotiation processes, creating internal databases, and an ability to learn from past negotiation experiences organization- wide, (b) broaden their measures of success by considering not only financial measures, but also the quality of negotiated solu- tions and the extent to which such solutions are implementable, (c) focus not just on the deal but also the relationship with the negotiation counterpart, including trust, information sharing, and collaborative decision making, and (d) have an organiza- tional approach to identifying best alternatives to a deal and identifying when to walk away (Ertel, 1999; see also Movius and Susskind, 2009).

Integrity

"Perceived integrity" includes three related elements. First, is the negotiator reliable and dependable? Second, does the negotiator keep his/her word and promises? Third, does the negotiator follow values and principles, whether moral or ethical or profes- sional, one agrees with? In the context of negotiation, these elements would be demonstrated by being truthful, professional, and principled during the negotiation process and also in the deal-keeping that follows. Behaviors such as using manipulative or unethical negotiation behaviors, or failing to honor past agreements, would obviously signal low integrity.

Of course, "integrity" can refer not only to an individual's characteristics, but also to a group's or organization's. In fact, in corporate negotiations, it may be the case that one trusts the individual negotiator, but not his/her company. Sometimes, the situation is reversed: One trusts the company but feels disinclined to trust the individual negotiator (Zaheer, McEvily, and Perrone, 1998). In negotiations for complex deliverables such as engineering and construction projects, agreements are made not just on what the company is willing to negotiate into the contract (price, specifications, completion dates, etc.), but also on whether the company will meet its contractual obligations. In fact, it is frequently the case that companies that are considered untrustworthy are not even invited to bid.

Benevolence

"Perceived benevolence" refers to the extent that another party is perceived to care for one's interests. Benevolence is distinct from ability and integrity in that it focuses not on the nature and character of the trustee, but on the motives of the trustee, particularly *vis-à-vis* the relationship between negotiators.

Like ability and integrity, benevolence may reflect an individual trait. All of us know individuals who are rather competitive and self-serving, tending to put their own interests ahead of others' interests. But we also know other individuals who are relatively selfless, and will often sacrifice their own interests for the benefit of another. Within organizations, the term "silo mentality" refers to the tendency of some individuals and groups to place their own selfish interests ahead of other groups' interests. In contrast, a benevolent individual or group will recognize the importance of superordinate interests, and the need for groups to sometimes subordinating their own selfish interests for the success of the entity as a whole. Externally, most corporations work assiduously to manage their reputations with respect to benevolence, often portraying themselves as finely balanced between pursuing the profits that stakeholders are interested in vs. the many other interests that stakeholders such as employees, environmentalists, and community members are interested in. Nevertheless, companies do also develop informal reputations as being more or less focused on profit vs. other concerns.

Benevolence perceptions can also be influenced by negotiation behaviors and deal structuring. Negotiators who adopt a win-lose orientation, sometimes even boasting about how they bested an opponent in a negotiation, will certainly earn a reputation for selfishness. Negotiators who demonstrate a sincere care and concern for their counterpart will be deemed benevolent and trustworthy. In integrative negotiations, expressing a clear interest in understanding the counterpart's interests and exploring ways of meeting those interests, is a key route toward earning trust. Of course, it is also valuable to interact with politeness and respect. Nearly three centuries ago de Callieres (1716/1983) recognized the importance of diplomats' courtesy and respect in negotiations with foreigners.

Perceived ability, integrity, and benevolence in combination

The Walt Disney-Hong Kong Government impasse provides an excellent example of how ability, integrity, and benevolence perceptions can affect trust and negotiation outcomes. The Hong Kong government's perceptions about Disney's ability were probably shaken by at least two occurrences. First, Disney failed to meet visitor targets or even turn a profit since opening in 2005. Second, Disney had serious difficulties managing volume, most notably in Chinese New Year 2006 when Disney underestimated the response to a discount promotion at the start of the holiday and, after meeting capacity, locked out hundreds of ticketed customers who had traveled from Mainland China to the Hong Kong Special Administrative Region to visit the park. This resulted in TV coverage of crying children, and angry tourists climbing fences to try to get into the park. The Hong Kong government also had reason to doubt Disney's benevolence. While negotiating with the Hong Kong government, Disney was also in negotiations with Shanghai officials to open a park in Shanghai, perhaps as early as 2014. Clearly, a Shanghai park would represent a serious competitive threat to Hong Kong Disneyland. The Hong Kong public were also given reason to doubt Disney's integrity. The Hong Kong government paid more than 80% of the US$2.9 billion cost of building the park, but received only a 57% share in the joint venture. Consequently, Disney's practice of not disclosing specific attendance or revenue figures rubbed Hong Kong citizens the wrong way, as it would only seem fair that a joint venture funded by Hong Kong's citizens should disclose pertinent information about the performance of the venture. In combination, we can easily surmise that skepticism about Disney's ability, integrity, and benevolence, even in conditions of high vulnerability, risk, and uncertainty, led the Hong Kong government to withhold funding even though this act threatened the very viability of its own investment.[2]

Of course, Hong Kong Disneyland provided us with an example of the consequences of weakened trust. Positive ability, integrity, and benevolence perceptions can equally contribute to stronger trust and positive negotiation processes and outcomes. Additionally, while ability, benevolence, and integrity perceptions may all be aligned in a positive or negative direction (as in the example of Hong Kong Disneyland), sometimes they are not. For instance, Jack Welch was considered an extremely able CEO, however considering his highly-publicized sex scandal and his "rank and yank" HR policies, many people would not consider him to be high in integrity and benevolence. In general, to fully gain another's trust, it will usually be necessary to be perceived as high in most or all facets of trustworthiness. For instance, research has

---

[2] The Hong Kong government did ultimately approve a financing plan to build three additional "lands" over the next five years at an estimated cost of US$448 million (Chmielewski, 2009).

specifically noted that to be seen as a trustworthy and attractive partner, it is necessary to be seen as having both ability *and* integrity (Dirks and Skarlicki, 2009). Individuals may be hesitant to negotiate with a 'shark' who has high ability but low integrity!

How Can I Gain Others' Trust?

How can I gain another's trust? To start with the obvious, it is crucial to be trustworthy. Ability can be demonstrated by one's record of successful past performances related to negotiation in question. Integrity can be demonstrated by ardently keeping one's promises and upholding the highest ethical standards. Both ability and integrity can be demonstrated interpersonally, and also built into organizations' culture and values. Benevolence can be demonstrated through negotiation behaviors, and also through deal structuring.

The above tactics all demonstrate trustworthiness directly to the trustor. One can also convey trustworthiness indirectly, through story-telling. For example, insurance agents, when meeting a new prospect, frequently tell a story of a past customer who requested a policy that the agent knew was unnecessarily costly and did not meet the customer's needs, so the agent recommended a cheaper policy that better fitted the customer's needs. Note that this simple story simultaneously conveys ability (of the agent to understand the customer's needs and identify a policy that meets those needs), integrity (honestly disclosing the best policy), and benevolence (placing the customer's interest ahead of the agent's interest of earning a large commission).

Another indirect way of gaining another's trust is through the identification of similarities (Hurley, 2006). It is quite natural, when meeting another person, to look for similarities such as common work history, affiliations with professional or leisure organizations (e.g., common clubs), similar personal interests, similar philosophies, and common backgrounds (e.g., country, language, education). Evolutionary psychologists understand that humans have become hard-wired to develop trust toward those who are similar, because in the course of human history humans have been more successful when they have relied on those are similar because they share a common fate, and therefore will look after each other's interests. In negotiation, identifying and communicating such similarities can help build trust, so it is advisable to systematically attempt to identify such similarities in the very earliest stages of building a negotiation relationship. This helps people to bond and better understand each other. Of course, the technique can also be used disingenuously. Car salespersons, for instance, are known to look in the back of customers' cars to discern the customer's interests (Cialdini, 2001). For customers with golf clubs, the salesman may say 'what a beautiful day, I wish I were golfing', whereas for customers with car seats, the salesman may say 'please forgive me if I have to leave suddenly, my young child is at the doctor with the flu'. For negotiators, it is worthwhile to invest time before and during the negotiation to identify similarities that can provide a foundation for trust.

One particularly powerful determinant of trust is the actual and perceived alignment of the parties' goals and interests (Deutsch, 1949). Perceiving one's interests as positively aligned with another's interests can lead one to behave in a more trustworthy and trusting way, and also cause one to perceive another's behaviors as more trustworthy, both of which engender trust (Ferrin and Dirks, 2003). In contrast, perceiving another's goals and interests as opposed to one's own can cause less trusting and trustworthy behavior and more negative perceptions. One practical way of managing alignment is to work toward constructing deals that actually align the parties' interests. In fact, one of the most fundamental processes through which negotiations can be made successful is interest discovery and alignment (Fisher, Ury, and Patton, 1991). If parties can understand the interests that are brought to the negotiating table, and then find a way to align those interests, then an agreement can be formed that makes it in both parties' interests to agree. Once this agreement is reached, one can rely on the counterpart to behave in a trustworthy way because doing so is actually in the counterpart's interest. Another way of aligning interests is through contingency contracts, which are "if-then" agreements that utilize negotiation parties' different forecasts or preferences and specify the actions negotiation parties are to take if a certain circumstance (a contingency) materializes (Bazerman and Gillespie, 1999). For example, in a buyer-supplier agreement, buyers will naturally suffer from any product defects, whereas suppliers may benefit from product defects since it allows them to procure and manufacture lower-quality products at reduced cost. A contingency contract that provides for penalties or rework can align interests between buyer and seller because the contingency clause provides incentives for each party to behave in ways that protect the interests of the other party.[3]

Social networks provide a powerful way of building trust. If it can be established that you are in a common network with a trustor, connected by one or more third parties whom you both trust, then one may gain trust in two ways (Ferrin, Dirks, and Shah, 2006): First, the other party will trust you via referral — by learning from a trusted third party that you are trustworthy; second, the other party will have confidence that if trust is violated, then sanctions can be applied not just by him/herself, but by other parties he or she trusts within the network. Naturally, the more third parties connecting the trustor and trustee, the stronger and quicker the trust. Thus, for negotiators, one valuable way of earning

---

[3] It is also important to recognize that ill-constructed contingency contracts can be destructive to trust building and inadvertently magnify negotiators' exposure to risk. As Kong (2010) noted, the credit-default swap (CDS), an over-the-counter derivative invented by JPMorgan Chase, is a kind of contingency contract between protection buyers and protection sellers — negotiation parties who are interested in covering losses on certain securities in the event of a default such as a bankruptcy or a credit rating downgrade. The market for these securities exploded over a decade to more than US$50 trillion in 2008. However, CDSs actually magnified the risk embedded in the global financial system (Philips, 2008), and they ultimately destroyed the trust between protection buyers and protection sellers, and among many other investors and stakeholders.

another's trust via social networks is to discover ways that one is connected to another via mutually trusted third parties.

There are also specific negotiating behaviors that can be used to build trust during the negotiation process. For instance, when negotiating, it is usually important to share information and give concessions. However, in most cases it would be inadvisable to unilaterally share all relevant information or make all of one's possible concessions at the outset of a negotiation because it would make you vulnerable to exploitation or forfeit all negotiation leverage. Yet at the same time, if one resists sharing information at all, or refuses to make any concessions, then there is a likelihood that the negotiation will end in impasse. Our recommended strategy is to build reciprocity: Share a small bit of information or make a small concession, then wait for the counterpart to reciprocate, and then gradually build trust through reciprocation of information sharing and concession making. If the counterpart does not voluntarily reciprocate, request that the counterpart reciprocate before providing further information or concessions.

There are even more subtle ways of building trust in the context of negotiation. Research has shown that mimicking the other negotiation party's behaviors can increase the other party's prosocial tendencies, and gain their trust, even without the other party's awareness (Maddux, Mullen, and Galinsky, 2008). Emotional expressions convey information about one's intentions, beliefs, and preferences, reinforce or correct the other party's behavior, and evoke complementary emotions from the other party (e.g., one's anger evokes the other's fear or anger) (Morris and Keltner, 2000). Emotions can be contagious (Bartel and Saavedra, 2000), and positive emotional contagion can improve cooperation and decrease conflict (Barsade, 2002). Indeed, research on emotional intelligence — individuals' abilities "to monitor one's own and others' emotions, to discriminate among them, and to use the information to guide one's thinking and actions" (Salovey and Mayer, 1990, p. 189) — suggests that emotionally intelligent negotiators gain more trust from their counterparts (Kong and Bottom, 2010).

How Can I Assess Another's Trustworthiness?

Thus far we have focused primarily on how one can earn the trust of another. Meanwhile, one of the most challenging aspects of negotiation is to accurately assess whether one's counterpart is trustworthy. How can one assess another's trustworthiness? Fortunately, the guidance above can be used not only to earn trust, but also to assess another's trustworthiness. If one wishes to assess another's trustworthiness, one can assess another's track record for professional ability, negotiation ability, integrity, and benevolence. One can consider whether there are *meaningful* similarities that could provide a foundation for trust such as shared moral philosophies or professional aspirations. One can consider whether there are third parties who can attest to another's trustworthiness and/or help enforce trustworthiness. One can also consider whether the other party mimics and/or expresses emotions in a way that provides a reliable indication of trustworthiness.

Another strategy is extremely simple and should be used whenever possible: Negotiate with parties whom you already trust!

Can one assess another's trustworthiness perfectly? Of course not. Investment guru Bernard Madoff has provided us with an instructive example of misplaced trust. Over many years, Bernard Madoff earned the trust of many friends and investors — many of them very successful investors and businesspeople in their own right — via a remarkably consistent record of investment performance (perceived ability), word of mouth recommendations from one investor to another (social networks), and perceived similarity (Madoff got to know many of the victims via membership in country clubs in New York and Florida). And, for years he systematically exploited his friends' and investors' trust by investing their funds into an elaborate pyramid scheme which finally collapsed in late 2008 (Frank *et al.*, 2008). Those investors had ample reason to trust Madoff, yet their trust was violated. Our recommendation is that negotiators should recognize that trust is vulnerability in the context of risk and uncertainty, and any time a relationship or agreement is entered into on the basis of trust, the negotiator should simultaneously recognise and be prepared for a failure of trust. This strategy would not have prevented Madoff's investors from losing money, but it would have led investors to diversify their investments across multiple investment advisors, and by doing so would have saved many from losing their entire life savings in one fell swoop.

Repairing Trust After a Violation

The worst case scenario has materialized: You have violated the trust of a negotiation partner. Is it possible to repair trust? Contrary to popular belief that trust cannot be repaired after a significant violation, recent research indicates that trust can be repaired through several different processes and in certain circumstances. First, it matters whether the violation related to expectations about competence vs. expectations about integrity; integrity violations are much more difficult to repair. Second, the key mechanism through which trust can be repaired is repentance: You must communicate that you regret the violation, you have worked to rectify it (by either repairing the damage or preventing future damage), and you have reformed (recognised the error and are committed not to repeat it). Repentance can be communicated in several different ways such as via verbal apologies, penance, and/or regulation or sanctions of future behavior (Dirks *et al.*, 2007).

In some instances, a negotiator's violation may be so severe that the only hope of restoring trust is to actually remove the negotiator from the negotiation. This is particularly the case in situations where the violation is considered to involve a serious lapse of integrity because integrity violations are seen as highly diagnostic of the underlying character of the trustee, and thus it is very difficult to reverse such perceptions even with positive subsequent behavior (Kim *et al.*, 2004). In 2003, Don Carty, the then CEO of American Airlines, had just successfully negotiated the largest restructuring deal in history with the 100,000+ employees of AA, when hours later the media publicized that he had also facilitated sweetheart deals for AA's top leaders. The anger from the AA workforce was so swift and severe that Carty's denials, apologies, and proffered penance could not repair trust. Carty ultimately stepped down, and it was only after his resignation that mediators could be brought in to repair trust and restore the negotiated agreement between employees and the airline (Wong and Maynard, 2003).

Summary

Trust is widely recognized as one of the most important factors in negotiation. We hope that this chapter gives negotiators a much deeper, more detailed, and practically useful understanding of how and why trust matters in negotiation. First, being perceived as trustworthy — which is the critical precursor to trust — involves not one but three different facets: ability, integrity, and benevolence. In most negotiations, it is critical to be perceived as trustworthy not only on a single facet, but ideally on all three. These facets are distinct from each other, and in many or most cases it will be necessary to give individual attention to each as one attempts to gain trust. Second, negotiators have many different ways of building and managing perceptions of trustworthiness, and we have highlighted a sample of some of the most useful approaches. Third, while it is obviously critical to be able to accurately assess the trustworthiness of a partner, we suspect that most individuals struggle to achieve this outcome, so agreements based on trust should always be made with the simultaneous recognition (and in many cases, a contingency plan) that trust may fail. Finally, it is possible to repair trust if one focuses on signaling repentance in a credible manner.

7

Power and Influence in Negotiations

Min Li
Carlson School of Management
University of Minnesota

Julie Sadler[1]
Labor Studies and Employment Relations
Pennsylvania State University

Introduction

Underlying any negotiation experience is power — the relative power of the multiple parties. We define power as the potential to influence others and regard influence as power in action. If you have absolute power and can dominate your counterpart, you do not need to negotiate since you could simply take what you want. However, rarely in today's world will one party possess so much power that he/she can impose and sustain his/her will over others. In this chapter, we focus on the interplay between power, influence, and strategies in the context of negotiation. We first provide an overview of the diverse set of sources from which negotiators could draw power. We then highlight power bases within the specific context of negotiation. In light of the prevalence of power asymmetry, we discuss the effects of power imbalance on negotiation processes and outcomes. As negotiations do not occur in a vacuum, we highlight the

---

[1]Both authors contributed equally to this chapter and the ordering of names is purely alphabetical.

contextual forces that alter the power dynamics such as societal, cultural, and organizational norms and pressures. Thus, we conclude our chapter by illustrating how to effectively translate power into influence in accordance with national cultures.

Negotiation — The Process of Power Dependence, Social Influence, and Joint Problem Solving

The term "negotiation" typically refers to any give and take process between two or more parties that seek to resolve a conflict, determine how to divide or share resources, or create an alternative solution that neither could accomplish on their own (Rubin and Brown, 1975; Lewicki, 1992; Lewicki, Saunders, and Barry, 2006). The parties involved could be individuals, groups, or organi-zations attempting to resolve an issue. Negotiations are entered into by choice because the parties believe they can get a better deal by engaging with the other party than simply acquiescing to what the other side offered them. In the pursuit of a better deal, each party seeks to convince the other(s) to make concessions so that the final outcome is aligned as much as possible to one's own preferences. In this "give and take" process, each party holds valuable resources desired by the other(s). Characterized by this inherent interdependence, negotiations is a joint problem-solving process where power and social influence become a critical and "the strategic issue" (Rubin and Brown, 1975: 260).

Power and Influence Defined

What is "power" and what does it mean within the social context of negotiation? Typically, *power* is defined as the potential or capacity of influencing someone to act, feel, or think in an intended manner, and in a way that the person(s) would not have otherwise. Having power does not necessarily translate into actual influence. The process of affecting behavior, thoughts, or feelings of others in a particular direction is influence (Pfeffer, 1993). In other words, *influence* is the outcome of power being exerted on a person and represents the actual degree of change in that person's actions, feelings, and/or thoughts. Simply put, influence is power in action. The term power typically has a negative connotation and hearing the word often insights visions of power mongrels or visions of people who abused their power. In reality, power is not predestined to subjugate or manipulate people to their detriment. The real questions are where do people acquire power (i.e., sources of power), what will people do with their power (i.e., their goals), and how will people use their power (strategies for converting power into influence). We now turn our attention to each of these questions.

Sources of Power

For anyone who wants to be effective and successful in negotiation, important questions to ask include: how is my power position in this negotiation, where does my power come from, where does your counterpart's power emanate from, and how do I gain power in this negotiations. A solid understanding of power sources will enable you to better gauge the situation and to make effective moves in negotiations. One of the earliest studies to explore sources of power was conducted by French and Raven (1959) and they identified five bases of power — legitimate, referent, expert power, reward, and coercive power.

French and Raven's bases of power

Legitimate power refers to an individual's capacity to alter another person's actions merely because he/she is granted formal authority over another person. Formal authority is typically granted to a role or title through the formal structure of the organization. A typical example used to illustrate legitimate power is the CEO of a company, who by virtue of holding that position has the capacity to alter his/her subordinates' actions.

Referent power over another person stems from the degree of personal connection or "oneness" the parties have with each other. Essentially, this source of power over another person stems from him/her liking you and wanting to be liked and around you. Think of those charismatic and popular people in high school or college that had the capacity to influence others because they want to remain in favor or be liked by him/her.

Expert power stems from an awareness that a person within the negotiation context has unique and valuable set of knowledge and expertise. Given that expertise, a party will be more susceptible or open to the "experts" efforts to convert power to actual influence. Think about the person who has received an undergraduate degree in accounting, has been working as an accountant for fifteen years vs. the recent college graduate who earned a degree in marketing, but who has filed his/her own taxes for the last two years — who are you likely to be most influenced by when they provide recommendations?

Reward power reward power is power derived from a person's ability to reward his/her counterpart in negotiations by exchanging a variety of different resources (ex. money, promotions, friendship, and information). An example of reward power is a parent, in "negotiating" with his/her teenager about baby-sitting his/her younger siblings, the parent may relax the teenager's curfew the following evening in exchange for the baby-sitting "service".

As with reward power, *coercive power* attempts to convert the capacity to change another person into actual change by manipulating outcomes. Exercising coercive power, akin to punishment, attempts to alter another by introducing negative consequences or the removal of a positive consequence if the person fails to conform to the wishes of the "power wielder". Think about a situation in which management, in the process of negotiating a collective bargaining agreement, threatens to close down a wing of the hospital and layoff that subset of employees, if the union does not agree to reduce the number of vacation days available to each employee.

A major criticism of French and Raven's initial work on power sources is that reward and coercive power are not two independent or unique sources but rather are two sides of the same coin (Podsakoff and Schriesheim, 1985). As such, we treat reward and coercive power as one source, whereby a person has the potential to change another person and persuade him/her to agree to the negotiation terms because he/she has the ability to add or remove resources.

Additional power sources and their advantages and disadvantages

Recent work by Kakabadse and colleagues (Kakabadse, 1999; Kakabadse *et al.*, 2005) reiterated the importance of three of French and Raven's initial sources (legitimate, reward, and expert power) and identified additional sources underlying power. Additionally, they elaborated on the advantages and disadvantages of relying on each of these sources. The following section reviews and expands on the sources and highlights potential advantages and disadvantages of each source.

Akin to French and Raven's legitimate power, *role power* refers to power granted to an individual as a function of holding a specific role within an organization's structural hierarchy. To successfully translate power into influence via legitimate power, the followers must acknowledge the legitimacy of the hierarchy of the organizational structure and system of rules. One reason that role power is effective is because it is typically bundled with access to various resources (i.e., reward and coercive power). A potential downside to using role power is that over time parties may rebel or push back when someone consistently relies on that formal authority to obtain an agreement.

Similar to French and Raven's conceptualization of reward and coercive power, *reward power* or resource power is defined as the ability of a person to control the resources desired by others. Resources include monetary and non-monetary or

144 M. Li and J. Sadler

non-material resources (i.e., prestige or privilege). As raised above, resources can be used in two broad ways — as a reward or coercive element. For reward power to successfully translate into actual change in another person, the rewards being offered (or withheld in the coercive version) must be desired by the counterpart and under the control of the person attempting to exert power. Managers and negotiation parties are likely to frame an exchange in reward framework and people do tend to respond to the use of positive outcomes. The short-term effectiveness of this approach is relatively high but long-term sustainability of relying solely on reward power to resolve a negotiations experience can be costly and ineffective. Overuse of reward power may, over time, inspire resentment and foster ill will in an on-going negotiations and exchange relationship. Given the delicate balance that the use of reward power (or coercive power) requires, sole reliance on reward power may not be an effective long-term strategy for negotiations. An additional concern is that to identify rewards that are considered by your counterpart as valuable and scarce requires considerable effort and may misdirect or hinder identifying alternative solutions that could be mutually beneficial to the parties.

Coercive use of reward power, whereby individuals use punishment-centered strategies to gain compliance or exert influence on another person in the short-term is an effective approach to resolving the negotiations in your favor. Unfortunately, coercive power, as French and Raven and others have pointed out, is effective at obtaining the on-the-surface goals (or superficial goals) to the detriment of the relationship-building goals (i.e., trust). Additionally, over time, people will come to resent the negative dynamic; thus, the long-term effectiveness of relying on coercive power is relatively low.

Akin to French and Raven's expert power, *expertise or knowledge power* is derived from a person's specialized knowledge about a task, role, or issue and is bestowed on people who are seen as achieving a mastery of a particular subject area. Being seen as an expert and displaying confidence about his/her knowledge on a particular issue or task is a highly effective strategy for altering your counterparts' thoughts and behaviors. The challenge or potential disadvantage is that expertise is context or negotiation specific and as such, it is unlikely that expertise power will transfer to other contexts. Additionally, expertise and credibility takes considerable time to accrue.

Akin to French and Raven's referent power, *personal power* is power derived from an individual's personality and how likeable and attractive he/she is to others. A challenge in exerting personal power over someone else within a negotiation process is that likeability is in the eyes of the beholder and not everyone will be attracted and drawn to the same person. Additionally, maintaining this personal connection and likeability is challenging when parties are not negotiating face-to-face or do not spend significant time in each other's presence.

Kakabadse and colleagues also identified additional sources of power including information, access, and corporate memory power.[2] *Information power,* also referred to as numbers game power, is derived from a person's access to data or information of critical importance to another person. Numbers and information can be used in divergent ways — such as to instill fear, impart information, and as a strategy for improving performance. How numbers and data are raised and brought into the negotiation process determines whether this information inspires anxiety and fear or serves as the foundation for information sharing and problem solving. For instance, parties to a negotiation may intentionally bombard their counterpart with a barrage of information to bury the critical issues under a mound of paperwork. Similarly, parties

---

[2] Kakabadse and Kakabadse (1999) identified two other sources of power — reverence and context power. However the connection to negotiations is less clear and as such are not discussed in this chapter.

may request further information at a strategic point in time, which could catch their counterpart unprepared and create a chaotic moment. As social scientists and our own personal experiences can validate, fear is a strong motivator, at least in the short run, and thus people who use fear aspects of information power can be successful in negotiating terms in their favor. However, the stress and anxiety that a counterpart experiences as a result of using information to inspire fear may hinder the negotiation process as they may respond with their own information warfare or by refusing to continue to negotiate. Another potential disadvantage is that it can be quite expensive to amass the data in terms of both time and resources. Successful use of information source requires parties to be educated about the data and issue to be able to provide a helpful and meaningful solution, which requires a degree of training and development of the parties. A unique advantage of information power source is that it is not exclusive in that anyone who can gather the data can use this power source. Certainly, there is skill in identifying the necessary facts needed to develop, define, and defend one's position but it is not dependent on demographic characteristics, such as age or gender. An additional advantage is that using data and numbers as the foundation for decision-making can result in enhanced solutions for both parties.

Access power refers to when a person has personal or professional access to a wide and potentially diverse set of people within and outside the organization and because of this access has the potential to influence another person. Individuals with access power develop dense networks with diverse individuals and groups. An example of someone within an organization that may possess access power is an administrative assistant to senior management. Because of the nature of the job, he/she serves as the gatekeeper to the top-level executive and may be able to exert influence over others within the organization due to having access power. One advantage of access power is that it can be highly effective in shifting your counterpart's perspective or behaviors in both the short and the long run. A potential disadvantage to access power is the time it takes a person to amass.

TABLE 1 Comparison of categorizations of power sources

French and Raven (1959)	Kakabadse, Bank, and Vinnicombe (2005)
Reward	Reward
Coercive	Reward
Legitimate	Role
Expert	Knowledge
Referent	Personal
	Network
	Information
	Corporate memory

Corporate memory power refers to knowledge that a person gains simply by virtue of spending a long time within a specific organization. Those with corporate memory power are those that a historical perspective can be drawn from for problem solving, know where and whom to go to for assistance, and how best to address an organizational problem. A disadvantage of this power source is that it takes time to accrue and those who possess it may be resented by those newer to the organization.

Power in the Context of Negotiation

So far we have focused on power sources that are applicable to a broad range of social settings, including negotiations. Negotiation, characterized by joint problem solving, interdependence and mutual influence, renders an additional set of factors that affects the power positions and dynamics.

Best alternative to a negotiated agreement

Typically, when we talk about power within a negotiations moment, researchers and practitioners alike point to the value of the negotiator's best alternative to the negotiated agreement, widely known as BATNA (Fisher, Ury, and Patton, 1991; Bazerman *et al.*, 2000).

It is reasonable to assume that if a negotiator has a very attractive alternative to the current negotiation, then he/she is willing to walk away from that negotiation if the proposals on the table are not optimal. Thus, having an attractive BATNA puts the negotiator in a powerful position as it reduces the value, dependency, and scarcity of resources that the counterpart possesses. However, obtaining an attractive BATNA is contingent on a person's power sources and the transferability of those power sources to the present and other negotiations contexts (Kim and Fragale, 2005). Research suggests that people who have a strong BATNA engage in different strategies and tactics than those with a weak BATNA, which in turn affects the quality of both the individual and joint outcomes of the negotiation (Pinkley, 1995). Pinkley (1994) demonstrated that negotiators with high BATNAs developed higher reservation prices, aspirations, and expectations than those with low BATNAs. These higher aspiration levels kept negotiators on track to push hard for their desired outcome and motivated negotiators to request and share more information in an effort to discover win-win agreements. In summary, the attractiveness of a negotiator's BATNA is critical to the quality of his or her outcome (McAlister, Bazerman, and Fader 1986). One practical advice that can be derived from the research findings on power through BATNA is that negotiators should create and improve alternatives to the current negotiation whenever possible.

Time pressure

Imagine that you are selling your house and you have received one offer that is the minimal price you are willing to accept but is far below your desired price. Likely, you will say no to the offer and stay on in hope of better offers. Now imagine again that you are about to relocate to another city where you have found a dream house to buy. You need to make the down payment in a timely manner so you are eager to sell your current house, preferably before your moving date, which is just three days away. All of a sudden, this low offer does not seem that unattractive anymore because it spares you from uncertainty and, more importantly, it saves you time. Time pressure, meaning how soon does a party need to conclude the negotiations, is another factor that could alter the power differential between negotiators. Time pressure can occur in negotiations either because of time costs, which are costs associated with the amount of time it takes to reach an agreement (such as lost income, opportunity costs, payment for a negotiation agent, and so forth), or because of negotiation deadlines. It has been shown that negotiation agreements tend to favor the negotiator with less time pressure for two reasons (Moore, 2004b; Stuhlmacher, Gillespie, and Champagne, 1998). First, negotiators with more time pressure are less demanding due to lower aspirations and an interest in making rapid concessions. Second, their opponents are empowered to threaten delays if more concessions are not made.

One way to reduce the effect of a time pressure, when in fact one party does have a time constraint, is for that party to share his/her condensed timeline with the counterpart. Assuming that both parties BATNAs are weak and they are interdependent on each other in terms of seeking to exchange resources and reach an agreement, informing the other party of the deadline puts him/her under time pressure too, because, regardless of the source of the deadline, when the deadline arrives, both parties must stop negotiating. As a result, the sharing of the deadline can lead the other party to have lower aspirations as well and to make concessions faster. This effect can be particularly useful to parties who are subject to time costs, because moderate deadlines can improve outcomes not only by sharing time pressure with the other party but also by minimizing the potential amount of time costs that accrue (Moore, 2004a; Moore, 2004b).

The Importance of Power Assessment

Disentangling where your power emanates from and contemplating the source of your counterpart's power sources will aid you in the preparation and in navigating the process of coming to an agreement. For instance, when two companies negotiate a merger deal, they are both likely to assess their own and their counterpart's potential to offer more financial gains, entail fewer legal liabilities, supply more technology advancement, and provide additional customer base. Demands are then likely to reflect each negotiator's perceived contributions of their own and those of their counterparts'. In preparing for a negotiation moment, you should contemplate your power sources relative to your anticipated counterpart and recognize the general advantages and disadvantages of relying on these various sources. Using the power sources identified above as a foundation, you can engage in a power assessment where you objectively think about your power relative to your counterparts. It may be helpful to enlist the perspective of trusted allies to provide insights and feedback regarding your power sources relative to your anticipated counterparts sources. Additionally, for each potential power source you possess, contemplate how attractive these sources are likely to be to your counterpart, how dependent your counterpart will be on you to obtain these resources, how scarce these resources are within the context, and what are the cultural and organizational norms exist that may alter the negotiations (Kakabadse and Kakabadse, 1999; Kakabadse *et al.*, 2005).

Engaging in a power assessment is one tool to aid you in determining your position, goals and objectives and help outline the strategies you may use in negotiations moment, given your counterpart and the context. Admittedly, it may not always be possible to have detailed information about your counterpart prior to the negotiations moment. However, once you start negotiating and have developed a sense of your counterpart's power sources over you, you can go through this assessment in an effort to acknowledge and potentially guard yourself against certain toxic dynamics. Alternatively, you can take a time-out from the negotiations moment to reassess your power relative to theirs and develop alternative goals and strategies based on this newfound information.

Power Imbalance

In social reality, power is rarely distributed evenly. In fact, power asymmetry may be one reason why individuals opt to resolve differences in preferences through negotiations rather than simply accept the status quo. When power is distributed unevenly, the more powerful parties are likely to have their interests addressed during a negotiation because their demands are deemed as more legitimate, or because they have higher aspirations and can afford to stick to their elevated goals. For similar reasons, the interests of the lower-power party may be ignored. If you think that high-power party is therefore likely to claim a larger share of the benefits, you are largely right. However, in an unequal-power relationship, the more powerful party could use his or power bases as leverage to exploit the less powerful party; the more powerful party, however, could also use the power in a cooperative way.

Power imbalance does not just determine the distribution of the negotiation outcome, it has more important implications on the maximization of the joint gain or the integrative nature of the negotiation (Mannix and Neale, 1993; McAlister *et al.*, 1986). Integrative potential exists when parties value or prioritize issues differently and thus they can make concessions on issues they value less in exchange for concessions on issues they value more. Through trading off between issues prioritized differently by negotiators, a mutually beneficial or an integrative agreement can be reached. For instance, the high-powered party could take the lead in information exchange by actively sharing information and encouraging the low-powered party to specify their preferences. Information exchange in turn enables the discovery of the integrative potential in the negotiation.

To the extent that the high-powered party is concerned about the outcome for the low-powered party, the asymmetry in power may even translate into higher joint outcome as well as better individual outcome for the less powerful parties. Howard, Gardner, and Thompson (2007) demonstrated that the impact of power on negotiator motivation and behavior is contingent upon the way negotiators define themselves in relation to others (i.e., self-construal). More specifically, power holders who view themselves as interdependent entities connected to others are more likely to take the perspective of others into account and orient their behaviors toward the pursuit of the goals of others. Consequently, they exhibit more benevolent use of power in dyadic negotiations, which is conducive to reaching an in integrative agreement.

One particularly interesting pattern emerges when one party is completely powerless. Recent research on ultimatum bargaining revealed a tendency for allocators to increase their offers when recipients are completely powerless as compared to when recipients have some minimal amount of power (Handgraaf *et al.*, 2008). The very act of seeing the recipients completely deprived of the power to defend themselves from an unfair offer triggers a strong sense of social responsibility among the more powerful, who then allocate more resources to the powerless. The above finding paints a much more complex picture of power imbalance in negotiation. You may get the impression that it could pay off to be powerless, however, you may not want to count on the goodwill of the powerful. Rather, you may want to work on the mechanisms that trigger the prosocial behavior from the powerful. You can achieve this by framing the situation in a way that highlights the social responsibility of the powerful, or by building strong identity that subsumes both you and the powerful, or simply by emphasizing to the powerful the need for them to maintain a positive social image.

Strategies to Tackle Power Imbalance

Negotiating without power (i.e., minimal power sources relative to counterpart and a weak BATNA) can prove challenging and it may not be possible to teach people how to overcome a severe imbalance — "No book on gardening can teach you to grow lilies in a desert or a cactus in a swamp" (Fisher, Ury, and Patton, p. 97). However, there are some strategies to minimize the damage or harm, while maximizing your strength and resources.

First, do not fall into the powerless or helpless mindset as that will prove self-defeating. Admittedly, one party may be at a disadvantage when entering into negotiations, but it is critical that parties remain engaged and focused on problem solving, rather than merely conceding to the wishes of their counterpart. Do not assume a position of complete helplessness or a defeatist posturing in a negotiation, even when you believe that your counterpart has more resources, a stronger BATNA, and more potential influence in the situation.

Secondly, you are not required, and it is often not desirable, to confess or impart to your counterpart how "weak" your power sources and BATNA really are relative to theirs. "You are only as weak as they think you are" and thus do not let on how weak you see your position to be compared to theirs.

Third, remember that your counterpart will have some weaknesses and your power and BATNA can be enhanced by diminishing their perceptions of power and BATNA.

Presuming there is a zone of possible agreement between the two parties (i.e., both parties' BATNAs overlap such that parties can offer an option that is better than their BATNAs), remember — how you negotiate is key (i.e., how you attempt to translate a power source into actual influence over your counterpart). You can enhance your negotiating power by developing positive working relationships with your negotiating parties. You will need to develop trust with your counterpart to engage in mutual problem solving and to shift from focus on power.

Additionally, communication and listening skills will be key and so focus on effective communication, be open to sharing your perspective and thought process, engage in active listening to their interests and concerns, and work to understand their underlying issues. Given all the information and rich dialog, you will need to be creative in identifying possible solutions of mutually beneficial nature. Lastly, you will need to actively seek to enhance your own BATNA in the short and long-run (Fisher, Ury, and Patton, 1991; Malholtra and Bazerman, 2007).

Influence Tactics

Now that we have explored power and its underlying sources, both broadly and within a negotiation setting, let us turn our attention to the various ways parties convert those power sources into actual influence or change in other person's actions, thoughts, or feelings. Early investigation into how people influence others focused on identifying various unique approaches to exerting power over others. The following tactics are the ten most commonly used to get people to do what you want them to do (Yukl and Fable, 1990; Yukl and Tracey, 1992; Yukl, Kim, and Falbe, 1996; Greenberg and Baron, 2008).

Rational persuasion refers to using information to pose logical arguments to persuade your counterpart that a desired result will occur. *Inspirational appeals* refers to persuading your counterpart by appealing to his/her ideals, values, and moral make-up to illicit enthusiasm. *Consultation* is a technique used whereby a party is asked to share ideas or solutions to an issue based on the idea that through participating in crafting the solution or content of the agreement he/she will be more likely to agree to that provision. *Ingratiation* tactic is when a person seeks to influence, or change another person's actions, behaviors, or ideas by getting the person to feel at ease by being likeable and getting them to be in a good mood.

An *exchange approach* is when someone's agreement to a request is made contingent upon receiving a benefit. The *personal appeal tactic* relies on appealing to a person's sense of loyalty or friendship before making a request of him/her. In a *coalition-building strategy* a person will attempt to persuade someone by asking for help from an array of people within a network or coalition and informing the target person that you are gaining or have the support of this coalition. *Legitimating* refers to when a party seeks to gain agreement to a request by asserting his/her formal authority or right to make such a request. They may legitimize their proposal by pointing to the policies, rules, practices or traditions operating in that environment.

Upward appeal tactic refers to when a person will attempt to persuade his/her counterpart by pointing out that his/her proposal or request has the support of upper management. Upward appeal is somewhat akin to coalition building albeit is more specific form of garnering support from those external to the immediate negotiations. A *pressuring tactic* is when a party works to reach an agreement by placing demands on his/her counterpart, uses intimidation and threats to coerce the counterpart. Beyond an understanding of the variety of influence options, it is important to determine when, or under what circumstances do parties use the various influence tactics and how effective are these tactics at achieving the desired outcomes.

Yukl and Tracey (1992) provided a conceptual model for organizing the interrelated factors that determine how frequently an influence tactic is used and how effective the tactic is when attempting to exert influence on peers, subordinates, and superiors. They suggest factors that affect the frequency and effectiveness of an influence tactic include: 1) the prevailing social norms and expectations about the use of the influence tactic within that context; 2) the agent's possession of an acceptable power source needed to use the influence tactic within that context, 3) the appropriateness for the goal or objective of the influence initiative; 4) level of resistance that the influence target puts forward, which is a function of his/her power and the attractiveness of the requested action, 5) potential costs or negatives associated with using the tactic relative to the anticipated benefits, and 6) the agent has the requisite skill to execute the tactic.

Underlying these factors is the presumption that most people attempting to change someone else's behaviors or thoughts in an intended direction will prefer to use and are more likely to accomplish his/her objectives if the tactics employed are: socially acceptable, feasible given his/her power sources relative to his/her counterpart, likely to be effective in accomplishing the goal given the resistance of the counterpart, and are not costly in time, effort, resources expended, or damaging to the relationship. How do power sources and influence tactics relate to each other? The relationship between power source, influence tactics used, and effectiveness has been investigated in only a handful of studies and have relied primarily on French and Raven's typology of power (Yukl, Kim, and Falbe, 1996; Schriesheim and Hinkin, 1990; Yukl, 1994). In an effort to synthesize the various streams of literature, we suggest that certain power sources and bases are more likely to relate to a specific influence strategy based on the theories and definitions promoted by other researchers. We highlight these expected relationships between power sources and various influence tactics in Table 2.

TABLE 2 Integration of influence strategies and power sources

Influence strategies and tactics*	Definition	Power source
Coalition tactics	A party builds alliances and seeks assistance of others to persuade you to agree to his/her terms or uses the support of other parties to gain your agreement.	Access Power[b]; Network Power[c]
Consultation tactics	A party seeks to change your behavior or thoughts by involving you in making a decision or in the planning for how to implement a proposed idea.	
Exchange tactics	A party implies or explicitly promises that you will receive tangible gains or rewards if you agree to the request or proposal. Or a party may remind you of a past favor that you are expected to repay or reciprocate.	Reward Power[ac]
Ingratiating tactics	A party gets you in a positive mindset and to think favorably about him/her before raising the terms of the negotiations.	Referent Power[a]; Personal Impact Power[b]; Personal Power[c]
Inspirational appeals	A party conveys a request or proposal in an emotional manner that attempts to appeal to your values, ideals, and sense of esteem in your abilities to accomplish the task.	Referent Power[a]; Role Power[bc]

(Continued)

TABLE 2   *(Continued)*

Influence strategies and tactics*	Definition	Power source
Legitimating	A party attempts to gain your agreement by pointing to his/her legitimate authority to make the request.	Role Power[a]; Personal Impact and Reverence Power[b]; Personal Power[c]
Pressure tactics	Party relies on coercive actions such as intimidation, threats, and demands to elicit compliance.	Coercive Power[a]; Reward Power[c]
Rational persuasion	A party used logic and facts to convince you that a proposal is appropriate and viable given the objectives.	Expert Power[a]; Expert and Numbers Game Power[b]; Expert and Information Power[c]
Upward appeals	A party attempts to persuade you that his/her proposal or request has been formally approved by, or at the very least has received support from, upper management.	Legitimate Power[a]; Role Power[bc]

*Yukl and Falbe, 1990; Yukl and Tracey, 1992; Yukl, Kim, and Falbe, 1996; [a]French and Raven, 1959; [b]Kakabadse and Kakabadse,1999; [c]Kakabadse, Bank, and Vinnicombe, 2005.

Effectiveness of Influence Tactics Across Cultures

In the previous section, we have identified ten major influence tactics. A question that naturally follows is: which influence tactics are more effective? The answer is: it depends. The effectiveness of different influence tactics varies a great deal across national and organizational cultures.

In some sense, we are all products of national culture, we all grow up in certain culture(s). Through socialization and learning, we internalize the dominant culture values, which influence our attitudes and behaviors in manners that we may not even be conscious of. Cultural values, which are stable beliefs about what is important, specify acceptable forms of interpersonal behavior, including influence tactics. For an influence tactic to be effective, it needs to be consistent with relevant contextual and cultural values. For instance, in a culture where power differential is readily accepted, influence tactics that utilizes authority and legitimate power may be better received than in a culture were inequality is not considered normal. The use of unacceptable influence tactics is likely to trigger negative affective reaction by the target person, which in turn would compromise the effectiveness of such influence tactics.

One detailed comparative study between American and Chinese managers largely confirms the intuition that the effectiveness of influence tactics are to a large degree determined by cultural values (Fu and Yukl, 2000). American managers considered rational persuasion and exchange to be more effective, likely because that rational persuasion is consistent with the preference of Americans for direct confrontation and use of reasoning to influence people in organizational settings. In contrast, Chinese managers regarded coalition tactics, upward appeals, and gifts as more effective influence tactics. Their preferences are a direct reflection of the strong collective orientation (i.e., defining themselves in terms of their group membership). In collectivist cultures, interpersonal relationships provide an important basis for power and influence. Managers bearing that cultural color emphasize the importance of relationships and they tend to use indirect forms of influence that elicit assistance of a third party, especially in difficult, controversial situations. Gifts, a cultural tradition for the Chinese, are used by Chinese managers to strengthen relationship in workplace, but are perceived by American managers as inappropriate and problematic.

The notion that national cultures are associated with cross-cultural differences in preferences for the use of influence tactics is further validated in a 12-country study. Several general patterns emerged: (1) In cultures where members feel comfortable with ambiguous and uncertain situations, managers considered relationship-based influence tactics (e.g., personal appeal, exchanging) as more effective than persuasive influence tactics (e.g., rational persuasion, inspirational appeal, consultation). (2) Managers in collectivist cultures, where group interests are put in front of individual interests, preferred relationship-based influence tactics over other tactics. (3) In cultures where long-term result is valued over short-term gratification, managers chose relationship-based over assertive influence tactics. Adding to the complexity, the same study demonstrated that preferences for influence tactics are also determined by managers' personal beliefs about how things work and how the social world operates. For instance, managers who believe that effort and the investment of one's resources will lead to success tend not to seek help from above; rather, they think logical arguments are more effective in demonstrating their skills and capability, thus they are more likely to endorse persuasive influence tactics over other types.

Today's work place is getting increasingly diverse in cultural composition. An accurate understanding of cultural differences is necessary for managerial effectiveness and successful negotiations. Parties need to actively and consciously apply cultural understanding to identify appropriate influence tactics in given situations. An additional point to note is that the organizational culture that individuals are operating in may also dictate the appropriateness of using power sources and influence tactics to alter peers, subordinates and superiors (Kakabadse and Kakabadse, 1999; Kakabadse *et al.*, 2005).

Summary

Negotiation is characterized by joint problem solving, power dependence, and social influence. When assessing power and exercising influence, we encourage you to focus on both negotiators (e.g., sources of power of both you and your counterparts) and the negotiation context (e.g., negotiation specific power sources, cultural context in which negotiations are embedded) (Li *et al.*, 2007). In closing our discussion on power and influence in negotiation, we wish to emphasize the following:

There is a wide range of sources upon which you can draw power. Having a comprehensive understanding of all these sources would help you utilize your power and influence in negotiations. However, you need to coordinate the power bases. Misuse of one power source could erode other power sources and derail the negotiations.

When assessing power and exerting influence, you need to factor in you and your counterpart's subjective evaluation of negotiations. Certain influence tactics may be effective in the short run, but may turn out to be detrimental in the end, especially with respect to the relationship.

Influence tactics should be carefully crafted based on not only what power you have, but also on important contextual factors — whom you are trying to influence, what is the culture of the organization you are embedded in, and what are the higher level cultural characteristics that may alter the effectiveness of your influence tactics.

Power and Influence in Sales Negotiation

Ababacar Mbengue
Reims Management School & University of Reims
REPONSE Research Center

Joël Sohier
University of Reims
REPONSE Research Center

Patrice Cottet
University of Reims
REPONSE Research Center

Negotiation is one of the most important aspects of selling and buying (Neslin and Greenhalgh, 1983) and is a very effective marketing vehicle (Roman and Iacobucci, 2010). The negotiations conducted while carrying out a sale involve two parties, a seller and a buyer, interacting voluntarily to come up with an exchange agreement which will be a compromise between each party's interests and expectations (Patton and Balakrishnan, 2010). This applies whether both stakeholders are firms (e.g., B2B with a purchasing manager as the buyer and a marketing manager as the seller) or where the buyer is an individual (e.g., B2C). Existing empirical research primarily focuses on one aspect of the sales dyad — the buyer. Over-emphasizing buyer behavior is misleading since the seller's negotiation orientation is just as critical to the outcome of dyadic interactions (Mintu-Wimsatt and Gassenheimer, 1996). The bilateral context of sales negotiation allows both sellers and buyers to have some monopoly power (Rapoport, Erev and Zwick, 1995). Typical examples are a buyer with a sole supplier or a vendor with a unique product that has special value for a particular industrial customer.

Power refers to the ability to influence or control others to act in a manner that one desires (French and Raven, 1959; Zartman and Rubin, 2000). Power is usually derived from the resources possessed by a person which are desired by someone else (Jasperson *et al.*, 2002). When someone has a resource that someone else desires, an asymmetric power relationship exists, and the more the second party desires the resource, the greater the power imbalance (Wolfe and McGinn, 2005; Johnson and Cooper, 2009). Power asymmetry enables the more powerful party to compel the other party to make certain concessions (Mannix and Neale, 1993; Johnson and Cooper, 2009).

Unequal bargaining power is quite common during negotiations, and negotiators with less bargaining power usually leave the negotiating table disappointed with the negotiating process (Drahos, 2003). Negotiators often face difficult situations in which they must examine and understand their own and their counterparts' power. This chapter stresses the importance of power issues in sales negotiations, outlines how power can affect the negotiation process and outcomes, and provides solutions to resolve power issues in sales negotiations.

Sources of Power in Sales Negotiations

The interaction between buyers and sellers is rooted in their different levels of bargaining power. Bargaining power refers to the ability to influence the setting of prices (Porter, 1980), and it varies across contexts. This variance is due to its origin in three different sources (Drahos, 2003).

Market share

First, the amount of bargaining power a firm has depends on its market share. Monopolistic or quasi-monopolistic suppliers (or similarly monopsonistic or quasi-monopsonistic buyers) have higher profit margins and can often negotiate better terms compared to their competitors. An example of an industry with powerful suppliers is the personal computers (PC) manufacturing industry, which is faced with the almost monopolistic power of operating system suppliers. For example, Microsoft has been frequently accused of abusing its power and has been reined in by competition watchdogs all over the world. Industries that use diamonds, such as jewelry and electronics manufacturing, also confront a powerful supplier in the form of the DeBeers organization. On the other hand, suppliers in certain industries have weak bargaining power. For example, food processing firms buy agricultural produce from many small and medium-sized farms. Retail stores also buy many of their products from small producers. Conversely, some industries have powerful buyers. For example, firms that are sub-contractors for car makers have a limited set of powerful buyers, each commanding a large share of their market. Similarly, defense contractors have a limited set of buyers (governments). On the other hand, other industries have weak buyers. For example, retailers interact with individual consumers who have little or no power. Consider the following example (*Bloomberg BusinessWeek*, October 5, 2010):

> With the global population adding 75 million people a year, food demand is set to put further strain on crops, increasing the need for fertilizer. The world's eight largest potash miners, whose market control already exceeds that of oil cartel OPEC, are poised to tighten their grip on prices of the crop fertilizer as proposed mergers consolidate sales channels. Consolidation among producers of potash, a form of potassium used to boost yields by helping plants withstand dry soil, has caused concern in countries such as India, the biggest importer last year, that prices will rise. Actually, there has been a fivefold surge in potash prices over 2007–2008, which led to at least eight class-action claims in the U.S. over alleged collusion. In the global

recession, potash producers cut output to prop up prices. Potash Corp. used a third of its capacity last year, while none of its seven largest rivals used more than 80%.

Critical information

A second source of bargaining power is critical information. Boundary spanners acting as gatekeepers of critical information are a good example of how power can accrue to those who have critical information (Russ, Galang and Ferris, 1998; Dalton and Dalton, 2009). Consider the following example (*Bloomberg BusinessWeek*, September 29, 2010):

> Since Chinese leader Deng Xiaoping made mastering of critical materials including neodymium and 16 other elements known as rare earths a priority, China dominates the market, with far-reaching effects ranging from global trade friction to U.S. job losses and threats to national security. Military officials are only now conducting an inventory of where and how U.S. suppliers use the rare earths — including those that silence the whoosh of Boeing Co. helicopter blades, direct Raytheon Co. missiles and target guns in General Dynamics Corp. tanks. Complicating matters is that even the Pentagon has been unsure of its own needs. It took U.S. Army's officials a month to learn that rare-earth metals are in the nose of the Excalibur missile, and they still were not certain of the exact supply route. The Pentagon has been incredibly negligent. There are plenty of early warning signs that China will use its leverage over these materials as a weapon. China once imposed a "*de facto*" ban on exports to Japan of the metals used in liquid crystal displays and laptop computers.

Large retailers, such as Best Buy or Wal-Mart, often obtain valuable information from their suppliers (through mandatory data exchange) and customers.

Enrolment power

A third source of bargaining power is enrolment power: the capacity of a buyer or seller to enroll other actors in a coalition (Braithwaite and Drahos 2000). For example, the Japanese have developed long-term, stable relationships with their partners (Hayes, 1981; Bard, 1987). In contrast, U.S. purchasing managers and their counterparts, marketing managers, have frequently been criticized for failing to deal constructively with their suppliers or buyers respectively. Very often, the buyer or supplier adopts an attitude of defiance during negotiations by threatening to either take his/her business elsewhere, or to integrate backwards or forwards so as to eliminate the other party's market. Business relationships thus tend to be based on mutual distrust, which can result in inefficient planning and operations (high inventories, long lead times, and reduced quality).

Building strong performance relationships with various stakeholders including competitors, employees, customers, vendors, suppliers, and the public in general (unions and citizens) may be crucial in sales negotiations. Consider the following example (*The Sydney Morning Herald*, October 31, 2007):

> BHP Billiton Ltd., the world's largest mining company, and the world's third-largest iron ore producer is fighting to introduce an iron ore price index similar to the globalCOAL energy coal index which connects big coal producers, such as BHP, Rio and Xstrata, with buyers. The new index would shift the power in the market much more towards suppliers (BHP, Rio Tinto and Brazil's CVRD). With the current situation where the bulk of iron ore is traded under the annual negotiations, consumers of iron ore (basically Asian steel mills) have a degree of market power from the ability to negotiate together. Introduction of an iron ore price index would really reduce the size of each individual transaction, it would be individual steel mills negotiating with individual suppliers. In that context an individual steel mill

would have a lot less market power. BHP's new strategy is to move its expiring contracts onto an 'iron ore index', with forward deliveries and financial swaps that better reflected the spot market than the extant annual benchmark pricing system. BHP has already threatened to sell some of its iron ore production on the spot market in the absence of an agreement.

Another famous illustration of enrolment power is Wal-Mart's 1985 "Buy American" program. In February 1985, Sam Walton wrote to 3,000 American manufacturers and wholesalers to announce that the chain wanted to buy more American goods. Walton implored fellow retailers, suppliers and manufacturers to "Buy American". In an effort to combat the growing trade deficit, Walton wanted to show that Wal-Mart was committed to being a steward of the American economy. Today, however, over 80% of Wal-Mart's 6,000 global suppliers are based in China.

Power Management in Sales Negotiation

Taking advantage of information asymmetry

It is well known that an impressive power base can accrue to those who have critical information, or access to such information, compared to those that do not (Russ, Galang and Ferris, 1998). In the context of sales negotiations, banks seem to take advantage of information asymmetry between suppliers and buyers to generate revenue. For example, customers are often surprised by the fees they are charged, as they are often not mentioned clearly up-front. Since information is valuable, firms may target that as their objective, instead of the quality of their ostensibly core product. Thus, banks can compete, even dominate their market, with low-quality products for consumers: they claim that customers benefit from the "free" features of these products (such as free checking accounts), even though the banks benefit substantially by obtaining valuable data on consumer spending patterns and the order in which transactions are processed. Bank profits seem to be rooted in a lack of consumers awareness of the implications of their transactional activities. When one bank gets away with a profitable anti-consumer activity, other banks begin to imitate it.

Consider another example, Providian, a company that sold credit in the "subprime" market (*PBS Frontline*, November 24, 2009). Providian provided credit cards primarily to the lowest income groups in the U.S. at high interest rates. The annual percentage rates (APR) charged by Providian were as high as 29.9%. Providian successfully targeted vulnerable low-income customers called "the unbanked". They were lower-income people-bad credits, bankrupts, young credits, no credits. Providian also innovated by offering "free" credit cards that carried heavy hidden fees called 'penalty pricing' or 'stealth pricing'. While there might be many things going on in this case, one important point was indicated by former Providian CEO Shailesh Mehta: "When people make the buying decision, they don't look at the penalty fees because they never believe they'll be late. They never believe they'll be over limit, right? Our business took off. ... We were making a billion dollars a year". Thus, like bankers and stakeholders in various buyer-seller contexts, Providian relied on information asymmetry to generate revenue. Beginning in mid-1999, however, a number of class-action suits were filed against the company regarding aggressive sales tactics for various "credit protection" services being sold to Providian credit card holders. In 2001, a settlement required Providian to pay over $100 million in cash, credits, and other benefits, and to stop certain practices that were at issue in the class actions. Combined with an earlier settlement with governmental entities, the award constitutes the largest settlement ever against a credit card company for alleged widespread unlawful business practices.

Taking advantage of the imbalance of power

The capacity to make credible threats is a critical determinant of a sales negotiation exercise. When suppliers can threaten to increase their prices or reduce production, they possess greater bargaining power, which they can use to increase their profit (Bard, 1987). On the other hand, if buyers have alternate sources of supply or can use substitute materials, they may apply some counter-pressure. When the buyer depends on a few suppliers, he may be at a disadvantage (Porter, 1980). A threat is not really a negotiation in the formal sense; rather, it is a demand that at best resembles a single issue negotiation (Dalton and Dalton, 2009). In the context of a sales negotiation, a buyer whom many sellers want to sell to is in a position to make credible threats. For example, Wal-Mart is often accused of systematically pressuring manufacturers to outsource their jobs (*WalmartWatch.com, Research Team*, May 29, 2008):

> Many American businesses like Huffy, Mr. Coffee, and Master Lock have suffered under the weight of Wal-Mart's pressure. When Rubbermaid asked Wal-Mart for a modest price increase, Wal-Mart said no, and stopped sales of Rubbermaid products and Rubbermaid ended up selling itself to a competitor. Wal-Mart has frequently instructed suppliers to settle in China. For example, to land a supply contract with Wal-Mart, the Lakewood Engineering and Manufacturing had to locate manufacturing operations in Shenzhen, China. Mr. Coffee faced similar pressure to shift production to China. Wal-Mart is known for pressuring suppliers to cut prices. With its $408 billion in sales in 2009 and its incredible buying power, the retailer has plenty of clout to persuade makers of goods sold in its big-box stores to create environmentally friendly packaging and exclusive product sizes, and to participate in joint advertising promotions, etc. Wal-Mart is now seeking to take over U.S. transportation services from suppliers in an effort to reduce the cost of hauling goods. The company is contacting all manufacturers that provide products to its more than 4,000 U.S. stores and Sam's Club membership warehouse clubs. The goal is to take over deliveries in instances where Wal-Mart can do the same job for less and use those savings to reduce prices in stores

(*Bloomberg BusinessWeek*, May 21, 2010). Interestingly, one important side-effect of the plan is that manufacturers may face increased transportation costs on deliveries to other retailers as they lose scale, which will increase Wal-Mart's bargaining power.

Even after having signed a supplier contract, large retailers like Wal-Mart are almost never compelled to buy anything, and their purchase orders may or may not follow. Large retailers also usually ask smaller suppliers to guarantee that their product will sell. What sets a small supplier apart is its innovativeness and knowledge of what sells in its region. Suppliers also have to understand the impact of national trends on large retailers like Wal-Mart and be prepared to adapt. The key to impressing a powerful buyer is to display an understanding of the potential market.

Becoming a central player

Consider the following example (*Bloomberg BusinessWeek*, December 10, 2009):

Best Buy, the last major consumer electronics retailer in the U.S., is committed to go beyond its traditional typical big-box retailer role of selling commodity products such as televisions and personal computers and become a central player in determining which products come to market. Rather than waiting for electronics makers such as Hewlett-Packard and Toshiba to ship Best Buy the same products that its rivals get, Best Buy is now collaborating with suppliers, influencing product development and design. The retailer is pushing suppliers to use standardized software and digital services so consumers can listen to music or watch movies on any device. And Best Buy has set up its own venture capital fund to pour millions of dollars into start-ups from Silicon Valley to Asia. The goal is to shape development of new technologies in promising fields such as green vehicles, digital health, and home monitoring. Best Buy wants to become the go-to store to test out the latest gear or get exclusive goodies. There is a big swath of customers that are going to want to get a little advice and to touch and feel that new gadget. Users come into Best Buy for reasonably good answers and solutions to the question of what is the right gadget to buy. Best Buy is promoting partnerships with suppliers for the common purpose of connecting more consumers to more devices.

One advantage of Best Buy's innovative strategy is to reinforce its bargaining power with suppliers. Best Buy is definitely in a position of strength with its suppliers because it is closer to the consumer. Being the entity with the strongest knowledge of and deepest relationships with consumers gives Best Buy real bargaining power. As a large-scale retailer with a sales force of 150,000, Best Buy has the golden opportunity to be the co-creator and sole source of all kinds of new, unique, and innovative things that people want, and to make a lot of money in the process. Best Buy's new role makes it a kingmaker for companies that play along and a serious threat for those that refuse. The company is already selling certain products in competition with suppliers, and will likely push other products off store shelves to make room for the products it is developing. Executives at several major consumer electronics companies worry privately about Best Buy's growing influence. They are concerned that Best Buy could block them from placing innovative products in front of customers or that it would favor Best Buy-backed goods.

A second advantage of Best Buy's new strategy is to reinforce its bargaining power with its customers. Best Buy is now able to play a greater advisory role for its clients. Buyers come to Best Buy to find sound advice, answers to their questions, and solutions to their needs. That is, Best Buy is in a position to exploit some "expert power", the kind of power accruing to those who have critical information that others do not (Dalton and Dalton, 2009; Russ, Galang and Ferris, 1998). Customers come everyday into Best Buy and ask for specific features that no existing device has. Best Buy can listen to its customers' unfilled needs, and use that unique information to urge manufacturers to develop the products that consumers want.

Today, Best Buy is no longer simply a dominant channel that can potentially favor one manufacturer over another; it is also a competitor. With so much technology manufacturing out-sourced, Best Buy can easily make the products it believes consumers want by itself, as it has done with TVs, if suppliers like Dell, HP, and Toshiba are unwilling to cooperate. Both Best Buy and Wal-Mart are using their bargaining power to influence sup-pliers' behavior. While Wal-Mart typically focuses on supply chain efficiency and/or data exchange, Best Buy is targeting product innovation and customer service.

Some U.S. farmers and ranchers are using their enrolment power to team-up with a labor union (the United Food and Commercial Workers International Union) and urge the Obama administration to broaden its antitrust inquiry into meat, dairy and seed businesses to include Wal-Mart. The retailer is accused of using its power to hold down prices in the agriculture industry (*Bloomberg BusinessWeek*, September 14, 2010).

Reaching integrative ("Win–Win") agreements

While negotiation occurs in various domains of life, its basic structure is the same: all negotiation situations share four com-mon characteristics (Murtoaro and Kujala, 2007): First, there are two or more parties; second, the parties can be creative and coop-erate to arrive at a joint decision; third, the payoffs to any party depend either on the consequences of the joint decision or alter-natives external to the negotiations; fourth, the parties can reciprocally and directly exchange information, honest or other-wise. Each party is also presumed to have defined a best alternative to a negotiated agreement (BATNA), which is the best course of action that the party could pursue unilaterally outside the given negotiations (Fisher and Ury, 1981). Thus, a basic test of a proposed agreement is whether it offers a better payoff than that side's best alternative course of action outside of the negotiations (Murtoaro and Kujala, 2007).

There are alternatives to the use of threats in negotiation. Actually, threats are not really negotiations. Rather, they are demands which at best resemble a single issue bargaining. Research shows that single issue bargaining should be avoided whenever possible (Dalton and Dalton, 2009). Consider a negotiation between a buyer and a supplier. If only price is an issue, it will be a single issue negotiation. But if there are additional elements like payment mode (cash or by schedule), penalties for late payments or deliveries, responsibilities for cartage or warehousing, sales and delivery timeframe, arbitration, and termination rights, and liability, the parties may well have different utilities for those different elements and, thus, be able to reach a mutually acceptable agreement based on something other than price alone (Dalton and Dalton, 2009).

Sales negotiations take place in a socio-political context which defines a power structure (Stern and Reve, 1980). Sales negotiators adjust their behavior to the balance of power. When they are in a weak position, their interests will lie in encouraging their counterparts to engage in mutually satisfying win–win solutions.

Negotiation behavior is commonly situated on an "integrative — distributive" continuum (Lewicki and Litterer, 1985). Integrative behavior seeks an agreement acceptable to both parties. The negotiator seeks to establish a climate of trust, reciprocity and mutual concession to reach a balanced agreement for both parties. Examples of integrative tactics include trading off across issues, exchanging information about priorities, and avoiding a zero-sum assumption. These common tactics are useful to generate joint gains, which is typical of a cooperative approach to negotiation. Distributive tactics, on the other hand, seek to create individual gain by acquiring unilateral concessions. Distributive behavior consists of a search for unilateral gain which may be to the detriment of the other party. It is translated into threats to force the negotiating partner to accept one's proposal. Distributive tactics are appropriate when issues are equally valued by both parties (Weingart, Hyder and Prietula, 1996).

Empirical research (see Johnston and Kristal, 2008) has established that when buyers and sellers work collaboratively, value (in the form of revenues, efficiencies and profits) may be created for both parties. Negotiators often fail to reach integrative ("win–win") agreements because they think that their own and other's preferences are diametrically opposed — the so-called fixed-pie perception (Pietroni *et al.*, 2008). It has long been stated that suppliers would take advantage of buyers if they become too important (Porter, 1980; Spekman, Kamauff and Myhr, 1998). This situation may be changing as the nature of competition among firms is shifting from the level of the firm to the entire supply chain (Carr and Pearson, 2002; Cousins, Lawson and Squire, 2008). For example, Procter and Gamble and Wal-Mart decided to collaborate when they realized that their relationship had expanded beyond procurement to include supply chain management and customer service. They built their relationship on a single objective: to eliminate inefficiencies across the entire value chain, from production processes and delivery lead times to customer service. Together, they reduced product ordering time by three to four days, improved billing accuracy from 15 to 95%, and expanded knowledge and insights about their customers (A.T. Kearney, 2010). Wal-Mart is also trying to increase its buying clout by teaming with suppliers to jointly purchase raw materials at better prices (*Bloomberg BusinessWeek*, October 7, 2010). Wal-Mart is jointly purchasing a growing share of raw ingredients with manufacturers of food and household products sold in its stores. The company envisions a day when it will do this for most of the goods it sells.

How to negotiate effectively with a sole supplier or buyer?

Consider a buyer negotiating with a sole supplier. Negotiating with a supplier who is a monopolist in a market is often a buyer's worst nightmare. In general, when negotiators have alternative parties to contract with, they are less dependent on any single entity; this weakens the power of the party they are negotiating with currently (Blau, 1964; Emerson, 1962). Several studies suggest that when negotiators have an alternative, they are more likely to reach integrative, win–win solutions than when both negotiators lack alternatives (Giebels, de Dreu and van de Vliert, 2003). It is therefore essential to define the upstream strategy and tactics of negotiation, including promising, bluffing, puffing, delaying, and even lying (Hackley, 2005). That is, understanding and strategies are required to work within such a situation where power, resources and control are unequally distributed (Johnston and Kristal, 2008).

Having a sole supplier is very uncomfortable for the buyer: the supplier does not have a particular interest in reducing its prices since it will definitely obtain an order. In addition, it can afford not to comply with a number of trade clauses, such as timeliness, quality or warranties. Consequently, buyers often feel helpless when dealing with suppliers who are monopolists. Empirical research on negotiation suggests that negotiators with a low level of power should use promises rather than threats, in part because doing so makes their powerless position less salient (De Dreu, 1995). Other strategies can also be adopted by the buyer. Below, we list ten ways for managing power imbalance:

- Build a stronger partnership with the supplier, with shared objectives, risks (a monopolist supplier represents a major risk for the buyer in case of failure) but also and above all, profits (Drahos, 2003).
- Attracting the supplier by convincing it of its interest to cooperate. By creating a climate of mutual trust, the buyer may succeed in encouraging the supplier to make a concession (Drahos, 2003).
- Creating a panel of so-called strategic suppliers to enable the monopolist supplier to understand its importance in a broader context.
- Writing, if possible, extremely precise specifications to obtain only what is the "just need". For example, by buying only some modules of a software and not the entire package.

- Grouping purchases to obtain volume discounts and other volume effects.
- Teaming up with other buyers to increase one's bargaining power. Forming coalitions is one natural response to power imbalance (Drahos, 2003). The capacity of a buyer to enroll other actors in a coalition (enrolment power) is a major source of bargaining power (Braithwaite and Drahos, 2000).
- Evoke a new source of products or services, and other suppliers (Giebels, de Dreu and van de Vliert, 2003; Hackley, 2005). This is especially important in situations of false monopoly. These are often the result of a lack of prospecting and sourcing, which obliges buyers to buy from one source, despite the existence of competition. Thus, there is sometimes a local monopoly which can be easily challenged by larger-scale sourcing.
- Appeal to second-ranked suppliers for the acquisition and development of new skills so that they can position themselves as competitors of historic suppliers (Giebels, de Dreu and van de Vliert, 2003; Hackley, 2005).
- Evoke a possibility of backward integration (you will do things yourself). For the supplier, this means losing a customer and earning a competitor, which may lead it to accept concessions (Giebels, de Dreu and van de Vliert, 2003; Hackley, 2005).
- When it is credible, suggest the eventuality of changing your technology or process and hence your supplier (Giebels, de Dreu and van de Vliert, 2003; Hackley, 2005).

Summary

Power is widely recognized as one of the most important factors in negotiations. We hope that this chapter gives negotiators a much deeper, more detailed, and practically useful understanding of how and why power matters in sales negotiations. As negotiators, we might or might not have taken time to think about where we stand with regards to power in negotiation. Most of us probably really care about power in sales negotiations. Perhaps, some of us think that we should build as much power as possible because the more powerful negotiator will probably try to take advantage of their power. In this chapter, we examined the self-interest motive for using power and exploring why it is necessary for us to be clear of the power issues that shape our actions during the sales negotiation process. Increasing our self-awareness of the role of power in sales negotiations paves the way for us to make effective use of power in the negotiation process, and may thus help us to revise our fixed-pie perceptions and discover mutually satisfying win–win agreements.

Negotiation Strategy

Brosh M. Teucher
J.L. Kellogg School of Management
Northwestern University

Introduction

On September 7, 2009, Kraft Foods Inc. led by its CEO, Ms. Irene Rosenfeld, made an unsolicited cash-and-shares acquisition proposal to Cadbury PLC, an iconic 185-year-old U.K. confectionary manufacturer led by the CEO Mr. Todd Stitzer, and Mr. Roger Carr, the Chairman. Kraft offered Cadbury 745 British pence per share, a 31% premium over last close value, (deal value of £10.2 billion or $16.73 billion). Cadbury insisted it was an undervalued offer, declined it, and stated it will remain independent.

After 19 weeks of public sparring, and after a £9.8 billion ($16.28 billion) hostile takeover bid launched by Kraft on November 10, 2009 (rejected by Cadbury), with a deadline of midnight Tuesday January 20, 2010, looming for Kraft to put the hostile offer directly to Cadbury's shareholders, Cadbury agreed to enter discussions with Kraft. Ms. Rosenfeld, who has had no contact with Mr. Carr since their meeting in London in August 28, 2009, just before announcing the initial bid, called him at home on Sunday January 18 and suggested to meet again. Mr. Carr responded that it would be worthwhile only if she "had adjusted her thinking on where a suitable price was". At 8:30 a.m. of Monday January 19, Ms. Rosenfeld and Mr. Carr brought their lawyers and met at a hotel in London.

Ms. Rosenfeld proposed an improved bid of 830 pence per Cadbury share. Mr. Carr responded that while he respected Kraft's increased offer, it still was far below an offer acceptable to Cadbury's shareholders. The discussion went on while at several occasions the two parties broke up to consult with advisers and then reconvened. Around 9 p.m., Ms. Rosenfeld offered the winning price of 850 pence per share. Mr. Carr said that with that price, he would ask the board to recommend Kraft's bid, which the board did. The two parties then went to the offices of the law firm advising Kraft, and spent most of the night fine-tuning the details.

On Tuesday January 20, 2010, both companies announced a deal that valued Cadbury at 850 pence a share or £11.9 billion ($19.4 billion). During the negotiations, in addition to increasing the value of its bid by 10% Kraft increased the cash portion to 60% (up from 40%). The price represented a 50% premium to where Cadbury shares were traded before Kraft's first offer in September 2009. Shareholders representing 71.73% of Cadbury's shares accepted the deal (Cimilluca and Carolan, September 14, 2009; Cimilluca and Rohwedder, January 20, 2010; Cimilluca, Rohwedder and McCracken, November 10, 2009; Curtin, September 8, 2009; Wall street Journal, February 3, 2010).

This example demonstrates how two business leaders complete a merger deal. However, to say that they have achieved that only through rushed negotiations over a 24-hour period would be simplistic. Moreover, such framing overlooks subtle but critical moves that are important for understanding the foundations of negotiation strategy, and how it is developed, deployed, and adapted to advance the goals of a negotiating party. Strategy formulation and execution are critical steps in deal making and in conducting and completing a successful negotiation. The goal of this chapter is to equip you with an understanding of what a negotiation strategy is and how it functions. The chapter defines negotiation strategy, summarizes key strategies, and discusses how to apply them effectively.

Definition of Negotiation Strategy

Negotiation is a social process that occurs whenever people (or parties) cannot achieve their own goals without the cooperation of others (Thompson, Wang and Gunia, 2010). Through this social process, negotiating parties attempt to enlist and secure the support or obtain the resources of others in order to promote their own goals. Negotiation strategy is a set of goal-driven behaviors applied to a negotiation (Weingart *et al.*, 1990). Parties that are involved in a negotiation pursue a goal or a set of goals. They have a choice of applying various sets of actions that aim to achieve these goals. While parties can negotiate without forming goals or strategies, this chapter focuses on the intentional use of goal-oriented strategies in a negotiation.

In the Craft-Cadbury merger, the two parties had explicit and focused goals. Kraft was interested in taking the leadership position in the global confectionary market (vs. Mars, Nestle and Hershey). By reaping synergies from acquiring and integrating Cadbury, it aimed to boost its long-term annual organic revenue growth to 5% or more, 1% better than for Kraft alone. Kraft was also interested in expanding the distribution of its own products (e.g., Oreo Cookies) to India and Mexico, where Cadbury had a strong presence, but also aimed at capitalizing on its network in the U.S., Brazil, China, and Russia to sell Cadbury's sweets (e.g., Crème Eggs, Crunch bar). Meanwhile, Cadbury was focusing on bringing up its underperforming share prices. It planned to do so by improving its lagging operating profit margin from 10% to 15% by 2011. When Kraft made its offer, Cadbury was in the midst of a restructuring plan to meet its goal. Expecting enhanced performance, Cadbury wanted to stay independent. Both Ms. Rosenfeld, pursuing Kraft's growth through acquisitions, and Mr. Stitzer pursuing Cadbury's growth through cost cutting, had fiduciary responsibility to deliver the best business outcomes and returns to their shareholders. Moreover, both had a strong personal stake, economic and reputational, in their positions. Their goals guided their respective negotiation strategies (Curtin, September 8, 2009;

Kesmodel and Rohwedder, September 8, 2009; Cimilluca, Brat and Jargon, September 8, 2009).

Basic Negotiation Strategies

Research on negotiation indentified four basic negotiation frameworks, each composed of a pair of simple strategies. These frameworks are: Competitive vs. Cooperative processes (Deutsch, 1973), Concern for Self vs. Other (See the dual concern model: Blake and Mouton, 1964; Pruitt and Carnevale, 1993; Rubin, Pruitt and Kim, 1994), Distributive vs. Integrative bargaining (Walton and McKersie, 1965), and Claiming vs. Creating value (Lax and Sebenius, 1986). The four frameworks have diverging origins and underlying assumptions. However, they converge on two basic strategies of negotiation: expansion of the overall value of the deal (by creating value, integrative bargaining, cooperative processes, and concern for other and self) and the division of that value among the negotiation parties (by claiming value, distributive bargaining, competitive processes, and concern for self). Moreover, all four frameworks emphasize the necessity of applying a mix of these two basic strategies to achieve satisfactory negotiation outcomes.

These four basic frameworks are concise and powerful analytical tools applicable to diverse negotiation situations. However, narrowing the strategic view of a negotiation to value expansion and division moves neglects the boarder context in which most deal-making and negotiations take place and where parties apply intricate negotiation strategies. The Kraft-Cadbury negotiations required strategic sophistication that exceeds the basic strategies' level. It exemplifies three advanced negotiation frameworks that supplement the basic strategies. These are the 3D Negotiation (Lax and Sebenius, 2006), Negotiauctions (Subramanian, 2010), and When Not to Negotiate (Malhotra and Bazerman, 2007).

3D Negotiation

The 3D negotiation framework expands on the basic value creating/claiming strategy and identifies three dimensions (hence "3D") of negotiation that parties should act upon: tactics, deal design, and setup (Lax and Sebenius, 2006).

Tactics

Tactics are the actions and reactions that parties make "at the table" or during the actual negotiation interaction. They focus on particular negotiation moves, on interpersonal and interparty processes, and on individuals and parties that are involved in the negotiation. For example, Mr. Carr rejected Kraft's offer and repeatedly made offensive remarks calling Kraft "an unfocused conglomerate" with "unappealing categories" led by a management that "under delivers" (Cimilluca and Rohwedder, January 20, 2010). Mr. Carr might have had a personal disliking of Kraft, but making these statements was clearly a negotiation tactic discrediting Kraft. However, what goal did Mr. Carr's tactics serve? Tactics flow from moves devised at the deal design level. Thus, Mr. Carr's deal design needs to be examined.

Deal design

Deal design is the process of meeting party's negotiation objectives by creating and claiming value and constructing a sustainable agreement. The process takes place "on the drawing board", or a step away from the negotiation interaction as parties evaluate and navigate the unfolding negotiation process. A party's focus at this level is on creating and claiming value to meet its desired negotiation goals. At this level, parties search for counterparty's interests, identify opportunities for joint gains, and apply value creating and claiming moves.

Kraft's unexpected takeover offer was a distributive move, focusing on the lowest price it could pay for Cadbury. Mr. Carr's possible deal design moves in response were either to avoid negotiating altogether and repel Kraft, or initiate a distributive move to claim the highest price for the company. Carr's tactical comments might have served the first move by aiming to offend Kraft's CEO to the degree that she would walk away from the deal. However, it is likely that Mr. Carr led the second move all along (Wiggins, September 8, 2009). To understand this possibility, one needs to consider the deal setup, as it dictates the deal design.

Deal setup

Deal setup is a set of decisions and moves that parties make "away from the table", or before the negotiation starts. The goal of these moves is to create optimal negotiation conditions before a party arrives "at the table" to engage in negotiation with the counterparty. The essence of this step is the focus on the "architecture" of the negotiation process, as Lax and Sebenius (2006) state:

> ... acting to ensure that the *right parties* have been involved, in the *right sequence*, to deal with the *right issues* that engage the *right set of interests*, at the *right table or tables*, at the *right time*, under the *right expectations*, and facing the *right consequences of walking away if there is no deal*. (p. 12, italics in source).

The setup is critical for having a solid deal design and ensuring the effectiveness of the tactics applied during the actual negotiation. If in mid-negotiation a party finds its setup incomplete, it should act to reshape or reset it to a more favorable state. From a practical standpoint, the setup stage requires a party to engage in detailed preparation guided by two insights: where would it want the negotiation to end up, and what are the obstacles that stand in the way of getting there. Based on this analysis, the party should develop a comprehensive strategy to overcome the barriers. The strategy should cover all three levels, starting with the setup. The setup design begins with setting the right negotiation, designing value-creating deals, and stressing problem-solving tactics. Next is selecting the right counterparties and taking into account all other players (e.g., other parties, principals, agents, and decision makers) that might affect the negotiation. Next is analyzing the interests and no-deal options of all sides. Once the scope of the negotiation has been determined, the design of the process takes place by mapping out the appropriate sequence of interactions, information flows, and negotiations with all related counterparties. After these steps are complete, the negotiating party can move forward by implementing its planned negotiation.

Consider the differences between the deal designs of Kraft and Cadbury on the day of the takeover offer. Examining Kraft's activities, it is evident that is was gearing up for acquisitions and eying Cadbury as target for some time prior to making its offer. After becoming CEO in 2006, Ms. Rosenfeld advocated and built the support among her managers and shareholders for a growth strategy based on global acquisitions and investment in major brands. She prepared the company by selling off weak brands and revitalizing key ones. In 2007, Kraft bought Groupe Danone SA's global biscuit business giving it brands with operations in more than 20 countries, and strengthening its global position. Kraft carefully timed its proposal to Cadbury. In August 2009 Kraft's second quarter profit topped Wall Street's forecasts and the company raised its earnings forecast for the whole year. Meanwhile, Cadbury was busy restructuring itself and its stock price was underperforming, which made it vulnerable for acquisition (Curtin, September 8, 2009; Kesmodel and Rohwedder, September 8, 2009).

Cadbury's deal design with respect to the acquisition proposal was nonexistent. Not planning to be a target, it had none of the deal setup's "right things" in place. Mr. Carr probably identified the opportunity in Kraft's proposal, and perhaps was willing to consider selling Cadbury for the right price. However, he surely realized that Cadbury was unprepared to negotiate. Similarly, should he wanted to ward off the takeover, he had to reinforce Cadbury's position. Thus, Mr. Carr first had to reshape his deal design according to his goals, and only then engage Kraft. In either case, the requisite first step was buying time by rejecting the offer and prodding Kraft to better it (Wiggins, September 8, 2009). The question is what kind of a setup and strategy could he have possibly come up with given this surprise offer?

Negotiauctions

Except for simple fixed price processes (e.g., buying groceries in the store), auctions and negotiations are the only mechanisms by which assets are transferred in a market economy (Subramanian, 2010). Moreover, pure "one-on-one" negotiations rarely take place in the business world. Deal making takes a complex dynamic that involves a blend of both negotiation and auction elements. Subramanian (2010) calls this process Negotiauction (*negoti*ation + *auction*). Such process requires a unique strategy.

Negotiation, auction, and negotiauction

A *negotiation* is a process in which a price or resource allocation is determined by a joint decision-making process in which the primary source of competitive pressure arises in "across-the-table" dynamics between a buyer and a seller. An *auction* is a class of sales where a price is neither pre-set nor determined by a negotiation but is discovered through the process of competitive bidding. The seller is a passive participant in the dynamic after setting the specific bidding process. Here, the primary source of competitive pressure arises from competition among buyers acting at the "same side of the table" (Subramanian, 2010). Note that the roles of seller and buyer in auctions are interchangeable. For example, buyers seeking to purchase services or assets at the lowest price possible can set an auction for potential suppliers. Sellers seeking to sell services or assets at the highest possible price can set an auction for potential buyers. Thus, referring to "seller" as auction setter is to ease reading. *Negotiauction* is the common situation and price determination process where negotiators are acting in two arenas: across the table [with counterparty] and simultaneously on the same side of the table [with known, unknown and possible competitors] (Subramanian, 2010).

Selecting and setting up a negotiauction

An *auction* is preferred to a negotiation under several conditions. These are when: there are many potential buyers, the asset is well specified, deal speed is important, and process transparency is critical. A *negotiation* is preferred when: the bidders are well known, buyers have good alternatives to the deal at hand, there are large differences in valuations of asset sold, there is a large value creation potential, where relationship and service are critical, if the seller has low risk tolerance, and if secrecy is important. To engage in a *negotiauction*, the seller needs to identify a potential negotiauction situation. Several circumstances characterize it: the seller interacts with three to ten potential buyers, the seller knows more about the situation than buyers do, there is ambiguity about who sets the process (as opposed to auctions), the seller can have one-on-one negotiation-like meetings with potential buyers, and the seller can initiate one or more rounds of auction-like bids among potential buyers.

As in the cases of negotiations and auctions, a party engages in a negotiauction to maximize its gains (via expanding the value of the deal and claiming its own share of it). Some situations call for initiating the negotiauction with an auction-like process. This stage aims to bring the deal price to the desired range of the focal party (e.g., the price range that Mr. Carr had in mind for Cadbury). This is done by identifying counterparties that are capable of meeting that range (e.g., Hershey, Nestle), and weeding out those that are not able or willing to meet it (e.g., smaller companies such as Lindt and Sprungli AG). In the subsequent stage, the focal party can engage in a series of sequential or simultaneous but discrete negotiations with a small group of qualified counterparties to create (and claim) more value, to identify the best matched counterparty, and to finalize the deal. Other situations call for opening the negotiauction with a set of negotiations. If the party does not have a clear specification of the asset or an understanding of the potential counterparties, it would need to generate that insight. Opening with negotiations could help mapping counterparties' interests and capacities, and assets or services' prices and quality ranges (e.g., a first-time car shopper refines his or her preferences to a specific make and model through preliminary meetings and negotiations with various car dealers). Capitalizing on information and insights gained at the negotiations, the party can initiate a bidding process to maximize value (e.g., following initial negotiations, the car shopper solicits and evaluates price quotes for a specific model received from several dealers).

Compared to the decision to negotiate vs. auction, in a negotiauction the decision to auction or negotiate is no longer a static choice made at the onset of the deal process. Instead, the deal process constantly evolves as the situation changes and the seller needs to adjust the process accordingly. The challenge is to determine which competitive source to utilize, and when. While auction-like and negotiation-like processes rely on different sources of competition, it is the strategic and dynamic blending and sequencing of these processes that is critical for value creation and claiming and for deal success.

Mr. Carr aspired to rearrange the deal setup and launch a negotiaciton strategy opening with an auction and moving to negotiations. He might have hoped that Hershey Co., who had the rights to manufacture and sell Cadbury products in the U.S., and Nestle SA, the third largest global confectionary manufacture (following Mars-Wrigley and Cadbury), both threatened by the possible Kraft-Cadbury merger, will submit competing counteroffers (Jargon and Ball, September 9, 2010; Brat, September 9, 2010; McCracken, Cimilluca and Brat, January 7, 2010). In mid-September 2009, Hershey hired four advisors to assess a potential bid. Whether Hershey and Nestle were real contenders was not important. The expectation of a bidding war pushed Cadbury's stock price past initial offer value (790 pence a share vs. 745) and pressured Kraft to improve its offer (Rohwedder, September 22, 2009).

Taking part in a negotiauction

A party might find itself maneuvered into a negotiauction and engage simultaneously or sequentially in bids against competitors (real or potential) and in negotiation with the counterparty (who initially had set up the negotiauction process). In such a case, the party has an interest in controlling or reshaping the negotiauction dynamic to its own favor. Thus, a negotiating party should take a proactive approach to engaging in a negotiation, determine whether the situation is a negotiauction, constantly asses its position and the viability of shaping the dynamic, and take action as necessary. Subramanian (2010) calls such actions "game-changing moves" and identifies three types: setup, rearar ranging, and shut-down.

Setup moves

Setup moves establish the terms of a party's entry into a negotiauction. In some cases, having an extra party (or any party) entering a deal-making situation could be of value to the counterparty that sets the process. Recognizing the positive impact of its entry on the negotiauction dynamic and on the potential deal value, the new entrant can set terms for its entry and ask for specific concessions in return to its entry. The critical element of setup moves is that the new entrant (e.g., Nestle or Hershey, following Kraft) should ask for them explicitly and that the focal party (e.g., Cadbury) needs to accept them. The focal party will accept these new terms only if it believes that it will be better off by accepting these new terms and having the new entrant as an additional counterparty, than otherwise. In other words, the setup move is a negotiation initiated by a party on the terms of entering a pending deal making situation. The new party should initiate this step prior to agreeing to enter the negotiauction; otherwise, that opportunity to shape the game in its favor will be lost.

Under U.K. Takeover Panel rules, Hershey had a week to counteroffer after Cadbury's board approval of Kraft's proposal made on January 20, 2010. However, any attempt to top Kraft's bid would have triggered a break fee of nearly $200 million (£122 million) (Farrell, January 20, 2010). Thus, revising its offer to Cadbury, Kraft initiated a variation of a setup/shut-down move making it harder for any competitor to enter the negotiauction.

Rearranging moves

Rearranging moves reconfigure the assets, the parties, or both in a way that adds value to the deal. Compared to setup moves, these moves can be made both at the beginning of the negotiauction or when it is already in process. Contrary to set up moves and shut-down moves, these moves aim at the counterparty (other side of the table) and enhancing the value of the deal, rather than blocking or removing the competition (same side of the table). Making these moves require a deep understanding of the situation and deal at hand. For example, Hershey, ranked fifth in global confectionary market, reluctant to bid for Cadbury on its own due to low cash reserves, tried to structure a takeover alliance with Ferrero SpA, ranked sixth and believed to have no cash limitations. The two companies identified potential synergies among themselves and with Cadbury that could be realized in a merger. Had this joint counteroffer materialized, this rearranging move would have had a significant effect on the negotiauction, and probably on its outcome and deal value (Brat, McCracken, Cimilluca, November, 18, 2009).

Shut down moves

Shut down moves are initiated by one of the competing parties in an attempt to cut off the same-side-of-the-table competition. If successful, reducing the negotiauction to a one-on-one negotiation between that party and the counterparty. These moves are composed of a unique offer that, ideally, persuades the counterparty to drop its negotiauction strategy, focus its attention on the party making that unique offer, pursue a deal with that particular party, and ignore all other actual or potential competing parties and offers.

Successful shut down moves build on affecting the perceptions of the party that runs the negotiauction regarding its alternatives at the time that the shut-down move is initiated. To have the desirable impact, the move or unique offer, should incorporate a credible threat that highlights the temporality of the offer. This threat negatively affects the targeted party's perception of the value and feasibility of its other alternatives. Thus, the offering party should structure and time the move carefully to affect the targeted party, leading it to believe that the offer is the best it could get, and has the best odds of materializing into a desirable deal, given the circumstances.

Kraft led an integrated setup and shut down move. On January 5, 2010, Nestle surprisingly announced its purchase of Kraft's frozen pizza operations in the U.S. and Canada for $3.7 billion in cash, adding that it would not bid for Cadbury. Kraft's secretive move with Nestle both eliminated a possible competitor, and infused it with cash towards its final offer for Cadbury (Gelnar, January 6, 2010).

Next, Kraft aimed its shut down move at Hershey that seemed be completing a counteroffer due within days past January 15 (Jannarone, January 16, 2010; McCracken Cimilluca, and Brat, January 16, 2010). Timing was critical: over the 19-week period between Kraft's first offer and just before the hostile bid's deadline, long-term shareholders sold 26% of Cadbury's shares, while the eight largest buyers of them were hedge funds and other short-term traders (Hodgson, February 10, 2010). Should Kraft's bid have gone directly to shareholders on midnight January 20, short-term traders might have sold their stock to Kraft at that bid price. Aiming to take full control of Cadbury and preempt Hershey's possible counteroffer, Kraft used the diverging interests of the two shareholder groups and the hostile bid's looming deadline to squeeze Cadbury. Mr. Carr, as Cadbury's chairman having a fiduciary responsibility towards all Cadbury's shareholders including long-term investors, had an interest in selling Cadbury for the best price possible, and well above Kraft's hostile offer. By calling Mr. Carr and willing to discuss the price, Ms. Rosenfeld led Mr. Carr to believe that negotiating with Kraft just before the deadline was the best way to secure a good deal, while avoiding the uncertainty regarding Hershey's intent to counteroffer (Hodgson, February 10, 2010).

When Not to Negotiate

Should Hershey have made a counteroffer in response to the Kraft-Cadbury deal? Among the most critical strategic decisions is whether to initiate and engage in a negotiation or not. Cases identified by Malhotra and Bazerman (2007) where negotiation might not be the best way to achieve a party's goals, and other actions should be sought are discussed next.

When time is money

Preparing for and engaging in an important negotiation is an intensive and resource-consuming process. Moreover, some negotiations are time-sensitive or are limited to a narrow window of opportunity. When several negotiations are pending, a party should identify the negotiations that could lead to the highest payoffs, or the more critical and time-sensitive ones, and pursue the critical and potentially higher paying negotiations rather than the trivial or less valuable ones. For example, Nestle, following its business strategy and objectives, chose to focus its attention and resources on the acquisition negotiations with Kraft over the pizza lines rather than bid on Cadbury (Gelnar, January 6, 2010).

When a party's best alternative to no agreement is bad — and everyone knows it

A party is advised not to negotiate when a reasonable analysis suggests that it will not be able to improve a deal (either create or claim value) relative to an offer a counterparty made. This is particularly important when it is known (or about to be public) that the party does not have any good alternatives to having a deal with that particular counterparty (e.g., receiving a single job offer after graduation during a recessionary economy). In such a case, the party should consider accepting the initial offer and try to improve the settlement after signing an agreement.

When negotiating sends the wrong signal

When a party extends an offer, the counterparty's initiation of a negotiation always sends a signal. Typically, that it requires more value before it is willing to settle. However, sometimes initiating a negotiation could be interpreted as distrust of the party, focus on counterparty's own gains rather than relationship, or questioning the validity of the initial offer (e.g., think of a person initiating a negotiation over joint financial arrangements in response to receiving a romantic marriage proposal). If there is a risk that initiating a negotiation will send the wrong signal, a party has three options. First, negotiate anyway if it expects the gains to outweigh the cost of the wrong signal. Second, actively change the signal by explicitly communicating the reasons for negotiating. Third, not negotiate if it evaluates the cost of a possible wrong signal as higher than expected gains. Note that with Cadbury, agreeing to negotiate immediately with Kraft after its first offer would have sent the wrong signal to Kraft, shareholders, and to potential bidders.

When relationships might suffer

The dynamic of a negotiation, even if all parties face a potential gain, could affect the nature of the relationship and future interactions among them. Attempting to "win" a negotiation by claiming the majority of value created might have long lasting consequences. Use of extreme competitive or claiming moves and tactics could create negative reputation for that party, affecting its future interactions. Moreover, reaching a settlement purely on economic grounds, without considering its emotional ramifications, could affect agreement implementation and future goodwill (e.g., how competitively should parents negotiate an hourly rate with a babysitter for their children?). When parties expect repeated negotiations, or a long-term agreement, they should evaluate the possible impact of the negotiation dynamic on the relationship. Indeed, Mr. Carr's negotiation tactics had an impact on his relationship with Kraft's CEO. He had not met Ms. Rosenfeld again after the January 19 meeting and less than two weeks afterwards he and his team announced their departure from Cadbury (Wall Street Journal, February 3, 2010).

When negotiating is culturally inappropriate

Each culture has a set of norms that define the realms of life where it is appropriate to negotiate, and how to do so. Sometimes, insisting to negotiate could violate strong norms and lead to negative consequences (e.g., attempting to bargain with a U.S. police officer over a traffic violation ticket). In other cases, unwilling to negotiate could go against accepted social rituals (e.g., when buying or selling a carpet in a Turkish bazaar). Moreover, cross-cultural variances in negotiation strategies could affect negotiation dynamics and outcomes. To engage in negotiations in countries and cultures they are not familiar with, parties must prepare and learn about the foreign culture prior to initiating negotiations, or postpone negotiations until they do so. Kraft, a U.S.-based company, was well prepared for the takeover move on U.K.-based Cadbury and employed a London-based consulting law firm. In addition, per Mr. Carr, Kraft benefited from British merger and acquisitions rules that enable hostile takeovers of U.K. companies by foreign companies (Hodgson, February 10, 2010).

When a party's best alternative to no agreement is better than the counterparty's best possible offer

Not every negotiation opportunity is a viable one, nor very negotiation should result in a settlement. When a party recognizes that it will not be able to advance its goals (or gain an improvement over its alternatives) via a negotiation with a particular counterparty, then there is no reason to initiate or continue negotiating with that counterparty. Moreover, if a party recognizes that instead of benefiting from the negotiation it is incurring costs and becoming worse off than its initial position, it should stop negotiating and seek other options. Although Hershey and Ferreo held contacts with Cadbury and identified possible synergies with it, and although Kraft was one of their major competitors that preferably be blocked, they both hesitated to counteroffer over Cadbury. Hershey realized that doing so would severely risk its investment-grade credit ratings and other interests, and avoided the bid (Brat, Ball and McCracken, January 20, 2010). Meanwhile, Ferrero, a private family-controlled and secretive Italian company was reluctant to break its traditions and publically expose its financial data for the bid, and avoided it as well (Meichtry, November 19, 2009).

Conclusion

Negotiation is a social process that occurs whenever people cannot achieve their own goals without the cooperation of others. Negotiation strategy is a set of actions applied to achieve these goals. This chapter focused on the intentional use of negotiation strategy and reviewed the central frameworks used to understand and formulate such strategy. Several key themes emerge from this review. First, prior to developing a negotiation strategy, a party must have a clear understanding of its own interests and goals. These should guide the selection, deployment, and evaluation of the negotiation strategy. Second, a party should also evaluate the goals of potential and actual negotiation counterparties and competitors and apply this understanding when devising its strategy. Third, strategy development for critical and complex negotiations requires a deep insight into the negotiation context and the nexus of key parties involved. This insight will guide the choice of counterparties, strategic use of information, the sequencing of strategic moves, and the sequencing of interactions with counterparties. Fourth, except for simple barraging cases, most negotiations require a blend of integrative (cooperative, value creating) and distributive (competitive, value claiming) strategic negotiation moves. Sometimes the situation calls for a negotiauction strategy, blending both auction and negotiation elements. Negotiating parties have the choice of timing, sequencing, overall emphasis, and intensity when applying and integrating these complex moves. Last, parties must recognize that initiating a negotiation is a strategic choice by itself, and that interests and goals should always guide this decision.

Personality and Negotiation

Alice F. Stuhlmacher
DePaul University

Christopher K. Adair
DePaul University

Omnicorp Technologies has scheduled its annual strategy and budgeting retreat. Once a year, the organization's directors convene for discussion of resources and strategic planning. This is a time for negotiating — for the organization, for one's department, or sometimes for one's own self interests. Those attending have very different approaches to the negotiations. Amy is confident in her ability to gain more staff and office space and is persistent in voicing her requests. During breaks, Juan indirectly gathers information on what others think of his new proposal for a joint venture so he can modify his "pitch". Evelyn deceptively overstates some market data to bolster her case for increased research funding. Jae-Hwa spends time talking with various groups and discussing how to help them get the resources they need. William mainly hopes that everyone leaves the meeting as friends and that they are willing to cooperate in the future. Each of these people has very different perspectives, and some may even conflict with those of other employees.

What drives these diverse responses in negotiations? One possible answer is that the variation is due to *individual differences*, those unique characteristics that each person brings to a situation. As shown in Figure 1, these individual differences influence the processes in a negotiation which then affect important outcomes such as satisfaction, settlements, and perceptions.

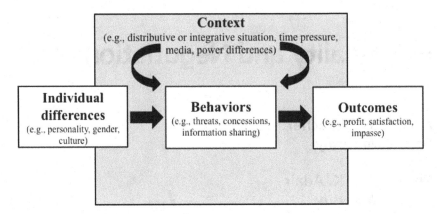

FIGURE 1   The impact of individual differences in negotiation

While individual differences include aspects such as gender, age, culture, experience, and cognitive ability, this chapter looks specifically at personality. Personality can be understood as the unique and relatively stable patterns of behavior and thoughts shown by individuals. Personality is one way we categorize ourselves and our negotiation counterparts. Even though some people's personalities stand out as particularly unusual or memorable, everyone brings some kind of a personality to the negotiation table. For instance, one person may tend to be gregarious and outgoing, while another tends to be reserved and shy. Predispositions, or traits, like these make up what we generally regard as personality. Additionally, it is important to understand what personality is *not*. Unlike moods, personality is not expected to fluctuate wildly over time or have extreme changes within a single day. We also find that personality is not the same as a negotiator's style, although personality may be a factor that influences one's negotiation style, among other things.

Various researchers have tried to classify personality types and it is worthwhile to consider the implications for negotiation. This chapter provides a brief background on why personality is important, how specific traits relate to aspects of negotiation, and what good negotiators should know about personality.

Personality in Negotiation

Personality plays a role in negotiation whether we are considering formal negotiations in a diplomatic summit, informal maneuvers for more departmental resources, or deciding with friends what to eat for dinner. The impact of personality can be seen in how negotiators initiate an offer, in how they plan and strategize, in the tactics they use (such as cooperation, aggression, deception, threats), as well as in the final settlements, perceptions, and satisfaction.

There are many interesting questions about the best traits for a negotiator. What kinds of personalities would you want to negotiate with? Someone friendly and warm or who strictly sticks to business? Which personality type would give you the best deal? Would *you* try to portray your personality in a negotiation as something you are not, such as tougher or more sociable than usual? When does personality play its biggest role in influencing behaviors and perceptions?

Even though it seems that personality always determines behavior, it rarely operates alone; situations have a strong influence on how people act. Throughout this chapter we consider how personality interacts with other variables. Figure 1 includes this as well; the situation can enhance or limit the influence of personality and other individual differences. This is referred to as an "interactionist" perspective, in that the effects of personality depend on the level of other (contextual) variables. For example, some personality traits may be more successful face-to-face than in an online negotiation, or the outcomes may depend on time pressure, or help women rather than men. Thus, personality interacts with the *context* of the situation.

Before we more fully consider how personality impacts negotiation, we have to think about the common negotiation situations we might encounter. One important distinction was set out by Walton and McKersie (1965) in their discussion of distributive and integrative negotiations. In the field of negotiation, these terms describe ways to approach negotiation as well as types of negotiation situations. Distributive negotiations are those characterized by competition, self-interest, and assertiveness. Distributive negotiations are sometimes called "win-lose" negotiations where there is a single fixed issue that must be divided. In other words, what one side gains, the other side loses. In contrast, an integrative negotiation (sometimes called win-win) involves the possibility of mutual gain, but generally requires problem-solving and information exchange to discover these areas of benefit. If we are in a negotiation that involves only a single, one-time issue (e.g., the price of a used bicycle at a rummage sale), we might see this as a distributive negotiation. But negotiating for the merger of two organizations has integrative potential; negotiators may discover better outcomes for both sides by exploring options. Some personality characteristics are better suited to distributive than integrative negotiations and vice versa.

In addition to the integrative/distributive aspects of negotiation, we need to specify the terms of "successful" negotiation or, typically, what outcomes are of interest. For example, one important outcome of a negotiation may be building positive relationships or maintaining reputations that will open doors in the future. Other times, people value feelings of competence or not "losing face". Sometimes, the perceptions or feelings of success are what matters most. Or, in other cases, the bottom line settlement may be the most important factor. More typically, multiple goals and outcomes are critical in the negotiation. So depending on the goals of a negotiator, some personality characteristics may be more helpful. However, it is important to remember that this is also dependent on various contextual or situational factors.

Now that we have broadly identified some negotiation situations and definitions of success, we can delve into the findings about personality. Many personality traits have been examined in negotiations, and we will present a few of the most common.

Relationship focused traits

One important set of traits deals with how sensitive negotiators are to other people, their social ties, and relationships in general.

Some examples of relationship focused traits in negotiation include interpersonal orientation (Rubin and Brown, 1975), relationship orientation (Greenhalgh, Neslin and Gilkey, 1985), relational self-construal (Gelfand *et al.*, 2006), social motives (DeDreu, Wiengart and Kwon, 2000), communal orientation (Thompson and DeHarpport, 1998) and unmitigated communion (Amanatullah, Morris and Curhan, 2008). While these are conceptualized as different traits, together they illustrate how predispositions about self and others affect negotiation.

Research provides some intriguing findings regarding various relationship-focused traits. For example, high unmitigated concern (high concern for relationships and low self-concern) influences various negotiation outcomes (Amanatullah *et al.*, 2008). When one of the negotiators has high unmitigated concern, he or she tends to earn less because of setting lower goals and concern about harming a relationship. When both negotiators have high unmitigated concern, they also have lower economic outcomes but higher relationship satisfaction than other negotiators.

Other relationship-focused traits are influential as well. Negotiators with a relationship orientation have more capacity for empathy, interrupt less, and attempt deception less than negotiators with a transaction orientation (e.g., non-relationship orientation) (Greenhalgh and Gilkey, 1993). Empathic and people-oriented traits are associated with more generous settlements (Greenhalgh *et al.*, 1985). Thompson and DeHarpport (1998) found that when friends with a communal orientation negotiate, the settlement is relatively equal. Settlements are less equal when friends are low in communal orientation. Interestingly, the pattern is opposite for unacquainted negotiators. Low communal dyads reach relatively equal outcomes perhaps because they are paying more attention to the actual distribution rather than giving and receiving help. Finally, a pro-social orientation (e.g., concern for mutual benefit) in integrative negotiations increases economic outcomes but only when the negotiators have concern for self interests and stand firm on their own interests (De Dreu *et al.*, 2000). If pro-social negotiators are overly accommodating, they leave value on the table.

In short, these findings suggest that a strong relationship focus may harm economic outcomes unless it is balanced with some concern for self-interests. It also suggests that for some negotiators it will be very important to leave on amicable terms. For some people, good interpersonal relationships would be important to calling a negotiation a success, and would drive the choice of future negotiation partners.

Contrary to the concern for positive relationships is Machiavellianism (Christie and Geis, 1970). Machiavellianism is a personality trait named after the writings of Niccolo Machiavelli which encourage a "whatever it takes" strategy for achieving goals without concern for morality or ethics. As such, a Machiavellian personality refers to a general tendency to manipulate or exploit others for one's own ends or purposes.

"High-Mach" individuals are convincing liars (Geis and Moon, 1981), which has implications for negotiations that are dependent on feelings of trust. High-Machs tend to be more successful in jobs where the rules are vague, since this provides more room to exploit others (Schultz, 1993). High-Machs also tend to be more open and upfront about feelings of mistrust. They tend to employ more manipulative behaviors and tend to seek power more than low-Machs. High-Mach individuals may feel more comfortable exploiting their power in a negotiation to reach selfish goals, and in fact may even *enjoy* doing so.

The Machiavellianism trait has relationships with individual bargaining outcomes, although the results are mixed (Barry and Friedman, 1998). It may be the case that high-Machs do better in distributive situations while low-Machs tend to do better in integrative situations. Given what we already know about the nature of these two different negotiation cases, this makes sense. Low-Machs may be less likely to exploit the other side, instead moving toward a cooperative solution. On the other hand, high-Machs' pursuit of self-interest would be fulfilled in distributive negotiations and may even enhance their outcomes.

Interestingly, low-Machs are at a disadvantage when bargaining in face-to-face negotiations with a high-Mach because low-Machs are susceptible to distraction by emotions (Christie and Geis, 1970). In other words, these individuals are distracted by issues not related to the task at hand, such as the disposition of the other party. This is less of a disadvantage for low-Machs when they negotiate with other low-Machs (Fry, 1985).

Knowing your personality tendencies and those of your counterparts can help you better understand and prepare for the bargaining situations. However, if your counterpart is a high-Mach, you may have to be attentive for deceptive negotiation tactics and to structure the situation so deceptive behavior can be detected. An awareness of these traits, as well as understanding whether you are in a distributive or integrative situation, can influence negotiation performance and satisfaction.

Five factor model

While relationship-focused traits are important, they are not the only traits that have been studied. One particularly popular way of classifying personality is the five-factor model (FFM) (Costa and McCrae, 1992; Costa and McCrae, 1995; Digman, 1990). This model suggests that there are five unique traits that describe someone's personality. The five factors (or dimensions) are extraversion, agreeableness, conscientiousness, openness to experience, and neuroticism. *Extraversion* is identified with outgoing, sociable, and assertiveness. High extraversion tends to be associated with higher job performance when interpersonal interaction is required. *Agreeableness* is a tendency to be cooperative and accepting (as opposed to confrontational). People high in agreeableness look to maintain harmony and seek positive outcomes for themselves as well as others (Jensen-Campbell and Graziano, 2001). *Conscientiousness* is a predisposition for attention to detail and has been a consistent predictor of individual performance, especially in sales jobs (Hurtz and Donovan, 2000). People high in *openness to experience* tend to be creative, intellectually curious, and value learning. There tends to be a higher level of innovation when openness is high. *Neuroticism* (or low emotional stability) is typically identified by feelings of anxiousness and stress.

Of these broad variables most research attention in negotiation has focused on agreeableness and extraversion. We will start with agreeableness. In conflict situations, high-agreeable individuals are more positive in their evaluation of opponents, and perceive less conflict than their more cynical low-agreeable counterparts. These individuals would tend to interpret the situation more positively, as well as proceed in the negotiation with a more positive outlook and using more constructive tactics. This trait influences the perception of the situation (i.e., what strategies one sees as effective). Agreeableness is expected to influence the perceptions of self and others, which in turn influences the intensity, tactics, and oppositions during a negotiation or conflict episode (Graziano, Jensen-Campbell and Hair, 1996).

The interactionist perspective suggests that the impact of highly agreeable negotiators depends on the circumstances. For example, if the person on the "other side of the table" has a tendency to be cooperative, some negotiators may feel a little more comfortable pursuing their own self-interests in order to exploit this trust. Low-agreeable individuals are more likely to support the use of criticism, threats, manipulations, and physical force in conflict situations (Graziano *et al.*, 1996). Additionally, to their detriment, high-agreeable people and their high levels of trust may be manipulated depending on the opposing party. On the other hand, highly agreeable negotiators may encourage reciprocal behavior from their counterparts, leading to a more positive negotiation process.

Agreeableness is particularly desirable in integrative situations — it helps to see conflict in a positive manner and to be open and cooperative to reaching a shared outcome. However, high-agreeable individuals may be more likely to settle for less, or end up settling for less, if they start the negotiation with an "agreeable" opening offer that has low economic value (Barry and Friedman, 1998).

Somewhat similar to agreeableness is extraversion. Extraversion also deals with how an individual interacts with others in social situations. Extraverted individuals are more likely to be active in the negotiation process, openly speaking their minds throughout the process. This trait is positively related to negotiation behaviors that require joint problem-solving and open discussion of the preferences of both parties. Therefore, in negotiation situations where open discussion is useful, extraversion is an advantage since sharing information will likely lead to a more favorable outcome for both parties. However, in more contentious negotiations, high extraversion can be a liability since full disclosure of information is not most effective in these cases (Barry and Friedman, 1998). High extraversion may undermine distributive performance because open communication is not as important as strategically learning information about the other side and sticking up for one's own self-interests.

Less can be said about conscientiousness, openness to experience, and neuroticism than extraversion and agreeableness because there are fewer studies about them in negotiation. It has been suggested that conscientiousness is positively related with problem-solving, creativity, and understanding (Barry and Friedman, 1998), while openness to experience predicts integrative behaviors but not distributive behaviors of negotiators (Ma and Jaeger, 2005). However, many avenues remained unexplored. More research needs to be done about the influence of the five-factor traits. Future research on these traits within a variety of contexts will provide a clearer picture of the role of personality in negotiation performance. Consistent with the interactionist perspective, we would expect that there are both advantages and disadvantages to each trait in the five-factor model.

Self-monitoring

Additional traits do not fall directly into the five-factor typology but warrant discussion. The trait of self-monitoring relates to the degree people evaluate and adjust their behavior when interacting, with the goal of giving a positive impression to others (Snyder, 1987). High-self monitoring has a positive relationship with a variety of work-related outcomes, such as job satisfaction, promotions, and performance (specifically in areas that require communication and interpersonal interaction). Persons who are able to adapt (or "mold") their behavior to fit with others (partners/opponents/constituents) are more likely to succeed than those who are less willing to change their style and behavior. This is because, in part, individuals who are high in self-monitoring can pick up on important social cues that help them succeed in presenting themselves.

The superior performance of high self-monitors makes sense, given that they are likely to have an advantage when impression management is important. These individuals are more adept at altering their behavior in response to changes in the environment. In other words, high self-monitors should be better able to mirror other individuals within the negotiation (Flynn and Ames, 2006). Interestingly, research on these situations finds that self-monitoring behaviors help women more than men to achieve higher outcomes, especially in distributive tasks. Perhaps self monitoring women are better able to counteract negative gender stereotypes pertaining to their negotiations with which men do not have to contend (Flynn and Ames, 2006).

The disparate relationship between men and women self-monitors and their negotiation performance again illustrates how personality's impact depends on interactions with other variables that may be outside of an individual's control. Just like the other traits, self-monitoring may be beneficial in some situations and detrimental in others.

Self-efficacy

Self-efficacy refers to an individual's belief in his or her ability to successfully perform a task. Imagine two individuals going into a performance review process: one is confident in her ability to negotiate a pay raise while the other is more skeptical and worried about her ability to do so. It seems plausible that the first individual (high self-efficacy) is more likely to succeed than the second (low self-efficacy), and research tends to support this relationship. The resulting process is a self-fulfilling prophecy. In other words, an individual with high levels of self-efficacy will be more likely to succeed at the task in question, which in turn will reinforce and encourage the initial (high) self-efficacy beliefs. In negotiation, those with higher self-efficacy have higher negotiation outcomes than those with lower self-efficacy levels (Gist, Stevens and Bavetta, 1991).

Individuals with low levels of self efficacy, on the other hand, anticipate failure and by focusing on these feelings are less likely to succeed and may even give up. Low self-efficacy can lead to a negative downward self-fulfilling prophecy. When they hit an impasse in a negotiation, negotiators with low self-efficacy are more likely to spiral into negative emotions, report negative perceptions, see their negotiations as unsuccessful, as well as report less likelihood to share information, work together, and behave cooperatively in the future than those with higher self-efficacy (O'Connor and Arnold, 2001). Those with high self-efficacy do not report such negative predictions about their future negotiations.

Somewhat distinct from other personality traits, self-efficacy can be developed. Self efficacy can develop through past experience (both their own and watching others). For example, paying attention to a negotiator who "models" successful behavior can increase the self-efficacy for future bargaining. Involvement in negotiation training or classes can also increase self-efficacy for negotiation. You may appreciate knowing that reading this book could increase your self-efficacy in negotiation to the extent it makes you more confident about your knowledge and ability to negotiate, which in turn, can increase your negotiation success.

Implications for Negotiators

First, we offer a word of caution on how personality is assessed and the validation of these scores. Most frequently personality is

TABLE 1   Sample items from personality measures

Personality trait	Sample measurement item
Communal Orientation	"When making a decision, I take other peoples' feelings into account" (Clark, Ouenette, Powell and Milberg, 1987).
Machiavellianism	"It is hard to get ahead without cutting corners here and there" (Christie and Geis, 1970).
Five Factor Model	(Goldberg, 1992)
Extraversion	"Am the life of the party."
Agreeable	"Am interested in people."
Conscientiousness	"Am always prepared."
Neuroticism	"Get stressed out easily."
Openness to Experience	"Have a vivid imagination."
Self-monitoring	"In different situations and with different people, I often act like very different persons" (Snyder, 1974)
Self-efficacy	How confident are you that you can negotiate a $50,000 salary?

measured by self-report, or people answering questions about themselves. Respondents answer sets of questions similar to those in Table 1.

To have confidence in using particular responses requires reliability and validity evidence for the scores. Reliability requires evidence of consistency in results. If someone took a Mach test, the results should not be drastically different from previous administrations, despite the time of day or other extraneous variables like the weather or setting. Once a personality characteristic has reliable scores, it is critical to find evidence supporting the use of the scores. This is the validation process and it is continual, such that a test and its scores need to be supported for each use. We bring this up because while a multitude of personality scales exist, many are not supported for serious use. In reality, it takes substantial research to have confidence in using personality scales as tools to make diagnoses or recommendations, in negotiation or other settings.

So while taking personality tests and labeling yourself and others can be very entertaining, the scores are not always truly informative, especially in untrained hands. However, in the hands of trained interpreters, personality scores and understanding of the traits have practical applications for you, the negotiator. Our review thus far suggests that good negotiators are people who are to some degree agreeable, extraverted, good self monitors, and have high self-efficacy or confidence in their negotiating ability. Having a relationship focus can improve satisfaction on both sides, but can limit outcomes if one is too accommodating. These characteristics can help negotiators maintain good relations as well as search for solutions that would expand the possible settlement range and find satisfying solutions for both sides. Additionally, certain characteristics like Machiavellianism may help a negotiator in the short run or certain situations, but may not create long term success and promotes unethical behavior and deception that especially flourishes in unmonitored situations.

But, where you stand on these traits does not necessarily mean you will or will not be a good negotiator. It is important to know that personality is not destiny. Even if you do not have the traits of a successful negotiation, you can incorporate the necessary behaviors that are associated with effective traits. Personality may provide a predisposition one way or another, but once you are aware of your personality tendencies you can make some modifications appropriate to the requirements of a task or situation. For example, someone who is not extraverted can make special efforts to exchange information and increase communication that will lead to improved mutual gain. Likewise, someone who is not highly conscientious can use tools and strategies to help plan, research, and prepare for a negotiation. Simple behaviors like goal-setting prior to a negotiation can be used and have a much stronger effect on negotiation outcomes than most individual differences (Zetik and Stuhlmacher, 2002). Negotiators can also work to improve their self-efficacy to increase confidence and persistence through the negotiation proceedings.

Once again, it is important to keep the interactionist perspective in mind. For example, too much self-efficacy can also have a dark side, making negotiators overconfident so that they do not walk away from losing situations, or seek outside help from a mediator or third party even if it may be in their best interests (O'Connor and Arnold, 2001). Or, certain expressions of personality may be seen as more appropriate for men than women. Due to gender roles, women may be expected to exhibit more cooperation rather than assertiveness in a negotiation and may experience backlash for being aggressive (Walters, Stuhlmacher and Meyer, 1998). Likewise, women who are high self-monitors do better in negotiations than women or men who are low self-monitors (Flynn and Ames, 2006), perhaps due to the expectation that women should be more sensitive to others. Similarly, high Machs can have more influence in ambiguous or weak situations, where the situation allows them to take advantage of others more than in a highly regulated and monitored environment.

Consider Michael who has the tendency to be abrasive, uncooperative, and concerned with his own self-interest above that of others. Certain situations may inhibit the expression of these traits. If Michael is meeting with his boss, he is more likely to cooperate and compromise with his supervisor's requests because it means keeping his job. But with a peer or subordinate, Michael's personality predisposition may assert itself more. Personality effects are more likely to emerge in weak situations — ones that have fewer prescribed norms on how to act.

It is also critical to know that many people enter into negotiation expecting that they must be competitive and inflexible and may try to exhibit those personality characteristics. This may be acceptable in one-shot negotiations over a single issue with a stranger, but more complex negotiations need a broader set of traits. In reality, decades of research have shown that cooperation starts negotiators on a path to higher profits and better relationships (for a review see Halpert, Stuhlmacher, Litcher, Crenshaw and Bortel, 2010). This is especially true in integrative negotiations, and most negotiations have potential for some kind of mutual gain.

How one is perceived by opponents is an important part of negotiation and personality plays a role in this perception. For example, portraying oneself as a difficult and competitive negotiator leads to more demanding negotiations than when the party is not labeled with a tough reputation, and ultimately the negotiator is less successful (Tinsley, O'Connor and Sullivan, 2002). Evaluations of another's behaviors may ultimately drive judgments of personality more than the counterpart's actual personality. Morris, Larrick, and Su (1999) found that when they manipulated the situation to require tougher negotiator behavior, this determined the opponent's impression of a negotiator's personality. Negotiators required to haggle more were seen as having more disagreeable personalities. Negotiators with ambiguous information going into the negotiation were seen as having low emotionally stable (or neurotic) personalities. This suggests that behaviors will be attributed to personality even if there are other possible reasons and this can also start a spiral of self-fulfilling prophesies within the negotiation process.

Conclusion

Personality applied to work settings has surged in popularity within the last 25 years and many organizations use personality tests for hiring and screening employees. The research and understanding of personality in negotiation also is regaining popularity. And like our story at the beginning of the chapter, personality is an explanation for the various behaviors we see around us. We hope you recognize in the scenario elements that suggest Amy's high self-efficacy, Juan's self-monitoring, Evelyn's high-Mach potential, Jae-Hwa's extraversion, and William's agreeableness and relationship concerns. However, while the temptation is to ask who will be more effective, we hope you gathered that personality is only one piece of the negotiation puzzle. Its effect depends on what kinds of resources are available, what kinds of settlements are sought, power differences between parties, and other individual and situational differences.

Despite this, we find personality a meaningful construct to examine in negotiation. First, although the relationships may not be extremely strong, they are still significant statistically and practically. As such, they are worth exploring. Personality is more likely to relate to behavior in weak situations — ones with more latitude in how to respond. This is helpful to understand what strengthens and weakens the overall impact of personality. Finally, personality is an interesting avenue of research, and people will likely continue to describe the unique traits of themselves and others for many years to come, so it pays to be informed on personality and its many complexities.

11

Judgment Bias and Decision Making in Negotiation

William P. Bottom
Olin Business School
Washington University in St. Louis

Dejun Tony Kong
Olin Business School
Washington University in St. Louis

Alexandra A. Mislin
Kogod School of Business
American University

The Paris Peace Conference at the end of World War I surely ranks among the most costly of diplomatic failures, a "peace to end all peace" (Fromkin, 1992).[1] After he directly contributed to some of the early mistakes made by the American delegation, Walter Lippmann observed these errors rapidly multiply as the negotiation process went awry. In the book *Public Opinion* (Lippmann, 1922) he developed a complex multilevel theory identifying certain psychological factors responsible for the cascade of mistakes committed by the negotiators along with organizational and political forces that sustained and magnified them (Bottom, 2010). Turning prescriptive, he urged social

---

[1] The German government officially fulfilled their financial obligations under the peace treaty with a final payment of reparations to the Allied governments on October 2, 2010 (Boyes, 2010).

scientists to undertake a systematic "study of error", one that would more fully reveal the operation and impact of these psychological factors.

His theory proved to be, as Herbert Simon (1985) later recalled, "the harbinger of the behavioral revolution". This was a revolution that Simon would subsequently do much to advance through his own work. The study of error developed quickest in Simon's own field of political science becoming the dominant paradigm by midcentury. Because of the prevailing rigid doctrine of behaviorism (Watson, 1913), which ruled out attempts to study mental life, psychologists made limited contributions to the study of error (e.g., Allport, 1925; Katz and Braly, 1933; Rice, 1926) until the cognitive revolution overturned dogma in the 1960's. Simon's insights on "bounded rationality" would inspire cognitive psychologists to identify information processing heuristics that combine with motivational factors to yield persistent biases.

A compilation of studies about these heuristics (Kahneman, Slovic, and Tversky, 1982) drove social scientists to explore social and organizational implications of cognitive biases. Especially successful was a "decision theoretic" perspective on negotiation that energized both research and teaching (Raiffa, 1981; Bazerman and Chugh, 2006). But scientists are boundedly rational so they focus on newly published work while adhering to prevailing disciplinary paradigms. So the origins of the behavioral approach, conceived out of a profound negotiation failure, have long been obscured.

This chapter places decision theoretic research on negotiator judgment in its wider historical and political context. Doing so enables us to more clearly discern what progress has actually been made toward Lippmann's "study of error". The focus will be on biases stemming from the availability, anchoring and adjustment, and representativeness heuristics most closely connected to Lippmann's original formulation of the bounded rationality model. The review also addresses the closely linked biases associated with overconfidence and perceptions of integrative potential that magnify bias stemming from the three heuristics.

Shifts in risk tolerance associated with issue framing are also addressed. This survey concludes by examining aspects of the original behavioral agenda that still require further research attention.

The Mental Models of Negotiators

In analyzing the mistakes made by Allied leaders, Lippmann came to an important realization. These negotiators had based their decisions on highly simplified mental models of the incredibly complicated problems of arms control, border determination, colonial exploitation, nation building, financial reparation, and institution building (e.g., the World Court). He deemed these cognitive representations "pseudo-environments", explaining how statesmen constructed them from knowledge structures in memory he called "stereotypes". From the outset he stressed the indispensable role these "pictures in the head" play in our ability to process information and formulate judgments (Schneider, 2004). But he also conjectured that stereotypes shape information search in confirmatory fashion so that biased sampling generates overconfident judgment that is far more impervious to correction.

This confirmatory bias left significant "blind spots" in the thinking of the conference leaders — blindness about their counterparts as well as particular issues they were attempting to resolve. Appalling overconfidence about the viability of their BATNA misled them to reduce a devilishly complicated diplomatic puzzle into a crude ultimatum game (Bottom, 2003). The coercive process they forced upon the German delegation compelled the desired concessions but precluded the information sharing that would have better educated them to German, Balkan, and Middle-Eastern realities.

Lippmann could discern the operation of stereotypes because they were employed so blatantly. This was not "modern racism" reflecting hidden prejudices (Brief, Dietz, Cohen, Pugh, and Vaslow, 2000). Generalizations about nationality were overt, crude and ubiquitous. To persuade his colleagues to impose harsh terms by ultimatum, for example, French Prime Minister Clemenceau asserted it would succeed because "the Germans are a servile race" (Mantoux, 1992: 184). The only direct communication the Allies permitted the head of the German delegation was a brief speech after they handed him the treaty for study. Afterward, American President Wilson dismissed his remarks by explaining to his colleagues that "the Germans really are a stupid people. They always do the wrong thing. They have no understanding of human nature" (Riddell, 1986).

In recent decades psychologists at last began studying how these knowledge structures operate. They rediscovered Lippmann's observation that stereotypes are essential for processing information in a way that economizes on scarce cognitive resources. Stereotype activation varies across situations as goals and cognitive resources fluctuate (Kunda and Spencer, 2003). Through the representativeness heuristic, people use the closeness of fit between new information and stereotype to gauge the probability of future events or the likelihood of different hypotheses (Kahneman *et al.*, 1982). Employment of a given stereotype depends on its accessibility in long term memory. "Exposure to the name of a familiar social category increases the accessibility of the traits that are closely associated with its stereotype" (Kahneman, 2003). Enhanced availability increases the likelihood a stereotype will be used for predictions or formulating strategies. Chronically accessible stereotypes shape processing and behavior without conscious awareness. These get activated by environmental cues, driving even complex molar behavior in ways unknown by the individual (Bargh, Chen, and Burrows, 1996).

Experiments with two parties bargaining over multiple issues demonstrate that negotiators working to resolve unfamiliar issues with unfamiliar counterparts suffer from a "fixed pie bias" (Bazerman, Magliozzi, and Neale, 1985; Pinkley, Griffith, and Northcraft, 1995; Thompson, 1990). In these situations a bit of logrolling or creativity could yield Pareto superior solutions to the advantage of both parties. But they fail to recognize such opportunities. The deals they construct leave sources of value unclaimed by anyone. This bias stems from the absence of individuating information about priorities and beliefs of the other.

Lacking such knowledge, we may attempt to "put ourselves in the other person's shoes" — guessing at their interests, predicting their reactions. Negotiating texts often dispense this advice (e.g., Fisher and Ury, 1981: 22). But this "projection" has a pernicious effect in negotiation because our mental model of the other negotiator becomes just a crude version of ourselves. Because the counterpart in the model has identical priorities and beliefs, there will be no evident basis for "integration" (Follett, 1926). Fostering the impression that the negotiation will be essentially distributive, this model actually restrains information sharing (Bar Gill, 2006; Bottom and Paese, 1998; Larrick and Wu, 2007), favoring contentious tactics or simple compromises. The Central Intelligence Agency, having suffered intelligence failures for just this reason, admonishes its analysts to avoid this "mirror image thinking". For real perspective taking, one must suspend personal beliefs and value judgments to map the counterpart's mental model. This means "jumping in imagination into another person's skin, imagining what it might be like to look out at his world through his eyes, and imagining how you might feel about what you saw. It means being the other person, at least for a while, and postponing skeptical analysis until later" (White, 1984: 160).

Harsanyi (1962) early on conjectured that negotiators rely on rough categorizations such as "sex, age, social position, education, etc". to infer their counterpart's utility function. To "persons of a given description" we tend to attribute "a stereotype utility function". The time consuming dance of offers in a negotiation represents a mechanism for testing hypotheses about deviations from this stereotype representation. The process permits mutual adjustment of expectations. As the storehouse of knowledge about people and issues, stereotypes provide negotiators with a source of hypotheses about how the other's priorities or beliefs may differ. Hsee and Weber (1999), for example, found that cultural stereotypes led Chinese and Americans to anticipate — correctly — that representatives of the other culture had very different risk tolerance. In negotiation such differences present opportunities for integration through risk shifting mechanisms. Stereotypes here reversed the actual pattern of differences. Chinese subjects were far more risk tolerant than Americans. But both groups predicted the reverse.

Depending on the knowledge and expertise represented in stereotypes, the hypotheses of difference may vary widely in accuracy as well. But by merely suggesting possible integrative potential, stereotypes can push negotiators away from hardball tactics toward exploration of tradeoffs needed to expand the pie (Bottom and Paese, 1998). Expertise among sales personnel, diplomats, attorneys, and other professional negotiators develops richer, deeper, more accurate stereotypes about categories of counterparts and issues (Lurigio and Carroll, 1985).

Bias induced by stereotypes does have troubling distributive consequences. Employing confederate actors varying by gender and race, Ayres and Siegelman (1995) showed that car sellers bargained harder females or black buyers than white male buyers employing identical scripts. Seller stereotypes held that white males were more knowledgeable about vehicles so they would hold out for a lower price. Such expectations become self fulfilling locking in discriminatory practice over time. When targets of unflattering stereotypes recognize they will be judged in this biased manner, their behavior changes in a way that perpetuates the stereotype. Labeling this "stereotype threat", Steele (1997) showed that it undermined achievement test performance. Anxious subjects aware of the expectations have a difficult time performing effectively. This phenomenon extends to the often tense negotiation process.

Evidence indicates that women generally perceive themselves in a relational manner but men in an independent manner. Female negotiators see the process as more relational than men (Gelfand *et al.*, 2006). Kray, Thompson, and Galinsky (2001) informed some subjects that stereotypically masculine traits of rationality and assertiveness were more associated with bargaining success than stereotypically feminine characteristics of emotional expression and accommodation. Although gender was not mentioned, indirect activation of the stereotype led to self confirming behavior with men claiming greater value through negotiation.

But the precise impact of stereotype threat on negotiator actions may be complicated. When informed these characteristics of effectiveness varied by gender, females actually bargained harder, claiming more value. Overt salience of the stereotype motivated them to disconfirming behavior. When the experimenter contrarily linked effective negotiation skills with stereotypically feminine traits such as empathy then female negotiators became more effective than their male counterparts (Kray, Galinsky, and Thompson, 2002). Outside the controlled laboratory conditions, with more diverse populations, it is difficult to gauge when reactance is likely to arise. But the importance of stereotypes and stereotype threat in understanding negotiation is clear.

Given the complexities of the multi-national negotiation fiasco he was attempting to explain, Lippmann focused much of his analysis on national stereotypes. Recent research on this subject demonstrates obstacles to communication that variation in stereotypes by culture can pose to effective negotiation. Brett and Okumura (1998) found that individualists and collectivists have differing schemas with regard to self-interest, power, and information exchange that impede the process of creating joint gains across cultures. Negotiating barriers posed by cultural differences in mental models of negotiation have been widely explored. But these studies obscure factors that make cross-cultural negotiation potentially more fruitful. Vast differences that complicate communication also yield enhanced opportunities for integration. Cross national differences in risk tolerance identified by Hsee and Weber (1999) form the basis for creative deal making. But negotiation experiments impose artificial preferences and beliefs that eliminate underlying variability in pie sizes arising from different resources, beliefs, and risk attitudes. Trade theory emphasizes enhanced integrative potential across borders but leaves out communication barrier while negotiation research has done the reverse. A complete descriptive theory of negotiation must incorporate both.

Anchoring and Adjustment

Negotiating parties must decide on the basis of incomplete information. Uncertainty about the counterpart's reservation price leaves negotiators highly susceptible to a form of bias known as anchoring. In formulating judgments people tend to 'anchor' on a readily available starting point, adjusting the estimate in the direction of the preponderance of the other relevant information about the unknown value. The starting point may be an arbitrary stimulus, but once utilized as the anchor value, it exerts disproportionate pull on the judgment (Slovic and Lichtenstein, 1971; Kahneman 1992; Epley and Gilovich 2001). Other, more relevant information is underweighted.

The anchoring bias occurs naturally in situations with uncertainty and incomplete information (Kahneman, 1992). Even the obviously irrelevant number generated by spinning a roulette wheel can skew judgments (Kahneman *et al.*, 1982). The sequence of offers comprising a bargaining process readily induces anchoring. Each party may have done sufficient preparation to establish their own limit prior to initiating discussions. So they know how far they will concede before walking away. But they can only judge the other party's limit. The initial offer establishes a highly salient anchor for that judgment. By making an extreme first offer, one that is not expected to be accepted, a negotiator can take advantage of this bias to distort a counterpart's perceptions shifting offers onto more favorable terms (Bottom, 2003).

Northcraft and Neale (1987) asked real-estate professionals to examine properties and estimate appraised value, a reasonable price, and minimum acceptable offer. Listing-prices that were above and below the actual listing price for the property were presented to subjects across four conditions. Anchors biased the professionals' judgments in the predicted directions even though these experts had informed the researchers that this number was not something they would consider in judging the value of the property. Strack and Musseweiler (1997) showed that expertise did not moderate the anchoring effect. Nor did financial incentives for accurate predictions diminish this bias. Extreme or implausible values were as likely to contribute to the anchoring bias as more realistic ones. Nor did group discussion mitigate the bias (Whyte and Sebenius, 1997).

The first offer anchors and adjusts a counterpart's expectations thereby providing an advantage in distributive negotiations (Liebert, Smith, Hill and Keiffer, 1968; Galinsky and Mussweiler, 2001). Ritov (1996) found this distributive advantage extended to contexts with considerable integrative potential. But Galinsky and Mussweiler (2001) showed the distributive advantage of the anchor could be offset by perspective-taking and proper focus. When negotiators were asked to focus on information that was inconsistent with the counterpart's first offer, either the lower-bound of the counterpart or their own aspiration level, the anchoring effect diminished.

Overconfidence and Egocentrism

These biases would pose lesser problems for negotiators were it not for the general tendency toward overconfidence. Alpert and Raiffa (1982) pointed out the prevalence of this pattern when people attempt to formulate probability judgment. Studies of inexpert judges have demonstrated considerable across different cultures (Yates *et al.*, 1998). But experts too are prone to overconfidence when the space of possible events is complicated, the events have low base rates, and discriminability is weak (Koehler, Brenner, and Griffin, 2005).

Such judgments may characterize appraisal of relative bargaining skill, a counterpart's reservation value, a counterpart's priorities, and risk tolerance (Lim, 1993). It could reflect judgments about the views of potential third parties who intervene in a dispute (Neale and Bazerman, 1985). Jury verdicts and arbitrator judgment represent uncertain events that a negotiator must forecast to devise appropriate strategy (Bar Gill, 2006). Overconfidence often results in less compromising behavior. A generous offer from a counterpart in negotiating a legal claim may be turned down because of overconfidence in personal ability or the likelihood a jury will return a favorable verdict if trial continues. Reflecting supreme confidence in his ability to persuade jurors, Jan Schlictmann turned down sizable offers from W.R. Grace and Beatrice Foods to settle liability for cancer deaths in Massachusetts. The ruinous trial costs and eventual decisions disappointed his clients and bankrupted his firm (Harr, 1996).

Excessive confidence in judgment skewed by anchoring or the representativeness heuristic discourages deeper investigation needed to correct it. Why spend time asking more questions, probing answers more deeply, or conducting further analysis if one already has an accurate estimate? Neale and Bazerman (1985) predicted that overconfident negotiators would achieve less successful outcomes and higher rates of impasse (Neale and Bazerman, 1985). In a laboratory study of final-offer arbitration, half the subjects were informed that, "Negotiators routinely overestimate their likelihood of being awarded the contract in final-offer arbitration". Subjects who were informed of the negotiator's tendency to be overconfident had more successful outcomes as measured by impasse rates, dollar value for the contract, and perceived fairness of the contract terms than those who were not in this treatment condition correcting for overconfidence. These subjects also made more concessions than the overconfident.

This bias is conflated with the tendency to associate one's self interest with what is morally proper or likely to happen. Thompson and Loewenstein (1992) discovered that subjects in a simulated collective bargaining situation where the alternative to settlement was costly strike judged a fair wage to be higher if they had been assigned to the union than if they were assigned to management. Information provided to both groups was identical and assignment was random. Interests in the situation biased their perceptions of fairness. Extent of the disparity between perceptions predicted the number of days of mutually costly strike the parties endured before settling. Bias diminished efficiency of the settlements.

Loewenstein, Issacharoff, Camerer, and Babcock (1993) investigated this further using a civil suit over injuries sustained in a motorcycle accident. Most such cases get resolved prior to a verdict through defendant and plaintiff negotiations. Here randomly assigned self interest warped the subjects' predictions about how a judge would rule. Predictions made after the subjects learned whether they were plaintiff or defendant were biased toward a more favorable self outcome. When subjects knew role before reading the case they more often deadlocked requiring a judge's decision Selective information processing inflated optimistic overconfidence so that impasse can arose even though the parties were aware of all relevant facts.

Risky Decisions and Framing

As Lippmann pointed out negotiators must construct a mental model, or pseudo-environment, to represent their problem. Using this model they simulate different future possibilities based on the choices they make. This mental cost benefit analysis requires some scaling of value to discriminate whether one approach is likely to lead to more appealing circumstances than another. Rational choice theory assumes individuals construct complete veridical "small worlds" for decisions. They can do so because they have coherent preferences including consistent risk preferences over every conceivable eventuality. Behavioral studies have demonstrated fluidity in actual preferences and predictable context driven shifts in attitudes toward risk.

According to prospect theory (Kahneman and Tversky, 1979), we actually construct mental models using a reference point to evaluate attractiveness of different possibilities rather than overall wealth positions we might experience after a given decision. People tend to be risk-seeking over outcomes below the given reference point but risk averse over outcomes above it. Losses loom about 1.5 times larger than equivalent gains (Kahneman and Tversky, 1979; Tversky and Kahneman, 1981, 1991). Because they determine valuation these reference points greatly impact negotiator behavior and settlement. As with overconfidence, the precise impact depends on the source of risk confronted in the negotiation.

In the typical multi-issue negotiation experiment between dyads, the greatest risk is the possibility that the parties fail to reach an agreement, leaving both sides with their best alternative to negotiated agreement (e.g., Naquin, 2003; Pinkley, Griffith, and Northcraft, 1995). The safe course of action in these experiments is to make a concession. Concessions increase the likelihood the other party will accept the offer, locking in a guaranteed positive return on the negotiation. Of course concessions diminish the attractiveness of the agreement. But since there is always a positive bargaining zone in these experiments concession making is a risk minimizing strategy. Threatening impasse or standing firm on a given offer put capitalizing on that positive bargaining zone at risk in the interest of possibly enhancing the reward.

A number of researchers have investigated the impact of framing by manipulating the reference point negotiators use to evaluate possible outcomes associated with different agreements. By establishing a very high reference point, it is possible to make agreements appear to be about losses of different magnitudes rather than gains. Because they more willingly accept risk, such "loss framed" negotiators will resist making concessions in these negotiations. This increases the risk of an impasse but also means they claim more value in the actual settlements that are reached (Bazerman, Magliozzi, and Neale, 1985; Bottom and Studt, 1993; De Dreu *et al.*, 1994; Neale and Bazerman, 1985; Neale, Huber, and Northcraft, 1997).

Rudy Giuliani's political ascendancy provides a case study in loss frame induced risk taking. Then U.S. attorney, Giuliani prosecuted members of the Wall Street establishment on charges of insider trading including James Sherwin of GAF who was charged with manipulation of the stock of Union Carbide. After previous mistrials, Giuliani elected to try the case a third time. As the jury deliberated, Giuliani gave Sherwin another offer. If he would admit having engaged in the actions on behalf of GAF, then the company would pay a fine but Sherwin would face no jail or financial penalty. The GAF board agreed but Sherwin personally rejected this offer that would have limited so much personal risk. The size of the bet became apparent within the hour when the jury returned a guilty verdict resulting in a six month jail sentence and $20 million fine. Sherwin appealed the verdict in another bid for complete exoneration. Two years and many legal expense fees later, the conviction was reversed. Giuliani's successor declined to try the case a fourth time ending the brinksmanship between two savvy professionals negotiating to avoid a loss (Liman, 1998). Sherwin's losses were measurable in freedom, reputation, and financial penalty. It is difficult to imagine Giuliani trying the case three times had it not jeopardized acclaim he accrued for initially making the high profile arrest.

As with overconfidence the link between risk taking and concession making depends greatly on the nature of risk involved. Many complicated business directly determine the terms of exchange of inherently risky assets. Greater willingness to take risks, which may come from loss framing or overconfidence, actually contributes to concession making through eagerness to consummate deals. The spotty financial record of large scale mergers between publicly traded corporations reflects this pattern. Trading cash or even shares in the acquiring firm for control of the target firm, is an inherently high risk undertaking. Judgment bias contributes to excessive deal making rather than impasse.

Overconfidence in forecasts of potential synergies between the two firms is one source of bias that leads acquirers to make excessively generous concessions to the shareholders of the target (Hayward and Hambrick, 1997). The vast complexity involved in making such complicated forecasts insures error. Managers with an inflated sense of self efficacy seem particularly prone to optimistic estimates that they will find cost efficiencies and capitalize on complementarities in combined operations.

But another class of failed mergers reflects loss induced excesses in risk taking (Morck, Shleifer, and Vishny, 1990). The overly generous premium CEO Robert Allen authorized AT & T to pay to shareholders of NCR for control of that computer maker in 1993 has, for example, been tied to prior losses sustained by the firm in its own computing business (Lys and Vincent, 1995). Rather than acknowledge the failures of that strategy, and cutting its losses, Allen chose to increase the bet on computing even further in an attempt to make it work. Conceding the premium to overcome NCR management's resistance to the idea was the price required to take that risk. When the hoped for synergies proved elusive, Allen was forced out as CEO. Performance of AT & T deteriorated so greatly that it was eventually acquired by one of its previous subsidiaries, SBC.

Bottom (1998) replaced the guaranteed payoffs in Pruitt and Lewis's widely studied three issue negotiation task with chances to win a risky lottery. So pairs were negotiating over how many chances they would receive to win a lottery. Failure to reach an agreement locked in a small gain (or in the negative frame a moderate sized loss) that was in between the possible lottery outcomes in value. In this context over control of a risky asset, loss framing indeed led to greater concession making than gain framing. In their eagerness to gain exposure to the risk, which was the only way they could have an opportunity to experience no loss at all, the loss framed negotiators ceded value to their counterparts. Put differently, their reluctant gain framed counterparts had to be paid off with a risk premium in order to agree to the transaction.

These results provide clear evidence that negotiator framing, based on reference point shifts, has a highly significant highly predictable impact on risk taking, on the likelihood of a deal being struck, and on the distribution of expected value the parties can anticipate from these deals. But whether loss framing pushes negotiators to be more conciliatory or more contentious depends on the nature of the risks involved. Negotiations researchers must move beyond the deterministic payoffs found in the standard three issue task otherwise the knowledge we accumulate about judgment bias will not generalize to the most significant business and diplomatic negotiation contexts where risk is omnipresent.

Conclusion

This chapter has reviewed progress researchers have made in the study of error in negotiation. Originating in the troubled aftermath of the Paris Peace Conference of 1919, the behavioral paradigm is predicated on understanding error in order to prevent or correct it. Decades of behavioral research has clarified significant details about boundedly rational decision makers and their negotiating effectiveness. The theory that Walter Lippmann initially constructed (Lippmann, 1922) from his participant observation in a failed negotiation process has proven accurate and general. The necessity of stereotypes in the formation of mental models is now well understood. The blind spots and persistent bias introduced by overconfidence in these models often forestalls negotiated settlement or results in very inefficient or unstable agreements.

Because the origins of the behavioral paradigm, in particular its roots in negotiation failure, have been so poorly understood, it has been difficult to clearly gauge this progress or ascertain what remains to be accomplished. Lippmann sought the construction of an accurate model of the social system that teachers could use to "make the pupil acutely aware of how his mind works on unfamiliar facts" in order to "prepare them to deal with the world with a great deal of sophistication about their own minds" to "see vividly, as normally we should not, the enormous mischief and casual cruelty of our prejudices" (1922: p. 256). By means of such an education, decision makers and negotiators would learn to take a more disciplined and scientific, a less biased, approach to solving complex problems.

The advent of decision (Howard and Matheson, 1982) and negotiation analysis (Sebenius, 1992), methodologies squarely based on social science, represents a partial step toward harnessing research to fulfill the behavioral agenda. These techniques, now widely taught at leading schools of business and government (Thompson, 2006), provide some of the necessary training negotiators need to understand and cope with bias. Certain descriptive studies of individual and negotiator bias have yielded effective technique for eliminating specific forms of bias (e.g., Babcock, Loewenstein, and Issacharoff, 1997; Galinsky and Mussweiler, 2001; Heath, Larrick, and Klayman, 1998; Jolls and Sunstein, 2005; Paese and Yonker, 1993). Thaler and Sunstein (2008) provide a useful overarching framework, "libertarian paternalism", for devising interventions at a system wide level. Yet Lippmann's larger goal of properly modeling the social system remains incomplete. Further research progress must move beyond cataloguing specific kinds of errors toward sound theory on the interrelation of these errors in different contexts.

Development of a multi-level, interdisciplinary theory must couple an accurate psychological model of the individual negotiator to a social model of the negotiation process and an institutional model of the wider system within which the negotiations take place. Walton and McKersie (1965) illustrated the kind of theory that is possible but based it on the subjective expected utility theory of choice. Research summarized in this chapter has shown that to be a flawed psychological model of negotiator decision making. Fortunately the general framework for the psychological model of the negotiator is now reasonably well understood with growing consensus across disciplines.

Game theorists are beginning to appreciate the sometimes sizeable gaps between the "psychological game" (Rabin, 1993) actors believe they are playing and the actual contingencies they confront. Psychological game is merely another expression for what Lippmann originally called the pseudo-environment and psychologists now call mental models. Fryer and Jackson (2008) developed formal theory of stereotype formation, showing how these generate particular cognitive biases. Compte and Postlewaite (2004) invoked "stereotype threat" to prove biased expectations about a game can be sustained in equilibria. Benabou and Tirole's (2010) theory explained "how pride, dignity or wishful thinking about one's options ('keeping hope') lead individuals or groups to walk away from 'reasonable' offers, try to shift blame for failure onto others, or take refuge in political utopias — leading to impasses and conflicts". Belatedly adopting Lippmann's behavioral formulation, abandoning the overly simplified "economic man of the classical economists", these theorists have begun to recognize that "the study of error" can be "a stimulating introduction to the study of truth" (Lippmann, 1922: 256). As we at last come to consensus about how a promising negotiation process can spiral into a "peace to end all peace" we may yet figure out how to prevent it from happening in the first place.

The Role of Gender in Negotiation

E. Layne Paddock
Singapore Management University

Laura J. Kray
University of California, Berkeley

The Role of Gender in Negotiation

Seemingly every few months a major media source highlights the salary differential between men and women, a difference apparent in nations around the world. Just recently Bernard (2010) wrote about this gender pay gap, pointing out that women in the United States earn 77 cents for every dollar earned by men. She highlighted the multiple explanations frequently used to explain this gap (e.g., women's time away from the workforce for childcare and resulting lesser experience than men, men's employment in higher paying industries than women) and that these explanations together do not fully explain why women earn less than men. She also, however, included a reason less frequently cited in the popular press until recently, but which is recognized in research as an important explanation of the gender pay gap: how gender impacts compensation negotiations. Compensation negotiations are similar in many ways to other types of negotiations. Thus, it is not surprising that our understanding of gender in compensation negotiations is informed by research relating gender to the negotiation process more broadly.

Systematic research focusing on gender's role in the negotiation process has grown, especially over the last decade, and evidence has accumulated to illustrate the nuanced ways gender impacts negotiations (Kray, 2007; Kray, Galinsky and Thompson, 2002; Kray and Thompson, 2005; Kray, Thompson and Galinsky, 2001). In this chapter we address *how* gender is conceptualized, *why* gender impacts negotiations, and *when* gender is likely to have a stronger impact on the negotiation process. Understanding these factors should help negotiators achieve stronger negotiation outcomes, for women and men alike.

Defining gender

We define gender in a manner consistent with negotiation research. Specifically, a distinction exists between *sex*, which biologically categorizes males and females, and *gender*, which includes both cultural and psychological markers of sex. Negotiation research typically gathers data by sex (indicating negotiators as male or female), and even two decades ago this was the most frequently tested individual difference in negotiation research (Walters, Stuhlmacher and Meyer, 1998). Even when measuring sex, however, research typically explains findings using a theoretical rationale that focuses on gender. For example men and women's actions are explained by prescriptive stereotypes dictating how they should act. As a result of this focus on gendered explanations, researchers suggest the term *gender* rather than *sex* be used in negotiation and gender research (Kray and Babcock, 2006). We use the term gender in this chapter.

As will become evident, this term makes sense given a second distinction related to gender — the idea of *gender roles* (e.g., Bem, 1974). To understand gender roles ask yourself how much you identify with each of the following traits: Do you consider yourself "analytical", "competitive", "dominant", or someone who "has leadership abilities"? Now, consider the following traits: Do you consider yourself "sensitive to the needs of others", "warm", "compassionate", or "gentle"? Quickly you can assess whether the first versus second set of traits better reflects you, and this should give you an idea of your own gender identity. These questions measure the extent to which you are masculine (high on the first set of items), feminine (high on the second set of items), or androgynous (high on both).

The idea of gender roles is important for understanding gender in negotiation for two reasons. First, gender roles highlight an important point about making comparisons among groups based on individual differences such as gender (men or women): Sometimes a man is more different from other men than he is from women, and the same is true for some women. Just think about the men you know; do they differ from each other in terms of gender roles? In your mind identify a woman who differs a lot from others of the same gender; maybe it is you. Because she violates aspects of the traditional feminine gender role this woman may upset a negotiation counterpart who is expecting that she will behave "like a woman should act". This is because gender roles typify what is expected of men and women. As will become evident in the following sections, these expectations, and associated perceptions and behaviors, play an important role at the negotiation table.

Do gender differences exist at the bargaining table?

Nearly four decades ago in 1975, in the first textbook on negotiation, authors Rubin and Brown included a section about women's versus men's performance; they argued that men and women held different foci at the bargaining table. Men's focus on maximizing their own earnings meant that they either competed or cooperated, depending on the situation. Women, on the other hand, held an interpersonal orientation and focused on relationships. These claims — for gender differences at the bargaining table — stood without much empirical evidence for decades. In fact, with few exceptions, contemporary negotiation textbooks continue to overlook the role of gender in negotiation. Possible explanations for this omission range from an apparent belief that gender accounts for little variance in negotiation outcomes (a view espoused by texts emphasizing cognitive biases driving negotiation outcomes; e.g., Bazerman and Neale, 1992) to a lack of definitive answers about gender's role at the bargaining table. However, given the surge of scholarly interest in this topic over the last 15 years, a body of research now explains gender's role in negotiation clearly and convincingly.

One particularly important empirical advance is the recognition that both gender and context must be considered (Kray *et al.*, 2002; Kray and Thompson, 2005; Kray *et al.*, 2001; Stuhlmacher and Walters, 1999; Walters *et al.*, 1998). Prior to this acknowledgment, the majority of research focused on gender in isolation and across contexts. This initial work left many vital questions unanswered because of discrepant findings across studies. Some individual papers show no gender differences at the bargaining table and others show significant gender differences. Helpful in summarizing these seemingly discrepant empirical findings are meta-analyses, which statistically combine disparate research findings across studies. Meta-analyses suggest the answer to our original question of whether gender differences exist is yes — men and women do show two reliable gender differences related to negotiations. First, men's behavior on average is more competitive than is women's behavior (Walters *et al.*, 1998). Second, men's economic negotiation outcomes are typically better than are women's economic outcomes (Stuhlmacher and Walters, 1999). Notably, however, these two gender differences are statistically small in size, meaning the simple effect of gender on negotiation outcomes does not help us explain much of the variance in negotiation outcomes.

At first blush, the small effects reported in these meta-analyses suggest gender's role in negotiation is unimportant. However, this is an incorrect conclusion for three main reasons. First, gender effects remain important because even small gender differences are likely to compound over time (Kray, 2007). Martell, Lane and Emrich's (1996) computer simulation of the impact of gender bias illustrates this point. Starting with a group of equal numbers of men and women, they introduced a 5% gender bias (against women) in evaluations. After multiple rounds of promotions, women accounted for only 29% of the top-level positions. So, what if the gender bias was less? Even introducing a 1% bias in evaluations resulted in women holding only 35% of the top-level positions. Likewise, negotiators facing a real-world salary negotiation showed that relatively minor gender differences in initiating a negotiation at the beginning of an individual's career can result in substantial lost income over a lifetime, as a lower starting salary results in a smaller base on which interest can grow and subsequent raises and bonuses are based, meaning income differences compound over time (Babcock and Lashever, 2003). Clearly even small gender effects, when aggregated over time, can have dramatic and detrimental effects. In negotiations, these negative effects are most often reflected in women's poorer economic outcomes (Stuhlmacher and Walters, 1999).

Focusing solely only on economic outcomes, however, is limiting and likely fails to capture the actual range of gender effects in negotiations. This results in the second reason it is unwise to ignore gender effects: we have not yet studied this topic completely. Whereas research on this topic is no longer in its infancy, it remains in its "adolescence". It made sense for earlier meta-analyses to focus on economic gain (whether in points or money) because it was and still remains the most commonly assessed negotiation outcome (Kray and Babcock, 2006). However, more subjective negotiation outcomes may better represent women's negotiation performance. Further, recent research focusing on subjective negotiation outcomes suggests this broader set of outcomes not only matter but may be better predictors of long-term negotiation satisfaction (Subjective Value Inventory, Curhan, Elfenbein and Xu, 2010). Understanding gender as it relates to economic *and subjective* outcomes would better represent the actual range of gender effects.

Third, considering gender in isolation is different than considering the effects of gender in combination with other variables considered at the same time (e.g., gender and status). We now know that, by collapsing across situational factors, we underestimate the impact of gender in negotiations. In certain situations gender plays a large role, whereas in other situations gender does not matter as much or at all. Understanding why gender differences exist will help us to identify when gender effects will be more or less pronounced. Thus, we now turn to the question of why gender matters.

Why do gender differences exist?

Explanations for why gender differences (or similarities) exist in negotiations differ, depending on which of multiple approaches researchers take; researchers have focused on the negotiation context, the negotiator, the counterpart, and specific interactions between these variables (Kray and Thompson, 2005). Related to each of these approaches, expectations of men and women help explain gender differences in negotiation.

Expectations are associated with individuals' status and power. As Ridgeway (2001) explains, status is a sign of greater social significance and general competence. Status is defined by the extent to which an individual is respected by others (e.g., Magee and Galinsky, 2008). Status is distinct from power, which is an individual's control of resources and often conferred by the roles an individual holds, including societal and organizational roles. However, often the terms are used interchangeably. When men and women have equal power in negotiations (e.g., their alternatives to the potential negotiated agreement are equal), they are equally effective at leveraging their negotiation power (Kray, Reb, Galinsky and Thompson, 2004). Men and women typically differ in their status and power both generally and within negotiations specifically. In general status differs based on gender, with individuals associating greater trait competence with men than women (Ridgeway, 2001). Likewise, within negotiations traits typically associated with men and not with women are related to being a competent negotiator. In fact, Kray (2007) referred to the traits typically associated with each gender — gender stereotypes — as the "linchpin connecting gender to negotiating effectiveness".

What exactly are gender stereotypes then? Gender stereotypes reflect the gender roles we outlined earlier. Men are rational, assertive, and highly protective of their own interests (Williams and Best, 1982). In contrast, women are passive, emotional, and accommodating of others' needs. It takes little to activate gender stereotypes. For example, stereotype threat studies of math ability show it takes as little as being presented with a "gender" checkbox prior to a difficult exam to create performance decrements for individuals threatened by a stereotype (Brown and Josephs, 1999). Research suggests group contexts where women are sole members of minority groups promote stereotype threat (e.g., Roberson, Deitch, Brief and Block, 2003). Imagine then what women of *Fortune* 500 boards feel, given women's under-representation on such boards (Catalyst, 2009). Of course, the minority status of women on Fortune 500 boards is not unique; women worldwide are under-represented within upper-management. Further, gender stereotypes are consistent across nations (Williams and Best, 1982).

Stereotypic traits associated with men are also associated with being an effective negotiator. As authors Kolb and Williams (2000, p. 28–29) note, "the effective negotiator… turns out to look remarkably like a man: independent, self-confident, active, objective, and unruffled by pressure. Thus, men are often perceived as better negotiators than women". As Kray and Thompson (2005) summarize, attributes associated with being an effective negotiator include "strong", "dominant", "assertive", and "rational" — all attributes associated with males. In contrast, attributes associated with being a weak negotiator include "weak", "submissive", "accommodating", and "emotional" — all attributes associated with females. More recent research focuses on additional traits associated with women and which are also disadvantageous in negotiations. For example, Kray (2010) focused on the gullibility component of the female stereotype, which suggests that women are more gullible or naïve than men (Bem, 1974; Prentice and Carranza, 2002). Presuming women are more gullible, deceiving women should be easier and thus more frequently attempted. Consistent with this hypothesis, in a buyer-seller real estate negotiation, women sellers were deceived more than were male sellers. This research makes clear that multiple aspects of gender stereotypes impact how negotiators are treated.

Given that negotiation is a task in which masculine stereotypes are positively associated, gender stereotypes easily become activated when individuals negotiate (Miles and Clenney, 2010). That being said, regardless of their level of cognitive accessibility, gender stereotypes have more of an impact in some situations than in others. Researchers have identified that contextual cues are important because they distinguish between strong and weak situations (Mischel, 1977). In strong situations, individual difference variables like gender play less of a role. In contrast, in weak situations gender plays a larger role. For example, when negotiation issues are unclearly defined, a weak situation exists and gender impacts the negotiation more, meaning gender effects should be larger. In contrast, if negotiation issues are clearly defined, a strong situation exists and gender should play less of a role, meaning gender effects are smaller. This idea of weak and strong situations was tested in the research of Bowles and colleagues (Bowles, Babcock and McGinn, 2005). They had career service professionals rate 13 industries in which 525 MBA students took jobs as either high- or low-ambiguity negotiation situations. In low-ambiguity situations (i.e., strong situations), MBA students were able to find specific information about salaries, so they better knew what salary to negotiate. In high-ambiguity industries (i.e., weak situations), MBA students were unsure of what salary to request. Results show no gender differences in the low-ambiguity context; when students knew how much to ask, men and women obtained similar salary amounts. However, in high-ambiguity situations women accepted salaries 10% lower than those taken by men. When the context was weak (ambiguous), gender played a larger role in negotiators' economic outcomes.

In weak contexts, gender stereotypes especially impact nego-tiations if the stereotypes are more salient. Stereotypes are more salient when negotiators carry gendered associations (e.g., the sex role stereotypes we discussed earlier) or if the context is gendered (Bowles and McGinn, 2008). The context can be oriented such that it is masculine, feminine or androgenous. Organization con-texts such as upper-level management are often male-dominated and masculine, which is related to the often-documented male advantage in negotiations (Kray and Thompson, 2005). Ayres and Siegelman (1995) provide an example of this within the male-associated context of car dealerships. They had women and men actors follow the same script to inquire about purchasing a car. Price quotes received by women were significantly higher than those received by men, a pattern of gender discrimination by car salespeople that placed women at a disadvantage for negotiating a car. Now consider negotiations related to traditionally female-stereotyped roles such as negotiating for aspects of the home domain (e.g., for childcare). Stuhlmacher and Walters (1999) sug-gested in such tasks male negotiators may not have an advantage, and empirical research supports this, showing no gender differ-ences in negotiations of childcare (Miles and LaSalle, 2008). That the task occurs in a female-stereotyped role may be enough to justify men's — and women's — competence in related negotia-tions (Miles and Clenney, 2010). Finally, in specific situations there may be no predetermined gender expectation. For example, a recent study of lawyers suggests women negotiators are viewed similarly to their male counterparts; it may be that, at least when lawyers participate in negotiations, the role of lawyer supersedes gender roles (Schneider, Tinsley, Cheldelin and Amanatullah, 2010). Even these authors are careful to note, however, that this effect may not generalize from specific legal case negotiations to more general aspects of being a female lawyer.

More often than not, women are viewed as less competent negotiators than men. Aware of the stereotype and the associated disadvantage, women negotiators may experience *stereotype threat* (Steele, 1997), which refers to the concern individuals feel when faced with a situation that may confirm a negative stereo-type about a group to which they belong. Kray, Thompson, and Galinsky's (2001) study shows the impact of stereotype threat in buyer-seller negotiations. One group of negotiators was told the task was indicative of their actual negotiation ability, a focus predicted to introduce doubt (stereotype threat) for women. The second group was told the negotiation was an exercise designed to introduce core negotiation concepts and to promote learning (no stereotype threat). Experiencing stereotype threat, women in the first group did worse than men. In contrast, women's performance in the second group did not differ from men's. The content of the stereotype also matters (Kray *et al.*, 2002). Whereas in less carefully controlled environments, including the real world, stereotypically female traits are generally linked to poor negotiation performance, multiple traits considered to be important in negotiation success are feminine in nature. Thus, it is possible to emphasize that either feminine traits or masculine traits lead to poorer negotiation performance, especially in more controlled situations. Kray and colleagues did just this and found that, when the link between stereotypically feminine traits and good negotiation performance were emphasized, women outperformed men.

Given that people typically link stereotypically masculine traits to negotiation success (Kray *et al.*, 2001), in the real world stereotype threat often results in women's lower negotiation performance. In part this is because stereotype threat can reduce individuals' goals (Kray *et al.*, 2002). In negotiations, men tend to set higher goals than women. For example, Bowles and colleagues (2005) found that male buyers set goals that were 9.8% higher than women's. Setting high goals in negotiation is very important because goals mediate the relationship between stereotype activation and performance. Activated stereotypes hurt women's negotiation performance by lowering the goals set by women (Kray *et al.*, 2002). Lower goals often translate into lower performance. For example, in a study of compensation men set goals 5% higher than women set them, despite understanding the negotiation situation equally (Stevens, Bavetta and Gist, 1993). By the end of the negotiation, men outperformed women. Notably, negotiators focused on a high goal make higher first offers and achieve better outcomes (Galinsky and Mussweiler, 2001; Galinsky, Mussweiler and Medvec, 2002).

Facing stereotype threat, can female negotiators overcome the associated negative outcomes? Yes, and they can do so by working to disprove the stereotype. We know that people psychologically react when they perceive a threat to their behavioral freedoms, often pushing against the perceived barrier (Brehm, 1966). Faced with the negative implications of a stereotype, people show *stereotype reactance*. Within negotiations women show stereotype reactance when reminded explicitly of stereotypes (Kray, Thompson and Galinsky, 2001). Negotiators reminded only of factors associated with performance in negotiations, such as being "relational and assertive" and demonstrating "a regard for [one's] own interests throughout the negotiation, rather than being emotional, passive, and overly accommodating", showed signs of stereotype threat; women underperformed when compared to men. In contrast, negotiators reminded of all of this and of gender stereotypes (that personality differs between genders and that "male and female students have been shown to differ in their negotiation performance") showed signs of stereotype reactance; women outperformed the men. In fact, just being reminded of sexist remarks endorsing gender stereotypes by a university authority figure — remarks not specific to negotiation — are enough to encourage stereotype reactance at the bargaining table (Kray, Locke and Haselhahn, 2010). So, what explains women's better performance in the stereotype reactance group? At least two factors do: setting higher first offers and expectations for performance at the bargaining table (Kray *et al.*, 2010). First offers are important because they anchor the negotiation (Galinsky and Mussweiler, 2001). When women are exposed to the blatant endorsement of gender stereotypes, they tend to give more assertive first offers. These assertive first offers provided an advantage through the entire negotiation process. Women faced with stereotypic remarks also set higher expectations for themselves than men did, and the women's higher expectations became self-fulfilling.

Of course, negotiators do not act individually, and we know that expectations shape *both* the behavior of the expectancy holder and his or her interaction partner (Snyder and Swann, 1978). The implication is that negotiators and their negotiation counterparts enter negotiations with expectations. Consider an example of the resulting dynamics: faced with a female negotiator, a male negotiator may expect weakness consistent with a feminine stereotype. Based on this expectation, the counterpart treats the female negotiator in a condescending manner. Perceiving this condescending manner she may find it hard to concentrate on the negotiation, resulting in her inability to fully understand all of the issues within the negotiation and how they might be optimally packaged in an integrative agreement. Clearly, expectations matter to the negotiator and negotiation counterpart.

The role of expectations in counterpart's reactions is especially apparent when negotiators deviate from expectations. Returning to the above example, what would happen if the female negotiator made an assertive first offer that was incongruent with what the negotiation counterpart expected of a female negotiator? Research indicates he likely would dislike her. Counterparts' negative responses to behaving in a counter-stereotypic fashion can take the form of social and economic reprisals — termed a *backlash effect* (Rudman, 1998). This backlash effect is apparent in organizations broadly. For example, women who are more successful at stereotypically male tasks are more personally derogated than men, which then impacts resource allocation at work (Heilman, Wallen, Fuchs and Tamkins, 2004). Likewise, research shows men who violate gender norms are viewed as more ineffectual and given less respect than women (Heilman and Wallen, 2010). Backlash is also apparent in negotiations. In compensation negotiations dominance is required. Dominant behavior is associated with men and directly contradicts the warmth or friendliness expected from women, and thus more backlash is experienced by women who initiated compensation negotiations than men (Bowles, Babcock and Lai, 2007). Further, when the gender of the person penalizing is included, men only penalized women negotiators and women penalized both men and women for initiating compensation negotiations. This is consistent with evidence showing higher-status individuals (men) penalize other higher-status individuals (men) less than lower-status individuals (women) penalize them (Bowles and Gelfand, 2010).

These findings suggest that it is not always good advice for women to act like men. Acting both masculine (competent) and feminine (nice) simultaneously may help mitigate backlash in contexts that do not include issues of dominance; however, it does not seem to work within negotiations, which inherently require dominance (Bowles *et al.*, 2007). There are, however, ways women may escape backlash. Women can hold a socially validated high-status role with clear role expectations. They can also communicate concerns in a gender-role consistent way.

Recall that evidence suggests female lawyers do not experience backlash when negotiating (Schneider *et al.*, 2010). Their externally-conferred, high-status position of lawyer may mean female lawyers' negotiation behavior is not seen as challenging existing status ranks; they already have high status granted to them by others. There are also clear normative behaviors expected of these women based on their occupational role. Finally, advocating on behalf of another person is consistent with gender stereotypes that dictate women show a high concern for others. In effect, it may be that their occupational expectations promote assertiveness in negotiations.

Additionally, women may lessen or avoid backlash by communicating their concerns in a way that is feminine (i.e., focused on the collective) rather than masculine (i.e., focused on self-interest). Evidence shows that women request more salary in response to a hypothetical compensation negotiation when requesting for another person than for themselves (Wade, 2001). What is the reason for this difference? Amanatullah and Morris

(2010) suggest negotiators' foci relate to the backlash they anticipate and their research results support this assertion. When women negotiate for themselves, they anticipate backlash and lower their level of assertiveness, using fewer competing tactics. When women advocate for another, women do not expect backlash and do not alter their assertive behavior, resulting in better outcomes. Thus, it is possible one way women may lessen or avoid backlash in negotiations is to behave in ways that are both competent and focused on others. However, given that only minimal research exists showing this solution, future research is needed to confirm the effectiveness of this strategy.

How can gender effects be reduced?

In concluding, we suggest several strategies to mitigate gender effects in negotiation. These include negotiators making sure they ask for what they want, taking care to avoid self-handicapping behaviors, and reacting to negative and focusing on positive stereotype elements with negotiations.

Do not avoid negotiating in the first place: Ask for what you want. Negatively stereotyped individuals, such as women, may avoid participating in negotiations. Whereas some studies show no differences between women and men in willingness to negotiate salary increases, at least some evidence suggests women ask less often. Think about what you would do: you perform work for money and expect you will be paid $10. Then you are told "Here's $3. Is $3 OK?" Now, think about a slightly different situation. You do the same work for money and expect you will be paid $3, you are paid $3, and then also asked "Here's $3. Is $3 OK?" Small and colleagues (Small, Gelfand, Babcock and Gettman, 2007) did exactly this and found that in the former situation while most people accept the $3, males were more likely than females to request more money. These results changed depending on how the situation was described. When this exchange was framed as "negotiating for more money", even more males asked for more money; however, when the exchange was framed as "asking for more money", the gender difference disappeared. Apparently, gender connotations are particularly strong for the task of negotiating. This research may help explain the consistent finding that men receive higher starting salaries and career advancement than women (Bowles and McGinn, 2008): regardless of the way the situation is framed, they ask. Interestingly, within compensation negotiations it may be women ask, but often ask for different things: women are more likely to ask for job components including work and travel schedules, notably factors that relate more closely than some other job components to household responsibilities (Bohnet and Greig, 2007). These different forms of compensation relate to others, thus following the explanation given earlier that women may be willing to ask for these forms because they anticipate less backlash.

In fact, across situations both men and women need to ask for what they want. A woman who finds it difficult to ask might consider altering her perspective and advocating for others — family, friends, clients, a work team, or other women overall — rather than herself. As Bowles states, "When a woman negotiates persuasively for higher compensation, she clears the path for other women to follow" (Bernard, 2010). Men are already asking, even when the situation is framed as a negotiation. Nonetheless, women and men should remember, for both themselves and others, to ask.

Do not self-handicap: Work at it. When stereotypes are activated in a situation, especially a salient situation in which an individual desires to avoid critical evaluation, it may lead an individual to self-handicap. Rather than try but have poor results, negatively stereotyped individuals may put forth little effort, providing themselves with a more palatable explanation for their poor performance (Keller, 2002). It is easy to see how someone who puts forth little effort in preparing for and carrying out a negotiation does poorly. Preparation is one critical aspect of negotiation. The ongoing development of alternatives provides negotiators with a stronger best alternative to a negotiated agreement (i.e., BATNA). Generation of alternatives may help in part because they allow women to feel less dependent on the other party and thus increasing their willingness to walk away from the table (Kray, 2007). Kray *et al.* (2004) showed that men and women with strong BATNAs were equally effective at leveraging them at the bargaining table.

Once an individual has entered into a negotiation, she should avoid falling into the trap of self-handicapping. By directing her efforts towards careful preparation and ongoing generation of alternatives, she will at best achieve high negotiation outcomes and at worst gain practice, which will make her a better negotiator.

Be aware of stereotypes: React to the negative and focus on the positive. As we have discussed, stereotypes are pervasive and impact negotiations. Understanding that gender stereotypes impact negotiations and the ideas of stereotype threat and reactance are first steps to mitigating the impact of negative gender stereotypes on negotiators.

Consistent with negotiations research, we have focused in this chapter on the negative ramifications of gender stereotypes for women and suggested individuals be aware of negative stereotypes and react to them when negotiating. While not faced with the negative stereotypes women are faced with, men negotiators too should be aware of the potentially negative consequences of their gendered behavior at the bargaining table. This point is highlighted by recent research on ethical judgments (Kray, Haselhuhn and Schweitzer, 2010). Women's greater concern with their counterparts may mean women are less biased by their own goals than are men. In contrast, men's greater pragmatism, evidenced by more egocentrism and instrumentalism, results in more leniency in judging ethically ambiguous actions than are women. Thus, both women and men should be aware of gender within negotiations.

Further, emphasizing the positive aspects of gender stereotypes may help women at the bargaining table. For example, women are associated with being both passive and empathetic. While being passive often has negative connotations, being empathetic does not. Emphasizing the positive — in this case women's empathy — results in more assertive goals and higher expectations and ultimately higher performance at the bargaining table. For example, recall when Kray *et al.* (2002) emphasized positive stereotype aspects, women outperformed men in a negotiation task. Further, they did so despite the fact that the task was framed as diagnostic of negotiators' core abilities, which is typically a trigger of stereotype threat. Focusing on the positive aspects of gender stereotypes helps to build confidence, and thus improving performance, for men and women alike.

Summary

Gender does impact negotiation, with women often at a disadvantage at the negotiation table relative to men. However, this difference is not set in stone; instead it is situation-specific. While discussion of gender differences extends back to the first negotiation text, systematic research on gender and negotiation is rather segmented. Whereas much of early research focuses on the focal negotiator, in the past decade research theoretically grounded in stereotypes has helped to integrate the focal negotiator with other perspectives (including the negotiation counterpart and situation). This research offers suggestions for individuals entering into important negotiations; careful consideration of these should help mitigate gender differences within negotiation.

Physiology in Negotiations

Smrithi Prasad
National University of Singapore Business School

Jayanth Narayanan
National University of Singapore Business School

Introduction

Negotiation is a process where two or more parties come together to either create something that neither party can by itself, or to resolve a dispute about the existing terms of engagement (Lewicki, Saunders, Minton and Barry, 2003). Negotiations can be studied with a variety of approaches within the social sciences, ranging from economics and psychology to political science and law. In this chapter, we investigate how physiological processes affect negotiation processes and outcomes.

Negotiations are mixed-motive interaction situations that involve a trade-off between co-operation and competition. Morton Deutsch proposed that the fundamental problem in such interpersonal situations is to resolve this co-operation/competition dilemma (Deutsch, 1949). During a negotiation, a negotiator faces two competing objectives: a) to create value overall, and b) to claim a portion of the value that has been created (Lax and Sebenius, 1986). The tactics used to create value, such as open information sharing, are based on co-operation and trust, and may undermine the negotiator's objective to claim value for oneself. In a similar vein, the tactics used to claim value, such as withholding information and using hardball tactics, undermine

247

the negotiator's objective to create value for both parties. This situation has been termed "the negotiator's dilemma". In this chapter, we use this framework to examine how physiological factors may affect these two fundamental motives.

Although there has been little research on the impact of physiological factors on negotiations, studies in allied disciplines such as psychology and economics have examined how biology affects behaviors that are related to co-operation and competition. In the next section, we provide an introduction to the physiological factors that are relevant. We then examine how physiological factors might impact the two fundamental motives of competition and co-operation. We conclude by suggesting that the negotiator's dilemma may be a result of the competing levels of activation of these biological systems.

Physiology Primer

The human body is a remarkably complex machine that has evolved over millions of years. Science has generated a remarkable amount of insight into our physiological functioning. However, the effect of our physiology on our social behavior is only being investigated now, and some recent studies have shown how our physiology can alter our social behaviors. For example, our propensity to trust can be altered by administering a nasal spray that contains oxytocin or a shot of testosterone, which alters whether we accept or reject an unfair offer. While our physiology is complex and can be studied at a number of levels, two primary drivers have been investigated from the standpoint of social behavior — changes in brain activity and changes in hormonal activity. The study of the brain is called *neuroscience* and the study of *hormones* is called *endocrinology*.[1]

---

[1] We provide an overview of some of the physiological terms in this section. A complete overview is outside the scope of our discussion and we refer the reader to very accessible introductions (see Camerer, Loewenstein and Prele (2005) for review of neuroscience and see Taylor, Klein, Lewis, Gruenewald, Gurung and Updegraff (2000) for review of endocrinology).

The brain is the centre of all information processing, including the processing of social information from the environment. The way the brain perceives and processes this information affects the social behaviors that are manifested. Several recent developments in the domain of neuroscience have enabled this research to flourish. Firstly, since behaviors can be localized to specific parts of the brain, we can map the role of this circuitry to social behaviors. For example, the *amygdala*, a pea-shaped part of the brain, is associated with the processing of emotional stimuli. Secondly, neuro-scientific methods, such as *functional magnetic resonance imaging* (fMRI) and *positron emission tomography* (PET), have enabled us to locate and study the role of different parts of the brain in social behaviors.

Hormones are chemicals produced by glands or tissues and are released into the blood stream (Zyphur, Narayanan, Koh and Koh, 2009). They initiate a chain reaction within the body and alter several physiological functions. For example, *epinephrine* changes the digestive, cardio and muscular processes within the body. Like the brain, hormones, drive biological processes, albeit in a more controlled manner (Brown, 1994). The hormones that are potentially relevant when studying negotiations are *cortisol* (produced in response to threatening or stressful situations), *oxytocin* (associated with trust and also known as the 'love hormone') and *testosterone* (male-centric hormone associated with social status and power).

Hormones can be measured in different ways. The *baseline measure* is the amount of a hormone that is present when we are at rest. This baseline measure is used to assess the degree of *reactivity* (change in hormonal levels) of the hormone in response to environmental stimuli. The changes in hormonal levels from the baseline in the presence of environmental changes is also measured and studied. The higher the baseline measures of a hormone, the greater the *reactivity* of that hormone and the greater the change in hormonal levels. In addition to these measures, other proxy measures of hormonal levels also exist. For example, the level of testosterone can be measured by the ratio of the 2nd digit (index finger) to the 4th digit (ring finger). This ratio (2D:4D ratio) is a measure of prenatal exposure to testosterone. Although only a few studies have shown a relationship between prenatal testosterone and adult testosterone, the digit ratio still predicts outcomes, such as sexual orientation, spatial ability, status, physical prowess and aggressive behaviors (Putz, Gaulin, Sporter and Burney, 2004; Bailey and Hurd, 2005; Bergh and Dewitte, 2006).

Competition

Individuals involved in negotiations are more likely to have a competitive, instead of a cooperative, mindset. Most people approach negotiations as though they were dividing a fixed pie. This "fixed-pie perception" is the main reason why a negotiation is seen as a contentious process. This mindset typifies the competitive motive that negotiators bring to the table. Negotiators with a competitive mindset want to know how they can maximize their share of the resources being bargained for. This mindset is stressful, and stressful stimuli from the environment may impel the negotiator to adopt a "fight" or a "flight" stance towards the situation (Cannon, 1932).

These responses are a result of our evolutionary conditioning. Human physiology is not designed to solve modern problems, but is instead adapted to the situations that our hunter-gatherer ancestors faced more than 10,000 years ago (see Tooby and Cosmides, 1992). For example, when a hunter-gather encountered a snake, the result should have been either a flight reaction, because snakebites were a common cause of death, or a fight reaction, in terms of an attempt to kill the snake. Although these negotiations are not as stressful as encountering a snake, our evolutionary conditioning behooves us to treat any threat or stress presented by the environment with a "fight or flight" response.

The flight or fight response is governed by a complex set of physiological processes. The presence of threatening stimuli in the environment activates the *limbic system*. This system consists primarily of the *amygdala*, a pea-shaped structure involved in emotional processing, and the *hippocampus*, the memory center of the brain. Threats also activate the *cortisol* hormone. The rush of cortisol into the bloodstream leads to a cardiovascular response, resulting in an increase in our heart-beat. Thus, the pounding of our hearts indicates an imminent threat. The increased heart-beat prompts more blood to flow to our muscles, which enables us to respond either by fleeing (a flight response) or fighting. Thus, from perceiving a stimulus, evaluating its salience, and then responding physically, the brain and body work together through these physiological means.

Negotiations are a stressful process and result in the cortisol and limbic system being activated. Besides the act of negotiation being stressful, the thought of competition is also stressful and will garner a similar response from the limbic system and cortisol. The activation of these systems initiates cognitive and behavioral changes. Increases in cortisol (the primary driver of reactions to stress) result in a reduction in cognitive functions such as social memory, processing speed and other forms of executive functioning (Lee, Glass, McAtee, Wand, Bandeen-Roche, Bolla, Schwartz, 2007). Thus, cortisol, which is produced in the presence of stressors, impedes brain functioning and thereby affects our behaviors.

Takahashi (2005) examined the relationship between the presence of a social stressor and memory function. He found that individuals who faced social stress showed an increase in cortisol levels, followed by a decrease in social memory. It can be argued that this lapse in memory occurs because of cortisol's effect on the memory areas of the brain (hippocampus). However, it is interesting to note that this study also found that the negative relationship between stress and memory was mitigated in the presence of trusting relationships. While the preparation for a competitive reaction (driven by cortisol) has a negative impact on brain function, this can be moderated by the presence of a positive cooperative initiative, as in this case- the presence of interpersonal trust. This interplay between the stress system and the affiliative system in humans is important for us to consider in negotiations and will be explored in more detail in the subsequent sections.

The physiological reactions to a threat or stressor (limbic system and cortisol) are complex and generate other bodily changes as well. Besides the stress of competition, other social processes are also implicated in negotiations. One of the primary drivers of a competitive mindset is an urge to win and dominate the counterparty. Seeking positions of power and high status is an evolutionarily in-built process and is also driven by our biological systems. The hormone synonymous with power and status relationships is *testosterone*.

Initially research in testosterone focused purely on male samples since this hormone is popularly known as an androgen (male-centric hormone) and men produce seven times more testosterone compared to women. However, recent developments indicate that this physiological correlate also affects the inclination of women to be socially dominant (Dabbs, Jr, Ruback, Frady, Hopper and Sgoutas, 1988; Cashdan, 2001; Grant and France, 2001). The level of testosterone indicates an individual's motivation to gain a position of power and dominance (Archer, 2006; Mazur and Booth, 1998). It is also positively associated with a reduction of fear (Hermans, Putman, Baas, Koppeschaar, Honk, 2006) and risk aversion (Sapienzaa, Zingalesb and Maestripieric, 2009).

Testosterone, like cortisol, is produced by the adrenal gland and affects the amygdala (the region in the brain that deals with emotion) and the hippocampus (the region in the brain that deals with memory). There is a baseline level of testosterone in the blood, but it also changes in response to environmental stimuli. Testosterone increases in anticipation of competition and also as a result of a victory in the competition (Booth, Shelley, Mazur, Tharp and Kittok, 1989). Testosterone increases people's desire to get even. A study by Burnham (2007) found that people with higher levels of testosterone are more likely to reject an unfair offer in an ultimatum game. Thus, testosterone causes individuals to punish others even at a cost to themselves in order to get even. Another study found that people who lose competitions and have lower testosterone levels are keen to engage in another competition to regain their lost status (Mehta and Josephs, 2006).

In addition to testosterone, cortisol is also related to changes in power: when people gain power, they show a drop in cortisol levels. In a famous study by Robert Sapolsky on free-range baboons in Africa, he found that baboons lower in the hierarchy had higher levels of cortisol (Sapolsky, 1990). As a higher level of cortisol means greater susceptibility to a range of cardiovascular diseases, Sapolsky's work helped explain why the rate of heart disease differed significantly across socioeconomic strata in human society.

Until recently, testosterone and cortisol were thought to operate independently. Researchers are now examining how testosterone and cortisol jointly determine human behavior. A recent study by Mehta and Josephs (in press) found that the testosterone system and the cortisol system interact to regulate competitive behaviors. Their findings suggest that a higher level of testosterone encourages competitive behaviors only when the level of cortisol is low. When the level of cortisol is high, a higher level of testosterone may actually decrease competitive behaviors. In essence, this means that, even when people have a high level of testosterone, they will not dominate unless they are not stressed by the situation.

A recent study examined how physical posture affects the levels of these hormones. Carney, Cuddy and Yap (2010) asked participants in an experiment to adopt physical postures of power (standing in a pose that symbolizes dominance) and powerlessness (standing in a pose of submission), and tracked changes in their levels of testosterone and cortisol. Individuals who enacted a pose of power not only showed an increase in testosterone levels but also a greater reduction in cortisol, compared to those in low power poses. This implies that merely adopting a physical posture of power could alter our hormonal levels, which in turn drives our behavior. For example, a decrease in cortisol will decrease the level of stress and lead to more risk-taking.

Testosterone and cortisol are the two hormones that primarily drive the competitive system in response to status challenges and stressful stimuli respectively. In addition to these social processes, an emotion that is prevalent in competitive contexts is anger. Anger is manifested as a mechanism to initiate a fight response. Anger is also accompanied by physiological changes: an increase in the level of cortisol, *heart-rate* and *blood pressure*. The expression of anger is generally associated with negative consequences. In support, studies have shown that individuals who are high on hostility (and thus tend to get angry easily) are likely to suffer more cardiovascular issues, resulting in poorer health and well-being (Smith, 1992). However, one must note that anger should not be viewed as having only negative connotations. Sometimes, the demonstration of anger can improve outcomes when it is legitimate and expressed appropriately (Daly, 1991). Indeed, studies have shown that people who demonstrate anger are also seen as more powerful (Tiedens, 2001; Lerner and Tiedens, 2006).

Co-operation

One of the primary objectives of negotiation research is to understand how to create conditions that result in creating a "win-win" outcome for both parties. This can be achieved by creating a climate of co-operation between the two parties. Such a climate will allow trusting behaviors to emerge between the parties. Trust and empathy have been shown to have physiological correlates. The hormone that drives these cooperative behaviors is oxytocin.

Oxytocin is a *neurotransmitter* that is better known as the 'love hormone'. Initially, oxytocin was known only for the biological use that it presented during child birth and lactation. However, today this hormone is extensively studied for its impact on social behaviors, such as trust (Kosfeld, Heinrichs, Zak, Fischbacher and Fehr, 2005), empathy (Singer, Snozzi, Bird, Petrovic, Silani, Heinrichs and Dolan, 2008) and altruistic behaviors (Barazza and Zak, 2009). Oxytocin works as both a neurotransmitter in the brain and as a hormone in the blood stream. As a neurotransmitter, oxytocin affects several brain regions, particularly the *nucleus accumbens*- the brain region associated with reward and the amygdala- the brain region that deals with emotion.

Research has indicated that when trusting behavior is exhibited towards an individual, the level of oxytocin increases (Zak, Kurzban and Matzner, 2004). The reverse is also true: the intranasal administration of oxytocin can result in an increase in trusting behaviors. Experiments (e.g. Kosfeld *et al.*, 2005) have been conducted to examine the role of oxytocin in trusting behaviors. In one of the experiments, individuals who received positive social cues from their trustor had a concurrent surge in the level of oxytocin, which was significantly higher than those who received an impersonal cue. This study also found that those who received money with a positive social cue returned almost 50% of the money they received, thereby establishing their investor's trust (Zak, Kurzban and Matzner, 2005). This experiment highlights that a social cue, a form of affiliation, not only resulted in a rise in oxytocin but also prompted cooperative behaviors.

Cooperative behaviors can also stem from a specialized human ability to not only 'imagine' the emotional turmoil another person is going through, but also experience the sensory state that the individual is in i.e. physical pain, commonly referred to as empathy (Singer, Seymour, O'Doherty, Kaube, Dolan and Frith, 2004). Guastella and colleagues (2008) found that when participants were shown the eye regions of faces and asked to predict the emotions that were being expressed; the participants who were administered with oxytocin were able to do a better job. Social neuroscience research has indicated that, in the presence of oxytocin, certain brain regions (the posterior superior temporal sulcus and the para-cingulate cortex) are also activated (Gallagher and Frith, 2003). These regions specialize in detecting how other individuals might feel or might act and are called 'theory of mind' regions.

The release of oxytocin works not only for facilitating cooperative behavior, but also for deregulating the stress response produced by cortisol. We know that when there is a threat in the environment, the level of cortisol surges to enable us to cope with the threat. The administration of oxytocin through an inter-nasal device dampens the cortisol response (Heinrichs, Baumgartner, Kirschbaum, Ehlert, 2003). In a business context, if negotiators want to adopt a competitive stance, it is possible that an externally administered spray of oxytocin will reduce the stress associated with making a competitive move and will in turn facilitate cooperative behavior.

Face-to-face negotiations allow individuals to engage in interpersonal interaction that goes beyond merely verbal communication. Other non-central aspects to the negotiation, such as posture, facial expression and even touch, also affect negotiation outcomes. Physiological research has examined how touch, a sign of affiliation, might impact social outcomes. Some of the early studies on touch indicated that a momentary or fleeting touch by a waitress or librarian prompted a more positive appraisal of the individual (Crusco and Wetzel, 1984; Fisher, Rytting and Heslin, 1976). Physical contact is known to produce oxytocin (Zak, *et al.*, 2005; Carter, 2006; Odendaal and Meintjes, 2003), and this might be the reason why the individual making the physical contact receives a positive evaluation.

In a business context, attempts have been made to study the role of touch in economic games. Morhenn and colleagues (2008) found that when participants were massaged before they responded in a trust game, their level of oxytocin increased and they displayed more trusting behaviors towards an anonymous counter-part. In the trust game, the money that is offered gets tripled; therefore, touch increased sacrificial behavior so that both parties would mutually benefit. This study also administered massages to the second player and found that this increased the tendency to return the money back or to reciprocate a trusting act.

Oxytocin could be a mediator between the act of being massaged and displaying trusting behaviors; however, it has been argued that touch could also have other physiological implications, such as reducing the levels of cortisol and adrenalin and thereby promoting less threatening situations. In another study, participants who were touched fleetingly with a handshake or a pat on the back took more risks in their economic decisions (Levav and Argo, 2010). Physical contact and increased cooperative behaviors seem to increase the level of trust that can be bestowed on others, as they create a feeling of safety by reducing the perception of threat.

Studies indicate that oxytocin is associated with *positive emotions* such as trust and affiliation. However, a recent study indicated that this might not be entirely true. Shamay-Tsoory and colleagues (2009) found that the inter-nasal administration of oxytocin affects negative emotions that involve social comparisons, such as gloating and envy. These emotions prompt individuals to engage in social comparisons, and therefore, oxytocin might have a role to play in eliciting emotions towards people who have some social salience in their lives. While on the one hand oxytocin presents itself as almost being synonymous with affiliate intentions, it also propels negatively connoted emotions like envy and gloating. Therefore, our physiological machinery is not very straightforward; instead, it is highly complex. Hence subjective self-reports are used to attribute value to physiological changes so that we can understand the relationship between physiology and the relevant emotions and cognitions.

Cooperation is positively evaluated by the recipients of the act. The act of cooperation can thus be viewed as being rewarding since it guarantees something pleasurable at the end. The biochemical reactions to rewarding stimuli have been well-studied in the neuroeconomic literature. Any rewarding stimuli will activate the 'pleasure' or the dopaminergic system in the brain. This system is driven by a neurotransmitter called dopamine, which affects two important reward areas in the brain- the *nucleus accumbens* (NAcc) and the *striatum*. The reward system in the brain does not work independently from other measures, such as personality (extraversion), arousal, and affect. These factors play a moderating role in the relationship between the presence of rewards and the extent to which the NAcc is activated (Peterson, 2004). Recent research has shown that the structure of the brain regions differ depending on personality (Engelmann, 2006; DeYoung and Gray, 2009; DeYoung, Hirsh, Shane, Papademetris, Rajeevan and Gray, 2010). This provides us with some evidence that personality measures might indeed have an anatomical basis.

Apart from the NAcc, the brain region that has been associated with rewards is the striatum. Like the NAcc, the striatum is also activated when the brain is anticipating a reward (Balleine, Delgado and Hikosaka, 2007). Singer and colleagues (2004) conducted a prisoner's dilemma experiment, in which participants were shown the faces of their opponents. Participants were informed during the game whether their opponents cooperated intentionally or unintentionally. Later, when the participants were shown the same faces of their opponents, the ventral striatum — the reward center of the brain — was activated only when these faces belonged to those who had cooperated intentionally. Therefore, rewards need not be visceral like food or money, but could entail even symbolic representations.

Conclusion

Negotiations involve a constant juggle between creating and claiming value. Different physiological systems are at work when people have a competitive versus a co-operative mindset. This is perhaps the underlying reason why people at the bargaining table feel a dilemma within themselves, as they try to create and claim value. While additional research needs to examine how these dilemmas are resolved, examining how these two physiological systems interact might help us understand how negotiators can resolve this dilemma.

Appendix: Glossary of the Physiological Terms Used

Amygdala	A pea-shaped region in the brain associated with the processing of emotional stimuli.
Baseline measure	The level of a hormone present at a resting state.
Blood pressure	The pressure exerted by the circulating blood on the blood vessels transporting the blood.
Cortisol	A hormone produced by the adrenal gland in response to stress.
Endocrinology	A branch of biology that studies the action and functions of chemical secretions in the body called hormones.
Epinephrine	A hormone and a neurotransmitter generates a cardiovascular response in order to prepare the body to make a fight-or-flight response.
Functional magnetic resonance imaging (fMRI)	A specialized brain scan that measures the relative change in brain activity across different brain regions. This is one of the new forms of neuroimaging.
Heart-rate	The number of heart-beats in one unit of time. This is also indicative of the amount of oxygenated blood that the body is able to pump to the rest of the body.
Hippocampus	A region of the brain associated with memory processing.
Hormone	Chemicals that are released from an endocrine gland or from other tissues into the blood stream and organs such

as the brain. These chemicals initiate and alter other bodily functions.

Limbic system — A brain system consisting primarily of the amygdala and the hippocampus. It is responsible for the processing of threatening and emotional stimuli.

Neuroscience — The study of the nervous system (which includes the network of nerves and the brain).

Neurotransmitter — A chemical messenger in the brain that sends signals from one neuron to another.

Nucleus Accumbens (NAcc) — A region of the brain associated with the processing of rewarding stimuli.

Oxytocin — A neurotransmitter produced during child birth, breast feeding, mating and other affiliative social behaviors.

Positron emission tomography — A neuroimaging technique that can produce a three-dimensional picture of the brain using gamma rays.

Reactivity — The degree to which a chemical will undergo a change.

Striatum — A brain region associated with processing of rewarding stimuli.

Testosterone — A hormone that is mainly present in males and is responsible for the development of secondary sexual characteristics. Testosterone is also implicated in social processes like dominance and power dynamics.

Understanding Negotiation Ethics

Kelvin Pang
Department of Management and Organisation
National University of Singapore Business School

Cynthia S. Wang
Department of Management and Organisation
National University of Singapore Business School

You have been getting erratic performance from your mobile handset the last few days and you decide to bring it back to the mobile service provider for repairs. At the customer service counter, the service representative examined the equipment and informed you that you have violated the warranty agreement. You have a choice to pay $300 for repairs or get a new phone at a rebated price of $400. You recall several occasions when you had exposed the phone to "extreme" weather conditions, however, instead of taking responsibility, you find yourself raising your voice at the customer service representative, indignant of any wrong doing, and insisting that no one had informed you of the non-service clause at the point of purchase. After a heated negotiation to get your phone repaired at no cost, both parties remained firm on their respective positions. You stormed out of the centre vowing never to patronize the shop again, leaving behind an "emotionally abused" customer service representative, and bewildered onlookers having doubts about the phone and the level of service provided by the company.

Have you ever been caught in similar situations whereby you misrepresent facts, raise your voice, or even lie, just to get the most out of a negotiation? At the end of the process, instead of feeling remorseful over your actions, you blame your opponent for their unethical behavior, justifying your choice of unreasonable tactics. Often when this happens, these behaviors escalate and we end up with strained relationships and potentially sub-optimal outcomes.

Negotiators often face difficult situations in which they must question their value system and ethical limits. Many a time, negotiators feel that their counterpart acted in an unfair manner. Yet, just as likely, negotiators engage in behaviors without realizing that they may have acted in way that may be seen as unethical by others.

The objective of this chapter is to bring to awareness situations where ethical dilemmas are often overlooked, understand our tendencies to behave in such situations, and discuss strategies for resolving them. Given that the discussion of ethics in negotiations is become more commonplace, it is essential for negotiators to be aware of and understand how to respond to the ethical dilemmas they face. We discuss various topics related to ethics using this framework, including how self-interest, norms, fairness biases, collective dilemmas, and cultural stereotypes affect the negotiation process and outcomes. We begin by addressing the question of why we are motivated to use ethically questionable tactics in the negotiation process.

"I want to win!" — Maximizing self-interest

You are in the running for the university club's presidency and you have been elected into the executive committee through a close alliance with the club's most popular candidate, and a close friend of yours. It is a few days away from the final elections and you decide the only way you can get your coveted title is to persuade your partner to step aside from the competition. Over coffee, the negotiations proved tougher than you expected. Despite your promises to do your best for the club and why you might be a more suitable candidate for presidency, your friend showed no signs of wanting to give up the fight for the title. Finally, you decided to show him some "photographs" that you had conveniently snapped on your mobile phone a few months back at his birthday bash. He was rudely shocked by your move, and glared at you in disbelief...

The photos misrepresented what actually occurred on the night of the birthday bash, but you knew that your opponent would not take the risk to have his reputation smeared. Was that an ethical move to use against your friend?

The above example suggests the use of ethically questionable tactics when you have a clear, fixed goal (e.g., Schweizter, Ordonez, and Douma, 2004). However, there are also many instances when the outcome is really not that important to us, yet we find ourselves using aggressive, perhaps unreasonable tactics just so as to win the negotiation. Consider the following situation:

> You are holidaying in a less developed country and trying to pick up some good bargains at the night market. Prices are considerably lower than what is available in your home country and reasonable for the quality of goods you are interested in. However, your friends and guidebooks suggest that you should never accept the first offer but mark down prices by at least 50%. Being an aggressive negotiator, and not wanting to get an unfair end of the bargain, you brace yourself for a tough "fight" with the stall owner, whose two undernourished kids sit by watching.
>
> Despite the fact that you have significantly more wealth and power than your opponent, why are you still so intent on winning the negotiation?

Both these examples serve the same purpose of highlighting an innate desire to win in every one of us, and how the strength of this self-interested motivation might drive us to use ethically questionable tactics to gain a power advantage over our opponent. Lying or manipulating the situation during the negotiation process allows us to gain an upper hand over our partner (Acquino, 1998; Boles, Croson, and Murnighan, 2000; Lewicki,

1983). Getting your opponent to believe in your side of the story and to be able to gather vital information about your opponents gives you an information-advantage (Lewicki, Saunders, and Barry, 2006). You can use this information to adjust your offers, to manipulate impressions and trust, and to strategize your options, all of which gives you additional power over your opponents.

Recognizing our natural tendencies in wanting to win

How then do we avoid using these ethically questionable tactics? It is an important first step to recognize our innate self-interested nature. Increasing our self-awareness allows us to pre-empt our tendencies to engage in unethical behaviors, allowing us to know how far we will go for the sake of winning. Not surprisingly, competitive individuals are more likely to engage in ethically questionable bargaining tactics than cooperative individuals (Robinson, Lewicki, and Donahue, 2000). As the incentive for winning increases, so does the likelihood for negotiators to use deception (Tenbrunsel, 1999). Interestingly, power might corrupt the thinking of the powerful, leading the more powerful to bluff more and communicate less with their counterparts who had less power during a negotiation (Crott, Kayser, and Lamm, 1980). This is contrary to conventional wisdom that more powerful individuals legitimately use their objective levels of power to get what they want; rather they use unethical tactics to win, yet reaffirming the notion that the desire to win is an important precursor to unethical bargaining behavior.

Often, we are not aware how competitive we can be during negotiation episodes, and it is imperative that we allow ourselves time to reflect on these natural tendencies of ours to pursue power and gains. Doing so will allow us to avoid falling into the trap of using ethically ambiguous tactics in our pursuit to win. Tightly coupled with this notion of wanting to win are the most common excuses we give for justifying our use of unethical tactics, which we turn our attention to next.

"Everyone is doing it, why shouldn't I?" — Unethical negotiation norms

You are a promising, fresh law graduate and have received a job offer at a prestigious law firm, due to start work in a week's time. You receive a phone call from a competitor who requested a meeting to discuss possibilities of joining them. During the meeting, the partners enquire of the remuneration package offered by their competitor and promised to match their offer. Knowing the importance of starting your career with the best possible first job, you contemplate whether you should inflate the initial offer to get a better deal...

Will you take this opportunity to misrepresent your initial offer to get a better remuneration package? Isn't that what all job seekers do?

Often, we find it easy to think that because everyone is using aggressive methods of negotiation, it is all right to follow suit because it is a norm to do so. Thus, you should have no qualms in inflating your offer because everyone does it. In fact, it is necessary for survival!

Yet another hurdle stands in the way of us doing our due diligence as ethical negotiators. Often, we justify our use of questionable bargaining tactics because the benefits of reaching an agreement (or sometimes the negative effects of an impasse) far outweigh the ethics involved in the process (Bok, 1978). Consider the police officer that offers a reduced sentence to a suspect in exchange for their willingness to testify in court against the main defendant. Different professions may have their own specific norms and acceptable use of ethically questionable negotiation tactics. An agent acting on behalf of a principal may also find it worthwhile to maximize his own interests at the expense of the principal's interests (Malhotra and Bazerman, 2007):

> You are representing your company's subsidiary to negotiate a merger with a competitor firm. Your company has given you flexibility and a set of parameters to work within to make the

final decision. During the meeting, your opponents have promised you a promotion, post-merger, if you can offer them a favorable proposal. Although they have requested for conditions that are within your boundaries, you are confident that you can negotiate a better agreement if you try harder. You wonder if there is a necessity for you to pledge full allegiance to your company...

Legally, you have not accepted any tangible benefits and you are working within the boundary set for you by your firm. As an agent of your firm, will you go all out to protect the firm's interests?

Knowing our ethical standards

Instead of merely making excuses on the grounds of self-defense and negotiation norms, a more responsible approach towards ethical negotiating should involve developing clear individual ethical standards to guide our actions. We outline four approaches can help us clarify how individuals choose to act when negotiating ethical dilemmas: utilitarian, individual, moral-rights, and justice (Cavanagh, Moberg, and Velasquez, 1981).

The *utilitarian approach* holds that an action that does the greatest good for the greatest number of people is ultimately the best course of action. The aforementioned negotiation of the police officer that exchanged a reduced sentence with a suspect for testifying against a drug kingpin would be seen as permissible under the grounds that reducing the punishment of one wrong-doer ends up providing a greater good for society as a whole.

The *individualism approach* suggests that promoting one's own long-term interests is of ultimate importance. With regards to ethics in negotiations in this framework, it is imperative for negotiators to consider the long-term effects of using deception on their reputation and the repercussions of engaging in short-term gains over long-term benefits when choosing to use unethical tactics. For example, Tinsley, O'Connor and Sullivan

(2002) found that expert negotiators that held a reputation for using claiming tactics performed worse than those that did not hold a reputation.

The *moral-rights approach* focuses on maintaining the fundamental rights and liberties of individuals taking part of a negotiation. For example, individuals have a right to speak their mind in a negotiation. Another example is that individuals have the right to life and safety in a negotiation, thus, should not be threatened by force to come to an agreement. Individuals have a key moral rights and should not be unfairly disadvantaged by the negotiation outcome and the process of arriving at that outcome. As negotiators, have we paid due consideration that we have not knowingly or unknowingly infringed on the rights of those affected by the negotiation?

The *justice approach* suggests that negotiators should act on the grounds of equity, fairness, and impartiality. These are some important questions that negotiators should consider from the perspective of justice: Are you treating your negotiating counterpart unfairly or differently because of some arbitrary characteristic, such as race, religion, or nationality? Is the final negotiation outcome distributively fair? Have you adhered to the mutually agreed rules of the negotiation process? Have you been unduly aggressive towards your negotiation partner or treated him or her in a procedurally unfair manner?

The four approaches present different ways of evaluating the appropriateness of the negotiation tactics that we use. It is important to recognize that there is not always just only one "ethically appropriate course of action"; rather, each individual differs in their preferences in ethical approach. Perhaps what is most important is that we are aware and clear of the ethical standards we are actually using to guide ourselves during the negotiation process. This also offers an explanation why the same tactic might be perceived by us to be ethical, yet perceived as unethical by our negotiating counterpart, and hence the need for us to consider the ethical norms being used by others.

These approaches help us be aware of the ethical standards we and our counterparts are using to guide behaviors during the negotiation process. Knowledge of these approaches can help to prevent us from making hasty, uninformed decisions on the tactics we use. Interestingly, even for the negotiator who professes adhering to the strongest ethical standards, we often find ourselves making decisions that are contrary to what we believe in — a notion termed "bounded ethicality". The subsequent sections discuss cognitive biases that affect our actions in a way that may be seen as unethical or unfair.

"I deserve more!" — Fairness biases

You believe that you deserve a better pay package than what your organization is offering you. You believe that the seller of the apartment you are interested in is inflating the price of the house and hiding defects from you. You believe that you deserve a larger share of the negotiated contract because the deal could not have gone through without you. You believe that as an agent, you are not obligated to protect your principal's full interests because you have already declared your conflict of interests.

There is no doubt that negotiators concerned would like to receive a fair share of any outcome in negotiations. However, problems arise because negotiators often view fairness in a self-serving, egocentric light, such that they view outcomes that favor themselves — such as thinking that they deserve more of the pie or that the other party is consistently acting unfairly (Babcock and Loewenstein, 1997). For example, negotiators who are provided information relevant to the negotiation tend to remember facts that favored themselves and not those that favor their counterparts (Thompson and Loewenstein, 1992). This self-bias is often not a conscious decision, with negotiators developing these egocentric standards without even realizing it (Banaji, Bazerman, and Chugh, 2003).

These differing perceptions of fairness can cause conflict. When one party views the other as acting unfairly, a significant barrier to develop a win-win outcome is instilled (Bazerman and Chugh, 2006). These biased perceptions increase the likelihood of an impasse (Thompson and Loewenstein, 1992; Babcock, Loewenstein, Issacharoff, and Camerer, 1995), increases the likelihood that negotiators will see their opponents as unethical (Kronzon and Darley, 1999), and often helps justify negotiations' use of questionable negotiation tactics (Bazerman, Curhan, Moore, and Valley, 2000).

Combating egocentric fairness biases

It is important to bear in mind that both your opponent and yourself are not immune to these biases. On your part, remember that fairness is subjective, and that you are likely to be egocentrically biases, thinking that you deserve more. How do we combat our own egocentric fairness bias?

One way is to increase one's own *self-awareness*, or directing attention inward such that consciousness is focused on oneself (Duval and Wicklund, 1972). Self-aware individuals tend to be less egocentrically biased, and adhere more to internalized justice norms (Greenberg, 1983). For example, high self-aware people are more likely to try to restore equity after receiving overpayment (Reis and Burns, 1982), less likely to steal (Beaman, Klentz, Diener, and Svanum, 1979) and cheat (Vallacher and Solodky, 1979). Moreover, self-awareness is particularly effective in the presence of *salient moral standards* (Batson, Thompson, Seuferling, Whitney, and Strongman, 1999).

In addition to decreasing egocentric biases, in order to combat fairness biases, it is also important to understand what the other side sees as fair. Novice negotiators often assume that the other side is only concerned about their own outcomes (e.g., maximizing their own gain). In fact, it might be about the process they undertake during the negotiation itself. Negotiators tend to focus on the procedure (Is the other side giving me voice? How was the process of negotiation?) Procedural justice encourages the acceptance of negotiated agreements, as well as leading to the opportunity for increased integrative bargaining (Hollander-Blumoff and Tyler, 2008).

Moreover, it is important to realize that negotiators are more about their relative than absolute outcomes, trying to avoid being disadvantaged compared to the other person (Lowenstein, Thompson, and Bazerman, 1989). For example, people were found to prefer an outcome of seven dollars for themselves and seven dollars for the other side over an outcome of eight dollars for themselves and ten dollars for the other party (Blount and Bazerman, 1996).

Moving away from egocentric fairness biases, another common situation arises in negotiators' pursuit of integrative gains for everyone at the negotiation table, but failing to see how decisions can affect external parties not present at the negotiation.

"For me or the group?" — Collective dilemmas

You are the owner of a bus transport company that provides travel to a neighboring state. You have been enjoying lucrative premiums on this exclusive route until last month when a competitor joined in the market, aggressively slashing prices. You are hesitant about engaging in a price war, however, you understand that if the situation persists, you will lose many of your price-conscious customers. The country's law does not explicitly ban price-fixing and you wonder if you can negotiate a price agreement with your competitor so that you can keep your premiums high.

> *Reaching a price agreement with your competitor effectively enlarges the pie for both as you both can reap higher profits. Have you violated any ethical principles in doing so?*

Negotiation classes extol the value of integrative bargaining, enlarging the pie such that it benefits everyone at the negotiation table. However, this can create collective dilemmas for negotiators. Collective dilemmas are situations in which self-interested decisions that maximize negotiators' own outcomes can lead to undesirable effects at some collective level. Often, negotiators focus on maximizing their own outcomes within a negotiation without considering the impact on a collective level, otherwise known as *parasitic value creation* (Malholtra and Bazerman, 2007).

The example above illustrates how parasitic value creation occurs: you may choose to fix prices with your competitor because it is beneficial for both parties, but fail to consider the deleterious costly effects on the consumers.

Ignoring how your choices affect the collective may also have disastrous social consequences, also known as *social dilemmas*. For example, fishermen have aggressively harvested Atlantic bluefin tuna because of its popularity in sushi restaurants, but overfishing has led to its near extinction. The overfishing case can also be seen as an intergenerational dilemma (Tost, Hernandez and Wade-Benzoni, 2008), when negotiators' self-interests in the present are in conflict with the interests of others in the future. In other words, decision-makers act in the present and it is future others alone who experience the future consequences of the decision. Another example of an intergenerational dilemma is a negotiator who is faced with the decision to use an energy source that is costly but conserves resources for future generations versus a less costly source that will pollute the environment.

All in all, it is often difficult to encourage individuals to consider the collective repercussions of their actions; if all negotiators decide to act in an individually rational manner and maximize their own profits within a given negotiation, negotiators may not only be unwittingly hurting related parties that are not at the negotiating table, but ignoring the collective can lead to the extinction of whole species and the decimation of forests, leaving little for our children's children to enjoy. Because of these dire consequences, researchers have concentrated on the various ways to increase collective cooperation.

Increasing cooperation

One way to increase collective cooperation is through a combination of *reminding people of past behavior* and *public commitment.*

272 K. P. and C. S. Wang

For example, Dickerson, Thibodeau, Aronson, and Miller (1992) found that people who found that people who made a public commitment to conserve water after being reminded of their past behavior motivated them to increase their efforts to conserve water (by taking shorter showers). Another method to increase cooperation is through *respect* and *social inclusion*.

DeCremer (2002) found that people who felt respected contributed more to their group's welfare, with respect leading to the greatest contributions by those who felt least included. In terms of intergenerational dilemmas, *decreasing psychological distance* between present decision makers and future others by increasing the connection across generations, eventually result in decisions benefiting future generations (Tost *et al.*, 2008). Also, even *how the dilemma is framed* can affect cooperation (Larrick and Blount, 1997); when a social dilemma is was framed as "The Community Game", players cooperated approximately twice as frequently as those in "The Wall Street Game" (Ross and Ward, 1995). Finally, while *sanctioning* (e.g., punishments non-cooperative behavior) can increase cooperation (Caldwell, 1976; Eek, Loukopoulos, Fujii, and Garling, 2002; Fehr and Gachter, 2002; McCusker and Carnevale, 1995; Van Vugt and DeCremer, 1999; Wit and Wilke, 1990; Yamagishi, 1986), recent research has suggested that sanctions can undermine trust, and can even reduce cooperation when trust was initially high (Mulder, Dijk, DeCremer, Wilke, 2006).

Does cooperative behavior always lead to individual loss?

Interestingly, cooperation does not mean that at the end, individuals do worse at an individual level. Weber and Murnighan (2008) found that cooperators who consistently contributed in a social dilemma not only causes others in the group to contribute more and cooperate more often, but doing so results in no apparent cost to the consistent contributor, with the contributors often gaining.

Finally, we turn to another perception bias that affects the way we perceive the ethicality of our opponents' actions and how others are interpreting our behavior: stereotyping. With cross-cultural negotiations becoming more commonplace, this has implications for how negotiators make sense of ethically accept-able bargaining tactics.

"They are all the same" — Cultural stereotypes

All Chinese bribe. All North Americans are aggressive. All women don't ask. All Japanese seek to avoid loss of face. All lawyers are greedy. All North Americans are time-sensitive. All Russians make high demands. All Latin Americans are highly emotional.

All of us have our implicit beliefs about the way we see the world around us. Sterotypes help us simplify the world and make quick assessments of the people we negotiate with (Hilton and Hippel, 1996). However, these same beliefs might also interfere with our ability to make objective, rational judgments. The question of ethics emerges when we subconsciously favor or discriminate certain groups of people we negotiate with. It also proves to be an issue when there is a lack of appreciation of the social norms different individuals subscribe to, giving rise to mis-construals that certain behaviors are unethical. Consider the following situation:

> You are a Chinese businessman, negotiating a business contract with your American counterpart. The last week had been a per-plexing experience for you. You had spent the last week trying to build relationships with the firm's representative, bringing her out for lavish dinners and buying her gifts. However, these efforts have been met with lukewarm response, and the previous two meetings seemed rather tense, with the representative aggres-sively pushing down the offer price. You had also seen your European competitor and the American representative going out for drinks at a pub two nights ago. You begin to wonder if the American firm is sincere in outsourcing their manufacturing activities to your firm and whether they can be trusted.

How did cross-cultural dynamics affect your ethical assessment of American representative's behaviors? Could the American representative have stereotyped your behaviors using her own set of lenses and misinterpreted your intentions as well? How would you handle the situation from now on?

Appreciating cultural differences in negotiations

In a globalized world, it is becoming increasingly important for us to understand how national cultures affect ethics in the negotiation process. Culture affects how negotiations are understood and what behaviors are deemed acceptable. For example, there exist significant differences in Asian and North American students' ratings of appropriateness in the use of 'false promises' and 'inappropriate information gathering' as bargaining tactics (Lewicki and Robinson, 1998). Asian students found it more appropriate than Western students to 'gain information about an opponent's position by cultivating his/her friendship through expensive gifts, entertaining, or personal favors', as these are common relationship-building practices in Asian cultures.

Furthermore, cultural differences exist in how people respond to deception and honest behavior in a negotiated situation, with East Asians using punishments more than Westerners, with the rationale due to their less mobile, more collective society (Wang and Leung, in press). In a similar note, Adam, Shirako, and Maddux (in press) found that expressing anger during negotiation elicited larger concessions from European-American negotiators, but smaller concessions from Asian and Asian-American negotiators. Both these studies suggest that it is important for negotiators to appreciate that there exist cross-cultural differences in the way individuals perceive and respond to unethical bargaining tactics.

Do I treat them all the same?

To overcome our bias, one must understand there are underlying differences in how other cultures negotiate, and what is ethically acceptable in that culture. While it is important to be aware of such distinctions, it is equally important that we keep an open mind to the specific person we are negotiating with as each individual is unique and might not behave stereotypically. Brett (2001) pointed out that while prototypical cultural differences exist in the use of negotiation behaviors, not *all* members of the same culture behave like the cultural prototype.

Final Thoughts

In this chapter, we began by examining the self-interested motive to use deception and exploring why it is necessary for us to be clear of the ethical standards that guide our actions during the negotiation process. Increasing our self-awareness in these two areas pave the way for us to make informed decisions on whether to engage in ethically questionable behaviors. We then proceeded to understand the notion of bounded ethicality, and the biases that hinder negotiators' ability to be as ethical as they wish to be.

As negotiators, we might or might not have taken time to think about where we stand with regards to ethics in negotiation. Perhaps, for some of us, the end is more important than the means to the end, and we don't really care about ethics, so long as we do not violate the law. For the rest of us, we might have clear, ethical standards we want to adhere to, but yet unknowingly find ourselves behaving contrary to our espoused beliefs. We hope this chapter leaves you with a better appreciation of the ethical pitfalls we avail ourselves to, and challenge us to examine the ethical standards we want to upkeep as effective negotiators.

15

Navigating International Negotiations: A Communications and Social Interaction Style (CSIS) Framework

Nancy R. Buchan
Sonoco International Business Department
University of South Carolina

Wendi L. Adair
Department of Psychology
University of Waterloo

Xiao-Ping Chen
Management and Organization
University of Washington

Entering into cross-cultural negotiations is a bit like heading out as the captain of the Titanic. When surveying the negotiation terrain, you will easily spot the most evident parts of culture — food, music, history, art, literature, language — these are the tips of the icebergs floating in the foreign sea. After studying these aspects carefully, it is possible to learn to navigate these parts of the cultural terrain. For example, discussions with your Chilean negotiation partner of Chilean literature, music and painting could help set the foundation for a relationship with them; it will demonstrate to them that you have an interest in their country and culture and that you are willing to take the time to get to know something about them prior to any discussion of business. Such extra measures could go far in helping to establish empathy and trust, particularly in a relationship-oriented culture, and could lead to a mutually beneficial negotiated agreement (Lewis, 2006).

However, when surveying the negotiation terrain, there are parts of culture that are not evident — these are the much larger pieces of the iceberg that are underwater and obscured; such hidden parts can doom a negotiation (and large seagoing vessels). This is because much of culture that is not evident is also unstated and implicit (Hall, 1976); individuals within a culture develop internalized "behavioral patterns", (Harris, 1968, p. 16), "unstated assumptions", "standard operating procedures" (Triandis, 1994, p. 6) and communication and social interaction styles unique to that culture (Adair, Buchan and Chen, 2009). Thus, not only do you not see these parts of culture, you may not understand them. To stretch the analogy even further, you have a situation where you cannot clearly view the iceberg underwater, but you may have run into it and not realize the potential damage it is causing. Take for example, the case of "Bilingual Labels:"[1]

Canada's largest importer of mobile phones and accessories, Nor-Phone Ltd. of Toronto, decided to start sourcing accessories in China. From an industry contact in Chicago, Vice President Pete Martin learned about Ever Sharp, a large manufacturer in Shenzen specialized in supplying the U.S. market.

After months of email correspondence, Pete flew to Guangzhou to finalize the purchase agreement for 10,000 accessory sets. Discussions with the Ever Sharp people proceeded amiably. Pete and the Chinese team needed a week of meetings to agree on specs, packing, delivery, price, payment terms and the other details of a large transaction.

Exhausted from these lengthy negotiations, Pete was really looking forward to the signing ceremony. At this point however, Pete learned that Ever Sharp had not yet exported to Europe or Canada, and thus might not be familiar with Canada's bilingual

---

[1] Case provided by Richard Gesteland, Global Management, LLC.

requirements. So he explained that all goods sold in Canada must have all product labels printed in both French and English.

This news caused the Chinese concern. They lacked French-language expertise and could only work with Chinese and English, but did not want to admit this to the buyer. So Managing Director Wang replied with a smile, "Mr. Martin, I am afraid that supplying labels in French and English will be a bit difficult. This question will require further study."

Pete Martin politely repeated that bilingual French/English labels were required by Canadian import regulations. "Please understand that we really have no choice on this — it's the law."

Mr. Wang replied with a smile: "Mr. Martin, we will give your request serious consideration. It will be quite difficult. We will do our best to solve the problem." Relieved to have settled this final detail, Pete signed the contract and said his formal goodbyes to Mr. Wang and his team.

Three months later Pete got a call from the quality-control chief at Nor-Phone's warehouse. "Mr. Martin, we have a problem. You know those 10,000 sets that just came in from China? Well, they've got bilingual labels all right — but they are in English and Chinese!"

Although the names of the persons and companies involved in this case have been changed to protect the innocent (but culturally ignorant), the events in this case were real, as was the consequence and cost of having to remove and replace the labels of 10,000 sets as well as the damage to the reputations of the people involved. Pete was unaware of the unstated and implicit cultural communication and social interaction norms in China, and as result, paid a heavy price for what he thought was a successful negotiation.

The goal of this chapter is to provide a framework for understanding the unstated and implicit portion of culture as it applies to negotiation, and to assist cross-cultural negotiators in identifying potential areas of opportunity and those of peril when they are navigating cross-cultural business negotiations.

Culture, Communication, and Negotiation

"Without communication there is no negotiation" (Fisher, Ury and Patton, 1991, p. 30).

"Communication is culture and culture is communication", (Hall, 1959, p. 169).

Communication is essential to negotiation. Without the ability to communicate with one another, parties could not exchange information. Without information exchange, negotiators could not inform one another of their interests. Without knowledge of one another's interests, it would be nearly impossible to negotiate mutually satisfying agreements. Thus, negotiation begins, continues and ends with communication. When negotiators are from different cultures communication becomes exponentially more complex.

The complexity arises from the fact that culture is a system that links individuals to the ecological context in which they live (Keesing, 1974; Gudykunst and Ting-Toomey, 1988). Context is acutely important in communication because individuals vary according to the degree to which they attend to context in communication and use contextual cues in their environment to reason and relate to others in social interaction (Hall, 1959; 1976). Anthropologist Edward Hall suggested there are two types of cultures; high and low context. Individuals from high context cultures pay great attention to and make extensive use of contextual cues in communication and social interaction. Individuals from low context cultures on the other hand, pay little attention to and make slight-to-no use of such cues in communication and social interaction. Hall generalized that most of the countries of Western Europe, Scandinavia, and the United States were relatively lower context cultures, while France, Russia, most Asian, Middle Eastern, Mediterranean, and Latin American countries were relatively higher context cultures (Hall and Hall, 2002).

Hall's conceptualization of communication as culture can be distilled into four key (correlated) components (Adair, Buchan and

Chen, 2009): communication style, relationship context, time context and space context. We propose that these four components comprise Communication and Social Interaction Style (CSIS), which we define as the standard operating procedures for communication and social interaction characterized by a culture's reliance on direct or indirect messages and attention to information in the relationship, temporal, and spatial contexts of the interaction. These four components are summarized in the following table:

	Reserved	Direct	Expressive
Communication Style	Indirect Holistic Listener oriented	Direct Linear Speaker oriented	Moderately direct Holistic Listener oriented
Relationship context	High relationship context Moderate work/non-work relation overlap Self and other face maintenance	Low relationship context Work/non-work relations distinct Self face maintenance	High relationship context High work/non-work relation overlap Self and other face maintenance
Time context	Fixed time and Fluid time, depending on social and relationship norm	Highly fixed time Fixed schedules and deadlines Serial process	Fluid time Flexible schedules and Deadlines Multitask
Space context	Distant, empty communication space Reserved Subtle body language	Distant, filled communication space Moderately expressive Moderate body language	Close, filled communication space Emotional Highly Expressive body language

Although Hall generalized that there are two main types of cultures — high and low context — we suggest that within these two cultures, the four components of communication style, relationship, time and space context provide for a multiplicity of communication and interaction styles. This notion is supported by the work of cross-cultural communications consultant Richard Lewis. For example, Lewis' work (2006) describes East and Southeast Asian cultures with words such as formal, reserved, silent, and respectful. Conversely, his descriptions of Latin, Mediterranean, African and Arab cultures include words such as emotional, expressive, and talkative. In Hall's dichotomy, all of the cultures just mentioned are classified as high context cultures. Yet, it is important to note that these differences are not just a matter of degree, i.e., paying more or less attention to contextual cues. The differences are in how the cues are used and the meaning they convey in high context communication. For example, in Japan, silence is not an empty space to be filled but a communicative act (Gudykunst *et al.*, 1996) Maintaining silent space can be a means of promoting harmonious social relations, or it can be a sign of crucial impasse in negotiations (Hodgson, Sano and Graham, 2008). In contrast, in Mexico, silence is an empty space to be filled. Mexican workers maintain camaraderie by avoiding silence and constantly interrupting one another (Hall, 1960), and Mexican negotiators rarely exhibit periods of silence during their negotiation sessions (Requejo and Graham, 2008). Thus, the category of "high context" is too broad to capture the distinctions in the use of spatial cues and modes of expression between high context Japanese and Mexican cultures.

Therefore, within the CSIS framework, the emphasis is on the four components of communication style, relationship, time and space context. An individual may vary in terms of how the contextual cues are used for each component and the meaning they convey in the communication. For example, among high context communicators there are likely to be two approaches to the components: for some individuals, both the contextual cues and meaning are very subtle and will be communicated in a *reserved* manner, for others, the cues and meaning will be more bold and will be conveyed via an *expressive* approach. Among the low context communicators, the cues will not be noticed or will not seem very relevant in communication, and all meaning will be conveyed in a *direct* fashion.

Component one: communication style

Japanese negotiators can say "no" in 16 different ways in a negotiation without directly saying "no"; for example, they will be silent, they will counter with a question, or they will leave the meeting without a response (Ueda, 1974). This is because Japanese negotiators might typically be considered reserved communicators.

Reserved. People with a reserved communication style are indirect and implicit in interaction. Their meaning is often very subtle, hidden in cues in the contextual environment. Nonverbal language (although sometimes hard for the non-reserved communicator to detect) is important and meaningful. The reserved communication style is listener oriented; the listener is a full partner in the communication and is expected to decode the message and understand its meaning. People with a reserved communication style tend to think and speak holistically, understanding a given point within the entire context in which it is presented.

Expressive. People with an expressive communication style are often direct and explicit owing to the open use of emotion and intense and rapid verbal expression in communication. Yet expressive communicators are holistic communicators as well in that they are attuned to the meaning conveyed in interaction not only through words but also through contextual cues in the interaction environment.

Direct. For people with a direct communication style, information is contained primarily in the verbal, coded, explicit part of a message. Their communication style is speaker oriented; there is no expectation that the listener will decode an implicit meaning because the message is clearly stated.

Just what is meant by a holisitic communication style? Hall notes that it is not the words that are used that matter, but rather *how* the message is conveyed, and that the receiver of the message is expected to work to interpret the meaning of the message sent.

> People raised in high-context systems expect more of others than do the participants in low context systems. When talking about something they have on their minds, a high-context individual will expect his (or her) interlocutor to know what's bothering him (or her), so that he (or she) doesn't have to be specific. The result is that he (or she) will talk around and around the point, in effect putting all the pieces in place except the crucial one. Placing it properly — this keystone — is the role of his (or her) interlocutor (1976, pg. 88).

Why do high context individuals take the trouble to walk around the point? This tendency toward indirectness and implictness is influenced by collectivism and individualism (Gibson, 1988). Collectivists have a need to maintain group harmony, to avoid bringing shame to the group, and to save face at all costs (Triandis, 1989), and therefore will use indirect, implicit messages whereas individualists are not as concerned about group harmony and therefore will use more explicit, direct communication.

Now we can start to unravel the Bilinguals Labels debacle. Mr. Wang was Chinese and thus was possibly a reserved communicator with respect to Pete Martin, from Canada, who was possibly a more direct one. When Mr. Wang told Pete that delivering the labels would be difficult, he was telling him "no", but not directly. It was Pete's job to figure out what was being said. Mr. Wang even said it would be "very difficult" a second time for emphasis. But Pete, a direct communicator who paid attention to the literal meaning of the words, (i.e., "it will be difficult" = "difficult but possible") still did not understand.

Why didn't Mr. Wang tell Pete directly? To say "no" to Pete would have brought shame to Mr. Wang and his company by forcing Mr. Wang to admit his inability to manufacture the labels; such admission would cause Mr. Wang to lose face. In forcing the issue, and causing Mr. Wang to lose face, Pete would also lose face, and the negotiation and relationship between the two men would have suffered a major setback.

What should have Pete done in this case? If Pete had understood Mr. Wang's implicit "no", an implicit option for resolving the problem would have been to bring samples of the labels in French and English with him to China, indicating to Mr. Wang that this is what the finished labels might look like. Pete would do this *without* suggesting that Mr. Wang might not know how to manufacture the labels. This would be a way to work with Mr. Wang and preserve what otherwise is seemingly a good relationship.

Component two: relationships

The United States is the home of the cold call. Only in the US and in a handful of other countries considered to be cultures where the populations exhibit a prominently direct communication and interaction style, is it possible to pick up the phone, call someone you have never seen, met, or have any connection to, and within 20 minutes, negotiate a deal with them. This is because one of the unstated and implicit channels through which information is conveyed in most other cultures — in cultures in which people have reserved or expressive communication and interaction styles — is the relationship between the negotiators.

Reserved. People who relate in a reserved manner are often very cautious in interactions with strangers, and rely on cues about stranger's backgrounds, their status (which may be indicated by age, title, wealth, education, gender) and particularly their network of colleagues. Time is needed to establish a relationship however once a relationship is established, the bond is extremely strong and long lasting. There is a heightened concern for face-saving (both self- and other-face maintenance) in the name of harmony within the relationship and the maintenance of social norms. For reserved negotiators, a moderate overlap between work and non-work relations typically occurs because (1) relationship building and business are often carried out after hours at dinner or over drinks at a restaurant or bar, etc. and (2) a heightened awareness of relationships and networks means reserved negotiators are likely to choose business partners with some sort of personal connection.

Direct. People who relate directly are low context, and as such do not infer or confer meaning from relational cues such as one's status, background, network, or the longevity or a relationship. Face maintenance by someone who relates directly concerns primarily the self, and would typically be for self-preservation purposes. It is their low attention to relationships and context that allows direct communicators to compartmentalize work and non-work relations. Rather than structuring one's life as one large network of contacts, relations at work remain in that restricted context, which is typically separate from relations outside of work.

Expressive. People who relate expressively are also cautious in interactions with strangers, and rely on cues about stranger's backgrounds, their status and their network of colleagues. As with reserved negotiators, expressive negotiators take time to establish relationships that are characterized by high trust and long-term commitment. Because of their concern for relationships, expressive negotiators will be cautious to save face for both the self and the counterpart. People who relate expressively see a strong overlap between work and non-work relations as quite natural. They rely heavily on personal contacts when developing business opportunities, and professional networks include people in their social and family networks. Work related activities may occur in after hours at restaurants, etc. or in the home.

McMillan and Woodruff describe how the Vietnamese, who are generally reserved with respect to relationships, rely on cues about strangers' backgrounds and networks in relationship building and negotiation, particularly given that a transparent legal system cannot be relied upon, "Firms often scrutinize prospective trading partners before beginning to transact, checking the firms' reliability via other firms in the same line of business or familial connections" (1999, pg. 638).

Furthermore, the importance of the relationship context is demonstrated in this recounting of negotiations in the Jamaican coffee industry (Kollock, 1993):

> When Hurricane Gilbert devastated the Blue Mountain coffee growing region in Jamaica in 1988, Japanese importers quickly offered to help rebuild the area. The grateful coffee growers allowed the Japanese importers to buy up the vast majority of their coveted crop, despite higher offers from American and European importers. As one Jamaican coffee manager put it: 'We have Americans and Europeans who call up all the time and say, look, we'll pay you $11 a pound' (the price at the time was $7.50). Well, that's fine for one shot, but what do you do four years hence, when the next hurricane hits? That's when you remember the Japanese, and the lesson for us has been taking care of clients like that first.

In this case, we see the importance of relationship over monetary utility, on knowing the partner's background and long term network over the immediate payoff for the generally expressively-oriented Jamaican negotiator.

Component three: time

Think of the adages people in the United States use that contain the word time; "Spend time", "Use time", "Waste time", "Save time", "Invest time", "Just in time". What do these adages say about how Americans view time? At least in part, time is regarded as a commodity, as something precious to be used as efficiently as possible. Compare this perspective with the following adages from cultures that are relatively higher context: "Time settles everything" from Italy, and "Hurry hurry has no blessing" from Western Africa.

Time is part of a socio-cultural system — it is socially constructed and reflects cultural variation in pace of life, time horizons, temporal focus, and simultaneous versus sequential task involvement (Bluedorn, 2002; Brislin and Kim, 2003; MacDuff, 2006). "Time talks. It speaks more plainly than words. The message it conveys comes through loud and clear". (Hall, 1959, p. 1). Thus, the way people attend to time and move through time is yet another of the unstated and implicit languages by which negotiators communicate and interact with one another. Hall suggested there are two orientations toward time: polychronicity and monochronicity (Hall, 1959).

Reserved. People who view time in a reserved manner, Chinese or Japanese negotiators for example, are typically more monochronic particularly in professional situations, and perceive it important to begin negotiations on time for the sake of the business relationship. Yet, reserved individuals, also tend to be very relationship oriented, thus are likely to become more polychronic once negotiations commence. They are attuned to cues in the interaction environment that may signal the need to be flexible with respect to deadlines and schedules. This is particularly true in the case of ensuring that maintenance of harmony and social norms in a relationship takes precedence over meeting a deadline. Direct negotiators need to be aware (and understand that their patience may be tested in situations when) the maintenance of social norms may mean a request for extra time to run a proposal past senior people who are not present at the negotiation (Hodgson, Sano, and Graham, 2008).

Direct. People who view time directly are monochronic both professionally and socially; they perceive time as a fixed commodity to be used efficiently, spent, invested, measured, or lost. They adhere strictly to fixed schedules and deadlines and process information in a serial fashion. For the mono-chronic person, being made to wait 30 minutes beyond the scheduled meeting time with their negotiation partner seems rude. Furthermore, the monochronic person may feel disre-spected when their polychronic partner allows constant interruptions for phone calls, messages, or continual sidebars (Gesteland, 1999).

Expressive. People who view time expressively are poly-chronic; they have fluid and flexible attitudes towards time (note the Indonesian phrase 'jam karet' — rubber time), and view punctuality and deadlines as artificial constraints relative to the reality of human relationships. They also tend to engage in simultaneous information processing, so multitasking dur-ing a negotiation, or breaking into frequent sidebars during negotiation in their foreign tongue is common. For the poly-chronic individual, catching up with a friend you've run into on the way to the office is much more important than arriving "on time" for a meeting, the deadline is a man-made construc-tion in a datebook, whereas the relationship is real (Gestland, 1999).

Greg Mortenson, head of the Central Asia Institute and advisor to the US military in the region, has built over 130 schools for girls in Afghanistan and Pakistan. In large part, he attributes his success in building these schools to his success in negotiating with the chieftains of numerous tribes including the Taliban, who have a stake in promoting (and preventing) women's education. He recounts the building of his first school and his restlessness and frustration with countless delays and interminable meetings and banquets with various tribal stakeholders, suppliers, and contrac-tors. During one of Mortenson's most frustrating moments, his mentor and the chief of the village where the first school was to be built, Haji Ali, sat Mortenson down and gave him a lesson:

> 'If you want to thrive in Baltistan, you must respect our ways', Haji
> Ali said, blowing on his bowl. 'The first time you share tea with a
> Balti, you are a stranger. The second time you take tea you are an

honored guest. The third time you share a cup of tea you become family, and for our family, we are prepared to do anything, even die', he said ... 'Doctor Greg, you must make time to share three cups of tea. We may be uneducated. But we are not stupid. We have lived and survived here a long time...'. 'That day, Haji Ali taught me the most important lesson I've ever learned in my life', Mortenson says. 'We Americans think you have to accomplish everything quickly. We're the country of thirty-minute power lunches and two-minute football drills. ... Haji Ali taught me to share three cups of tea, to slow down and make building relationships as important as building projects' (p. 150, 2006).

This case actually shows the value of two of the unstated components relating to interaction style — the relationship and time components. Both are equally important. In cultures with expressive and reserved interaction styles, it is crucial that negotiators take time to build relationships and trust with their negotiation partner. Building that trust means spending time with the partner — sometimes in their home drinking tea, sometimes in a smoky bar in Ginza singing off-key karaoke, sometimes talking about partner's family late into the night in Athens. In polychronic, relationship-oriented cultures, the relationship precedes the deal, not the other way around, and relationship building takes time. In fact, in these high context cultures, the amount of time you are willing to invest in the relationship often communicates much more than any words could say. Once this time is invested, the likelihood of creating and gaining value in your negotiation is exponentially increased.

Right now Baltistan may seem too far away to imagine in terms of international business negotiation since the main negotiations occurring there involve military personnel, the UN and NGOs. However, the story of Mortenson and Haji Ali is not that different from the anecdote commonly told to MBA students in "Negotiating in Japan" classes:

Question: "What do you tell your Japanese negotiation counterpart when he asks you 'when is your return ticket?'"

Answer: "I don't have one. I'm here as long as it takes us to get this partnership working."

Rationale #1: Negotiators from many other cultures, particularly polychronic ones, are highly practiced at the use of time as a negotiation tactic. If you tell your counterpart you have a ticket booked in a week, even two or three, they will certainly outlast and outmaneuver you in the negotiation.

Rationale #2: More importantly, in a polychronic culture, one week means nothing in terms of a relationship. In essence, you are signaling to them that all you want is THE DEAL. You might as well have not made the trip at all. If you are serious about working in that culture, you need to invest the time and work on the relationship first. Once that is in place, negotiating the deal will go much more smoothly.

Component four: space

Space is the last component in the unstated and implicit realm of communication. The most obvious dimension of space is the level of the physical boundary. Ambassador Richard Holbrooke, who helped broker the Dayton Accord following the 1992–1995 war in Bosnia, described the value of being able to control the space in which the negotiation occurred:

> So we decided to give a dinner for all the participants, and we chose the great museum, the air museum at Wright-Patterson, the largest and best military aviation museum in the world.... . And they have these huge hangars.... . They picked the biggest hangar and we put the tables out in front of it. And all the presidents came, and we seated them under the wing of a B-52. Some of the Europeans thought this was a little militaristic.... . I said, well, why not? Let them be reminded of this.
>
> So we sat them under this. And Milosevic started looking around as we went in. It was very emotional. And one of my colleagues took Milosevic over to the wall and said, that's a Tomahawk missile. A Tomahawk missile is about 18 feet long.

And Milosevic just looked at it. He stopped. He said, you
did all that damage with that little thing? And my colleague
said, yeah.

So I don't want to leave you with the impression — I don't
know whether any of this made any difference. I'm just giving
you the atmospherics. But I think it did. We brought generals out
there. We made absolutely clear that the bombing could resume
if we didn't get an agreement. And they agreed to stay until we
got an agreement (PON Harvard Law School, 2004).

Perhaps less dramatic, but a means of communicating power
just the same, are the seating arrangements for a Japanese negotiation. The most important Japanese executive will be seated
(a) in the largest chair (b) that is farthest from the door, (c) in the
location that is the center of the focus of the room (Hodgson,
Sano and Graham, 2008).

Less obvious is when space communication works at the
level of the other senses. "Few people realize that space is perceived by all the senses, not by vision alone. Auditory space is
perceived by the ears, thermal space by the skin, kinesthetic
space by the muscles, and olfactory space by the nose" (Hall and
Hall, 2002, p. 11). Thus, factors such as the use of silence, interruption, emotion, and body language also come into play. How
people define and interpret these different forms of space in
communication and social interaction provides another piece of
contextual information that differentiates low and high context
cultures.

Reserved. While reserved communicators may consider their
counterpart a close and valuable partner, they will still show
physical restraint and distance in social interaction due to social
norms for restraint and formality. For reserved communicators
auditory space remains empty. Silence is not an empty space to
be filled but rather the emptiness itself signifies a communicative
act. Silence may indicate disapproval or impasse, but can also signal truthfulness, seriousness or support for the counterpart; thus
maintaining silence can be a means of promoting harmonious

relations. Also due to social norms for restraint and formality, reserved communicators are very subtle in their expression and body language.

Direct. People who relate to space directly tend to be low context. As if they do not want to immerse themselves in their surrounding context, they are protective of their own "space bubble" in communication; they stand a good distance from one another. Insensitive to communication cues from their environment or conversational pauses, they prefer a filled communication space; that is, they perceive that fewer silences and more conversational interruption and turn-taking signals better interaction management. Those who view space directly are moderately expressive with their tone of voice and use moderate body language.

Expressive. People who relate to space expressively prefer to stand close to the person with whom they are interacting, often close enough so that they can frequently touch the person. By sharing space with their interlocutor, expressive communicators bring their partner into their own context. They like a filled communication space with few silences, and feel most comfortable when people are regularly interrupting one another or ending each another's sentences — this demonstrates a sense of camaraderie and closeness among the speakers. Those who relate to space expressively convey their meaning through emotion and expressive body language.

There is great variation across cultures in the aspects of negotiation communication related to the space context. A 15 culture study of the behavior of groups of six negotiators demonstrated that Japanese negotiators were comfortable with silence, and furthermore rarely interrupted their counterparts. This contrasted with Spaniards on the other hand who had no silent periods in their negotiations and Brazilians who had 28 interruptions in the 30 minute encounter (Requejo and Graham, 2008). According to Hodgson, Sano and Graham, for American negotiators, particularly, who are unaccustomed to silence, this opposition in styles can lead to a perilous situation *vis-a-vis* Japanese negotiators

(2008). The Japanese are masterful at the use of silence and will employ long periods of silence particularly on the occasion of an impasse. American negotiators, uncomfortable with silence, will often fall into the trap of filling the void with talking, thus possibly (a) making unreciprocated concessions and (b) almost certainly lessening the chances of learning more about the Japanese counterpart's interests.

Emotion and body language are also important elements of the language of space. The tone of conversation or the volume of speech is one cue, as are facial expressions, and body language (Cohen, 1991; Hall, 1966). As would be expected, individuals in high context cultures (those individuals who relate to space in a reserved or expressive manner) are more likely to be attuned to auditory and physical cues. Thus, as with time, both attention to space and space itself communicate information. In the study of negotiators from 15 cultures, one of the starkest differences demonstrated was that Brazilian negotiators spent 74.6 minutes looking at one another versus the six Japanese negotiators who looked at one another for a total of only 3.9 minutes. Brazilians touched each other 5.7 times in the course of the 30 minutes, Japanese did not touch each other at all (Requejo and Graham, 2008).

For Greg Mortenson and his right hand man, Sarfraz Khan from Pakistan, understanding spatial cues in communication was crucial at all times to the success of their negotiations to build school for girls, and in certain situations was a matter of life and death.

In any given situation, regardless of whether it involved an all-night negotiation with a group of conservative mullahs or a five-minute break at a roadside tea stall, Sarfraz paid keen attention to the body language of everyone involved. Who sat where and why? Who sipped his tea first and who hung back? Who spoke and who remained silent? Who was the most powerful person in the room, who was the weakest, and how did their respective agendas influence what they were saying?

There can be many layers and shades of meaning within each of these distinctions, and by responding to all of them with equally subtle adjustments of his own, Sarfraz strove to avoid drawing unwanted attention either to himself or to me (2009, p. 107).

Communication and culture: closing the deal

One of the toughest sticking points in closing a cross-cultural deal is drawing up the contract. This is because the view of the contract differs so radically from culture to culture. For lawyers who communicate directly and have a direct perspective on relationships and time, the preferred contract is likely to obsessively document the rights and responsibilities of the parties and spend little time on why the deal is being done or the philosophy of the relationship that got the parties to the point they are. The result is an extremely long, dense, detailed contract, "documented in a forensic way that says this is black, and by the way, black is not white, yellow, orange or red, and no shade of gray is acceptable.' In the end you have 250 documents with every single clause the lawyers could have imagined", (Glass, 2007, pg. 16).

On the other hand, for business people who communicate indirectly and have a reserved or expressive perspective on relationships and time, the approach to contracts is much more philosophical and focused on the relationship and trust. Asian agreements, for example, are much shorter and purpose-oriented; contracts are viewed as documents that live and breathe and move forward with the relationship. Rupert Pearce, general counsel of a mobile communications company says, "If you go straight to your legal rights as soon as you can, you cause a breakdown in a relationship that may otherwise prove to be valuable, because the thing that does not compute in Asian minds is having their noses rubbed in a paragraph in a circumstance where things have clearly moved on," (Glass, 2007: 17).

Obviously both sides to the negotiation seek contractual stability and assurance that the terms of their agreement will be respected in the future. Yet, it is clear that no one can foresee every possible change in circumstance. The traditional approach to resolving this dilemma is to provide for every contingency in a written contract. However, for reserved and expressive negotiators, this written contract captures the relationship between the parties imperfectly and incompletely. For them, the relationship is the foundation of the deal; if the context of the deal changes, the two parties will work together and adjust accordingly. This is simply part of the ebb and flow of the relationship.

It is because of these differing cultural views of contracts that renegotiation clauses have become much more widely used in many parts of the non-Western world. A renegotiation clause provides that at specified times, or as a result of specified events during the term of the contract, the parties may renegotiate or review certain provisions (Salacuse, 2001). Some executives setting up long term international projects acknowledge that despite lawyers' intentions, it is extremely difficult to predict real working conditions and relations many years hence, and at best, what can be provided is an informal framework for renegotiation. "Once the contract is signed, we put it in the drawer. After that, what matters most is the relationship between us and our partner, and we are negotiating that relationship all the time," (Kolo and Walde, 2000: 45). In other instances, parties will set up formal renegotiation clauses. For example, an oil exploration contract between a foreign oil company and the Government of Qatar provided that the two sides would negotiate future arrangements for the use of natural gas not associated with oil discoveries if commercial quantites of "non-associated" gas were found in the contract area (Salacuse, 2001).

Conclusion

Effective communication and information exchange is essential to negotiation. But when the negotiators are from different cultures, communication becomes exponentially more complex. This was demonstrated in research between Japanese and American negotiators in the experimental negotiation Cartoon. In this negotiation Japanese negotiators primarily used indirect methods of information exchange; American negotiators primarily used direct methods of information exchange. When Japanese and American managers were negotiating intraculturally, the joint gains were $4.02 mn and $4.19 mn respectively. However, when Japanese and American managers negotiated *interculturally*, the joint gains fell to $3.22 mn, a significant decrease (Brett and Okumura, 1998).

Interestingly, in the intercultural negotiations, Japanese negotiators adapted to the negotiation style of the Americans; Japanese negotiators increased direct information sharing and decreased indirect information sharing relative to the base rate in intracultural negotiations (Adair, Okamura, and Brett, 2001). In making the adaptation, Japanese intercultural negotiators understood the interests and priorities of their American counterparts, but the US negotiators did not understand those of the Japanese — contributing to the lower joint gains.

It is not surprising that it was the Japanese negotiators who adapted to the American negotiators and not the other way around. The Japanese are likely to be more reserved, or high context, communicators. Thus, they are always attuned to cues in their communication environment and reading meaning from them. They may have sensed the need to modify their method of information exchange. Americans on the other hand, tend to be direct communicators and do not normally attend to contextual cues. This does not mean that US negotiators are insensitive or don't want to build relationships. One survey of experienced US and Japanese negotiators showed that both US and Japanese negotiators report that they adjust to their counterpart's style (Adair, Taylor, and Tinsley, 2009). However, the behavioral evidence shows it is only the high context, relationally attuned Japanese that successfully adjust their communication and strategies.

The lesson here is that *both* negotiators need to learn as much as they can about their own and their counterpart's communication and social interaction style prior to the negotiation, and to become practiced and comfortable in the other's approach as part of their negotiation planning. Without such preparation, it will be difficult to achieve the highest joint gains possible in cross-cultural negotiations. Without the ability to communicate and to exchange information between partners effectively it is likely that the parties will complete the negotiations leaving value on the table for both sides.

Communication, being part of culture, is complex because it encompasses more than the words spoken. Like the iceberg, there is so much more to it than simply what meets the eye. However, if one can master the unspoken language, the implicit and unstated assumptions that are wrapped up in communication and in the contexts of relationships and time and space, they will have prepared themselves to venture into cross-cultural negotiations.

Building Intercultural Trust at the Negotiating Table

Sujin Jang
Harvard Business School

Roy Chua
Harvard Business School

In 1988 Komatsu, Japan's leading construction-equipment man-ufacturer, and Dresser, a giant in the American energy industry, combined their resources in a joint venture. The partnership was seen as a match made in heaven; the companies expected it to create what they called "a mountain of resources" for both sides. But as talks progressed, it became increasingly difficult for Dresser and Komatsu to stay on the same page, let alone to trust each other. As conflict escalated and trust faltered, the joint venture's market share plummeted and 2,000 employees were fired. Ultimately, in 1994, the partnership was dissolved. The experience of Komatsu and Dresser is not rare. The business world bristles with stories of intercultural negotiations gone wrong.

Intercultural negotiations are marked by difficulties at every turn. This chapter will examine the dangers that plague negotiation across cultural boundaries, and the critical role of trust in the negotiation process. We will discuss what trust is, why it matters, and why it is so elusive in intercultural negotiations. Then we will offer guidelines for building trust, with particular emphasis on the cultivation of cultural intelligence to prepare negotiators for intercultural interactions effectively.

The Perils of Intercultural Negotiation

Intercultural negotiation is tough. Cultural differences can shape the negotiation process in subtle and unforeseen ways, and even an experienced negotiator may become frustrated and confused when negotiating with someone from a different culture. Researchers Wendi Adair of Cornell University and Jeanne Brett of Northwestern University compare the negotiation process to a dance between two parties. Like dance, negotiation has a universal flow that transcends cultures. But just as different rhythms and movements characterize different dance styles, negotiation has *culture-specific* components as well (Adair and Brett, 2005).

Suppose we paired up a tango dancer and a ballerina. Though they might share the goal of dancing well together, it would be extremely difficult for them to synchronize their movements. This is because each style of dance has its own script, which governs its specific patterns of movement. Think of a script as an organized pattern of thought that guides action. Because the ballerina and the tango dancer do not share the same script, it is more difficult for them to move in synchrony with each other than it would be for them to dance with someone who shares the same background and knowledge.

The same is true of intercultural negotiations. Negotiators with different cultural backgrounds may share an objective — to reach an optimal negotiated outcome, say — but in the process of negotiating they will inevitably encounter difficulties. Different cultures have different norms of behavior and different conceptualizations of the negotiation process, making it tricky to find common ground and establish trust. This is why intercultural negotiation is often frustrating, and apt to produce suboptimal outcomes.

This is a serious issue, with the global economy increasingly introducing organizations from different cultures into each other's arenas. Today cross-cultural interactions abound at all levels of organization: employees assigned to global virtual teams communicate on a daily basis with team members from diverse cultures, managers cross cultural boundaries to create globe-spanning value chains, and leaders compete and collaborate with counterparts all around the world. Intercultural interaction also occurs at the organizational level. A common example is cross-cultural mergers and acquisitions (M & As) like that of Dresser and Komatsu. Cross-cultural M & A transactions require continuous negotiation, and can be viewed as an extended and particularly complex negotiation process. Between 1992 and 2000 the annual number of cross-border M & As involving American companies rose from 570 to 2648, a 365-percent jump. A closer look reveals, however, that few of these deals are successful; most fall short of expectations, and many even result in substantial erosion of shareholder returns.

In both the laboratory and the field, study after study has found that cross-cultural negotiations are less likely than single-culture negotiations to result in outcomes that are favorable for both parties. Jeanne Brett of Northwestern University and Tetsushi Okumura of Shiga University, for example, found that joint profits suffered significantly when Japanese and American managers negotiated over a business deal, compared to when they negotiated with counterparts from their own cultures (Brett and Okumura, 1998). Brett and Okumura attribute this effect to different negotiating scripts or schemas. We defined a script earlier as an organized pattern of thought that governs behavior; similarly, a schema is a mental structure or framework that determines how an individual makes sense of the world. Like the ballerina and the tango dancer, negotiators from different cultures bring different behavioral norms and cognitive assumptions to the negotiation table.

The Role of Trust in Intercultural Negotiations

What makes intercultural negotiation so difficult? A critical factor is the lack of trust. All negotiations, both intra- and intercultural, involve considerable risk. Negotiators must constantly ask themselves, "Should I disclose or hide my preferences? How much information should I reveal? Will my actions be reciprocated, ignored, or taken advantage of?" A negotiator may consider sharing sensitive information or offering a compromise in hopes of triggering a comparable response from the other party. But he or she must weigh the risk that the other side will be uncooperative, or even exploit their sincere intentions. It is this risky nature that makes trust so critical in any negotiation.

In *intercultural* negotiations, where the other party's motives and social norms are even less clear, negotiators share less common ground from the outset. According to Deepak Malhotra of Harvard Business School, trust is especially difficult to establish in situations characterized by high stress and high stakes, such as when negotiating with foreign parties or coping with sharp differences (Malhotra, 2004). It is important to note, however, that trust can make the biggest difference in these very situations. A recent article in the *Harvard Negotiation Law Review* by Yan Ki Bonnie Cheng (2009) specifies the potential positive outcomes of trust: "In a partnership founded upon trust, parties are more likely to share information, abstain from taking competitive advantage, and engage in longer-run exchange of favors".

As Cheng points out, negotiating parties who trust each other are more likely to share critical information. Roy Chua, Michael Morris and Shira Mor found, more specifically, that trust promotes the sharing of new ideas across cultures, such as coming up with new business initiatives and ways to get work done (Chua, Morris and Mor, 2010). Sharing new ideas with others is inherently risky; good ideas might be stolen, and bad ideas might be ridiculed. Trust increases one's willingness to take the risk of sharing untested ideas. In a similar vein, Aimee Drolet of Stanford University and Michael Morris of Columbia University have argued that trust leads to better rapport, which increases willingness to cooperate with others in mixed-motive conflicts (Drolet and Morris, 2000). In other words, trust promotes cooperation and moderates a climate of excessive competitiveness. Why is this important in a negotiation context? Because information sharing and cooperation enhance positive outcomes for both parties. In a study of 344 auto-maker/supplier relationships, Jeffrey Dyer of Brigham Young University and Wujin Chu of Seoul National University (2003) found trust to correlate with reduced transaction costs and greater information sharing. In fact, the study found that the costs of doing business with suppliers were nearly *six times higher* for the least-trusted automaker than for the most trusted.

Trust also has a long-term impact on the negotiating parties' relationship. Researchers have found that trusting partners are likely to abstain from short-term exploitation at the expense of the other party, and to engage in longer-term value exchange. Thus, building trust in negotiations also enables the parties to develop and maintain a positive relationship over time. Given that most negotiations are not one-shot deals but episodes in a potentially long and mutually beneficial relationship, the long-term value of trust is especially important.

In sum, trust leads to better negotiation processes, and enhances both the short- and the long-term outcomes of negotiations.

Unpacking the Concept of Trust

Trust has been defined as the willingness to make oneself vulnerable to another party despite uncertainty about the other party's intentions and future actions (Kramer, 1999; Mayer, Davis and Schoorman, 1995; McAllister, 1995; Rotter, 1967). Trust consists of both knowledge that the other party has the power to act beneficially or harmfully, and confidence that he or she will behave in ways that are beneficial. In short, when you trust someone, you willingly risk putting some of your welfare and interests in that person's hands.

How does trust develop between people? Following Daniel McAllister (1995), psychologists typically distinguish two paths toward trust. Think of someone you trust and ask yourself why you trust this person. One reason may be that you know him or her to be competent and reliable; you have come to trust this person based on what you know about his or her skills, motives, and past behavior. This path leads to cognition-based trust, or "trust from the head", on which many professional relationships are built. Alternatively, you may trust someone simply because you like him or her and believe you have a good personal relationship; you may also feel that this person has your welfare and interests at heart. Such affect-based trust, or "trust from the heart", characterizes most friendships and personal relationships.

In short, trust can arise via either of two distinct psychological processes: a cognitive evaluation of the other party's competence and reliability, or an affective experience of liking and rapport. The former is based on expectations of task-related competence and involves an analytic and utilitarian assessment of the other party; the latter is closely linked to empathy and rapport, and arises from emotional closeness. These two types of trust closely resemble two central dimensions of social perception: warmth and competence (Fiske, Cuddy and Glick, 2007). Affect-based trust is strongly linked to perceived warmth, and cognition-based trust to perceived competence.

The two types of trust also generate different behavioral tendencies. For example, Kok-Yee Ng of Nanyang Business School and Roy Chua of Harvard Business School (2006) found that, in a social-dilemma game, high affect-based trust among team members increases cooperation but high cognition-based trust can actually reduce cooperation. Why is this so? When people have high cognition-based trust in their co-workers, they tend to believe that they can rely on these co-workers to do most of the work. This actually makes them more likely to free-ride on others' contributions to the team. Conversely, when people develop affect-based trust in their co-workers, higher trust does not lead to withholding contribution to the team. Because they care about the interests of their co-workers, they are more willing to share the workload. Given these findings, it is crucial to distinguish between the two types of trust, and to examine how different cultures think about and build both.

Trust in Different Cultures

How would you go about winning the trust of an American executive? By giving him a shining résumé documenting your work experience and skills? By directly demonstrating how competent you are at your work? By asking a mutual acquaintance to vouch for you? By getting acquainted over a beer? Take a moment to think about what your strategy might be. Now imagine that you are trying to win the trust of an executive from China. Would your approach be the same?

If you answered yes to the last question, you may be in trouble. Practitioners and researchers have found that people from different cultures conceptualize and develop trust differently. Specifically, collectivistic and individualistic cultures differ, as do high-context and low-context cultures, in how their constituents think about and build trust. Psychologists Hazel Rose Markus and Shinobu Kitayama, of Stanford University and the University of Michigan respectively, describe *individualistic* cultures as characterized by a focus on the individual rather than the collective. Constituents of these cultures see themselves as independent social beings whose self-concept is not built on their relationships with other individuals. In individualistic cultures, the uniqueness of the individual is emphasized and celebrated. *Collectivistic* cultures, on the other hand, exhibit a stronger focus on community and society, and emphasize the rights of the collective over those of the individual. Constituents of these cultures tend to adopt interdependent self-concepts which are inextricably linked to their relationships with others (Markus and Kitayama, 1991).

Another dimension of culture, identified by the late anthropologist and cross-cultural researcher Edward Hall, entails whether constituents engage primarily in high- or low-context communication. In a *high-context* culture, many things are left unsaid; shared cultural knowledge fills the gaps. A few words can communicate a complex message to other constituents of the same culture. In a *low-context* culture, communication is much more explicit; much more is spelled out in words, rather than relying on context or shared knowledge (Hall, 1989).

How is trust conceived of and cultivated in these different kinds of cultures? Oana Branzei of the Richard Ivey School of Business and colleagues (2007) found that individualistic and collectivistic cultures have distinct "grammars" for developing trust. In individualistic cultures, where people forge relatively shallow dependence relationships at work, trust arises from knowledge of an individual's *ability* to accomplish specific tasks. In collectivistic cultures, where people seek deeper dependence relationships at work, trust stems from *feelings* of familiarity, caring, and empathy. In other words, the basic building blocks of trust in individualistic cultures are the capability-based processes that psychologists refer to as "trust from the head", or cognition-based trust. In collectivistic cultures, the foundations of trust are affect and rapport, leading to what psychologists call "trust from the heart", or affect-based trust.

Researchers have found that the degree to which the two types of trust are distinguished also varies across cultures. For example, Roy Chua and colleagues (2009) discovered that Chinese managers tend to mix personal and professional concerns in the workplace more than their American counterparts do; hence cognition- and affect-based trust are less easily distinguishable in the Chinese workplace. Generally speaking, in Western societies, where individualistic and low-context cultures are prevalent, the predominant work ethic deems it unprofessional to mix work with personal concerns, and spillover between the personal and professional domains is rare. Here, personal and affective matters are put aside at work in order to maintain a strong focus on the task (Sanchez-Burks *et al.*, 2003). Hence work relationships are characterized by "trust from the head", but not necessarily "trust from the heart". Conversely, in collectivistic, high-context cultures such as those found in East Asian and Middle Eastern societies, the distinction between the professional and personal realms is less clear. These cultures put much greater emphasis on relational and affective matters in the workplace; building personal ties and developing affective trust is a precondition to working effectively with others. Here, trust from the head and trust from the heart are often intertwined and difficult to distinguish.

Because the two types of trust operate differently in different cultures, it is important to be aware of these differences and develop the ability to cultivate the two types as needed in cross-cultural interactions. But the context of intercultural negotiations makes it extremely difficult to build both cognition- and affect-based trust. In the following part, we will discuss why trust is especially elusive in when negotiating across cultures.

Why Trust is Difficult to Build in Intercultural Negotiations

There are three primary reasons why trust is particularly difficult to build in intercultural negotiations.

First, differences in *cognitive* schema impede the building of trust. When negotiating across cultures, you and your partner do not share the same implicit scripts, norms, and assumptions. "Human cognition is not everywhere the same", according to psychologist Richard Nisbett of the University of Michigan (Nisbett, 2004: xvii). According to Nisbett's research, there are scientifically measurable differences in the way people of different cultures think. For example, East Asians are measurably more holistic in their perceptions, while Westerners tend to have a "tunnel vision" perceptual style, focusing on the prominent focal object. In the context of negotiations, one common finding is that Americans are apt to approach negotiations with a competitive mindset, whereas Japanese negotiators tend to see negotiation as a process of working together to reach a mutually agreeable conclusion (Lituchy, 1997). Such incongruence in approaches to negotiation can hinder the development of a shared understanding of the task, impeding the process of building cognition-based trust. As noted earlier, cognition-based trust stems from knowledge of the other person's task-related competence. In cross-cultural negotiations, incongruent negotiating mindsets or schemas stand in the way of effectively exchanging such knowledge.

Second, *behavioral* differences between cultures also inhibit trust. Negotiators draw on their own norms of appropriate action, enacting behavioral sequences that are taken for granted in their own cultures. For example, when it comes to communication styles, negotiators from low- and high-context cultures employ different types of behaviors to create joint gains. Those from low-context cultures (like the United States) tend to favor direct communication, explicitly stating their preferences and opinions. Conversely, those from high-context cultures (like Japan) often resort to indirect communication, communicating their thoughts and preferences in a roundabout way (Adair, Okumura, and Brett, 2001). These differences often make for inefficient communication. They also impede the establishment of rapport, and may even annoy and frustrate the participants. Recent studies by Hajo Adam of the Kellogg School of Management and his colleagues at UC Berkeley found, for example, that expressions of anger had different effects on European American and Asian American negotiators. Expressing anger elicited larger concessions from European Americans, but had the opposite effect on Asians and Asian Americans (Adam, Shirako and Maddux, 2010). This is because there are different cultural norms governing the appropriateness of certain behaviors — in this case, expressing anger in negotiations. In short, negotiators from different cultures have different behavioral norms and patterns, and the mismatch in communication styles that follows can ultimately erode cognition-based and affect-based trust.

Finally, *motivational factors* can also undermine trust. The sheer difficulty of arriving at a shared understanding of the task can make cross-cultural negotiators less likely to work toward a common goal, resulting in lower motivation to create joint gains. And the unfamiliarity of interacting with someone from another culture can also lead to anxiety, discomfort, and stress. Studies have found that Chinese negotiators are more likely than Western negotiators to withdraw from stressful situations, such as dealing with an aggressive counterpart (Graham and Lam, 2003; Tse *et al.*, 1994). However, Chinese negotiators are by no means the only ones to be affected by stress. The pressures of dealing with a dissimilar counterpart in the absence of a common goal can easily discourage cross-cultural negotiators on both sides of the negotiating table. Rajesh Kumar of the Nottingham University Business School noted that negative affect such as agitation or tension may result in "withdrawal or agreement at any cost" in negotiations (Kumar, 1999: 299). Needless to say, when negotiators are not motivated to build trust, neither cognition- nor affect-based trust can flourish.

In sum, negotiators from different cultures are likely to think and act differently, and to become discouraged in their efforts to communicate with and understand each other. These obstacles inhibit the development of both cognition-based and affect-based trust.

Establishing Trust in Intercultural Negotiations

Fortunately, you can change the odds. There is no fail-safe formula, but there are things you can do to overcome obstacles and promote mutual trust in cross-cultural negotiations. Establishing trust with someone from another culture requires effort on three dimensions: gaining an *understanding* of the other party's norms of interaction, adapting your *behavior* flexibly and appropriately, and maintaining the *motivation* to persevere. These are the three pillars of *Cultural Intelligence (CQ)*, a form of competence that has been identified as crucial to successful cross-cultural interactions (Earley and Ang, 2003).

Cultural intelligence is defined as "a person's capability for successful adaptation to new cultural settings" (Earley and Ang, 2003: 9). Christopher Earley of the University of Connecticut's School of Business and Soon Ang of Nanyang Business School, pioneers of the concept of cultural intelligence, emphasize that CQ is different from, and should not be mistaken for, emotional intelligence and social intelligence. Emotional intelligence refers to a person's ability to effectively understand and regulate emotions (Mayer and Salovey, 1997); social intelligence refers to one's ability to understand and manage people (Salovey and Mayer,

1990). Missing in these concepts is the *cultural* context and a person's ability to function in different cultures. This is where CQ comes in. Cultural intelligence refers to "a component of intelligence that is key for adjusting to, and interacting with, cultures other than one's own" (Earley and Ang, 2003: 7).

What good is cultural intelligence in the context of intercultural negotiations? Researchers Lynn Imai and Michele Gelfand of the University of Maryland recently found that negotiators with higher CQ exhibit more cooperative motives and higher motivation in intercultural contexts, and engage in more effective negotiation processes (Imai and Gelfand, 2010). This constellation of attitudes and behavior in turn enables them to achieve higher joint profits than negotiators with lower CQ. Empirical research has also shown CQ to be an important predictor of affective as well as performance-related outcomes in culturally diverse situations. In fact, CQ was found to predict success in intercultural situations over other constructs such as personality traits, emotional intelligence, and social intelligence.

Fortunately, cultural intelligence is not fixed; rather, it can be developed in psychologically healthy and willing people. You can enhance your CQ by cultivating all three dimensions of CQ: the cognitive, the behavioral, and the motivational. In this next part, we base our discussion and suggestions on the framework developed by Christopher Earley and Elaine Mosakowski (2004).

Let's start first with the cognitive dimension. Cultivating cognitive CQ does not mean simply collecting information on different cultures. Having an acquaintance with the characteristics of a given culture is certainly helpful, but such knowledge alone will not fully prepare you for every situation that could arise when engaging in intercultural negotiations. Instead, you need to have a *learning strategy* that will allow you to perceive and understand another culture's norms, customs, beliefs, and idiosyncrasies. Recent work by Roy Chua and colleagues found that individuals who think reflectively about cultural knowledge — that is, those who have an effective learning strategy — are more likely to succeed in creative collaborations across cultures

(Chua, Morris and Mor, 2010). An effective learning strategy involves constantly checking your assumptions and thinking about the different mental models that you and the other party bring to the table. Having an effective learning strategy will enable you to make sense of clues to a culture's hidden meanings and shared understandings.

But trust does not stem from knowledge alone. To establish trust with someone, your *actions* — both verbal and non-verbal — must also show that you have entered his or her world. That is, you must also cultivate *behavioral* CQ, the ability to adapt appropriate verbal and non-verbal behavior in different cultural contexts. Why should mimicking someone's behavior lead to higher levels of trust? Earley and Mosakowski posit that "by adopting the habits and mannerisms [of someone from another culture], you eventually come to understand in the most elemental way what it is to be like them. They, in turn, become more trusting and open". (Earley and Mosakowski, 2004: 3) Other researchers have found empirical evidence that supports these claims. For instance, a recent study by Jeffrey Sanchez-Burks at the University of Michigan (2009) found that job candidates who were able to adopt some of the mannerisms of culturally different recruiters were perceived in a more favorable light, and thus more likely to receive job offers. Earley and Mosakowski write, "whether it's the way you shake hands or order a coffee, evidence of an ability to mirror the customs and gestures of the people around you will prove that you esteem them enough to be like them". (Earley and Mosakowski, 2004: 3)

The final dimension of Cultural Intelligence is *motivational*. Motivational CQ refers to a person's desire and willingness to function effectively across diverse settings in spite of challenges and setbacks. Interacting with someone from another culture is not always easy. Because of the cognitive and behavioral differences we discussed above, trust will not be easily built. You will inevitably come across misunderstandings and other difficulties, and perhaps face a few unpleasant surprises along the way. As such, negotiating across cultures in a high-stakes environment can frustrate and discourage even the most skilled negotiators. However, motivation is crucial to success. To engage culturally different others and reach an optimal outcome, one must persevere in the face of difficulties and stay confident and motivated throughout the negotiation process.

Every negotiation is unique, and there is no magic formula for effectiveness. But evidence from research suggests that fostering cultural intelligence leads to greater mutual understanding and a higher level of trust. A person with high cultural intelligence can accurately assess the other party's capacities and motives, act accordingly to build mutual trust, and persevere in spite of hardships and challenges. Cultivating the three dimensions of CQ, therefore, can better prepare you to navigate the challenges of intercultural negotiations.

Conclusion

"A basic fact about negotiation, easy to forget in corporate and international transactions, is that you are dealing not with abstract representatives of the 'other side', but with human beings". With these words, Roger Fisher, Professor Emeritus at Harvard Law School, and William Ury, co-founder of Harvard's Program on Negotiation, remind us that negotiators are "people first" (Fisher and Ury, 1991: 14). It is this very humanness of negotiators that makes trust both important and difficult to develop. Trust is often called the lubricant that makes the wheels of business turn, but it does not spring up automatically; trust must be earned and built up over time.

For many, doing business in the twenty-first century means doing business around the world. Thus, it is crucial that business leaders know how to interact and negotiate effectively with people and organizations from different cultures. Each step of the negotiation process is risky, and challenges lurk at every turn. Under these circumstances building trust may seem daunting, but it is important to know that it can be accomplished. The first step is to understand what trust is and why it matters. The second crucial step is to cultivate cultural intelligence: to learn about the other culture, adjust your behavior accordingly, and stay motivated throughout the ups and downs of the negotiation process. Despite the hardships you will inevitably encounter, awareness and careful preparation for this process will put you in a much better position to negotiate effectively across cultures.

Negotiating the Renault-Nissan Alliance: Insights from Renault's Experience

Stephen E. Weiss*
Schulich School of Business
York University

In early 2010, the Renault-Nissan Alliance was the 4th largest automotive group in the world. With 350,000 employees and operations in 190 countries, the Alliance had sold 6.1 million vehicles — more than 9% of the world total — and taken in revenue of €86.5 billion (US$120 billion) in 2009.[1] The Alliance had performed so well over the past decade that it was widely touted as a model for successful partnership ("All together now", 2010).

When news first broke about the alliance, auto executives dismissed it as "the most improbable marriage in the world" (Thornton *et al.*, 1999). Observers skeptically emphasized the

* This chapter is a modified and updated version of the author's article in French (with C. Marjollet and C. Bouquet), titled "Perspective d'analyse en négociation: Le cas de l'alliance Renault-Nissan", *La revue française de gestion*, 2004, 30(153), 211–234. My thanks to Eric Chernin for editorial assistance.

[1] In addition to Renault and Nissan, Alliance brands include Infiniti, Dacia (Romania), and Samsung (South Korea). All financial figures in this chapter are expressed in unadjusted nominal values. For annual figures, currency translations are based on exchange rates at the end of the fiscal year.

contrast in national cultures, complexity of the undertaking, and opposition from various stakeholders. In the latter stages of negotiations to form the alliance, even Renault CEO Louis Schweitzer bleakly assessed the odds of reaching an agreement at 50/50 (Lauer, 1999a).

How was an agreement reached? What lessons can negotiators and managers draw from Schweitzer and Renault's experiences not only during, but before and after these negotiations?

The story begins with the environmental imperatives that brought the parties to the negotiation table.

Conditions in the Auto Industry

In 1998, world auto sales had been flat for 3 years. With reduced demand, huge overcapacity in production, and strong competition from Japanese companies, the auto industry was consolidating in established markets, namely, the U.S., Europe, and Japan. Analysts distinguished automakers as "big players", "likely [acquisition] targets", and "distressed or inefficient" firms (e.g., respectively, GM and Toyota, Volvo and Honda, Fiat and Nissan) (Vlasic *et al.*, 1998). Generally placed in the third group, Renault was considered "ripe for takeover".

Renault S.A. (hereafter "Renault") produced a full range of cars, commercial vehicles and parts. The 2nd largest automaker in France, and 10th largest in the world, Renault employed over 138,000 employees and generated €31.7 billion ($35 billion) in revenue in 1997. The 100-year old company had grown significantly after World War II but fell into a deep financial crisis in the early 1980s. After 6 years of "shock treatment" involving plant closings, layoffs and divestitures, and a repeat round of cost-reductions in 1997, the transformed company had in many ways turned the corner. At the same time, the French government, which reduced its majority equity share in 1996, still owned 44.2% of Renault, and the company remained heavily dependent on its home and nearby European markets.

Nissan Motor ("Nissan") was Japan's 2nd largest automaker. The internationally-oriented firm had production sites in 22 countries and sales in over 180. Nissan spearheaded the Nissan Group which comprised hundreds of subsidiaries and employed 130,000 people. With this workforce, the Group achieved substantially more than Renault in consolidated net sales: ¥6,659 billion ($56 billion) in FY1998. A proud, 90-year-old organization, Nissan had a longstanding reputation for engineering excellence. But in 1998, the company was floundering competitively, burdened by debt, and losing money for the fifth time in 6 years.

Schweitzer's Strategic View

"... [Renault] saw an opportunity that comes up once every 50 years".[2]

Renault's *président directeur générale* (effectively, the Chairman and CEO) was Louis Schweitzer. He had joined the company as Chief Financial Officer in 1986, after serving in the French ministries of finance and industry, and played a central role in Renault's historic restructuring. Appointed CEO in 1992, he was 4 years into his term when he ordered the 1997 round of cost reductions. While the move was controversial, Schweitzer was later credited with restoring the company's reputation.

In 1998, Renault was in better shape than it had been for decades but its position in the world auto industry was still precarious. Then in May, two major automakers, Daimler and Chrysler, announced a "mega-merger". That event shook Renault's top management into deeply questioning their company's future (Ghosn and Riès, 2003:173).

---

[2] See "Kenneth S. Courtis," 2000.

Interests

Schweitzer and his team identified several key interests for the company:

- improved global competitiveness in quality, cost and delivery
- accelerated internationalization of the company
- critical mass within the global auto industry
- a worldwide reputation for product innovation
- protecting domestic market share
- continued momentum as a revived enterprise

While Schweitzer's predecessors had targeted volume and profit, he wanted to shift the corporate focus to quality. He was also determined to shrink Renault's 36-month R&D cycle to the 24-month cycle common in Japan. Renault had no presence in the U.S. market, which represented 23% of the world total, and had either no reputation or a poor one in Asia and other non-European markets. Schweitzer felt the company could capitalize on its innovativeness in product design. Some interests were interconnected. For example, achieving critical mass would work both to improve competitiveness and fend off attacks from hostile acquirers.

The Renault CEO had presided over the unconsummated — some say "failed" — merger negotiations with Volvo in 1989–1993. As a matter of personal interest, he certainly had no desire to repeat that experience (Lauer, 1999a).

Options

Renault had two main strategic options: "go it alone" or join another major automaker. Renault held sufficient cash reserves to fund its own entry into the U.S. and could continue to enter limited-scope agreements with small automakers to plug operational deficiencies. However, these measures would neither accelerate internationalization nor create sufficient scale in a short time horizon.

With respect to a major partnership, Renault did not have much to offer any of the world's Top Five (GM, Ford, Toyota, VW and DaimlerChrysler). Schweitzer and his team drew up a list of potential Korean and Japanese partners but soon decided that the Korean companies had little to offer Renault. The team concentrated on Japanese firms.

Considering Nissan

Nissan had been the top Japanese automaker in the U.S. and top Asian automaker in Europe for decades, yet it had lost both positions by 1998. It held only 5% of the U.S. market. Customers and analysts perceived Nissan vehicles as dull and expensive. Beyond the red ink on its bottom line, Nissan suffered from a debt burden represented by a 5 to 1 debt-equity ratio. The company had to cover approximately ¥4,600 billion ($33 billion) in current liabilities by March 1999. On top of these problems, its business environment at home presented various constraints and challenges for operations, including a virtually sacrosanct commitment to lifetime employment.

From various sources of information, Renault executives could glean several Nissan interests:

- debt relief
- protecting the Nissan identity and brand
- returning to profitability
- reestablishing a strong position in the critical U.S. market
- improving its competitiveness in Asia and Europe
- ensuring the company's long-term health
- preserving jobs
- developing an effective solution for debt-ridden Nissan Diesel

Nissan Diesel was a truck and bus manufacturer in which Nissan Motor held a 39.8% share.

The president of Nissan Motor, Yoshikazu Hanawa, had been appointed to his position (effectively CEO) in June 1996. Having spent 40 years at Nissan, he was a dedicated "company man" but also a strong-willed leader. He had a personal interest in seeing his company recover and pull out of its current condition.

Pre-Negotiation Moves

Making contact

In June 1998, a month after the DaimlerChrysler announcement, Schweitzer wrote Hanawa a letter broadly proposing that they explore ways to enhance their companies' competitiveness. Schweitzer sent a similar letter to Mitsubishi Motors. However, Hanawa replied promptly.

Additional preparation

Renault executives initially prepared to talk to Nissan about a limited collaboration such as a manufacturing tie-up in Mexico. Schweitzer's inner circle for the tightly guarded "Pacific Project" included Executive Vice-Presidents (EVP) Georges Douin and Carlos Ghosn. Douin, who oversaw product and strategic planning and international operations, conducted the early studies of potential Asian partners. Ghosn was a cost-cutting expert who masterminded Renault's post-1996 restructuring. It did not take long for the group to look beyond a one-country relationship with Nissan.

Renault and Nissan had many common and complementary interests. They were "minnows living among sharks" trying to survive in the short term and thrive in the long term. Both CEOs were intent upon improving their companies' competitiveness, rebuilding the organizations, and enhancing the companies' reputations.

At an operational level, EVP Douin (2002:3) concluded that the two companies had an "almost miraculous complementary relationship". Renault's emphasis on product innovation fit Nissan's need to depart from dull, undistinguished cars. Each company sought to strengthen its standing in the other's strongest market: Nissan wanted to recoup its position in Europe (and the U.S.) while Renault wanted to expand into Asia. The list went on.

There were no previous conflicts between the two companies or CEOs to impede a relationship. Conversely, there was no strong foundation on which to build. Moreover, while there were many examples of U.S.-Japanese collaboration between automakers, there were no salient Franco-Japanese ventures. In Japan, according to Douin (2002:3), the French had a "poor image ... [as] not an industrial [power] ... arrogant, not very serious, and volatile". As a result, the Renault team felt they would have to prove themselves.

Nissan's options

To pursue Nissan's interests, Hanawa had few appealing courses of action in June 1998. Additional borrowing from commercial banks would have been costly due to Nissan's low credit rating, issuing additional equity or selling shares to raise capital would be ill-timed since shares had depreciated by 50% in the past year, and spinning off Nissan Diesel and other subsidiaries would not raise sufficient cash. Besides, these options would only satisfy creditors and not address fundamental strategic imperatives.

With respect to potential partners, the large Japanese automakers — arch-rival Toyota and Honda — probably viewed Nissan as undesirable, and smaller Japanese companies could not afford or digest a large firm. Meanwhile, the American majors GM and Ford were already allied with Toyota and Mazda, respectively. Ford had collaborated with Nissan in a limited way on a mini-van project but was, by this point, actually managing Mazda.

These conditions left Hanawa with the option of an internally led restructuring based on the Nissan Corporate Planning Department's 1-month old "Global Business Reform Plan" and short-term assistance from fellow members of Nissan's industrial group, the Fuyo *keiretsu*. Given the scale and scope of Nissan's needs, this was a rather weak option. (Later on, Hanawa's alternatives would improve at crucial points.)

Moving forward

From the outset, Schweitzer eschewed the idea of pursuing a typical acquisition or merger with Nissan (Korine *et al.*, 2002:22). He believed key stakeholders and the Japanese public would oppose a foreign takeover. Instead, he envisioned an alliance — a "subtle balance" — between the two companies (Douin, 2002:3).

Issues

The meta-issue for the companies to negotiate was the basic nature of a relationship. Specific agenda items included the scope of their collaboration, their respective contributions, and an organizational structure.

Whatever the basic relationship, management control and equity valuations were bound to be sensitive issues. Given Nissan's history and prominence in Japan's industrial sector, Hanawa and his team would be protective of the company and determined to ensure that Nissan Motor had a future. At the same time, while Renault had $2 billion in cash to spend, the company's financial history and government supervision necessitated that Schweitzer proceed prudently.

The Negotiations

"It's a question of seducing rather than imposing".[3]

Hanawa's reply to Schweitzer's letter set in motion a series of communications and negotiations that lasted from June

---

[3] Attributed by Diem (1999) to consultant Grégoire Van de Velde.

1998 to March 1999. This 9-month period may be divided into five phases:

1 — Exploring Interest in Collaboration	(June–July, 1998)
2 — Identification of Possible Synergies	(August–September, 1998)
3 — Evaluation of Possible Synergies	(October–December, 1998)
4 — Striking the Deal	(January–March 13, 1999)
5 — Finalizing Details	(March 14–27, 1999)

The following sections describe the various actors and each phase of the negotiation process.

Participants and stakeholders

As is typical of high-stakes corporate negotiations, the number of direct participants in the Renault-Nissan talks started small — less than 10 on each side — and grew as the discussions intensified. The two CEOs formally initiated the talks and remained engaged throughout the process. EVP Douin, who spearheaded the advance work for the CEOs' first meeting, served as chief negotiator of Renault's four-person team. Nissan's three-person negotiation team included General Manager of Corporate Planning Yutaka Suzuki.

Both executive teams were advised by investment bankers: Merrill Lynch for Renault, Salomon Smith Barney for Nissan. Internal specialists supported the negotiation teams. Three months into the negotiations, the teams drew 120 resource personnel from their companies and organized joint teams to study specific areas of company operations in detail.

The number of actors and arenas in such an undertaking is difficult to grasp and track without what some negotiation analysts have called a "party map" (Watkins, 2002:11). Figure 1 depicts direct participants, staff, stakeholders, and other relevant

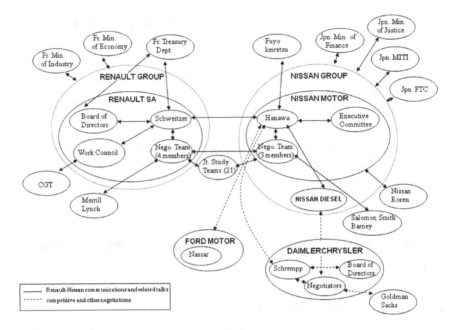

FIGURE 1   Parties and linkages in January 1999

parties evident in January 1999, a little over halfway through the negotiations. While not every germane actor appears in the figure (e.g., European Union Competition Bureau), it illustrates the complexity of the negotiation and provides a guide for the play-by-play account in the next section.

To consider these actors, albeit briefly, let us start on the left side of the figure. Renault's Board of Directors had to authorize any major strategic initiative and formal agreement. French and European Union labor laws required companies to inform and consult employees on important decisions, which entailed communication with the Work Council. Roughly 60% of Renault's workforce was represented by six activist unions, the largest being the Confédération Générale du Travail (CGT). Only 15 months before his letter to Hanawa, Schweitzer had faced a multi-country strike prompted by the closing of Renault's plant in Vilvoorde, Belgium.

The French government, led by a Socialist prime minister, was involved via multiple regulatory roles and as part-owner of Renault. The Treasury Department oversaw this stake. Though not a majority stake in financial terms, it was a "golden share" that gave the government veto power over board decisions.

On the right side of Figure 1, Nissan's largest shareholders and creditors in the Fuyo *keiretsu* were Fuji Bank, Industrial Bank of Japan, and Dai-Ichi Mutual Insurance. Nissan Roren, the largest labor union at Nissan, had clashed with management intensely throughout the company's history. Lastly, three ministries in the Japanese government could influence Nissan, as they did most Japanese business: the Ministry of International Trade and Industry (MITI), Ministry of Finance, and Fair Trade Commission (FTC).

At the bottom of the figure, additional players include automakers that could affect the Renault-Nissan negotiations. In July 1998, after nearly a year of talks through Daimler-Benz, DaimlerChrysler concluded an agreement with Nissan Diesel to co-produce a light truck. Hanawa subsequently talked to DaimlerChrysler co-CEO Jurgen Schrempp and to Ford CEO Jacques Nassar, but let us return to the Renault-Nissan story before we take up these encounters.

Phase one

In June 1998, after the Schweitzer-Hanawa exchange of letters, a select group of Renault and Nissan representatives met secretly to explore their respective interests in strategic collaboration. By the middle of the month, they were preparing for their CEOs to meet. Six weeks later, Schweitzer and Hanawa met for the first time in Tokyo.[4] They established rapport quickly (Korine *et al.*,

---

[4] A few weeks after announcing their light-truck agreement with Nissan Diesel, DaimlerChrysler also announced their intention to buy Nissan Motor's entire stake in Nissan Diesel.

2002:42–43) and put the wheels in motion for studies on potential benefits of collaboration. (For a detailed chronology, see the appendix.)

Phase two

During the 7 weeks from August 1-September 10, working groups in and from both companies conducted preliminary analyses on purchasing, engines and gearboxes, car platforms, production, distribution, and international markets. Results were promising. Nissan's capabilities in large cars, research and advanced technology, factory productivity, and quality control complemented Renault's talent in medium-sized cars, cost management, and global strategies for purchasing and product innovation (Douin, 2002:3; Renault, S.A., n.d.).

Highlighting the trust he felt they had established, Schweitzer proposed to Hanawa that they strengthen their relationship by holding each other's shares. Hanawa replied that Nissan had no money to spend on buying Renault stock. Schweitzer said they could talk about the subject again in the future though he also underscored how critical their collaboration was to Renault's future (Morosini, 2005:5).

On September 10, the two CEOs met in Paris and signed a memorandum of understanding committing their companies to evaluate synergies more extensively in an exclusive arrangement for the next 3½ months.

Phase three

From September to December 1998, 21 intercompany teams assembled from specialists on each side thoroughly examined the companies' respective operations. The teams held meetings at nearly every one of the companies' sites worldwide, visited plants, and exchanged cost and other proprietary information. As one reporter (Lauer, 1999a) later observed, information exchange of this kind was remarkable in an industry where companies jealously guard their manufacturing secrets.

Top management facilitated collaboration within the study teams as needed (Lauer, 1999a), and a coordinating committee reviewed progress monthly. (Communication between study teams was prohibited; teams reported directly to the chief negotiators.) The executives' main concern during this period was development of a business strategy; specific financial issues were left for the final rounds. Schweitzer and Hanawa — and the negotiation teams — continued their meetings at venues ranging from their headquarters to cities in Thailand, Singapore, and Mexico. (Ultimately, the CEOs met 12 times.)

Within Renault, Schweitzer and his executives concentrated on refining their concept of an alliance. They drew on their experience with Volvo (Korine *et al.*, 2002:46) and examined the Ford-Mazda partnership as a model, paying particular attention to financial and cultural dimensions (Barre, 1999a; Lauer, 1999a). Ghosn and 50 Renault researchers began taking daily Japanese classes (Diem, 1999). Schweitzer subsequently said the team was guided by the French maxim, "To build a good relationship, you do things together and look in the same direction together" (Eisenstein, 1999). In the same vein, one alliance scholar (Morosini, 2005:5) described the first 6 months of the Renault-Nissan discussions as "a corporate experiment in living together before marriage".

By October, the negotiations centered on a Renault investment in Nissan. Schweitzer had sounded out French government officials about the alliance and obtained support from Prime Minister Lionel Jospin, among others. For his part, Hanawa set four pre-conditions for a deal: retaining the Nissan name, protecting jobs, support for the organizational restructuring already underway at Nissan with Nissan management leading the effort, and selection of a CEO from Nissan's ranks.

In mid-November, Nissan's board of directors took the extraordinary step of inviting Schweitzer, Douin and Ghosn to Tokyo to present their vision of the alliance. The presentation was so well-received that the Renault team deemed it a turning point in the negotiations (Ghosn and Riès, 2003:178.)

Later in the month, Hanawa paid a courtesy call to DaimlerChrysler co-CEO Schrempp in Stuttgart. Schrempp proposed to go beyond his interest in Nissan Diesel and make an investment in Nissan Motor itself.[5] Hanawa then flew to Paris to inform Schweitzer personally of his intention to follow up on Schrempp's offer. This was not Hanawa's first contact with alternative partners. He had also sounded out Ford CEO Nassar (Ghosn and Riès, 2003:176), who showed no interest.

In December, as the Renault and Nissan negotiating teams discussed the legal form of a relationship, they hit an impasse. Renault had suggested a subsidiary or joint venture. Nissan rejected both concepts.[6] EVP Ghosn, who did not regularly participate in the negotiations, proposed an informal alternative that both sides accepted (see "The Deal" below).

At the end of December, with the approaching expiration of the September memorandum, Schweitzer and Hanawa negotiated over, among other things, a clause "freezing" Hanawa's contact with other potential partners until the completion or end of talks with Renault. Hanawa demurred from locking in just yet. On the 23rd, the CEOs signed a letter of intent, minus a freeze clause, for Renault to make an offer on Nissan Motor by March 31, 1999, Nissan's fiscal year-end. Hanawa asked Schweitzer to include Nissan Diesel in the offer.

Phase four

The fourth phase of the negotiations began with Renault's first public, albeit guarded, acknowledgement of its talks with "potential

---

[5] With a stake in Nissan Diesel, Schrempp could pre-empt Renault and strengthen DaimlerChrysler's position in commercial vehicles. By simply expressing his interest in Nissan Motor, he could bid up the price Renault had to pay and thereby weaken Renault. If he actually bought into Nissan Motor, he would increase DaimlerChrysler's limited presence in Asia and firm up the mega-merger's global status.

[6] As one outsider opined, "You've got two cultures here that are extremely nationalistic and believe that their way is the right way. There will be some major control issues" (Edmondson *et al.*, 1999).

partners… including Nissan", but the period was punctuated by developments in the competing Nissan-DaimlerChrysler negotiations (Lauer, 1999a). DaimlerChrysler was not simply a foil for Hanawa to leverage in the Renault negotiations; it had real pull of its own with Nissan management. They admired Daimler (Mercedes) and knew DaimlerChrysler had deep pockets. In contrast, they saw Renault as "no better off than Nissan in terms of future viability and survival" ("Gallic Charm", 1999; "Shuttle Diplomacy", 1999).

On the Renault-Nissan agenda, Renault's cash contribution was a tough issue. Nissan sought $6 billion. Renault initially expressed interest in a 20% stake, and if Nissan were valued between $8.7 billion (market value) and $12 billion (a comparable companies valuation), a 20% stake would yield no more than $2.4 billion for Nissan.[7] Nonetheless, Nissan was not ready to move quickly from its position. It had DaimlerChrysler in the wings and breathing space afforded by a long term, ¥85 billion loan ($740 million) from the state-owned Japan Development Bank. Fluctuating share prices and exchange rates further complicated matters.

The negotiating teams continued their discussions through the winter, meeting several times in Bangkok. In late February, a Nissan spokesman denied that a Renault deal was imminent and asserted that talks with DaimlerChrysler were "continuing".[8] This may have reinforced Schweitzer's fears that DaimlerChrysler was the favored partner.

---

[7] The market value is based on a Nissan Motor share price of ¥400, 2.513 billion shares outstanding, and an exchange rate of ¥116 per US dollar whereas the comparable companies estimate rests on earnings per share of ¥39.79 and an average multiple of 17. Note, however, that share prices ranged from a low of about ¥300 in November 1998 to a high of ¥450 in March 1999. In addition, the exchange rate fluctuated by as much as 20% between June 1998 (¥142/$1) and March 1999 (¥118/$1).

[8] This statement contradicted Schrempp's disclosure on February 19, in a speech at the Executives' Club of Chicago, that DaimlerChrysler was only interested in Nissan Diesel.

Two weeks later, on March 10, Renault's position completely changed when Schrempp formally withdrew his bid for Nissan Motor. The DaimlerChrysler Board of Directors, leery of Nissan's financial condition and understated debt at Nissan Diesel, had pulled him back (Barre, 1999b). Hanawa probed Ford's CEO yet again about a linkage, but without success. Schweitzer realized Hanawa's choice was now "Renault or nothing" (Ghosn and Riès, 2003:176–179).

What happened then has been described differently by different sources. Ghosn and researchers who interviewed principals at both companies (Ghosn and Riès, 2003:179–180; Korine et al., 2002:45) contend that Schweitzer restated the terms of his standing offer. The rationale for not reducing it, even with DaimlerChrysler gone, was consistency of intent. Schweitzer was trying to develop a cooperative relationship, and he did not want Hanawa to feel Renault would later exploit Nissan.

A news article written 2 days after the deal was done ("Shuttle Diplomacy", 1999) reports that Schweitzer sent Hanawa the following confidential message, "There is hope that Renault will be able to make a larger investment than we proposed earlier". Schweitzer did not specify the amount and asked Hanawa to trust him, but he also insisted that Hanawa agree, by March 13, on freezing contact with other potential partners. Schweitzer needed that commitment in order to go to his board.

Hanawa flew to Paris on March 13 and after a 5-hour meeting with Schweitzer and his team at Roissy Airport, signed a preliminary agreement for Renault to acquire a stake in Nissan. The agreement was announced publicly.

Phase five

On March 16, at the beginning of the 2-week final phase of the negotiations, Schweitzer obtained the internal approvals he needed from the Renault Board of Directors and Work Council (Renault Communication, 1999). These decisions centered on a 35% stake in Nissan for $4.3 billion (Lauer, 1999a cf. Korine et al., 2002).

This amount exceeded the 33.4% threshold for an investor to gain veto power on a board in Japan and remained below the 40% level at which French accounting standards would require Renault to consolidate Nissan's debt. With the approvals in place, Renault issued a press release about its intention to purchase 35% of Nissan. At this time, Schweitzer offered to start exclusive negotiations with Nissan without delay.

The negotiations intensified. Nissan executives withheld their approval of an alliance for several days (Lauer, 1999b). When an agreement was finally reached, Renault's investment had risen to $5.4 billion for 36.8% of Nissan Motor and stakes in other Nissan entities.[9]

The Deal

The "global partnership agreement" signed by Schweitzer and Hanawa on March 27, 1999 committed Renault and Nissan to cooperate to achieve certain types of synergies while maintaining their respective brand identities. The strategic direction of the partnership would be set by a Global Alliance Committee co-chaired by the Renault and Nissan CEOs and filled out with five more members from each company. Financial terms included an investment of ¥643 billion ($5.4 billion) by Renault. For ¥605 billion of the total, Renault received 36.8% of the equity in Nissan Motor and 22.5% of Nissan Diesel. With the remaining ¥38 billion, Renault acquired Nissan's financial subsidiaries in Europe. The agreement included options for Renault to raise its stake in Nissan Motor and for Nissan to purchase equity in Renault. With respect to management, Renault gained responsibility for three positions at Nissan (Chief Operating Officer, Vice-President of Product Planning,

---

[9] Public information does not make clear whether previous offers included "other entities", but they likely did not. If the bundles of Nissan assets associated with the 35% and 36.8% offers were the same, Renault's cash offer in the second instance would have represented a 19% increase in the valuation of those assets.

and Deputy Chief Financial Officer). One seat on Renault's board of directors was designated for Hanawa. At the alliance level, plans called for the formation of 11 cross-company teams to work on key areas of synergy (e.g., vehicle engineering, purchasing, product planning) and to coordinate marketing and sales efforts in major geographic markets.

The Aftermath

Before Schweitzer signed the Alliance agreement, he had made sure that Ghosn was willing to assume Nissan's top operating position (Ghosn and Riès, 2003:180), and when the deal was done, Ghosn did just that. In June 1999, the Global Alliance Committee met for the first time (and monthly thereafter), and cross-company teams were set up with a leader from one company and deputy leader from the other. English was adopted as the working language in the Alliance.

Ghosn, the cost-cutting expert, moved quickly at Nissan. In October 1999, he announced the closure of five plants in Japan, 21,000 job cuts (in the land of lifetime employment), and cost reductions of $9.48 billion over 3 years. By the end of the 2000, when Ghosn was promoted to president, Nissan turned a profit, and it continued to do so until 2008 when all automakers were hit by the global recession. Nissan achieved operating margins among the highest in the industry. The company paid off all debt by 2004 and in 2007, surpassed its net sales for 2000 by 78%, hitting ¥10,824 billion ($92 billion). In effect, the Alliance agreement met Nissan's main interests.

How has Renault fared since 1999? The investment in Nissan easily paid for itself, since the income alone from it averaged more than $2 billion per year from 2002–2007. In December 2009, Renault's shares in Nissan were worth more than Renault's total market value.

In terms of its own performance, Renault saw annual revenues drop twice after 2000 then recover, in 2004, to €403 billion ($50 billion). Operating margins, which ranged from 1.3 to 5.2%, were less than half of Nissan's. At the same time, the company realized improvements in its defective parts ratio and increased productivity through its adoption of the Nissan Production Way (see Miller and Zaun, 2002).

In 2005, when Schweitzer retired, Ghosn became Chairman/ CEO of Renault as well as CEO of Nissan. He set ambitious targets for Renault's 2009 unit sales and operating margins (Betts, 2010) but missed them by large margins. Renault lost €3.1 billion ($4.5 billion) in 2009, notwithstanding savings from sharing platforms with Nissan, establishing a joint purchasing organization, and other synergies. In 2010, *The Economist* observed, "For much of the past decade, Renault has been a disappointingly mediocre performer" ("Daimler and Renault-Nissan join forces", 2010). By itself, Renault continued to hold only 4% of the global auto market. Then again, without the Alliance, the company may well have been in worse financial shape during this period.

As to Schweitzer's original interest in accelerated internationalization, Renault acquired a majority stake in Samsung Motors (South Korea) in 2000 and subsequently expanded its presence in the largest emerging markets by purchasing 25% of AvtoVAZ of Russia and securing joint production agreements with automakers in China and India. With Renault still not established in the U.S. market, the Alliance approached GM in 2006, and then Chrysler in 2008, about joining forces, but neither effort panned out. In April 2010, in an ironic twist, the Alliance welcomed the company that originally shocked Renault into action. Daimler, whose merger with Chrysler failed famously, agreed to collaborate in small car design and swap a small percentage (3.1%) of shares.[10]

The Renault-Nissan relationship has evolved since 1999. Beyond adding partners to the alliance and sharing a CEO, the

---

[10] Renault also gained more freedom from its home government as an investor. The French government reduced its stake to 25.9% in 2002 and then to 15.01% in 2009.

two companies have increased their cross-shareholding (see the appendix) and expanded their organizational linkages (Ghosn, 2002). In 2009, these included 2 joint companies and 7 steering committees that manage over 30 cross-company teams, functional task teams, and task teams.

Lessons

Automakers' have negotiated international collaborations for decades and will continue to do so well into the future, but the Renault-Nissan negotiation stands out in many ways. Many observers did not expect it to lead to an agreement, let alone to a relationship that would become a model for industrial partnerships. So there are important lessons for negotiators and negotiation analysts to draw from Renault's experience.

Some of these insights relate to and reinforce recommendations from other case studies. For example, Sebenius (1998) concluded that parties should be clear about the industrial and strategic logic of a proposed partnership and the value it will create; price should not "bulldoze" other considerations. Further, leadership and top-level support appear to be critical for progress in complex negotiations (see Weiss, 1987; 1997).

Beyond these examples, however, the Renault-Nissan negotiation offers six distinctive lessons.

(1) *Go beyond ostensible differences; probe parties' interests and capabilities for "fit".* Unlike news reporters who emphasized cultural, linguistic and organizational differences, Schweitzer and his team focused on Renault and Nissan's common long-term goals, complementary interests and respective capabilities. Their fit on multiple dimensions motivated, directed and sustained the negotiators. Some differences matter less than others and not all differences imply incompatibility; in fact, they may offer substantial benefit.

(2) *Prepare extensively, continuously, and jointly as well as internally.* Renault took a broad view of preparation for negotiation. The company's executives and staff carried out thorough internal analyses but also spent months working with Nissan personnel even before a letter of intent was signed. The joint preparation before formal negotiations was more comprehensive and intensive in this case than in many others.[11] The negotiations were far from the quick, superficial courtship — the "shotgun marriage" — that some commentators (Woodruff, 1999) labeled them.

(3) *Consider conceiving a new (unusual) form of relationship.* Ideas based on a conventional acquisition, merger, joint venture or subsidiary were all set aside. Renault executives went "outside the box" and conceived a structure by which the two companies could be "together but distinct". High-level coordination and cross-shareholdings may have been familiar domestic business practices in both France and Japan (recall the *keiretsu*), but they were not common internationally in the auto industry where one-way holdings prevailed. Renault's innovation reminds us of a fundamental principle of negotiation: the design of an acceptable relationship is entirely up to the parties.

(4) *Behave not only as a negotiator but also as a prospective partner.* Negotiators typically pursue their own interests and take their counterparts' into account as needed to reach an agreement, whereas Renault negotiators paid extra attention to Nissan's concerns and to life after an agreement. They were keenly aware of the companies' limited history together, the opportunity that the negotiation offered them to demonstrate their qualities as a long-term partner, and the impact that their negotiation conduct would likely have on the implementation of an agreement. (In contrast, consider

---

[11] Appropriately, Renault's approach resembles the Japanese practice of *nemawashi* — consulting all involved parties before making a decision or change.

Daimler CEO Shrempp's misleading "merger of equals" negotiation with Chrysler and its aftermath.) These factors also shape a negotiator's reputation in an industry, and in the auto industry, initiatives to collaborate occur often and future partners cannot always be predicted.

(5) *Manage the influence of the counterpart's no-deal alternative (options).* In Hanawa, Schweitzer had a counterpart who had a formidable alternative (Chrysler) and kept working to improve it. The Renault team perceptively tried to limit how much Hanawa's maneuvers affected their position in the negotiations. Among other techniques, they stayed true to their vision of a partnership, pressed Nissan by putting ideas in print (e.g., a mock press release), announced commitments in public statements at strategic times, and most directly, asked Hanawa to sign freeze agreements. Schrempp ultimately eliminated the Chrysler alternative, but Renault executives probably did as much as they could under the circumstances.

(6) *Assess the quality of an outcome by its effects as well as its content.* Negotiations tend to be evaluated in terms of their immediate outcomes. While the Alliance agreement attracted a great deal of media attention (see Tagliabue, 2000), its main effects on Nissan and Renault can only be fully appreciated several years later. Back in 1999, few, if any, analysts anticipated Nissan's amazing recovery. At the same time, Renault "won the prize", but its subsequent performance is a more complicated and mixed story.

In conclusion, Renault's experience with Nissan offers many insights about negotiation. Even in this short chapter, one can see various incentives and obstacles to reaching a satisfactory agreement and the admirable efforts of Renault executives before, during, and after negotiation. They constitute a highly instructive example of negotiations to establish interfirm collaboration in the auto industry and in international business generally.

Appendix

Key Dates for the Negotiations and Aftermath

Phase 1: Exploring Interest in Collaboration

1998	June	Schweitzer writes to Hanawa to suggest "thinking strategically together"
	June 11	company representatives meet in Tokyo for general discussions
	July 11	teams from both firms begin developing a framework for cooperation
	July 22	first Schweitzer-Hanawa meeting occurs at Nissan headquarters in Tokyo

Phase 2: Identification of Possible Synergies

Aug 1	internal studies begin on a range of subjects such as purchasing and car platforms
Aug 31–Sep 1	review of preliminary studies and identified synergies
Sept 10	Schweitzer and Hanawa sign memorandum to evaluate synergies fully and exclusively by Dec. 23; joint study teams organized

Phase 3: Evaluation of Possible Synergies

Oct	Schweitzer prepares mock press release ("Nissan and Renault join forces") and shows it to Hanawa as a basis for discussions
Nov 1	Schweitzer and Hanawa meet in Singapore
Nov 10	in Tokyo, Schweitzer, Douin, and Ghosn present the "big picture" for an alliance to the Nissan Board of Directors; Ghosn describes Renault's own restructuring experience
Nov 11	Schweitzer and Hanawa meet in Tokyo

Nov	Hanawa visits DaimlerChrysler co-CEO Schrempp in Stuttgart, and Schrempp proposes to invest in Nissan Motor and Nissan Diesel
Dec	impasse over the legal form of a Renault-Nissan relationship; Ghosn suggests an "alliance" and informal, cross-company teams
Dec 23	Schweitzer and Hanawa sign a letter of intent, valid until March 31, 1999, for Renault to make an offer to Nisan after completing an audit

Phase 4: Striking the Deal

1999 Jan 18	Renault publicly acknowledges for first time its "discussions with a number of potential partners in Asia, including Nissan"
Jan 21	Hanawa meets with DaimlerChrysler co-CEOs Schrempp and Eaton
Feb (early)	two DaimlerChrysler board members arrive in Japan for talks at Nissan
Feb 10	credit rating firms warn Nissan of potential drop to junk bond status; Moody's places Nissan under review
Feb 25	Nissan releases statement denying Renault deal is imminent and referring to "continuing discussions" with DaimlerChrysler
Mar	Nissan team negotiates in parallel with DaimlerChrysler and Renault
Mar 10	Schrempp informs Hanawa in Tokyo that DaimlerChrysler is withdrawing from the talks
Mar 10–12	Hanawa attempts to connect with Ford CEO Nassar; Schweitzer offers to try to increase Renault's investment if Hanawa agrees to a freeze

Mar 13   in Paris, Schweitzer and Hanawa reach preliminary agreement for Renault to acquire
a stake in Nissan

Phase 5: Finalizing the Details

Mar 16   Schweitzer obtains approval for an alliance
from the Renault Board of Directors and
Work Council

Mar 16   Renault issues press release stating that it is
"convinced of the merits of a strategic
alliance" and intends to purchase about
35% of Nissan

Mar 19   Nissan executives reach consensus on
alliance with Renault but defer final decision

Mar 23   Nissan executives at a crossroads over the
alliance with Renault

Mar 27   global partnership agreement signed by
Schweitzer and Hanawa at Keidanren in
Tokyo

Aftermath

May 28   closing of the Alliance agreement

Nov 1   Nissan announces unprecedented move to
close five plants and cut 21,000 jobs in
Japan and elsewhere

2000 June 20   Ghosn becomes President of Nissan (CEO)
after one year as COO

2002 Mar 1   Renault increases stake in Nissan to 44.4%
at cost of €1.9 billion, then Nissan takes
15% (nonvoting) stake in Renault for
€2.2 billion

2005 April   Ghosn becomes Renault's Chairman/CEO
while continuing as Nissan CEO

2006 July–Oct   GM meets with Renault and Nissan about a
three-way alliance, but GM breaks off talks

2007 March   Volvo acquires Nissan Diesel (later renamed
UD Trucks)

2008	Oct	Nissan talks to Chrysler about joining the alliance
2009	Mar 27	10th anniversary of the Alliance
2010	Apr 7	Daimler joins Renault-Nissan Alliance by taking 3.1% stake in each partner, and the Alliance takes 3.1% of Daimler

Sources: "Negotiations Chronology" at http://www.renault.com, and news articles (see References).

The Arcelor and Mittal Steel Merger Negotiations

Gregor Halff
*Singapore Management University, Lee Kong Chian
School of Business*

The Arcelor and Mittal Steel Merger Negotiations

The largest industrial merger of this century began with a night-time phone conversation: steel entrepreneur Lakshmi Mittal contacted Guy Dollé, Arcelor's CEO, and announced that he would publicly offer 18.6 billion Euros for Arcelor the next morning. The India-born and self-made multibillionaire, who operated steel mills around the globe, had long been searching for opportunities to merge his company, Mittal Steel, with the European conglomerate on an equal basis. Guy Dollé and the Arcelor-board preferred to remain independent and to search for acquisitions themselves. On the evening of Thursday, 26 January 2006, the gloves came off and the stage was set for a confrontation between Arcelor and Mittal Steel, both of which claimed to be the world's largest producer of steel (in terms of production volume and revenue respectively).

After hanging up, Guy Dollé called in the help of Maurice Lévy, CEO of Publicis, one of the world's largest communication agencies, who spun a global network of media relations professionals to defend Arcelor before the European stock exchanges opened the next morning.

Once the night was over, so was the dyadic structure common in many negotiations. The offer by Lakshmi Mittal was not addressed to Guy Dollé (although he was the CEO, he was not a member of Arcelor's board), but instead to the owners of Arcelor, the multitudes of institutional and individual shareholders. Mittal offered them (via various combinations of cash and Mittal Steel shares) 28.21 Euros for each of their Arcelor shares. Furthermore, the proposed deal would only succeed if other stakeholders were also included in the negotiations. This was because the deal needed the approval of 7 national regulators and the European Union, the support of the Luxembourg and French governments, the backing of the industrial labor unions as well as the non-interference of Nippon Steel, Baosteel and other international steel conglomerates who might seize the opportunity to acquire Arcelor as white knights.

Mittal's offer represented a premium of 27% on Arcelor's most recent share price. Nonetheless, it was rebuffed as 150% hostile by Guy Dollé in his first reaction to the press waiting outside Arcelor's headquarters in Luxembourg. Furthermore, Guy Dollé twice referred to the sum as '*monnaie de singe*', in an interview with the French newspaper *Le Monde* and during a live radio broadcast on the Monday after the bid. This is a pejorative French term for loose change, which literally means 'monkey money'. It was, of course, the literal translation that made it into the world press and sharpened the tone of the negotiations from the outset.

Arcelor's Shareholders

Mittal's negotiating partner was like an anonymous fellowship that never met. The shareholders of Arcelor were scattered and mostly unknown to each other. Nonetheless, their decision to sell to Mittal would be an individual as well as a collective one, since his offer was only valid if he acquired a majority of the shares. Mittal's goal was to induce collective behavior from a group of people who were not even organized as a collective. The public defense of Arcelor would therefore have to go much further than garnering support for its independence. At first, it would have to ensure that the anonymous fellowship of shareholders remained truly scattered and that as few as possible of them would sell their shares to Mittal. Secondly, even if a majority of shareholders were willing to sell their shares, the perception would have to be formed that there was no such majority (and it would thus be meaningless for individual shareholders to sell). In short: the majority of shareholders would have to have the impression that there was no majority willing to sell (regardless of their personal willingness to sell).

The creation of such majorities in public opinion is described as the "spiral of silence" [Noelle-Neumann 1984]. The spiral of silence assumes that people are reluctant to distance themselves from majorities if doing so represents a risk to them (for example, losing the opportunity to sell Arcelor's shares to Mittal for a premium or selling the shares too early). Once a majority seems to be forming in the near future, individuals with contrary opinions tend to quiet down, leaving the arena to the proponents of the future majority, and thus further accelerating its swell (hence the 'spiral of silence'). The caveat is that people are unable to sense majorities in public opinion, much less their movements or majorities/minorities in the future. They are thus highly susceptible to impressions created about future public opinion. Moreover, they base their overt opinions and behavior on these impressions, which at times leads to self-fulfilling prophecies.

Who creates those impressions? Anyone who observes, structures, channels and comments on the public debate, especially the news media. But, they too cannot predict future public opinion and are therefore impression-mongers themselves, commenting not just on news items but also on assumed public opinion about them. According to the spiral of silence concept, the news media and their sources craft future majorities by predicting them.

The Defense

The predictors in the steel industry are the global communities of bankers and journalists. Investment bankers and analysts at UBS,

Merrill Lynch, BNP Paribas and Deutsche Bank encouraged their clients to hold or buy Arcelor shares. The journalists worked for all major television networks and high-quality daily newspapers such as the *Financial Times, Wall Street Journal, Le Monde, Times of India, FAZ, Handelsblatt, la Reppublica, El País,* and *Hürriyet.* The brief by Maurice Lévy and Guy Dollé to the media relations team was clear: to strengthen Arcelor's hand in the negotiations, the media had to be convinced that there was no majority for Mittal's hostile bid among Arcelor's shareholders. This meant creating public involvement in the negotiations, identifying as many opponents as possible among global shareholders and stakeholders, and connecting these opponents to the journalists to make their voices heard and quoted.

From 27 January onwards, the media team started working in India, Luxemburg, France, Spain, Turkey, Germany, Italy, USA and Canada. Personalization is a key aspect of news reporting anywhere in the world. Hence, in the first few days, it was easy to create a debate about Lakshmi Mittal, his newcomer status, and his personal intentions behind the hostile bid. The media (except in India) were generally apprehensive about the Indian billionaire. The governments of France, Luxemburg and Spain issued statements of support for Arcelor's independence on 31 January. Fuelled by sound-bites from, among others, Luxemburg's Prime Minister Jean-Claude Juncker and France's Minister of Economy Thierry Breton, Germany's *FAZ* initially described him as a 'modern maharaja' and France's *Liberation* as a 'father who satisfies any caprice of his children'. Italy's *la Reppublica* even saw in him India's 'attack to conquer the West'. Bullying elephants were also found in the caricatures. Quickly, however, after journalists had taken the time to carry out background checks (no doubt assisted by Mittal's communication team), they realized that Mittal, who lived in London and whose company was listed in Amsterdam, was not so exotic after all. This led to the *Wall Street Journal* describing him as 'the poster-magnate of globalization', and Germany's *Frankfurter Rundschau* being in awe of the 'boss of steel' and his business acumen.

To dissuade Arcelor-shareholders from selling to the 'boss of steel', a perception had to be created that a majority of share- and stakeholders would never find it in their interest to do so. To do so, the opinion leaders had to openly second-guess Mittal's ability to create value from the merger and warn that Arcelor was too alien an organization for an entrepreneur like Mittal to handle.

Stakeholder balance is pivotal in Europe. The governments of France, Germany and Luxembourg, in particular, have long sustained an industrial policy that balances labor interests with shareholder value. Dominique de Villepin, the French Prime Minister, christened this balance 'economic and European patriotism'. Any 'merger synergies' promised by Mittal to the shareholders would spell 'job losses' to de Villepin and other European leaders as well as the labor unions. Since Mittal lived in London's most expensive private residence and had feted his daughter's wedding guests at the Palace of Versailles, it seemed easy to pit the steel industry's blue-collar workers against him. Hence, the German labor unions were quickly persuaded to publicly demand job guarantees for their 9000 workers at Arcelor.

However, barely two weeks after his initial offer — and long before his first look at the actual labor costs of Arcelor — Mittal silenced the stakeholder critics by approving what they had hoped for, vowing not to reduce the headcount at existing Arcelor plants in Germany. Meanwhile, Mittal also discovered how useful it was to mention in interviews his support for the British Labour party, his humble background and his impressive charity work. For example, Mittal Steel sponsors numerous universities in India and churches in Romania, and supported relief work after Hurricane Katrina. Mittal finally pushed the labor issue from public sight in March by unequivocally stating that he would honor all of Arcelor's existing contracts and obligations. On 15 March, Luxembourg's government announced that it would (read: could) not bar an acquisition on legal grounds.

Corporate governance was the obvious next theme. Would a self-made man like Mittal accept independent officers and directors after the acquisition? Would someone who had picked and groomed his son Aditya as second-in-command surrender the overwhelming intra-corporate influence of his family? The financial press was quick to worry about the interests paramount to Mittal — his own or those of the shareholders? Since the spiral of silence is most effective when the public agenda revolves around a binary issue, corporate governance was a strong line of defense for Arcelor and the media relations team. In April, the *Financial Times* published several articles that scrutinized in much detail and disgust the financial links Mittal Steel's directors had with Lakshmi Mittal, his double voting rights, the provisions made for sustaining his family's majority stake, and the alleged recruitment of poor members of his extended family as additional directors. Not surprisingly, when first asked to vote at the shareholders' meeting on 28 April, the majority of Arcelor's shareholders voted against Mittal's offer.

Ten days later, Mittal dramatically showed that he had understood these concerns. On 9 May, he announced that his family would give up its special voting rights, hold less than half of the equity in the combined company, and would accept a balance on the board of directors. The financial regulators of Luxemburg, France and Belgium were appeased and approved a possible take-over by Mittal a week later on 16 May.

With the two main defensive themes gone, the world's media began to focus on the business rationale of Mittal's bid and discovered its merits. By mid-May, the press was more often quoting the deal's supporters (for example, a headline in the *FAZ* said 'Investment funds put pressure on Arcelor') or becoming as adamantly partial as the *Financial Times* ('Sensibility over Pride') or Germany's *Süddeutsche Zeitung* ('Arcelor should negotiate'). It helped that Mittal had raised his offer by another 34%, luring Arcelor stakeholders with 37.74 Euros for each of their shares and offering a total of 25.8 billion Euros in what France's *La Tribune* suspected was an overreaction to Arcelor's feisty defense.

Another Billionaire

Shareholders had a month to accept or decline Mittal's latest offer. Arcelor thus had a month to expand its defense. A week later, on 26 May, it announced a friendly merger with Severstal ('Steel of the North'), a Russian steel conglomerate run by its main shareholder, the 39-year old Alexej Mordashov, whom no one had expected to be a 'white knight'. Mordashov intended to personally pay 1.25 billion Euros, fuse Severstal into the new company, and obtain 32% of its new shares. Arcelor would then buy back its own shares for a total of 6.5 billion Euros, or 44 Euros per share. The two European companies would merge their mines and operations, achieve 590 million Euros in savings and — most importantly — become the world leader in steel, far too big for any competitor to swallow. In an interview with *Financial Times Deutschland*, Mordashov rubbed it in that no one would ever become a majority shareholder now, stating that he wouldn't mind if Mittal ('neither friend nor foe') wanted up to 30% of the new Arcelor.

The European Commissioner for Economy, Joaquín Almunia, publicly called Arcelor's latest move 'sensible', as did the Russian Finance Minister, Alexej Kudrin. Mittal Steel issued a press statement claiming to fear for Arcelor's shareholders in this 'second-rate' deal, as they would be ceding control over their company for no premium at all. A column in *Süddeutsche Zeitung* agreed and ended rhetorically: 'Let's see if Arcelor's shareholder will swallow that'. They did not. The next day, Arcelor's share price dropped by 3%.

At the same time, however, Mittal's share price climbed by 3%, and Arcelor's media team wondered: could this be portrayed as a sigh of relief by Mittal's shareholders that they too had been spared an unfriendly acquisition of Arcelor? But by now, the competition for attention in the world's media was between two equity stories: Mittal's twice-increased offer with corporate transparency and job guarantees versus the independence secured by a new minority shareholder.

The Deal Closes

The spiral of silence was turning against Arcelor by early June. Shareholders were speaking up against the deal with Mordashov. The *Financial Times* and *Bloomberg* ran stories on the weekend of 17 June about Romain Zaleski, who held around 5% of Arcelor shares and opposed the buy-back as a scheme to 'transfer cash from Arcelor to its shareholders without value creation'. Getting Severstal as a dominant shareholder was seen as a very negative move by existing shareholders, according to Zaleski. In the following week, José María Aristrain (whose family owned 3.6% of Arcelor) had the letter he had written to Arcelor's chairman in which he opposed the Severstal deal leaked to the media.

On 21 June, Severstal issued a press release with an improved offer (3.25 billion Euros) for a smaller stake in Arcelor (25%).

Five days later, on 26 June 2006, Arcelor and Mittal announced their merger at a press conference in Luxembourg. The Arcelor board recommended that its shareholders accept the latest higher offer from Mittal of 40.40 Euros per Arcelor share.

France's left-leaning newspaper *Le Monde* commented wryly that it was a 'victory of the market over the state'. But was it really? Germany's *Handelsblatt* hailed a 'true champion', but who was that in the end? The media relations team carefully saved all the media analyses they had sent from across the world to Guy Dollé at 7 am every morning. This archive, they thought, may be useful for evaluating the success of the negotiations in the future.

The Emotional Underbelly of Collaboration: When Politics Collide with Need

Daniel L. Shapiro
Harvard International Negotiation Program

The Problem

You receive a phone call from a top advisor to the Prime Minister of a developing country. The situation is urgent. The advisor explains that the Prime Minister was overwhelmingly elected as the populist leader of a coalition replacing more than a decade of authoritarian rule. Yet within the Prime Minister's first year in office, his nine-member leadership council is already fragmenting. Each member of the council represents a different interest group or sector of the population comprised of and not limited to Muslims, Hindus, Roman Catholics, Anglicans, and local African tribal spiritual groups, all drawn from a population that originates from Africa, India, the Middle East, China, England, Spain, Portugal, and natives to the land. The population is further segmented by geography, class, and even linguistic differences. The Prime Minister holds a precarious balance of power as the unifier of these disparate groups, each with its own powerful voice clamoring for its own "urgent" needs to be addressed. The situation is further complicated by the personal political ambitions of the leaders that form the coalition. While all these factors, combined, may seem like a recipe for disaster, the Prime Minister sees the situation as a singular opportunity for the liberation of his nation. He believes there is one common denominator: that none of the coalition leaders — and certainly the majority of the electorate — wish to return to the previous dictatorial regime that ruined the country. Disunity would mean a certain resumption of power by the very political party that presided over the most damaging political period in the nation's history.

The challenge now is to form a consensus around this common denominator and to create a formula for rapprochement within both the government and society at large. So the Prime Minister calls upon you to lead a negotiation seminar for him and all of his key government ministers of this troubled and expectant nation. You realize the urgency of the need. The country has great economic potential but currently suffers from crime waves, political intransigence, and a rotting educational infrastructure. The Prime Minister came to office last year on a platform of broad-based unity, security, anti-corruption, and political and educational reform, and he gained power as leader of the largest party in a 9-party governing coalition. But political in-fighting threatens coalitional productivity, and public displays of discord thwart progress.

You are warned that, although the Prime Minister has an academic background, he is not interested in armchair theorizing. He needs a pragmatic framework to foster coalitional effectiveness — or he risks losing power and the country's fragile democracy.

As you accept the invitation to work with the Government, three questions come to mind. What are the sources of this relational tension? What might be a useful framework to address the tension? And practically speaking, what specific ideas do you want to leave in the minds of the government officials to boost collaboration?

These were the questions that appeared in my mind upon receiving such a phone call. In this article, I share the basic approach to my seminar and, more generally, introduce the reader to an empirically supported framework I have developed to address the relational complications of negotiation (Shapiro, 2002; Fisher and Shapiro, 2005; Shapiro, 2010b). I show how the framework was used to diagnose core relational concerns impeding the government's collaboration. I close the paper by illustrating how this framework's guiding principles offered a roadmap for more effective government collaboration. To protect confidentiality, I guise the actual country, involved parties, and situational data, but do not change the critical structural and emotional aspects of this specific case.

Diagnosis

My conversations with various officials and advisors to the government pointed toward two key sources of relational tension. First, despite the Prime Minister's attitude of unity, the coalition held an underground norm of adversarial relations. While the coalition needed to work together to effect policy and avoid a return of the opposition government, an "us versus them" attitude lurked close to the surface. A political analyst encapsulated this attitude by noting that many of the officials in the governing coalition wanted more power and were not reluctant to manipulate the process of governing to serve their own myopic and often personal ambitions, even if that meant resorting to cut-throat politics and justifying those measures as being in the interest of the people to whom they were duly elected to serve.

Second, officials lacked a practical framework to understand and address the relational tensions within and between parties. These leaders were like fish in water: They were heavily influenced by the full range of emotions connected to their political positioning and maneuvering, yet lacked effective tools to recognize and deal with those emotions. These officials swam in a pool of pride, hope, ambition, fear, envy, and resentment, but had no clear map to navigate through the emotional undercurrents and political waves. Without such a map, they were easy prey to the perils of negative emotions.

Diagnosis	Strategy
1. Norm of adversarialism	1. Encourage norm of cooperation
2. Lack of framework to address relational tensions	2. Draw on "Core Concerns Framework"

Chart 1. Diagnoses and strategies to address governmental negotiation challenges.

A Strategy to Build Cooperation

To address these diagnoses, I drew upon two key strategies: (1) encouraging the officials to build a norm of cooperation and (2) equipping them with the core concerns framework support the norm of cooperation. (See Chart 1.)

Encouraging a norm of cooperation

I worked with leaders of the coalitional government to help them see the benefits of turning their underground norm of adversarialism into a norm of cooperation. At the beginning of our seminar, I asked each official to share three adjectives that he or she felt described him or her as a negotiator. Most of the officials shared sunny words like "open" or "win-win." However, these self-assessments failed to suggest their behavior in the subsequent negotiation activity: the "Oil Pricing Exercise" (Fisher, 2008). In this prisoner's dilemma game, participants enroll as members of an Oil Pricing Board of either the country Alba or Batia. They learn that the oil pricing market for a third country, Capita, is controlled completely by Alba and Batia. Each Oil Pricing Board's goal is to maximize the profits of their own country. Monthly profits for each country are based entirely upon the price each country sets and how it compares with the other country's price. If one board undercuts the other's pricing, the former board reaps substantial financial reward, while the latter fares poorly. If the boards compete, both reap minimal reward. And if both groups cooperate, they equally benefit fairly well. I have run this exercise dozens and dozens of times but have rarely seen boards as competitive and double-crossing as these. Two boards each explicitly conspired about how best to exploit the other board through deception and outright lies. During face-to-face meetings, several board members committed to an agreement with the other side — and shook hands — but failed to live up to that agreement. Several boards also intentionally skipped a meeting with the other board. The norm of adversarialism took charge from the outset of this exercise and became self-reinforcing.

When reviewing this exercise and sharing the pricing data with the participants, they quickly saw the dangers of an adversarial approach to negotiation. If boards were to cooperate, everyone would have performed substantially better than they had, yielding greater cumulative profits. But for some of these officials, particularly those scarred in the rough ride of politics, a self-defensive psychology appeared to overshadow pure rationality. The level of mutual mistrust between parties was so great that some officials felt obliged to engage in adversarial behavior. They feared that any form of cooperation put them at grave risk of being victim to exploitation. I understood their fear, and we discussed it. If one individual cooperates and others compete, the cooperator will be exploited. Adversarialism trumps cooperation, at least in the short-term. The group came to realize that it is only through the willful efforts of the coalition as a whole — starting with the Prime Minister himself — that the norm of adversarialism can be changed. During a conversation later in the day, the Prime Minister stated unequivocally his will to use political capital to make that cooperative alternative a reality.

Addressing core concerns

Once the officials saw the dangers of adversarialism and the benefits of cooperative relations, the challenge now was to offer a framework that could help them better understand and address the emotional dynamics driving their behavior. I have developed

Relational Identity Theory (Shapiro, 2002; Shapiro, 2010b), a model to illuminate key motivational and emotional variables that stimulate constructive or destructive conflict management. I drew upon the theory's practical variation, the Core Concerns Framework (Fisher and Shapiro, 2005), which Roger Fisher and I created after both an extensive review of the relevant scholarly literature and an analysis of the emotional dimensions of our practical experiences as negotiators, mediators, and advisors in real-life negotiations and conflict situations. To inform development of the framework, we drew on our experiences consulting for world leaders, business executives and managers, lawyers, doctors, military officers, mental health professionals and patients, academics, and disputing ethnopolitical factions.

The Core Concerns Framework offers a pragmatic approach to address the emotional dimensions of negotiation. Any negotiation involves a dynamic, complex intermix of dozens of nuanced, powerful emotions, such as shame, anger, resentment, contempt, hope, pride, fear, guilt, love, joy, and enthusiasm. The Core Concerns Framework suggests that rather than trying to identify, analyze, and manage such an overwhelming, constantly changing set of emotions, negotiators can simplify their task by turning their attention to a handful of core concerns that tend to stimulate many of those emotions.

Core concerns are fundamental motives that press for satisfaction, especially in the context of negotiation (Shapiro, 2010a). Motives can be classified as core concerns if they: exist across cultural and organizational contexts; hold relevance across professional and personal relationships; offer practical utility in negotiation; and are supported by empirical research. A convergence of research across domains points toward five such core concerns (Shapiro, 2010b):

- Appreciation (recognition of value)
- Autonomy (freedom to feel, think, take action, or decide)
- Affiliation (relational connection to others)
- Status (standing compared to that of others)

- Role (effectiveness and meaningfulness of job label and related activities)

The power of the Core Concerns Framework rests in the dual function of the core concerns. First, these core concerns can be used as a *lens* to understand the emotional dimension of negotiation. A better understanding of a party's core concerns can illuminate what I call the *semantic landscape* of a negotiation (Shapiro, 2010a). This is the emotional meaning that parties consciously or unconsciously attach to their interaction, often in the form of narratives that describe how parties see themselves in relation to one another. Who are we in relation to one another? How do we each want to be perceived from our own perspective — and in the eyes of the other? Second, the core concerns can be used as a *lever* to stimulate positive emotions and cooperative behavior. As a lever, a party's perception of how their core concerns are treated tends to impact their subsequent emotional and behavioral tendencies. If an individual or group's core concerns are addressed constructively, positive emotions and cooperative behavior tend to manifest. If these core concerns are unaddressed, negative emotions and adversarial behaviors are more likely to result.

Tactics: Applying the Core Concerns Framework

During our session, we discussed how to apply the core concerns as a *lens* to understand the emotional dimension of their relations and as a *lever* to stimulate a more productive emotional climate within which they could collaborate (Fisher and Shapiro, 2005).

As a lens

The officials and I discussed each core concern one by one, and we jointly reflected upon their relevance to the coalition's efficacy.

We started with a discussion on *appreciation* — the need to feel heard, understood, and valued. We referred back to their experience in the prisoner's dilemma game. One policymaker noted that the group, as a whole, had failed to understand and value one another's perspective, despite virtually everyone believing during the game that they had full understanding. Another policymaker then connected this theme to their real-life responsibilities, raising the problem of budget allocation. He noted that conflicts sometimes emerge when other ministries do not seem to understand the relative urgency of his ministry's financial priorities. Others alerted him to the need to appreciate their ministries' priorities as well. This crucial human need for appreciation has been demonstrated in numerous experimental studies (e.g., McCraty and Childre, 2004), and its practicality importance became salient in the political context.

We moved to the importance of *affiliation*, the relational connection between individuals or groups. A high-ranking minister noted that politics is replete with the challenges of building connections, allying with one group over another, and avoiding being cast as the scapegoat or outlier. Our discussion focused on recognizing what these officials experienced daily but rarely had opportunity to reflect upon: the impact of political backstabbing, party betrayal, and interpersonal rivalries on their affiliation to one another. The topic is a sensitive one, and we approached it at an abstract level. Yet the point hit home. The leaders of two of the coalition's major parties, for example, have a history of political and personal tension. One controls government finance; the other controls a critical coalitional party. Each views the other with strong suspicion, creating a major rift within the coalition. Through our discussion, these two leaders, among others, noted the political constraints of adversarial relations on coalitional stability and party success.

As the leaders realized the substantial consequences of negative affiliation on their behavior, our conversation flowed into a discussion on *autonomy*, the freedom to make decisions without the imposition of another person or group. One minister expressed the challenge of staying true to the coalition while simultaneously maintaining the integrity of his own party's doctrine. Numerous ministers agreed that there is a struggle to balance affiliation to the coalition with autonomy to their party (see Brewer, 1991; Shapiro, 2010b). One manifestation was the fear some parties expressed of being "absorbed" into the coalition, losing their identity. These parties talked about ways to increase their "brand presence".

Our conversation shifted to the core concern of *status*, one's standing in relation to other individuals or groups. It was inevitable that status played a role in the interactions of the ministers. They were from multiple competing parties, each representing a variety of competing constituencies, and each ministerial position held more or less influence than others. Furthermore, numerous individuals within each party had personal ambitions for an elevated position in the government and within their own party's rank. A few of the Ministers were rumored to want the position of Prime Minister and wondered why they were not in that seat now. During one break, one Minister quietly voiced feelings of inferiority at being selected for a relatively less influential post. All of these status factors affect the emotional experience of the ministers and ultimately their motivation to collaborate.

The final core concern we discussed was *role*: Do these ministers play effective, fulfilling roles? This core concern came to life as the Prime Minister and I talked during a break in our seminar. In the middle of our discussion, he looked over my shoulder and shook his head in angry disappointment. I turned around and saw, in a nearby restaurant, four ministers arguing. The Prime Minister explained: "They are arguing over who should write the check for one of my most important campaign promises: new curriculum materials for students!" The Prime Minister said, "Why can't they just get along! They forget the point of their roles: To serve the children!" Here, the Prime Minister wisely noted that poorly crafted roles can impede effective collaboration.

As a lever

The ministers now realized the power of these core concerns on their political lives, and they were motivated to make constructive change. We discussed five broad themes for prescriptive action. While our conversation took several hours, I now will summarize the major points. First, we discussed key steps for officials to express authentic appreciation. We touched upon three major aspects to appreciate the perspective of another: (1) understanding both what the other is saying and, more importantly, what the other is leaving unsaid, (2) finding merit in the other person's perspective; and (3) communicating that understanding (Fisher and Shapiro, 2005). An official commented that appreciating is not the same as agreeing with the other's perspective. This comment alerted the group to the notion that appreciating is a particularly useful tool for building relationships within their diverse government coalition. Second, we moved to a discussion about ways to respect the autonomy of the coalition membership. As an antidote to backstabbing, the ministers resonated with the importance of consulting before deciding on decisions important to others in the coalition (Fisher and Shapiro, 2005). Third, we considered tactical approaches to building affiliation. The Prime Minister emphasized to all of the coalitional parties the need to hold together as a cohesive entity — or else to risk a return to the dictatorial powers of the past. The Prime Minister had built a track record as an able politician who could bring disparate parties together. While his general style leaned toward rapprochement, during a break he shared with me his willingness to be strong-armed both toward promoting cooperation and reprimanding those who betray the coalition's goals. Fourth, the ministers acknowledged the need to better deal with the core concern of status. The officials identified ways that they could better respect one another's particular areas of expertise and experience in order to enhance governmental relationships and reach the coalition's wide-ranging goals. Finally, we discussed the importance of officials crafting constructive roles to help them attain their shared and differing political goals. Officials noted that, when differences arose, they often reverted to long-standing roles as adversaries. Through our conversation, they came to see that they could choose between multiple roles when negotiating political differences.

They could debate and argue, or they could structure roles conducive to joint problem-solving and mutual gains.

Preliminary Evaluation

Two months after the training, I met with the Prime Minister, other key officials, and support staff to informally evaluate the effectiveness of the training program. We spent several hours reviewing the current status of the governing coalition's relations, as well as what worked well and what might be done differently with the training. Three points stood out. First, the training has had a sustainable impact on the coalition's motivation to collaborate. The Prime Minister reported that the Oil Pricing Exercise remains a haunting reminder of the kind of relations his coalitional government does *not* want to replicate. Second, the Prime Minister reported on the particular utility of three of the core concerns: Appreciation, autonomy, and affiliation. The Prime Minister stated that, since the workshop, he has repeatedly emphasized to the ministers the need to understand and find merit in the perspectives of both fellow politicians and constituents. A key advisor to the Prime Minister noted that this emphasis on appreciation has improved the general attitude of parties toward one another. In terms of autonomy, the Prime Minister reported a noticeable increase in the government's practice of consulting before deciding. Awareness of autonomy has apparently increased the ministers' sensitivity to the dangers of making decisions "behind another person's back." In terms of affiliation, the Prime Minister commented on his increased urging of ministers to think about policymaking as a task of inclusion, not exclusion. He discussed his evolving approach to coalitional leadership, which includes building a strong personal connection with the ministers and empowering them. Third, the Prime Minister stated the need for additional negotiation training. No single, day-long training can fully change long-term habits, attitudes, and deeply embedded political divisions. Additional training would incentive use of the skills and would better prepare these officials for the complexities of multi-party negotiations. Our team is now in discussion with the Prime Minister's Office about follow-up training.

Summary

The goal of this chapter was to illustrate how one might go about dealing with the emotional complications of a real-life negotiation between stakeholders who hold a great amount of power. I focused on my consultation for government officials struggling to reduce the relational tensions inherent to a multi-party governing coalition. I introduced the Core Concerns Framework as a practical approach to understand and address the emotional dimension of negotiation, and I discussed ways in which the officials applied this framework to their relational challenges. These efforts equipped the officials with a set of tools to better collaborate within a sea of contentious interests toward a brighter, shared future.

The Role of Negotiation in Building Intra-Team and Inter-Team Cooperation

Helena Desivilya-Syna
Department of Sociology and Anthropology
Max Stern Academic College of Emek Yezreel

This chapter focuses on two wide-spread social and organizational phenomena: teams and negotiation. Understanding the intersection between teamwork and negotiation becomes vital in the era of globalization with its mounting competition and concomitant growing interdependencies among individuals, groups and organizations. Effective collaboration within team structures may provide a competitive advantage and foster sustainability (Richter *et al.*, 2006). Consequently, teams of practitioners collaborate with academics in developments projects, business organizations form strategic alliances, leveraging their advantage over other companies and residents in communities build partnerships and networks to muster scarce resources (Tomlinson, 2005).

The chapter focuses on informal negotiations within and between teams, addressing attempts to reach consensus and mutual understanding, albeit without formal procedures, such as setting the time and place and sitting around negotiation table. Often, the parties do not view these efforts as negotiation or are unaware of being in the midst of negotiation process (Kolb and Williams, 2000). We endeavor to integrate theory and practice, therefore, present and discuss three cases throughout the chapter.

The chapter commences with definitions of central terms, subsequently discusses the challenges and complexities of team negotiation, focusing on the processes of team negotiation and their consequences. We wrap-up by addressing the factors which promote the constructiveness of team negotiation, in turn, fostering effective team cooperation.

The Interface between Teams and Negotiation

Teams constitute increasingly popular organizational structures designed to improve quality, increase efficiency, and organizational sustainability. A widely accepted definition of a team refers to a small group of people who pursue common goals and who are mutually accountable (Katzenbach and Smith, 1993). Recent definitions embrace a dynamic orientation, viewing teams as knots, loosely defined and changing in accordance with contextual and historical transformations (Engeström, 2008).

Scholars in the area of organizational behavior and management have argued that the quality of a team's interpersonal bonds and consequently its outcomes is significantly affected by the group's ability to manage conflicts. The organizational reality of a highly diverse work group composition increases the propensity for conflicts, thus turning effective dispute management into a vital asset (De Dreu, 2006; Desivilya, 2008).

Negotiation constitutes a common way of engaging conflict. Social psychologists defined it as a social process designed to resolve differences by means of give-and-take (Lewicki, Saunders and Litterer, 1999; Pruitt and Carnevale, 1993). Other scholars construed this phenomenon as a process of consensus seeking, underscoring the process of mutual belief revision (Dunlop, 1984; Zhang *et al.*, 2004). Researchers and practitioners in the organizational behavior arena extended the concept to *negotiating reality* denoting the parties' interacting and coordinating of shared and individual understandings; namely, developing mutually acceptable subjective models of their social interactions within the specific organizational context (Eden *et al.*, 1981;

Friedman and Antal, 2004; Kolb and McGinn, 2009; Putnam, 2003). The latter extended definition appears highly relevant to the context of teams and inter-team relations, where subjective experiences of individuals have a considerable impact on the teams' functioning.

Proponents of critical conflict resolution theory conceptualized negotiation as social advocacy working against oppressing institutions to attain social justice; or in other words, redefine power relations (Hansen, 2008). In a similar vein, Collier (2009) construed negotiation as processes designed to define cultural identities and inter-group positions, or in general terms — negotiating relationships — as put by this scholar: "*Negotiation refers to communicative processes in which parties are engaged in developing, challenging, and reinforcing their group and individual positions in relationship to each other and the context*" (p. 289).

This chapter draws on the latter definitions, viewing negotiation as a process aimed at coordinating by means of informal communication individual or group understandings concerning mutually accepted terms of intra-team or inter-team relations.

The characteristics and functions of team negotiation

Case 1: Team Negotiation — What is it?

A psychology department in one of the academic institutions in Israel has embarked on a process of internal evaluation — an initiative carried out in recent years by the Council of Higher Education. The department chair assembled a department meeting aimed at forming a team responsible for materializing this mission. The mere attempt of a team creation raised tensions and disagreements among faculty members, department chair and the department administrative coordinator. A senior faculty member declined any task: "*I am just about to start my sabbatical year…*". Another

(Continued)

> ### Case 1: (*Continued*)
>
> faculty member voiced his dissatisfaction with joining the team, explaining: "*I am up for promotion to senior lecturer, I have to write and publish or else I perish...*". A junior adjunct faculty member expressed her reservation at investing extra time on a voluntary basis: "*I don't have to tell you how much I like working in this department, all of you know that I have always been involved in what happens in the department and volunteered to "open days", organizing meeting... but this is too much to ask without getting paid...*". The meeting was concluded with some very general decisions, at that point hardly operational.
>
> Shortly after the meeting, one of the faculty members (a senior lecturer) was injured and could not teach his winter semester courses. The department chair decided to appoint him as person in charge of the internal evaluation. She then reconvened another faculty meeting to discuss the procedures to be employed and division of labor. The faculty member in charge was involved in decision-making processes by means of virtual communication. Procedures were set and tasks were divided. Some faculty members have harbored ill feelings, which were voiced later on. Others volunteered to help. Division of labor was redefined several times by means of formal and informal communications, involving the department chair, the faculty person in-charge and the administrative coordinator of the department. The latter voiced her reservations with regard to her own involvement in the process of internal evaluation: "*I do not think these are my duties...*". Nonetheless, continued performing the coordination tasks.

What constitutes team negotiation and what purposes does it serve? Case 1 above illustrates some of team negotiation content and its functions. The department chair sought agreement with other faculty members with respect to an *ad hoc* team formation — its composition and division of responsibilities. Beyond these tangible elements, team negotiation penetrates into deeper layers, dealing with communication concerning status, power and influence of various individuals within the existing and emerging team. The department chair exercised her authority, but was contested by a peer male faculty member who declined any role in the evaluation process due to a sabbatical, another male faculty member, who expressed his reluctance as a consequence of a promotion procedure and a junior adjunct teacher who refused to undertake voluntary activities. Moreover, seemingly individual 'negotiators' embody representatives of various groups, such as senior faculty members versus junior faculty, women versus men and other possible social groups, who negotiate status hierarchies for their virtual and real constituents.

Thus, the adjunct teacher's statement expressed the sentiments of junior and temporary staff with respect to their inferior status, refusal to be exploited and attempts to 'bargain' for quid pro quo; namely, fair exchange relationship — getting pay for their work on the internal evaluation tasks. The informal and implicit communication was indeed a trigger for a more formal negotiation of the department chair with the head of academic administration, which resulted in a favorable outcome for the junior academic staff, i.e., pay for their contribution to the internal evaluation process.

The implicit or hidden aspects of negotiation have been labeled by Kolb and Williams (2000) *shadow negotiation*. As expressed by the authors: "*The shadow negotiation is where hidden agendas and masked assumptions play out. Often it is defined by a whole array of attitudes of which the participants are only dimly aware. These hidden agendas drive the negotiation as much as explicit differences over issues*" (p. 11).

Achieving actual influence in team relations is largely dependent on recognizing and dealing with this implicit layer of negotiation. Partners often do not acquiesce to overt request of their counterparts, but the reasons behind such refusals are not clear altogether, leading to misunderstandings, erroneous

attributions of invidious intentions and eventually conflict escalation (Desivilya and Yassour-Borochowitz, 2010; Friedman and
Desivilya, 2010). Consequently, exposing hidden agendas,
unvoiced assumptions and negotiating the terms of engagement
becomes essential for actual cooperation within and between
teams. The advice offered in many negotiation texts, to focus on
the problem while evading personal attacks — *"separate the people
from the problem"* — can hardly be implemented because in team
interactions people often constitute the core of the problem (Kolb
and Williams, 2000). Thus, negotiation cannot be constrained to
rational behavior, but rather involves feelings team members har-
bor towards one another, biases, stereotypes and prejudice held
by one social group towards another and identity-related issues,
which may impinge upon their relationships. Such irrational elements of negotiations are especially likely to emerge in an era of
globalization where encounters between various groups and
diverse individuals prevail. Notwithstanding seemingly or gen-
uinely common interests and goals, the preexisting differences
and the impact of socialization cannot be easily removed, pre-
cluding sole focus on problem-solving approach in negotiation.

As stated earlier, conflicts in team context are ubiquitous
(DeDreu, 2006; Desivilya, 2008; Tjosvold, 2006). These discords
often emanate from divergent goals and expectations of different
group members (such as discrepancies concerning strategies and
tactics) and attempts to muster control over the team's work and
outcomes. Thus, power issues either explicitly or symbolically,
underlie many of the conflicts in team context. The intensity of
such conflicts may mount especially when there are disparities in
the members' or partnering organizations' status, with the less
powerful parties needing greater assurance that their interests are
taken into account than the high status partners.

The Intricacies of Team Negotiation Processes

The pervasiveness of conflicts within teams and inter-team
interactions makes negotiation a frequent coping mechanism.

The following Case 2 illustrates the processes of inter-team negotiation.

Case 2: The Working of Team Negotiation

The case is derived from an evaluation study of a new municipal social program: The Unit for Prevention and Treatment of Violence against the Elderly (the Unit), which targets elderly residents and victims of family violence. All staff and executive committee members are experienced social workers. The Unit aims to provide services for the elderly population in all districts of the municipality by means of individual treatment, group and community work. The evaluation research team collaborated with the Unit's staff, and its executive committee in order to develop and implement a tool kit for documentation and follow-up of cases, considered essential for building a comprehensive database. In the long run, the inter-team collaboration was to attain three goals: a. Establish a knowledge base about the treatment of elderly victims of family violence b. Promote the professional development of the staff c. Ensure the sustainability of the program. To accomplish these goals the partners had to create some mechanisms of coordination. The research team initiated individual meetings with the Unit coordinator, followed by two focus groups: one with staff members and the other with the executive committee. The purpose of the individual and group meetings was to talk about inter-team relations: to explain the intended aims and rationale of joint work, clarify the interests, needs, ideas; and solicit specific suggestions for subsequent steps from the staff, the executive committee, and the research team. Many hurdles surfaced at the initial phase. The staff expressed suspicion and distrust concerning the motives of the research team, including concern that its priorities included

(Continued)

Case 2: (*Continued*)

publishing in scientific journals and reporting program pitfalls to the funding agency it was accountable to, and would neglect the needs and priorities of the program's staff in promoting the practice and the Unit's success. The staff stressed that their immediate concern was providing treatment to the patients, rather than "wasting" time on "paperwork," and feared that the additional tasks would further increase their already heavy workload, and would interfere with the relationships and accountability to their respective district department heads. The research team expressed its concern with regard to the potential loss of knowledge unless systematic documentation, follow-up, and learning were established and maintained. Additional issues emerged in the focus groups: Who decides which kind of knowledge is legitimate, and how is information gathered and stored? The staff felt much more in control about deciding about the legitimacy of the type of knowledge, due to their professional expertise in the field, whereas the research team claimed greater control concerning research methodology, such as modes of data collection and data analysis. Moreover, the parties jointly decided to divide responsibilities: the research team would subsequently review existing tools used by the social services systems, and on this basis prepare a draft designed for the Unit. Next, the draft formulated by the research team was presented to the executive committee and the Unit's staff. The comments of both groups were then incorporated into the second draft of the proposal, followed by a pilot phase for pre-testing the tools in the field. The implementation of the pilot was slow. The staff strongly resisted compromising the requirements of their daily practice and violating their accountability requirements to their superiors and to patients. The slow

(*Continued*)

Case 2: (*Continued*)

pace in the field was clearly contrary to the research team's expectations. In order to avoid such obstacles in the future, one member of the research team conducted a workshop for the staff, designed to draw lessons from the pilot phase. This session attempted to demonstrate the usability of knowledge generated by the tool kit for the daily practice and in the long run for the generation and integration of knowledge concerning elderly victims and perpetrators of family violence. The workshop facilitator convened dyads of staff members who jointly reviewed their respective forms, attempting to integrate potential insights concerning case profiles and criteria for evaluating the success of the treatment of patients. This strategy appeared quite successful in changing the Unit staff's perceptions with regard to the utility of the collected information. The staff members did realize that systematically collected data yielded useful insights for daily practice, as well as for developing professional practice in a new arena.

The case above depicts the basics of inter-team negotiation between two major partners: the Unit staff and executive committee (the practitioners) and the research team (the academics). The inter-team relationship that evolved can be classified as a "strategic partnership" according to Wilkinson, Browne and Dwyer's (2002) typology. Its objective was to create a trust-based partnership in order to foster multifaceted knowledge; the focus, then, was creating *coordination* between the partners. In line with this aim, the research team initiated individual meetings with the Unit coordinator, followed by two focus groups: one with staff members and the other with the executive committee. The purpose of the individual and group meetings was to *negotiate the meaning of the partnership* and determine the "rules of engagement" (Amabile *et al.*, 2001; Hinds and Mortenson, 2005; Tjosvold, 2006; Tomlinson, 2005). Although the process was led by the research team, the underlying goal was to merge the needs of each partner and create knowledge in a synergistic fashion by means of building a trust-based rather than power-based partnership. This was a difficult endeavor, given the considerable conflict in logic and practice between the research team and the practitioners. Active and continuous participation of both partners was considered crucial (Amabile *et al.*, 2001).

Stumbling blocks, such as mutual distrust and different motivations, were manifested at the first stage of inter-team relationship building. Disparate professional identities and values were expressed as a result of cultural differences, as suggested by Amabile *et al.*, (2001) and Desivilya (2001), emerging as a result of diverse professional socialization. The staff stressed their *practitioner* professional identity, reflected in the declared main concern with respect to patients' care, whereas the research team emphasized *their scientist/researcher* professional identity as reflected in their concern regarding loss of knowledge. The parties needed to negotiate their understanding and somehow bridge such contrasting professional identities.

In addition, issues of power and control had to be negotiated: legitimacy of different kinds of knowledge, modes of data collection and storage of information with each party claiming distinct professional expertise. The Unit staff preferred deciding about the legitimacy of the type of knowledge, while the research team expressing preference for making decision concerning research methodology. Discovering these different priorities formed an initial basis for negotiation. Nevertheless, there was a clear need for more systematic *coordination* in the partnership (Swan and Scarbrough, 2005). This meant establishing mechanisms for knowledge integration, including both the content and relational aspects:

- Overcoming barriers resulting from the use of different terminologies — research-based terminology employed by the evaluation team, and practice-based terminology used by the Unit staff;

- Using different rules in processing information — formal documentation by researchers versus sporadic note-taking and "storing information in memory" by the staff.
- Employing different patterns of action — systematic, pre-planned actions by the evaluation team versus spontaneous, crisis-related actions by the staff.

In line with the arguments and findings of several scholars (Amabile *et al.*, 2001; Tomlinson, 2005), division of areas of responsibility clearly facilitated the building of the inter-team collaboration. A series of separate working sessions followed by joint meetings actually formed a process of negotiation: each party preparing its proposal and subsequently discussing it and searching for consensus in joint meetings. Difficulties emerged again in the implementation phase. The staff members were highly reluctant to modify their priorities: incorporating the new methods of documentation into work routines while at the same time maintaining the requirements of their daily practice and not violating perceived accountability requirements to their superiors and patients. The research team was also resistant to changing their priorities with respect to the pace of implementation and adjusting to the conditions of the Unit's work context. The pilot phase again reflected the discrepant values of the two partners, pointing to the need for coordination and synchronization of time perspectives; namely, negotiating the terms of engagement (Standifer and Bluedorn, 2006).

In order to avoid the obstacles associated with power issues and different professional identities, it was necessary to work on organizational and social processes by means of engaging inter-group conflicts with regard to legitimacy of information, its usefulness and time perspective (Amabile *et al.*, 2001; Desivilya, 2008). Analysis of the case revealed that a workshop format promoted mutual understandings concerning potential gains of the pilot process, especially for the Unit staff, and synchronized expectations with respect to power relations, thereby providing a forum for *negotiating reality* (Eden *et al.*, 1981; Friedman and

Antal, 2004; Kolb and McGinn, 2009; Putnam, 2003). The negotiation process seemed effective in changing the staff members' views concerning the contribution of systematically collected information to the quality of practice and professional development. The implicit negotiation process made the voice of the Unit staff resonate quite clearly, while also promoting the research team's objective of building systematic data base.

As Case 2 demonstrates, the processes of building inter-team collaboration often reflect disparities in understanding of power-relations. These perceived incompatibilities in turn elicit conflicts which, the parties attempt to engage by means of implicit negotiation processes: negotiating reality and terms of engagement.

Engaging Identity Conflicts by Means of Team Negotiation

Conflicting perceptions of social relations are particularly likely in situations where the parties differ in formal or symbolic status. Such gaps often emanate from high levels of demographic diversity. Tajfel's and Turner's (1986) *social identity* and *social categorization* theories and Byrne's (1997) *similarity-attraction paradigm* explain the triggering effect of diversity on conflicting perceptions of social relations, which need to be negotiated in a team context.

The basic tenet of the social categorization and social identity conceptual framework posits that people tend to define and distinguish themselves from others based on their group membership. Encountering individuals from different groups sets up the categorization process and gives rise to a tendency to form a more favorable image of one's own group in comparison to the attitudes toward dissimilar groups. This process allows individuals to protect and maintain positive social identity. The similarity-attraction paradigm offers a different explanation to the biased tendency to favor members of one's own group over "outsiders". According to this model, people are more attracted to and prefer interacting with similar individuals because they expect thereby to reaffirm their values and beliefs. Both explanations point to the same outcome of *in-group favoritism*, which accentuates preexisting stereotypes and prejudice, enhances antagonism between diverse team members, increasing the odds of conflicts. In a similar vein, the identity framing of inter-group relations views inter-group conflict as rooted in threats to people's individual and collective purposes, sense of meaning, definitions of self, and fundamental human needs, such as dignity, recognition, safety, control, purpose, and efficacy (Rothman, 1997). Case 3 illustrates the complexities involved in negotiating power relations and terms of engagement in demographically, professionally and politically diverse teams in the context of protracted national conflict. Such processes underscore the importance of *shadow negotiation* aside to overt negotiation on substantive issues.

**Case 3: The Complexities of Negotiating Power Relations —
Engaging Identity Conflicts**

The case is based on a research follow-up of a partnership project between a Jewish nation-wide environmental NGO (A1) and an Arab Planning NGO (A2). The project was designed to promote legal and planning solutions to environmental problems in Arab communities. The research attempted to broaden knowledge and understanding about Arab-Jewish professional partnerships in leading joint projects: identifying the strengths of these cooperative efforts, difficulties and necessary modifications. The case describes the final phases of the joint project aimed at developing a tripartite alliance with another regional Jewish-Arab NGO (funded by the same organization and considered as one of its highlight projects), thereby potentially increasing the impact of the collaboration. Informal conversations with the two partnering organizations and the funding organizations

(Continued)

Case 3: (*Continued*)

alluded to differences in each party's perception with respect to the meaning and essence of a potential tripartite alliance. Consequently, the research team decided to convene separate meetings with each of the organizations in order to systematically learn about their views on that matter: the essence of new partnership, change in modus operandi and directions of future operations, designed to promote the collaborative project. The separate meetings pointed at several common issues. Each of the partners declared their interest in continuing the collaboration, albeit qualifying such readiness by presenting some '*red lines*': A2 stated that the partnership must not impede the high prestige and regard of the organization in the eyes of their Arab constituents; A1 presented 3 '*red lines*' — dealing with issues of environmental justice, refraining from political flavor and allocation of adequate resources, so that further investment in expanding the project is justified. The funding agency stressed the necessity of devising operational plans in order to allow continuation of the partnership. The separate meetings also raised the need for renewed definition of the partnership in terms of its content, finances and organization. The issue of financial administration deemed crucial for A2. Aside to similarities in the parties' perceptions, each raised some unique concerns. A2 saw the new alliance as an extension to new communities but also to new activities. A1 viewed the new partnership as switching from local or regional emphasis to cross-national orientation. The funding agency envisioned the new alliance as incubation of ideas, operations and organizational structure, therefore unlike the current partnership should not be bounded by time constraints. A1 and A2 also emphasized the need to define the role of the funding organization in the new alliance. The information collected at the

(*Continued*)

Case 3: (*Continued*)

separate meetings yielded an agenda for a joint meeting:
a. clarification and sharpening of the concept 'tripartite;
b. Discussion of ambiguous and controversial issues;
c. Definition of the funding organization's role in the new
partnership and renewed definition of the roles of A1 and A2.
Senior representatives of each organization attended the
joint meeting, which was facilitated by the research team. A1
and A2 presented their joint proposal for the tripartite
alliance which was then discussed by the group. The group
discussion allowed further crystallization of A1 and A2's
emphases. The funding organization reacted to the proposal
of the two partners and presented its own proposal.
Ambiguous and controversial issues were uncovered,
including surfacing of potential weaknesses of the tripartite
alliance versus its potential strengths. Finally, a tentative
time schedule was worked-out. The meeting was concluded
with several remaining ambiguous and controversial issues:
mode of interfacing of the existing partnership between A1
and A2 and the Jewish-Arab NGO so that the tripartite
alliance will be able to maintain its autonomy; the role of
other local organizations and modes of cooperation with
them and; types of activities within the Arab communities.
These issues along with their organizational and financial
aspects were to be elaborated in preparation of operational
plans by A1 and A2.

Drawing on Kolb and McGinn's (2009) construction of the
term negotiation as an ongoing activity in organizations, the two
partnering NGOs and the funding organization have engaged in
negotiating *authority* (legitimacy of their positions and ideas),
value (getting recognition and reward), *support* (developing coalition) and *commitment* (definition of "successful" project). A1 and
A2 engaged the challenges of inter-team relations by each party

attempting to speak in a distinct voice, which exerts an impact and is considered legitimate. These negotiation attempts were by no means trivial. The two original partners experienced difficulties in positioning themselves in the negotiation process with the funding organization, due to their dependence on resources for sustaining the joint project. This difficulty was especially salient for A2 as this party was bound in a symbolic inferiority due to its minority status. Both partners *vis-à-vis* the funding organization and A2 *vis-à-vis* A1, were good negotiators on the overt level, clearly defining their central interests and identifying viable options for bridging them, however they displayed weaknesses in 'shadow negotiation' — defining relations with the other party. Thus, various controversial issues remained ambiguous. A2 was not sufficiently resolute with regard to the legitimacy of its group position (full involvement in financial decisions and joint administration with A1 of the project's budget). Both A1 and A2 refrained from spelling out their limits ('*red lines*') *vis-à-vis* the funding organization (refusal to relinquish their leading position in the project and becoming accountable to the new partner). This might have hindered them unless the research team had suggested separate meetings, which actually fostered uplifting the *shadow* aspects of the negotiation process (Kolb and Williams, 2000). This forum allowed A2 to voice dissatisfaction with respect to its group actual exclusion by A1 from financial decisions and administration of the project's budget, subsequently moving this hidden issue to the 'forefront of the stage'. It also allowed A2 to express its fear concerning potential '*loss of face*' with its Arab constituency. A separate meeting with A2 facilitated clarifying its concerns with regard to maintaining professional identity (focus on environmental justice) and pointing at the importance of matching the funding with the scope of activities. A separate meeting with the funding organization helped in defining its hidden agenda of enhancing the visibility of its organization and nationwide impact on improving Jewish-Arab relations in Israel.

In line with the argument held by Amabile *et al.* (2001), Tjosvold (2006), and DeDreu (1997; 2006), constructive *engagement* of various kinds of conflicts among partners constitutes a crucial ingredient in the process of building team relations. The separate meetings provided an initial platform for such a process: facilitated attending to identity-related conflicts (minority-majority relations, professional identities of the parties and political identities — relations with constituents) and thereby improving the shadow aspects of negotiation. This process allowed members of each team to protect positive social identity, accord a sense of meaning and maintain fundamental human needs, such as dignity, recognition, safety, control, and efficacy (Rothman, 1997; Tajfel and Turner, 1986). The joint meeting allowed dealing directly with some of the power and identity issues, which surfaced at the separate meetings, and negotiate the terms of engagement among the parties. Such constructive engagement of identity and power-related discords through negotiation promotes learning and attainment of desirable outcomes as well as further strengthen the team bonds.

Concluding Thoughts

The last section integrates the insights concerning constructive negotiations which in turn promote building effective cooperation.

Tjosvold's (1994) maintains that constructing team relations on principles of cooperation requires developing a **shared vision, commitment** to realizing shared goals and interests, and engendering a feeling of **empowerment**. The prescribed processes include conflict engagement; namely, exposing and analyzing the dynamics of power in the partners' relationships, thereby promoting mutual understanding of the structural and dynamics aspects of discord. The latter facilitates on-going cooperation while attempting to formulate a joint direction, muster commitment and create a sense of empowerment among partners. In other words, constructively engaged conflict may constitute a positive force, enhancing cooperation within and among teams. Cases 2 and 3 reflected at least partial implementation of conflict engagement by means of *merging overt* and *shadow negotiation*.

Amabile *et al.* (2001), Tjosvold (2006), and Tomlinson (2005) also indicate the importance of developing shared meaning and vision through *open communication* (frequent face-to-face meetings), and of mutual understanding about roles and responsibilities. These authors have also underscored the need to create new shared identities and build trust between partnering teams. Trust is an important precursor of constructive team relations. Developing a shared meaning and understanding of partnership, shared identity, and mutual commitment may foster trust-based realtionships, but there is also a need to manage power relations on three levels: overt, covert, and latent (Schemer and Schmid, 2007). One way of promoting the power balance in the overt and covert levels, is through effective use of the capabilities of each partner by means of explicit division of tasks and responsibilities and subsequent exchange of feedback (Amabile *et al.*, 2001). The process ingredients, just mentioned, may mitigate the impact of preexisting social categorization processes and diminish threats to one's group identity thereby preventing in-group favoritism (Tajfel and Turner, 1986) and entail engaging potential of power-based conflicts (Friedman and Desivilya, 2010; Foucault, 1994; Rothman, 1996). Such attempts were indeed undertaken in all three cases, presented in this article, especially in the latter two.

In a similar vein, Swan and Scarbrough (2005), acknowledge the importance of negotiating and developing relationships by means of both formal and informal relationships, especially through *trust building, sharing information, and resources.* They emphasize the key function of *coordination* in the process of building relations among teams by means of *negotiating reality.*

Our review of literature and analyses of cases indicate that the processes of developing intra-team and inter-team collaboration entail *building relationships* among the parties, which subsumes four key aspects: (1) negotiation (2) coordination (3) power balancing (empowerment) (4) reflection and learning. This involves devoting concomitant attention to both structural as well as process aspects of the alliance. Attending to structural elements entails managing the interdependence and power-relations between the partners by means of appropriate division of tasks and empowerment. The process aspects involve negotiation of purpose (goals and interests), joint definition of the partnership (shared vision, design and practices), building mechanisms for coordination of communications, knowledge sharing and integration, decision making and conflict management, which allow openly engaging disparities and tensions in a constructive manner. Concurrent consideration of the structural and process aspects appears crucial for forging commitment to a team, developing trust among partners and creating synergy between espoused cooperative values and consistent action.

In sum, use of *negotiation*, while integrating its overt and shadow elements, in the course of different stages of relationship building fosters constructive conflict engagement, which in turn plays a central role in effective collaboration within and between teams. Failure to constructively engage conflicts in team relations can exacerbate internal tensions: increase perceived threats to social identity, dampen a sense of security and efficacy, enhance in-group favoritism and intensify power struggles. Such adverse process of conflict escalation impedes cooperation within the alliance. Grasping and actually implementing the potential of negotiation process in a team context entails integrating theory with practice — applying Kurt Lewin's famous tenet: "*There is nothing more practical than a good theory*" (1951, p. 169).

The Role of Communication Media in Negotiations

Shira Mor
Columbia Business School, Columbia University

Alexandra Suppes
Department of Psychology, Columbia University

Introduction

Negotiations are increasingly being conducted with the aid of computer technology. What's more, the infrastructure to facilitate such negotiations is on the rise. Price negotiation of over $3 billion in trades have been handled using anonymous instant messaging chats through Harborside Plus (Global Investment Technology, 2003). Similarly, auction sites such as Fididel.com allow buyers and sellers to engage in price negotiation via instant messaging (Business Wire, 2008).

However, negotiators often neglect to take into account the role of communication medium on negotiation outcomes. To highlight to negotiators the importance of communication media, Times Online published a series of podcasts by Robert Cialdini, an expert in the systematic study of persuasion, compliance and negotiation (Cialdini, 2007). In his podcasts, Caldini discusses important strategies for being persuasive over email, suggesting that communication media have become increasingly important in people's lives and, more importantly, for business professionals. According to Cialdini golden rules of email negotiations, negotiators should: (1) Take time early on to share personal information with their counterparts and ask personal questions before they get down to business; (2) Take time to individualize their personal emails rather than sending mass group emails. Cialdini finds that self-disclosure and individuation are likely to increase the success of any negotiation process or email negotiation. However, there are many more important pitfalls negotiators should be aware of when using different forms of media such as telephone and Instant Messenger (IM).

The aim of this chapter is to detail to negotiators the advantages and pitfalls of negotiating over different communication media. First, we discuss how Computer Mediated (CM) negotiations influence, for better or worse, the relationships with negotiation counterparts and provide readers with practical guidelines to master CM negotiation. Next, we address how CM negotiations present unique challenges to our ability to accurately perceive negotiation counterparts' personality and goals. Here, we highlight how a CM negotiator can use a medium to their advantage to glean a more accurate impression of their negotiation counterpart as well as ensure that they are giving off the right impression to their counterparts. Beyond the effects of media on perceptions of counterparts and social processes in negotiations, we also discuss how communication media affects negotiation outcomes in both distributive and integrative agreements.

How do Communication Media Differ?

In this chapter, we will focus on differences between five different media through which negotiations can take place. Table 1 illustrates what we see as the most important differences in these media. First, negotiations that take place face-to-face are the most basic: communicative channels are synchronous because responses between negotiators are immediate and all parties have full access to visual and vocal information that their counterpart is presenting. In this medium, there is the least psychological

TABLE 1 Attributes of communication media

	Synchronous	Visual cues	Vocal cues	Grammatical cues	Emoticons	Psychological distance
Face-to-Face	✓	✓	✓			Least
Phone/Skype	✓		✓			Moderate
Instant Message (IM)	✓			✓	✓	Moderate
Email				✓	✓	Greatest

distance between negotiators; they are physically co-present and immediately respond to one another's behavior, both conscious (e.g., what the other has said) and unconscious (e.g., emotions the other has expressed through changes in voice and face). Furthermore, face-to-face interactions signal understanding by facilitating the exchange of subtle signals to one's counterpart that one is attending to what is being said. They do so by back-chanelling, both by making vocal utterances ("Uh huh", "Yes", "I see") and using visual gestures (nodding, smiling and making eye contact) while their counterpart is talking.

Second, negotiations can take place over the phone and, increasingly, through internet phone services like Skype. Like face-to-face negotiations, phone negotiations are synchronous and all parties have access to their counterpart's vocal information, but not to their visual information. Psychological distance over the phone is greater when compared to face-to-face interactions because negotiators are not co-present and, while they can communicate with auditory backchannels, their physical gestures like nodding, smiling, and eye-contact cannot be seen by their counterpart.

Third, negotiations can take place over text-based instant message chats, such as IM, Facebook or Gmail chats, where counterparts respond synchronously to one another's statements. Because visual and vocal cues are absent, psychological distance is greater. Negotiation counterparts cannot see or hear the emotional tone of their partner. At the same time, there are new ways to communicate emotions, such as emoticons (e.g.,) to indicate a smile). What's more, negotiators can engage in concurrent unrelated tasks (e.g., checking email, taking a phone call, etc.) and they are not able to provide as vocal or visual backchannel. However, new communication cues are "revealed" such as language abilities and style of communication (formal or informal). Fourth, unlike IM, when negotiating over e-mails, negotiators face greater loss of communication synchrony with their counterparts. In other words, a counterpart can take hours or even days to respond to emails with terms or offers. The relative advantages and disadvantages of these media are summarized in Table 2.

Are Computer Mediated Media Good or Bad for Relationship Building?

Early research in the role of CMC suggests that any non face-to-face medium of communication was inherently impersonal and would hinder the development of interpersonal relationships, including those that potentially form between business partners after a successful negotiation. This line of research argues that CMC deprived negotiators of the vocal and facial cues that are necessary for relationship development. CMC was thought of as best for task-oriented interactions, and that CMC could not accommodate the more nuanced social relations processes that take place in face-to-face negotiation (Culnan and Markus, 1987; Hiltz, Johnson, and Turoff, 1986). Similar findings have been reported in the negotiation literature such that negotiators who could not see their counterparts were more contentious and less cooperative than those who did (Turnbull, Strickland, and Shaver, 1976). Furthermore, there are more miscommunication over email than in phone conversations (Kruger, Epley, Parker, and Ng, 2005). In turn, miscommunication hinders rapport building and interpersonal trust — important components of negotiations success (Drolet and Morris, 2000). And even more so, the ability to speak to and

TABLE 2 Examples of advantages and disadvantages of communication media in negotiations

Medium	Advantages	Disadvantages
Face-to-Face	• When social relations are less established. • Can help build rapport and trust, important if future negotiations are foreseen.	• When visual salient information (such as race, ethnicity or gender) may play a negative role in relationship building.
Phone	• Loss of visual cues can reduce saliency of negative visual cues (such as nervousness) that can hinder trust and rapport.	• Loss of visual cues reduces the quality of communication which has negative effect on rapport building.
Email	• Loss of synchrony may allow one to have more time in making a decision or contemplating one's BATNA.	• Loss of vocal cues may decrease one's ability to sense a change in tone which may imply a lower sense of trust and rapport.
IM	• Greater synchronicity relative to email — important when negotiators are in different geographical and locations, such as international negotiations. • Better than email when you can "fast talk" through technical information.	• When negotiations require elaborate time to think about options. • Individuals may use the fast-pace tempo of this medium to dominate their counterparts.

hear counterparts increases the use of cooperative tactics in negotiations (Lim, 2000; Smith, 1969). In sum, these studies suggest that negotiators should prefer to use richer media (such as face-to-face and phone) over email or IM.

More recently, communication researchers have argued that the quality of social relations matters more than the loss of communication channels in CM negotiations. These communication theories are grounded on the assumption that peoples' behaviors in non-face-to-face interactions are not driven by technological characteristics, but rather by counterparts' social roles, group identities, and even shared personal history (Fulk, Schmitz and Steinfield, 1990). Specifically, the Social Relations Approach argues that the presence of positive social relations, for example, long-term interpersonal relationships, group cohesion, or the presence of shared social identities, can help overcome the difficulties associated with non-face-to-face encounters and override the impact of communication cues on social interactions. Thus, negotiators should also be aware that having strong interpersonal bonds with their negotiation counterparts may alleviate the difficulties of negotiating over communication media that are less rich, such as email or IM.

Consistent with this view, we find that people can form meaningful relationships during CMC with people that they have not met in person as long as they are provided enough time to interact with them (Walther *et al.*, 1994). Moreover, research suggests that lack of visual cues does not reduce cooperation when individuals are working as part of a group they identify with (Spears *et al.*, 2002) or if they share a positive interpersonal connection with their counterpart (Walther, 1996). Morris and colleagues (2002) found that negotiators who spoke over the phone and exchanged personal information before an email negotiation were more successful than those who did not. This finding suggests that relationship building before an email negotiation can provide negotiators with a way to mitigate the negative effects of loss of visual cues and synchrony on negotiation success.

Furthermore, another line of research that extends the social relations approach suggests that negotiations via CMC can be more successful than face-to-face negotiation. The phenomenon in which CMC is experienced as more intimate than similar face-to-face communication is known as "hyper personal communication"

(Walther, 1996). Because of the perceived distance in CMC and relative anonymity, people may reveal more than they normally would in real life (Cooper and Sportolari, 1997). If one partner feels liberated to share intimate information about him or herself, the other will tend to view him/her more favorably, and should in turn respond with his/her own self-disclosure. This cycle of mutual disclosure sustained by CMC will lead to a sense of great relational closeness. According to Walther's hyper-personal perspective, when individuals communicate via computers, they may feel more comfortable and intimate with their partners and initiate disclosure of private information. For instance, today's young professionals may feel more comfortable negotiating over email or IM than negotiating over more traditional media (phone, face-to-face).

Taken together, the evidence supporting both approaches to CMC suggests that individual differences (such as gender) and situational factors (such as fleeting versus long-term relationships) can turn the use of media in negotiations to an advantage or disadvantage. For example, recent findings by Swaab and Swaab (2009) reveal that when two male negotiators cannot see each other, the quality of their agreements is better than when they can see each other. However, we should also note that, for women, visual contact enhanced shared understandings between negotiators and led to higher quality agreements.

Perceiving Negotiation Counterparts Over Different Communication Media

With access to different communication cues, the impression that negotiators form of one another will vary based on the type of medium they are negotiating over. Forming an accurate impression of a negotiation counterpart's goals, intentions and personality are important factors that influence people's success or failure in negotiations. For example, the absence of non-verbal cues or a-synchronicity in delivery and response can alter one's perception of personality traits. Past findings suggest that people rely on textual cues to infer personality traits in CMC. For example, people who wrote more lengthy exchanges in CM chats were perceived as more competent and more engaged (Liu and Ginther, 1999). In addition, past research finds that people are less confident and less accurate in their impressions over asynchronous media such as internet chats or personal websites (Hancock and Dunham, 2001; Markey and Wells, 2002; Vazire and Gosling, 2004). Thus, it seems that people might be using more non-valid cues when negotiating over non face-to face media that reduce negotiators' ability to make accurate impressions of their counterparts.

Furthermore, first impressions over non face-to-face media can lead to greater discrepancies between online and offline impression on certain personality traits. For instance, to a shy person, who takes time to open up to others, the lack of visual cues may allow him or her to feel more comfortable at opening up to another person. Thus, when negotiating for the first time with a business counterpart that one suspects is shy, one may prefer to ask him or her to negotiate over email or phone to increase their comfort as they may be more likely to exchange personal information over email than face-to-face.

Moreover, aside from using non-accurate cues to form impressions over email, we are also more likely to use stereotypes to infer personality traits over emails. In face-to-face negotiations, we would use tone of voice and pitch as additional cues. These cues are discriminately different from one another and may lead one to divergent or inflated impressions. Epely and Kruger found (2005) that racial stereotype and bogus expectancies influence people's impressions of a person more strongly over email than voice interactions. Thus, negotiators should be aware that they are more likely to use stereotypes (such as inferring race from a person's name) to form an impression of a negotiation counterpart over email than over the phone.

In addition to stereotyping, people are also more likely to make inferences about what their counterpart is in general, rather than recognize their counterparts are behaving in ways consistent with the situation. For example, a person who is assertive during a negotiation may not be domineering in other professional settings. In CMC, negotiators are more likely to overlook situational causes of behavior and ascribe people's behaviors to stable dispositions (see Gilbert, 1998 for an overview). In other words, negotiators are *more* prone to overlook situational causes for behavior when they simply don't have any over email or instant messaging. For example, when we meet Jessica face-to-face we know she is waiting for the CEO's approval to give us our last salary offer. However, over email, we focus only on her lack of response, rather than the situation that is preventing her from responding quickly. Thus, computer mediated communication can lead us to often assume that a person's behaviors are dispositional in nature. This kind of attribution error can have important implications during negotiation, which often requires counterparts to behave in a manner that is more assertive or domineering than they would in a different context. Therefore, negotiators should be aware of their biases and ask for situational explanations when negotiating over CMC to be able to make more accurate predictions about their counterpart's intentions and behaviors.

Disclosure Over Computer Media

Self-disclosure has been found to be a central ingredient in developing rapport and forming accurate impressions between two people. New acquaintances tend to match each other's level of self-disclosure: one partner will disclose more if the other person discloses, and will hold back when the other withdraws (Hendrick and Hendrick, 1983). As a result, it's important that negotiators understand how CMC affects self-disclosure during negotiations. First, when meeting face-to-face, negotiators are more likely to reveal truthful information (Valley, Moag, and Bazerman, 1998) and are more likely to disclose information regarding their own interests (Bazerman, Gibbons, Thompson, and Valley, 1998). There are many real-life examples for situations in which colleagues withhold information from their counterparts by using different forms of communication media strategically. One such example is an architect in New York City frustrated with his colleagues in Copenhagen when negotiating over Skype:

"When I'm being broadcast into a conference room full of people, I often become frustrated. I feel that they're either ignoring what I'm saying, or they can't hear what I'm saying, or they're talking amongst themselves.... I simply can't tell if they understand things or not".

The architect's frustration is inherent to the state of ambiguity that CMC can present and sheds light on the risks that technology plays in the role of reducing what negotiators are disclosing. Out of these frustrations, we see that the architect cherry-picks what issues will enter into the Skype negotiation and what will be attend to later:

"If it's something really critical I'll speak up, but a lot of times with low-level decisions I decide not to bother to explain because it's not worth the effort. Smaller details are often better described in an email or a sketch than over the phone".

And, while smaller scale issues are often better left to email, larger issues run the risk of being overlooked when communicated via email. As described by an East Coast project manager negotiating between teams in Silicon Valley at a major internet corporation:

"I realized early in the project that [the team was] ignoring our emperor-has-no-clothes emails over major issues. Those kinds of emails were never answered. Progress was about forcing those issues and that had to be done over video conference".

In both of the examples provided above and in empirical research, we see how CMC can inhibit disclosure during negotiation. On the other hand, there is evidence that CMC can introduce advantages to the process of self-disclosure particularly among strangers, as is the case with online trades through organizations such Harborside Plus. The perceived distance in CMC and relative anonymity leads people to sometimes reveal more than they normally would face-to-face (Cooper and Sportolari, 1997). If one partner feels liberated to share personal information about him or herself, the other will tend to view him/her more favorably, and should in turn respond with his/her own self-disclosure. This cycle of mutual disclosure sustained by CMC will improve negotiators' trust of one another. However, self disclosure of emotional content in CMC might not only strengthen relationships, but also enhance accuracy of perceiving negotiation counterparts (Andersen, 1984). For negotiators, self-disclosure is particularly important for withholding or forgoing important information that can deter one's negotiation outcomes if revealed. Thus, negotiators should remember to self-disclose personal information as needed in order to smoothen exchanges with counterparts over non face-to-face media.

Finally, there are occasions during negotiation when one does not want to encourage increased disclosure and information sharing from counterparts. That is, when negotiating over minor issues or when the negotiator is interested in maintaining the status quo, rather than introducing change, CMC can be used to one's advantage. As a Software project manager elaborated:

> "When you want no reaction out of the person — email is the best way to go. People will talk if they're given the opportunity to talk".

Impression Management

Unlike face-to-face first impressions, negotiators need to utilize new cues for forming accurate impressions of counterparts and providing favorable impression of themselves. Different communication media enable negotiators to hide some traits (such as extroversion) while revealing other traits (such as conscientiousness). For instance, two traits that negotiators can often misread are emotional stability and conscientiousness, both of which interviewees have used to mislead potential employers into viewing them more favorably (Barrick, Patton and Hugland, 2000).

These findings lead us to assume that emotional stability and conscientiousness are managed more than any other personality trait. Furthermore, self presentation online might be even more extreme than in face-to-face interactions when observers have no access to non-verbal behaviors that reveal visible personality traits such as extroversion, such that online, introverts may "transform" into extroverts. Moreover, the absence of physical interaction in CMC allows participants more flexibility in their expression of who they are. A negotiator's impressions of an online negotiation partner are based upon whatever information the partner *has chosen* to reveal about him or herself (Cooper and Sportolari, 1997; Walther, 1992). As Bell and Daly (1984) observed, people in general try to present themselves in socially favorable ways and try to get others to like them. Consequently, it follows that the impression a negotiator creates about an online negotiation counterpart is likely to be more positive than that which might have been formed if the interaction had occurred offline.

Furthermore, in face-to-face conversations, much emotional and cognitive energy is spent trying to correctly construct and understand everyday speech (which tends to be spontaneous, sometimes simultaneous, and thus difficult to comprehend), paying attention to the numerous different cues, and following conventions of turn-taking. In contrast, asynchronous modes of CMC, in which each individual logs on content separately and there are delays between communications (e-mail), allow communicators more time to reflect upon, prepare, and self-censor their messages at their own pace (Walther, 1996). As online communicators are better able to concentrate on message construction at their own pace, their communication may end up being more socially desirable and effective than in face-to-face interactions. The extra time and energy afforded by asynchronous communication also allows online negotiators to further improve their self-presentation to their partners. Thus, negotiators should use to their advantage their ability to manage online impressions when forging new relationships with new business partners.

Communication Media and Negotiation Outcomes

Overall, negotiations and communications studies provide competing predictions for the role of communication media on negotiation outcomes. For example, empirical evidence fails to provide consistent conclusions as to how communication media and the potential loss of sight, sound, and communication synchronicity (the ability to provide direct feedback in real time), affect negotiation outcomes. Some studies find that the loss of these communication cues decreases integrative outcomes (Valley, Moag, and Bazerman, 1998; Arunachalam and Dilla, 1995), whereas others studies find no effect (Croson, 1999; Morris, Nadler, Kurtzberg, Thompson, 2002; Naquin and Paulson, 2003), and others find an improvement in negotiation outcomes (Carnevale, Pruitt, and Seilheimer, 1981). We also find mixed results when looking at outcome over fixed-sum negotiations: where gain to one negotiator directly translates to loses for the other. Sometimes negotiating over CMC leads one party to perform better than they would in face-to-face negotiation (Croson, 1999), while sometimes it seems inconsequential to either party (Naquin and Paulson, 2003), or, inequalities can be exaggerated (McGinn and Keros, 2002).

Consistent with the Media Richness Approach, integrative negotiations can be harmed due to loss of communication cues which in turn lead negotiators to be less effective at integrating interests (McGrath and Hollingshead, 1993). Furthermore, negotiators are less likely to share information and integrate interests when they use asynchronous text-based communication such as email instead of synchronous text-based communication such as instant messaging (Loewenstein, Morris, Chakravarti, Thompson, and Kopelman, 2005). In addition, Drloet and Morris (2000) found that, in comparison to face-to-face negotiations, the lack of visual cues reduces rapport building, synchrony, and negotiation outcomes.

At the same time, theories highlighting the role of social relations in CMC find that the absence of vocal cues does not always lead to impaired negotiation outcomes. For example, members of virtual teams who rely predominantly on text-based communication media can be equally successful as face-to-face teams if they first build trust (Jarvenpaa, Knoll, and Leidner, 1998), develop a strong team identity, or anticipate long standing interactions (Maznevski and Chudoba, 2000; Wiesenfeld, Raghuram, and Garud, 1999). Negotiation research has provided comparable evidence by showing that integrative outcomes are not affected by the loss of vocal cues when negotiators anticipate an ongoing relationship with their counterpart (Purdy, Nye, and Balakrishnan, 2000). Although the impact of communication synchronicity is studied less frequently than that of visual and vocal cues, it has been suggested that its absence does not necessarily deteriorate social interactions (Dennis and Valacich, 1999). Negotiation research finds that compared to synchronous negotiations, asynchronous communication does not decrease integrative outcomes when negotiations are held between acquaintances (Barsness and Tenbrunsel, 1998; McGinn and Keros, 2002). Along similar lines, negotiations over Instant Messaging (where negotiators could not see or hear the other side) can yield more integrative outcomes than face-to-face negotiations (Citera, Beauregard, and Mitsuya, 2005).

One important predictor of how a negotiator will fair in a CMC negotiation compared to a face-to-face negotiation is the degree to which the negotiator's tactics are compatible with features of their communication medium. For example, in a study by Lowenstein and colleagues (2005), MBA students were asked to negotiate the sale of a car over email or IM. The researchers trained half of the sellers with complex, technical arguments of the sort that car dealers use and gave the other half simple arguments. Buyers and sellers received points for gaining advantage on eight different elements of the negotiation, such as price and warranty details. The results revealed that the complex arguments gave a clear advantage in IM (leaving their counterparts "at a loss"), but neither kind of argument gave negotiators an advantage in e-mail. The study illustrates that it is easier to overwhelm the other side with complexity when they have little time to respond, but when the medium is conducive to slower information exchange, the advantage disappears.

Another issue negotiators should remember is that conventional wisdom about negotiation tactics do not always apply to CM negotiations. One such example is making concessions: sending a message about an intent to cooperate that is usually met with reciprocity and no harm to negotiation outcomes when done judicially (Cialdini, 1993; Eisenberger *et al.*, 2001). However, when communicating over IM, the negotiator who makes the first concession is often not met with an equal concession from their counterpart (Johnson and Cooper, 2009). This happens because of lack of social pressure to reciprocate in kindness, and because of the meaning ascribed to the concession. In IM, a concession can be perceived by a counterpart as a sign of weakness whereas during face-to-face negotiation a concession is usually interpreted as a gesture of good faith and evidence of the shared goal to reach a mutually beneficial agreement.

To summarize, negotiators should be aware that negotiation outcomes can be either hindered or improved over different media and that some of the factors which influence negotiation outcomes are negotiators' social relations and the compatibility between their strategy or role and the negotiation medium.

Conclusion

Overall, we find that there are a number of key theories in CMC and negotiations that can improve negotiators' understanding of negotiations over CMC versus face-to-face. First, negotiators should be mindful of the differences between communication media and when one can be more appropriate than others. Second, negotiators should learn what communication cues they use when forming impressions of counterparts via different media and what potential biases can arise as a result of negotiating via each medium. Last, rather than perceiving technology a barrier, negotiators should find creative ways in which technology can facilitate interactions with business partners from different professional, racial or cultural backgrounds.

Negotiation via Email

Noam Ebner
Werner Institute for Negotiation and Dispute Resolution
Creighton University School of Law

Negotiation — Here, There, Online and Everywhere

Negotiation interactions are increasingly taking place through channels other than face-to-face encounters. Negotiators find themselves using e-communication channels, primarily e-mail, but also other media such as instant messaging and videoconferencing.

Given the broad definition granted to the term negotiation in the literature, and the many types of interactions and relationships we now conduct online, many us are often engaged in online negotiation. This is now obvious in the business world: two lawyers email offers and counteroffers in an attempt to settle a case; a team leader sends out a group message urging his team to work longer hours; a purchaser in Chicago writes to ask for a bulk discount on the price-per-unit from her supplier in Singapore. All are engaging in the allocation of scarce resources (Thompson, 2004), conducting back and forth communication aimed at reaching an agreement (Fisher and Ury, 1991) and in short, negotiating — online.

With the explosive increase in internet usage and online communication, and the surge in e-commerce, online negotiation can only become an increasingly widespread method of interaction.

Negotiating Online is Unavoidable — and Unavoidably Different

The proliferation of e-communication media has presented us with a world of opportunity for negotiation interactions. However, the ease with which so many people transferred so many of their interactions online conceals a hidden, yet crucial, truth: online negotiation is significantly different from face-to-face negotiation. While many people intuitively recognize this, the differences are either ignored and dismissed as inconsequential — or seen as insurmountable, a cause to avoid negotiating any significant matter online at all. However, in today's world, we can neither bury our heads in the sand, nor can we avoid online negotiation — we need to understand it, and learn how to conduct it well.

The professional and academic negotiation fields have also, for the large part, ignored this topic in training and teaching. Negotiators were trained for interactions 'at the table' — always assuming that there would, indeed, be a 'table' — some *physical* setting where the parties convened and negotiated. Only recently has a call to incorporate online negotiation as a core topic in negotiation education been voiced, as co-authors Anita Bhappu, Jennifer Brown, Kimberlee Kovach, Andrea Kupfer Schneider and I tried to capture the key elements of e-negotiation that teachers and trainers need to include in their curriculum and to provide ideas for how these can be taught (see Ebner *et al.*, 2009). This chapter, aimed at students and professionals, is in a sense an implementation of (some of) those recommendations.

This chapter will zoom in on the medium for online negotiation most commonly employed, particularly in a professional context: negotiation via e-mail. It opens with a theoretical model explaining the effects that communication media have on the content and dynamics of communication conducted through them. Next, it focuses on e-mail communication, delineating seven particular areas in which this media affects elements or dynamics of negotiation. A discussion of the challenges posed by the medium in each area will also include some potential benefits the medium offers. Finally, each section will make recommendations for practical applications based on the literature presented and best practices noted in the field. While the usual caveats regarding 'tips' and 'recommendations' in negotiation pertain, these should help to bridge theory and practice — and give negotiators ideas for avoiding common pitfalls while taking advantage of the opportunities presented by the medium.

The Medium and the Message: A Theoretical Model

The communication channel through which negotiations are conducted is neither passive nor neutral. Any communication medium influences both ends of the communication loop, affecting what information negotiators share and how that information is conveyed (Carnevale and Probst, 1997; Friedman and Currall, 2001; Valley, Moage and Bazerman, 1998), as well as how that information is received and interpreted. These effects are called 'media effects'.

Intuitively, we are all aware that some information could be easy to communicate face-to-face, but difficult to convey in an email; other messages might be hampered by a face-to-face setting. We might have one response to something we are told face-to-face, but respond in a completely different manner to the same message, conveyed by email. What underlies these differences? It is helpful, in this regard, to understand two dimensions of communication media (Barsness and Bhappu, 2004):

1) *Media richness*: The capacity of any given media to supply 'contextual cues': body language, facial expressions, tone of voice, etc. Face-to-face communication is considered a "rich" medium: it allows for all of these, which account for a significant proportion of a message's meaning (DePaulo and Friedman, 1998). Email, however, is considered a "lean" medium because it transmits neither visual nor audio cues;

we cannot see the other's gestures or facial expressions, or hear their tone of voice. Denied these contextual cues, negotiators both transmit and receive information differently.

On the transmitting side, this affects presentation style: email negotiators rely more heavily on logical argumentation and the presentation of facts, rather than emotional or personal appeals (Barsness and Bhappu, 2004). It also affects the content of the information negotiators share: The ability to transmit visual, audio and verbal cues allows a medium to provide more immediate feedback — and this, in turn, facilitates communication of information of a personal nature (Daft and Lengel, 1984). Email communicators are more task-oriented and depersonalized than those engaged in face-to-face interactions (Kemp and Rutter, 1982).

Media richness also affects the reception and interpretation side of the communication cycle: Information exchanged in email tends to be less nuanced than information exchanged face-to-face (Friedman and Currall, 2001; Valley *et al.*, 1998), and the elimination of important back-channel and clarifying information such as speech acknowledgements (e.g., "uh-huh" or "huh?") and reactive body language (e.g., nods) (O'Connaill, Whittaker and Wilbur, 1993) compounds this. Communicating through lean media, negotiators focus on the actual *content* of messages (Ocker and Yaverbaum, 1999), lending much more importance to the words that are chosen, and their interpretation. While email does allow for limited visual cues through color, font, and emoticons, these cues are crude, un-nuanced, and are often misused and misinterpreted. Their use — relatively rare in professional communication — could give rise to more confusion than clarity. In email negotiation, as discussed below, ambiguous messages trigger some of the greatest challenges to the process.

2) *Interactivity*: The potential of the medium to sustain a seamless flow of information between two or more negotiators (Kraut, Galegher, Fish and Chalfonte, 1992).

Interactivity has two dimensions. The first, a temporal dimension, captures the *synchronicity* of interactions. Face-to-face communication is synchronous and co-temporal. Each party receives an utterance just as it is produced; as a result, speaking "turns" tend to occur sequentially. Email is typically asynchronous: negotiators can read and respond to others' messages whenever they desire — and not necessarily sequentially. Minutes, hours, or even weeks can pass between the time a negotiator sends a message and the time their counterpart reads it, and reading messages out of order is a common cause of misunderstandings.

The second dimension of interactivity is parallel processing, which describes a medium's ability to allow negotiators to *simultaneously* transmit messages. In face-to-face communication parallel processing is overt. Email, however, permits the simultaneous exchange of messages, but negotiators will not necessarily *know* that this is occurring — 'crossing messages' is ubiquitous and confusing.

These two characteristics of email — asynchronous, and allowing for parallel processing — have profound effects on the way messages are transmitted and the way they are received. On the transmission side, the use of asynchronous media may accentuate analytical-rational expression of information by negotiators, as opposed to an intuitive-experiential mode (Epstein, Pacini, Denes-Raj and Heier, 1996). This favors individuals who tend to rely more heavily on logic and deductive thinking, and to engage in developing positions and reservation points, logical argumentation, and factpresentation. By contrast, individuals tending towards appealing to emotion and sharing personal stories (Gelfand and Dyer, 2000) may be put at a disadvantage.

On the receiving side, email imposes high "understanding costs" on negotiators. Negotiators' understanding is challenged by the lack of contextual cues. The timing and sequence of the information exchange further hamper negotiators' efforts to accurately decode messages they receive (Clark and Brennan, 1991). In addition, the tendency of email negotiators to "bundle" multiple arguments and issues together in one email message (Adair, Okumura and Brett, 2001; Friedman and Currall, 2001; Rosette, Brett, Barsness and Lytle, 2001) can place high demands on the receiver's information processing capabilities.

In summary, these two elements, media richness and interactivity, account for important differences across media in the structure, style, and content of information exchanged (for more detail, see Ebner *et al.*, 2009). How do these significantly alter email negotiation dynamics — and what can we do about it?

Negotiating Via Email: Seven Major Challenges

Building on this understanding of media effects on communication, we can now examine specific media effects affecting negotiation dynamics. We will focus on seven major elements:

1. Increased contentiousness
2. Diminished information sharing
3. Diminished inter-party process cooperation
4. Diminished privacy
5. Diminished trust
6. Increased effects of negative attribution
7. Diminished party commitment, investment, and focus

1. Increased contentiousness

Communication at a distance is more susceptible to disruption than face-to-face dialogue. Parties communicating via telephone were found to be prone to more distrust, competition, and contentious behavior than those in comparable face-to-face interactions. (Drolet and Morris, 2000). These findings are intensified in e-communication, which tends to be less inhibited than face-to-face communication due to physical distance, reduced social presence, reduced accountability and a sense of anonymity

(Griffith and Northcraft, 1994; Thompson, 2004; Wallace, 1999). The lack of social cues in e-communication causes people to act more contentiously than they do in face-to-face encounters, resulting in more frequent occurrences of swearing, name calling, insults, and hostile behavior (Kiesler and Sproull, 1992).

Early research on negotiation showed the same tendency for parties-at-a-distance (such as parties negotiating over the phone) to act tough and choose contentious tactics (Raiffa, 1982). Examinations of e-negotiation brought to light the effects of further-diminished media richness: the social presence of others is reduced (Short, Williams, and Christie, 1976; Weisband and Atwater, 1999) and the perceived social distance among negotiators increases (Jessup and Tansik, 1991; Sproull and Kiesler, 1986). This might explain why e-negotiators seem less bound by appropriate, normative behavior than face-to-face negotiators. This translates into an increased tendency to threaten and issue ultimata (Morris, Nadler, Kurtzberg and Thompson, 2002); to adopt contentious, "squeaky wheel" behavior; to lie or deceive (Naquin, Kurtzberg and Belkin, 2010); to confront each other negatively, and to engage in flaming (Thompson and Nadler, 2002). In short: email negotiation is a rough playing field!

Advantages

Can the tables be turned on this state of increased contentiousness? Returning to email's characteristics, it would seem that conscious utilization of email's 'lean media' nature might sometimes offer opportunity to *reduce* contentiousness. Used properly, lean media may facilitate better processing of social conflict exactly because these media do *not* transmit visual and verbal cues (Bhappu and Crews, 2005; Carnevale, Pruitt, and Seilheimer, 1981) and defuse triggers caused by the visible, physical presence of an opponent (see Zajonc, 1965). Additionally, email has been found to reduce the impact of unconscious biases which often serve to trigger or escalate conflict, such as group differences and attribution related to gender, race, accent, national origin, etc. (Greenwald, McGhee, and Schwartz, 1998). Keeping the 'interactivity' element in mind, asynchronicity dictates a different interaction-pace. This can help parties avoid being "emotionally hijacked" into conflict escalation — or into costly avoidance (see Goleman, 1995). The physical separation between parties, coupled with asynchronicity, might make it easier for parties to take time to "step out" of the discussion and respond thoughtfully, rather than suffer the consequences of a knee-jerk response, potentially limiting conflict escalation even further (Bhappu and Crews, 2005; Harasim, 1993).

In practice

1) Unmask yourself: The mutual invisibility inherent in email negotiation facilitates adversarial, contentious, behavior. It is easier to cause damage to a faceless other — particularly when we feel protected by a shield of anonymity and physical distance, causing us to assume that we can get away this behavior, and to lower any moral inhibitions we might have against doing so (Nadler and Shestowsky, 2006). By adopting a proactive agenda of unmasking ourselves — making ourselves human, present, and real in the other's eyes — we can protect ourselves from these dynamics. This unmasking process can include sharing personal information, building rapport, and reducing the perception of distance through shared language, or shared geographical or cultural references.

2) In the unmasking process, decide carefully what to share about yourself, taking advantage of the masking effect to avoid any anticipated bias.

3) Unmask the other: Remember, there is a person behind the other screen as well, whether they have had the foresight to engage in unmasking themselves or not. They are not computers or inboxes — they will respond to your messages on emotional, cognitive and behavioral levels which you will then have to deal with (see Mayer, 2000).

4) Use email's asynchronicity in order to think and work proactively: Read a received message twice instead of banging out an angry reply. When you do write a response — delay sending it, and read it again before clicking send.

2. Diminished inter-party process cooperation

As we've noted, information exchanged in email negotiations is likely to be constrained, analytical, and contentious. This might explain why email negotiators suffer from reduced accuracy in judging the other party's interests (Arunachalam and Dilla, 1995). This affects their ability to accurately assess differential preferences and identify potential joint gains — and therefore, one might posit — their desire to engage in this type of cooperative activity in the first place. Reduced social awareness in lean media causes parties to engage more heavily in self-interested behavior when negotiating by email. Focused inwardly, negotiators may simply ignore or fail to elicit important information regarding the other party's interests and priorities. The use of email may, therefore, accentuate competitive behavior in negotiations (Barsness and Bhappu, 2004). Email communication is conducive not only to parties acting uncooperatively, but to parties feeling *justified* for choosing this pattern of behavior (Naquin, Kurtzberg and Belquin, 2008). Combine this with increased contentiousness, and with the comparative ease of walking away from the process (see below), and we are faced with a recipe for diminished process cooperation.

Advantages

Email has the potential to *increase* information exchange. As a lean media with diminished social context cues (Sproull and Kiesler, 1991) and reduced salience of social group differences (Bhappu, Griffith and Northcraft, 1997), the mathematics of social influence which dictate who speaks up, who keeps quiet, who is listened to and who is discounted are fundamentally changed. This might result in higher participation rates, by more players — allowing more information to find its way to the table, and be paid attention to. The nature of email interactivity supports this tendency toward increased participation and more diverse information. Parties cannot shout each other down or interrupt. The nature of email parallel processing further throws traditional dynamics into skew, as it prevents one party taking control of an entire discussion, at the cost of others' expounding, sharing or suggestion-making (Nunamaker, Dennis, Valancich and Vogel, 1991). Parallel processing has advantages beyond its supporting of wider and fuller participation; it allows for the tendency and ability to simultaneously discuss multiple issues, a characteristic that encourages the search for joint gains (Barsness and Bhappu, 2004). Having pie-expanding possibilities right there on the same 'page', which negotiators relate to one after another, can easily lead into differential valuation, prioritization and logrolling dynamics to occur. A caveat: "over-bundling" too many issues (usually entailing delivering a lot of information simultaneously) might overload the receiver's information processing capabilities. This may be a reason that negotiators have more difficulty establishing meaning and managing feedback in asynchronous media (DeSanctis and Monge, 1999). As a result, negotiators can be left with partial and disconnected information — hardly the type that is necessary to form and integrative agreement.

In practice

1) Use interest-related language intentionally, and often, when discussing your own position and inquiring about theirs. Use process-cooperative language overtly, and try and set the tone for others to do so. This might give process-cooperation a much-needed boost.

2) Take the stage: You have the opportunity to speak your mind, state what you want and explain why you should get it. No one can shout or shut you down. Utilize this clear stage.

3) In a multiparty interaction, if one party is dominating the conversation and others are quiet, you might invite them in, either in a "Let's hear what some others have to think" email to the group, or in a private, behind-the-scenes message to reticent parties.

4) Use bundling intentionally, highlighting connections between the issues, and perhaps using language you fell might trigger similar thinking in your negotiation opposite.

5) A familiar source of confusion in email negotiation occurs when your opposite party relates to some of the issues you raised in an email, but not to others. This might not be a deliberate, contentious omission — it may simply be information overload. Consider whether you want to call their attention to this as an oversight, before assuming there is some underlying meaning in the omission.

3. Reduction in integrative outcomes

The potential for email negotiation to result in lower rates of integrative outcome is partially connected to the previous challenge of reduced process cooperation. Indeed, many experiments measuring these two indicators indicate significant challenges: First, that e-negotiation entails lower rates of process cooperation, and lower rates of integrative outcomes, when compared to face-to-face negotiation (Arunachalam and Dilla, 1995; Valley *et al.*, 1998; see also Nadler and Shestowsky, 2006) (for contrasting research, see Galin, Gross and Gosalker, 2007; Nadler and Shestowsky, 2006; Naquin and Paulson, 2003). Second, that the potential for impasse appears to be greater than in face-to-face negotiation (Croson, 1999).

These findings don't clearly explain *why* email negotiation results may be less integrative. Is it an outcome of reduced process cooperation? Of increased contentiousness? Of the difficulty of establishing rapport in email? Of reduced interparty trust? Or, perhaps of a combination of some or all of these elements? This crucial issue — which determines if email negotiation might be, inherently, a value-*diminishing* playing field — is sure to intrigue researchers over the coming years.

Advantages

One effect of email's asynchronous nature is negotiators' tendency to bundle multiple issues together in one letter; we've also noted that this might encourage process cooperation dynamics. These same dynamics, such as logrolling and prioritization — should they reach fruition — might well result in integrative agreements in a manner that separate discussions of each issue might not. Another effect is that time allows for reflection and for careful, overt use of cooperative language, which may increase the odds of reaching an integrative outcome.

In practice

Most of the suggestions made above (regarding process cooperation) apply here as well. In addition:

1) Consider using the multimedia potentialities used in e-mail in order to portray integrative offers or ideas. Charts, graphs, presentations — all easily attached to an email — are powerful tools for overcoming the challenges of lean media.
2) Frame: In email negotiation, every message is an opportunity to set a new frame around the interaction, much more than rapid-fire statements and reactions in face-to-face processes. Intentional and repeated integrative framing might have an effect on the outcome.

4. Diminished privacy

Maintaining a negotiation process' privacy is never an easy task. In face-to-face negotiation, absent a confidentiality agreement (and too often, in practice, even when one exists!) parties can and do share information about the negotiation with their friends, families and colleagues, and occasionally with wider circles. However, you can meet in a private setting, physically shut out the rest of the world, or relate something confidentially in a lowered voice. Anything shared with external parties will always be subjective, after-the-fact, secondhand (and in legal terms, hearsay). In email negotiation, by contrast, you never know who is 'in the room' with you. Is your opposite is showing your letter to their boss, to their colleagues or to your competition? The messages you transmit are recorded, and forever archived somewhere beyond your control; they can be adjusted or tampered with, altering what you wrote. Personal or proprietary information you send might be made public to wider circles than intended, whether due to the other's bad intentions or their technical shortcomings. Who among us has never clicked "reply all" instead of reply, and sent a personal message into a public domain?

Advantages

Consulting with others is an excellent way to diminish many of the challenging media effects of email we've noted in this chapter. Email provides asynchronicity and recorded messages — allowing us to consult optimally.

Getting practical

1) Consider each address field carefully. To whom should a message be sent? Should anyone appear in the "cc" field? Do you want anyone invisibly lurking on the conversation, from the "bcc" field?
2) Use the lack of privacy to your advantage: Record the interactions, return to them when things get unclear, and relate to them when it seems the other party is being inconsistent. Share messages with anybody you feel you need to share them with, and consult — often — about the process.
3) Increasingly, individuals' online activities are becoming public, widespread, sought out by future opponents and admissible

in court. Be cautious of what you write in an email, particularly before trust is established. A good rule of thumb might be: Don't write anything in an email that you wouldn't want shown on the news.

5. Diminished degree of interparty trust

Diminished privacy is but one factor that affects the much wider issue of inter-party trust. This issue has been identified as playing a key role in enabling cooperation (Deutsch, 1962), problem solving (Pruitt, Rubin and Kim, 1994), achieving integrative solutions (Lax and Sebenius, 1986; Lewicki and Litterer, 1985), effectiveness (Schneider, 2002) and resolving disputes (Moore, 2003). "Build trust!" is a key edict in any negotiation teaching or training.

Communicating via email, negotiators must cope with threats to trust that are inherent in the medium and in its employ (Ebner, 2007). Email negotiators trust their counterparts less than negotiators in similar face-to-face interactions — at all stages of the process. Before the process' inception, e-negotiators report a comparatively low level of trust in their opposite. This low trust-level persists throughout the course of the negotiation, resulting in diminished process cooperation and information sharing (Naquin and Paulson, 2003). E-negotiators are more likely to suspect their opposite of lying, even when no actual deception has taken place (Thompson and Nadler, 2002). Post-negotiation, e-negotiators trust their opposites less than do participants in face-to-face negotiations, manifesting in lower degrees of desire for future interaction with them (Naquin and Paulson, 2003).

Advantages

The online venue requires negotiators to be much more conscious regarding trust — something often missing face-to-face — people seeing trust as something that "happens". The slowed-down interaction pace provides e-negotiators with time and opportunity to recognize, and proactively initiate, trust-building opportunities.

In practice

The following practices are helpful for building trust in email interactions (for more on these and other methods, see Ebner, 2007):

1) Build rapport: Try to "bond", building an instant relationship with your opposite.
2) Apply social lubrication: Take the time, at the beginning of a negotiation and in its course, for light conversation. While this does not come naturally in email interactions as it does face-to-face, email doesn't make icebreaking or small talk superfluous — the contrary is true. Even minimal pre-negotiation, socially-oriented contact, such as preliminary email introductory messages, can build trust, improve mutual impressions, and facilitate integrative outcomes (Morris *et al.*, 2002; Nadler and Shestowsky, 2006).
3) Mix media, if possible: Holding a preliminary face-to-face meeting can assist in setting the stage for a trust-filled e-negotiation. (Rocco, 1998; Zheng, Veinott, Bos, Olson and Olson, 2002). Meeting face-to-face in the middle of the process can also be beneficial (Cellich and Jain, 2003).
4) Show e-empathy: Showing empathy performs multiple roles in negotiation (Mnookin, Peppet, and Tulumello, 2000; Schneider, 2002; Ury, 1991), including trustbuilding. E-negotiators who show empathy are more trusted by their negotiation opposites more than those who do not (Feng, Lazar, and Preece, 2004). This cannot be neglected just because the medium seems to be 'cold' and impersonal. Utilize email's characteristics which allow considered, careful language to intentionally show e-empathy (see Ebner, 2007).

6. Increased attribution, increased misinterpretation

Communicating through lean media increases the tendency toward the fundamental attribution error: parties perceive negative actions or statements on their opposite's part, and interpret these as outgrowth of the other's negative intentions and character — rather than as unintended results of circumstance. Reduced social presence and few contextual cues lend a sense of distance and vagueness to the interaction. The media richness element of interactivity compounds this: E-negotiators ask fewer clarifying questions than face-to-face negotiators — leaving more room for assumptions to form and take root (Thompson and Nadler, 2002). Attribution dynamics will cause these assumptions to tend toward the negative. Analysis of failed email negotiations shows that they tend to include unclear messages, irrelevant points, and long general statements (Thompson, 2004), each of which provides ample breeding ground for attribution.

Advantages

Used intentionally, email allows for well-crafted messages, which try to preempt lack of clarity and misunderstandings. Negotiators can consult with others — about the perceived meaning of a message they received, or about the potential interpretations if their own writing. Asynchronicity facilitates real-time interpretations and their accompanying negative attributions to be replaced by considered understanding of meaning, intent and character.

In practice

1) Increase your social presence: constantly remind the other of the real person opposite them.
2) Write clearly, taking into account negative interpretations. Clarify much more than you do face-to-face. Several rules of thumb for enhancing email clarity:
   a) Avoid unnecessary length — don't overload your opposite.
   b) Use "In summary" sentences to highlight your main points.

c) Use the subject field intentionally. This introduces your letter (preparing your opposite for the content), provides a frame through which it will be read (diminishing negative interpretation), allows your opposite to find it when they want to review it for clarity before responding, and helps organize messages bundling multiple issues.

d) Avoid use of emoticons — particularly in early message exchanges.

3) Waiting and perceived delay cause anxiety, which is conducive to negative attribution. Manage both sides of this cycle: Don't expect immediate answers to your own emails, and do your best to provide prompt responses to your opposites (see Thompson and Nadler 2002; Wallace, 1999; Walther and Bunz 2005).

4) Be very careful when using humor: While humor has been shown to be a valuable tool in online negotiation, leading to increased trust and satisfaction levels, higher joint gains and higher individual gains for the party who initiated the humorous event (Kurtzburg, Naquin and Belkin, 2009), humor is often misunderstood, misinterpreted and misattributed — and can easily backfire.

5) When you are concerned that all this mindfulness and caution might not suffice, don't leave it to email: Recognize situations in which you need to pick up the phone and call, or meet in person with, your negotiation opposite.

7. Diminished party commitment, investment and focus

Parties to e-mail negotiation might be less motivated than face-to-face negotiators. They have not displayed the minimum commitment of getting up, getting dressed and coming to the table; indeed, there might not be any sunk costs at all. Email may be the easiest medium there is for making 'shot in the dark' approaches (perhaps best exemplified by the 62 trillion spam e-mails sent yearly (McAfee, 2009), most of which are 'shot in the dark' scamming or marketing efforts). This might provide partial explanation for reports of higher rates of impasse in email negotiation (see above) and for the familiar phenomena of email negotiations simply evaporating, with one party simply dropping out of the conversation, either disappearing in a whiff of smoke or dissolving into a cloud of 'I'll get back to you'.

E-negotiators, even if committed and invested at the same level one might encounter in face-to-face negotiation, are likely to suffer media-related effects including confusion, low cognitive retention of previous messages and diminished concentration. This is due to several factors, including time passage between information exchanges, the tendency to answer emails in spurts and sections rather than finding the time to write full messages, and the tendency to answer emails in less-than-optimal surroundings and circumstances. In addition, email is often not something we train our full attention on, but rather something we do as part of our media multitasking. We check our email as we surf the web, and we surf the web as we read or reply to our email — perhaps holding in-person or phone conversations at the same time. Recent research addressing this issue indicates that we are not as good multitaskers as we like to think we are. Heavy multi-taskers suffer a range of shortcomings as opposed to 'focusers', many of which are pertinent to negotiation: They are not good at filtering out irrelevant information, and are easily distracted. They tend to have low detail recall, and despite their tendency to switch between tasks rapidly — they are not skilled at this, as their brain is always somewhat focused on the task they are *not* doing (Ofir, Nass and Wagner, 2009). Negotiators suffering from any of these, due to their multitasking tendency, work surroundings or email-management habits, might be confused and unfocused.

Advantages

The low commitment and investment level required to engage in email negotiation might certainly help negotiators engage in negotiation, at low cost. This can allow negotiators to engage in multiple processes, expanding their knowledge and improving their BATNA. It is also beneficial by providing a low-intensity interaction environment to negotiators who are conflict averse or tend towards avoidance as a conflict strategy.

Getting practical

1) Stay on top of things: Provide regular contact, keeping your counterpart engaged — without getting pushy (see Shipley and Schwalbe, 2007, for some guidance on this balance).
2) Bridge time gaps: Try to create the illusion or experience of an uninterrupted conversation. For example, write "As I wrote you..." and then copy and paste a quote from your previous letter.
3) It could happen to you: The implications of this section are not only about roping in and maintaining contact with your opposite. You yourself might be prone to underinvestment and a low level of commitment. Email negotiation tends to confuse us in this regard; keep a constant eye on your motivation level, and make sure it matches your commitment and the resources you invest.
4) Stay focused: The greater the importance of the negotiation to you, the more it pays to concentrate on it. Read and write messages in an environment that allows you to concentrate. Close your Internet web browser while reading and writing email.

Conclusion

Communicating by email, negotiators face a rougher playing field, a more contentious opposite and numerous process-challenges. The good news is, that armed with some knowledge and a healthy dose of awareness, negotiators can navigate these challenges and even turn use of the media to their advantage. Given the anticipated increase in e-negotiation processes, the sooner negotiators get started on improving their skills and awareness in this area, the better.

References

Kearney, A. T. (2010). A fleeting opportunity: Expanding the traditional buyer-seller relationship. *Executive Agenda, 13*(1).

Acquino, K. (1998). The effects of ethical climate and the availability of alternatives on the use of deception during negotiation. *International Journal of Conflict Management, 9*, 195–217.

Adair, W. L. and Brett, J. M. (2005). The negotiation dance: Time, culture, and behavioral sequences in negotiation. *Organization Science, 16*(1), 33–51.

Adair, W. L., Okumura, T., and Brett, J. M. (2001). Negotiation behavior when cultures collide: The United States and Japan. *Journal of Applied Psychology, 86*(3), 371–385.

Adair, W. L., Taylor, M. S., and Tinsley, C. (2009). Starting out on the right foot: Negotiation schemas when cultures collide. *Negotiation and Conflict Management Research, 2*(2), 138–163.

Adam, H., Shirako, A., and Maddux, W. W. (2010). Cultural variance in the interpersonal effects of anger in negotiations. *Psychological Science, 21*(6), 882–889.

Adler, S. P. and Kwon, S. (2000). Social capital: The good, the bad, and the ugly. In Lesser, E. (ed.), *Knowledge and Social Capital: Foundations and Applications* (pp. 89–115). Boston: Butterworth-Heineman.

Adler, S. P. and Kwon, S. (2002). Social capital: Prospects for a new concept. *Academy of Management Review, 27*, 17–40.

Aiello, J. R. and Watkins, D. M. (2000). The fine art of friendly acquisition. *Harvard business Review, 78*(6), 100–107.

Allport, F. (1925). The psychological bases of social science. *Psychological Bulletin, 22*(10), 561–574.

Alpert, G. and Raiffa, H. (1982). A progress report on the training of probability assessors. In D. Kahneman, P. Slovic, and A. Tversky (eds.), *Judgment under Uncertainty: Heuristics and Biases*. Cambridge: Cambridge University Press.

Amabile, T. (1996). *Creativity in Context: Update to the Social Psychology of Creativity.* Boulder, CO: Westview Press.

Amabile, T., Patterson, C., Patterson, J., Mueller, T., Wojcik, P., Odomirok, M., and Kramer, S. (2001). Academic-practitioner collaboration in mangement research: A case of cross-profession collaboration. *Academy of Mangement Journal, 44*(2), 418–431.

Amanatullah, E. and Morris, M. (2010). Negotiating gender roles: Gender differences in assertive negotiating are mediated by womenís fear of backlash and attenuated when negotiating on behalf of others. *Journal of Personality and Social Psychology, 98,* 256–267.

Amanatullah, E., Morris, M., and Curhan, J. (2008). Negotiators who give too much: Unmitigated communion, relational anxieties, and economic costs in distributive and integrative bargaining. *Journal of Personality and Social Psychology, 95,* 723–738.

Ambady, N. and Skowronski, J. J. (eds.) (2008). *First impressions.* New York, NY: Guilford Press.

Andersen, S. M. (1984). Self-knowledge and social inference: II. The diagnosticity of cognitive/affective and behavioral data. *Journal of Personality and Social Psychology, 46,* 294–307.

Anderson, J. R. (1985). *Cognitive Psychology and Its Implications,* 2nd Edition. San Francisco, CA: W. H. Freeman.

Archer, J. (2006). Testosterone and human aggression: An evaluation of the challenge hypothesis. *Neuroscience and Biobehavioral Reviews, 30,* 319–345.

Argyris, C. and Schön, D. A. (1996). *Organizational Learning II: Theory, Method, and Practice.* Reading, MA: Addison Wesley.

Arunachalam, V. and Dilla, W. (1995). Judgment accuracy and outcomes in negotiation: A causal modeling analysis of decision-aiding effects. *Organizational Behavior and Human Decision Processes, 61*(3), 289–304.

Ayres, I. and Siegelman, P. (1995). Race and gender discrimination in bargaining for a new car. *American Economic Review, 85,* 304–321.

Babcock, L. and Lashever, S. (2003). *Women Don't Ask.* Princeton, NJ: Princeton University Press.

Babcock, L. and Loewenstein, G. (1997). Explaining bargaining impasse: The role of self-serving biases. *Journal of Economic Perspectives, 11,* 109–126.

Babcock, L., Loewenstein, G., Issacharoff, S., and Camerer, C. (1995). Biased judgments of fairness bargaining. *American Economic Review, 85,* 1337–1343.

Babcock, L., Loewenstein, G., and Issacharoff, S. (1997). Creating convergence: Debiasing biased litigants. *Law and Social Inquiry, 22,* 913–925.

Bailey, A. A and Hurd, P. L. (2005). Depression in men is associated with more feminine finger length ratios. *Personality and Individual Differences, 39,* 829–836.

Balfour, F. and Einhorn, B. (March 17, 2009). Hong Kong Disneyland's future is in danger [Electronic Version]. *Bloomberg Businessweek.* Retrieved September 28, 2010.

Balleine, B. W., Delgado, M. R., and Hikosaka, O. (2007). The role of the Dorsal striatum in reward and decision-making. *The Journal of Neuroscience, 27,* 8161–8165.

Banaji, M., Bazerman, M., and Chugh, D. (2003). How (un)ethical are you? *Harvard Business Review, 81,* 56–64.

Bar Gill, O. (2006). The evolution and persistence of optimism in litigation. *Journal of Law, Economics and Organization,* 490–507.

Bard, J. F. (1987). Developing competitive strategies for buyer-supplier negotiations. *Management Science, 33*(9), 1181–1191.

Bargh, J. A., Chen, M., and Burrows, L. (1996). Automaticity of social behavior: Direct effects of trait construct and stereotype priming on action. *Journal of Personality and Social Psychology, 71,* 230–244.

Barraza, J. and Zak, P. (2009). Empathy towards strangers triggers oxytocin release and subsequent generosity. *Annals of the New York Academy of Sciences, 1167,* 182–189.

Barre, N. (1999a, March 15). Renault dans le capital de Nissan — Les négociations se sont accélérées. *Les Échos,* 14.

Barre, N. (1999b, March 19). Renault-Nissan — L'accord devrait être entériné à Tokyo le 27 mars. *Les Échos,* 12.

Barrick, M. R., Patton, G. K., and Haugland, S. N. (2000). Accuracy of interviewer judgments of job applicant personality traits. *Personnel Psychology, 53,* 925–951.

Barry, B. and Friedman, R. A. (1998). Bargainer characteristics in distributive and integrative negotiation. *Interpersonal Relations and Group Processes*, *74*, 345–359.

Barsade, S. G. (2002). The ripple effect: Emotional contagion and its influence on group behavior. *Administrative Science Quarterly*, *47*, 644.

Barsness, Z. and Tenbrunsel, A. E. (1998). Technologically-mediated communication and negotiation: Do relationships matter. Paper presented at the *International Association for Conflict Management*, College Park, USA.

Barsness, Z. I. and Bhappu, A. D. (2004). At the crossroads of technology and culture: Social influence, information sharing, and sense-making processes during negotiations. In M. J. Gelfand and J. M. Brett (eds.), *The Handbook of Negotiation and Culture*, 350–373. Palo Alto, CA: Stanford University Press.

Bartel, C. A. and Saavedra, R. (2000). The collective construction of work group moods. *Administrative Science Quarterly*, *45*, 197–231.

Batson, C. D., Thompson, E. R., Seuferling, G., Whitney, H., and Strongman, J. A. (1999). Moral hypocrisy: Appearing moral to oneself without being so. *Journal of Personality and Social Psychology*, *77*, 525–537.

Bazerman, M. and Chugh, D. (2006). Decision-making without blinders. *Harvard Business Review*, *84*, 88–97.

Bazerman, M. H. and Chugh, D. (2006). Bounded awareness: Focusing failures in negotiation. In L. Thompson (ed.), *Negotiation Theory and Research*. New York: Psychology Press.

Bazerman, M. H. and Gillespie, J. J. (1999). Betting on the future: The virtues of contingent contracts. *Harvard Business Review*, *77*, 155–160.

Bazerman, M. H. and Neale, M. A. (1992). *Negotiating Rationally*. New York: Free Press.

Bazerman, M. H. and Tenbrunsel, A. E. (1998). The role of social context on decisions: Integrating social cognition and behavioral decision research. *Basic and Applied Social Psychology*, *20*, 87–91.

Bazerman, M. H., Curhan, J. R. Moore, D. A., and Valley, K. L. (2000). Negotiation. *Annual Review of Psychology*, *51*, 279–314.

Bazerman, M. H., Magliozzi, T., and Neale, M. A. (1985). Integrative bargaining in a competitive market. *Organizational Behavior and Human Decision Processes*, *35*, 294–313.

Bazerman, M. H., Gibbons, R., Thompson, L., and Valley, K. L. (1998). Can negotiators outperform game theory?" In *Debating Rationality: Nonrational Aspects of Organizational Decision Making*, J. Halpern and R. N. Stern (eds.), 78–98. Ithaca, N.Y.: ILR Press.

Beaman, A. L., Klentz, B., Diener, E., and Svanum, S. (1979). Self-awareness and transgression in children: Two field studies. *Journal of Personality and Social Psychology, 37*, 1835–1846.

Bell, R. A. and Daly, J. A. (1984). The affinity-seeking function of communication. *Communication Monographs, 51*, 91–115.

Bem, S. L. (1974). The measurement of psychological androgyny. *Journal of Personality and Social Psychology, 42*, 155–162.

Benabou, R. and Tirole, J. (2010). Identity, morals, and taboos: Beliefs as assets. *Quarterly Journal of Economics*, forthcoming.

Benoliel, M. (2010). Personal communication based on interviews with master negotiators in North America and Asia.

Benoliel, M. and Cashdan, L. (2005). *Done Deal: Insights from Interviews with the World's Best Negotiators*. Avon, MA: Platinum Press.

Bergh, B. V. and Dewitte, S. (2006). Digit ratio (2D:4D) moderates the impact of sexual cues on men's decisions in ultimatum games. *Proceedings of the Royal Society of B: Biological Sciences, 273*, 2091–2095.

Bernard, T. S. (May 14, 2010). A toolkit for women seeking a raise. The New York Times. Retrieved November 4, 2010 from http://www.nytimes.com/2010/05/15/your-money/15money.html.

Betts, P. (2010, April 29). Carlos Ghosn gets second chance to rev up Renault. *Financial Times*, 18.

Bhappu, A. D. and Crews, J. M. (2005). The effects of communication media and conflict on team identification in diverse groups. *Proceedings of the 38th Hawaii International Conference on System Sciences*, 50–56. Los Alamitos, California.

Bhappu, A. D., Griffith, T. L., and Northcraft, G. B. (1997). Media effects and communication bias in diverse groups. *Organizational Behavior and Human Decision Processes, 70*, 199–205.

Blake, R. R. and Mouton, J. S. (1964). *The Managerial Grid*. Houston, TX: Gulf.

Blau, P. (1964). *Exchange and Power in Social Life*. New York: Wiley.

Bloomberg BusinessWeek, December 10, (2009). Why Tech Bows to Best Buy.

Bloomberg BusinessWeek, May 21, (2010). Wal-Mart Asks Suppliers to Cede Control of Deliveries.

Bloomberg BusinessWeek, October 5, (2010). Potash 'Oligopoly' to Strengthen on Mergers as BHP Eyes Entry.

Bloomberg BusinessWeek, October 7, (2010). Wal-Mart Wants More Buying Clout.

Bloomberg BusinessWeek, September 14, (2010). Wal-Mart Targeted by Labor Union, Farmers on Antitrust Claims.

Bloomberg BusinessWeek, September 29, (2010). Pentagon Losing Control of Bombs to China's Monopoly.

Blount, S. and Bazerman, M. (1996). The inconsistent evaluation of comparative payoffs in labor supply and bargaining. *Journal of Economic Behavior and Organization, 30*, 1–14.

Bluedorn, A. C., Kalliath, T. J., Strube, M. J., and Martin, G. D. (1999), Polychronicity and the Inventory of Polychromic Values (IPV). The development of an instrument to measure a fundamental dimension of organizational culture. *Journal of Managerial Psychology, 3*, 205–230.

Bodley, H. (October 25, 2006). Deal brings labor peace through '11 [Electronic Version]. *USA Today.* Retrieved October 9, 2010.

Bohnet, I. and Greig, F. (2007). Gender matters in workplace decisions. *Negotiation, 11*(4), 4–6.

Bok, S. (1978). *Lying: Moral Choice in Public and Private Life.* New York: Pantheon.

Boles, T. L., Croson, R. T., and Murnighan, J. K. (2000). Deception and retribution in repeated ultimatum bargaining. *Organizational Behavior and Human Decision Processes, 83*, 235–259.

Booth, A., Shelley, G., Mazur, A., Tharp, G., and Kittock, R. (1989). Testosterone and winning and losing in human competition. *Hormones and Behavior, 23*, 556–571.

Bottom, W. P. (1998). Negotiator risk: Sources of uncertainty and the impact of reference points on negotiated agreements. *Organizational Behavior and Human Decision Processes, 76*(2), 89–112.

Bottom, W. P. (2003). Keynes' attack on the Versailles treaty: An early investigation of the consequences of bounded rationality, framing, and cognitive illusions. *International Negotiation, 8*, 367–402.

Bottom, W. P. (2010). Essence of negotiation: Explaining appeasement and "the great Munich stereotype". *Negotiation Journal,* in press.

Bottom, W. P. and Paese, P. W. (1998). False consensus, stereotypic cues, and the perception of integrative potential in negotiation. *Journal of Applied Social Psychology, 27,* 1919–1940.

Bottom, W. P. and Paese, P. W. (1999). Judgment accuracy and the asymmetric cost of errors in distributive bargaining. *Group Decision and Negotiation, 8,* 349–364.

Bottom, W. P. and Studt, A. (1993). Framing effects and the distributive aspects of integrative bargaining. *Organizational Behavior and Human Decision Processes, 56,* 459–474.

Bourdieu, P. (1985). The forms of capital. In Richardson, J. G. (ed.), *Handbook of Theory and Research for the Sociology of Education* (pp. 241–258). New York: Greenwood.

Bowles, H. and Gelfand, M. (2010). Status and the evaluation of workplace deviance. *Psychological Science, 21,* 49–54.

Bowles, H. R. and McGinn, K. L. (2008). Gender in job negotiations: A two-level game. *Negotiation Journal,* 393–410.

Bowles, H. R., Babcock, L., and McGinn, K. L. (2005). Constraints and triggers: Situational mechanics of gender in negotiation. *Journal of Personality and Social Psychology, 89,* 951–965.

Bowles, H., Babcock, L., and Lai, L. (2007). Social incentives for gender differences in the propensity to initiate negotiations: Sometimes it does hurt to ask. *Organizational Behavior and Human Decision Processes, 103,* 84–103.

Boyes, R. (2010). For Fritz, the war really is over — but it has taken 91 years to pay the winners. *The Times,* October 2, 48.

Bradsher, K. (September 8, 2005). It's a small park: Hong Kong Disneyland faces overcrowding [Electronic Version]. *The New York Times.* Retrieved September 28, 2010.

Braithwaite, J. and Drahos, P. (2000). *Global Business Regulation.* Cambridge: Cambridge University Press.

Branzei, O., Vertinsky, I., and Camp, R. D. (2007). Culture-contingent signs of trust in emergent relationships. *Organizational Behavior and Human Decision Processes, 104*(1), 61–82.

Brat, I. (2009, September 10). Corporate news: Exclusive Hershey pact looms on horizon in Cadbury battle. *Wall Street Journal.* Retrieved from http://www.wsj.com

Brat, I., Ball, J., and McCracken, J. (2010, January 20). Kraft wins Cadbury: Hershey on its own has limited options. *Wall Street Journal.* Retrieved from http://www.wsj.com

Brat, I., McCracken, J., and Cimilluca, D. (2009, November 19). Hershey plot Cadbury bid: Chocolate maker could link with Italy's Ferrero to counter Kraft's 16 billion offer. *Wall street Journal.* Retrieved from http://www.wsj.com

Brehm, J. W. (1966). *A Theory of Psychological Reactance.* New York: Academic Press.

Brett, J. M. (2001). *Negotiating Globally: How to Negotiate Deals, Resolve Disputes, and Make Decisions Across Cultural Boundaries.* San Francisco CA: Jossey-Bass.

Brett, J. M. and Okumura, T. (1998). Inter- and intra-cultural negotiation: U.S. and Japanese negotiatitors. *Academy of Management Journal, 41*(5), 495–510.

Brewer, M. B. (1991). The social self: On being the same and different at the same time. *Personality and Social Psychology Bulletin, 17,* 475–482.

Brief, A. P., Dietz, J., Cohen, R. R., Pugh, S. D., and Vaslow, J. B. (2000). Just doing business: Modern racism and obedience to authority as explanations for employment discrimination. *Organizational Behavior and Human Decision Processes, 81,* 72–97.

Brislin, W. R. and Kim, E. S. (2003). Cultural diversity in people's understanding and use of time. *Applied Psychology: An International Review, 52,* 363–382.

Brown, R. (1994). *An Introduction to Neuroendocrinology.* Cambridge: Cambridge University Press.

Brown, R. P. and Josephs, R. A. (1999). A burden of proof: Stereotype relevance and gender differences in math performance. *Journal of Personality and Social Psychology, 76,* 246–257.

Burnham, T. C. (2007). High-testosterone men reject low ultimatum game offers. *Proceedings of the Royal Society of Biology, 274,* 2327–2330.

Burt, R. S. (1992). *Structural Holes: The Social Structure of Competition.* Cambridge, MA: Harvard University Press.

Burt, R. S. (1997). The continental value of social capital. *Administrative Science Quarterly, 42,* 339–365.

Business Wire. (2008). Introducing Engagement Commerce: Fididel Launches First Site with Real-Time Negotiation to Give Buyers More Control of the Online Shopping Experience. http://findarticles. com/p/articles/mi_m0EIN/is_2008_May_5/ai_n25379499). Retrieved Oct. 26, 2010.

Butler, J. K., Jr. (1999). Trust expectations, information sharing, climate of trust, and negotiation effectiveness and efficiency. *Group and Organization Management, 24*(2), 217–238.

Byrne, D. (1997). An overview (and underview) of research and theory within the attraction paradigm. *Journal of Social and Personal Relationships, 14,* 417–31.

Cadbury executives quit in the wake of Kraft takeover. (2010, February 3). *Wall Street Journal.* Retrieved from http://www.wsj.com

Caldwell, M. D. (1976). Communication and sex effects in a five-person prisoner's dilemma game. *Journal of Personality and Social Psychology, 33,* 273–280.

Camerer, C., Loewenstein, G., and Prelec, D. (2005). Neuroeconomics: How neuroscience can inform economics. *Journal of Economic Literature, 43,* 9–64.

Campagna, R., Bottom, W. P., Kong, D., and Mislin, A. (2010). Flying bagels and social graces: The impact of strategic expressions of emotion on distrust and post-settlement behavior. Paper presented at the IACM 23rd Annual Meeting, Boston, MA.

Caney, D. R., Cuddy, A. J. C., and Yap, A. J. (2010). Power posing: Brief nonverbal displays affect neuroendocrine levels and risk tolerance. *Psychological Science, 21,* 1363–1368.

Cannon, W. B. (1932). *The Wisdom of the Body.* New York: Norton.

Carnevale, P. J. (2006). Creativity in the outcomes of conflict. In Deutsch, M., Coleman, P. T., and Marcus, E. C. (eds.), *Handbook of Conflict Resolution* (pp. 414–435). San Francisco, CA: Jossey-Bass.

Carnevale, P. J. and Probst, T. (1998). Social values and social conflict in creative problem solving and categorization. *Journal of Personality and Social Psychology, 74,* 1300–1309.

Carnevale, P. J. and Probst, T. M. (1997). Conflict on the internet. In S. Kiesler (ed.), *Culture of the Internet*, pp. 233–55. Mahwah, NJ: Lawrence Erlbaum Associates.

Carnevale, P. J. D., Pruitt, D. G., and Seilheimer, S. D. (1981). Looking and competing: Visual access in integrative bargaining. *Journal of Personality and Social Psychology, 40*, 111–120.

Carnevale, P. J., Pruitt, D. G., and Seilheimer, S. D. (1981). Looking and competing: Accountability and visual access in integrative bargaining. *Journal of Personality and Social Psychology, 40*, 111–20.

Carr, A. S. and Pearson, J. N. (2002). The impact of purchasing and supplier involvement on strategic purchasing and its impact of firm's performance. *International Journal of Operations and Production Management, 22*(9), 1032–1053.

Carter, C. S. (2006). Biological perspectives on social attachment and bonding. In Carter, C. S. (eds.), *Attachment and Bonding: A New Synthesis* (pp. 85–100). Cambridge, A: MIT Press.

Cashdan, E. (1995). Hormones, sex, and status in women. *Hormones and Behavior, 29*, 354–366.

Catalyst. (2009). *2009 Catalyst census: Fortune 500 women board directors.* http://www.catalyst.org/publication/357/2009-catalyst-census-fortune-500-women-board-directors

Cavanagh, G. F., Moberg, D. J., and Velasquez, M. (1981). The ethics of organizational politics. *Academy of Management Review, 6*, 363–374.

Cellich, C. and Jain, S. C. (2003). *Global Business Negotiations: A Practical Guide.* Mason, OH: Thomson/South-Western.

Cheng, Y. K. B. (2009). Power and trust in negotiation and decision-making: A critical evaluation. *Harvard Negotiation Law Review.* Retrieved September 21, 2010, from http://www.hnlr.org/?p=207

Chicago Tribune. (September 18, 1997). Rodman Contract Talks Hit Snag On Incentives.

Chmielewski, D. C. (July 10, 2009). Hong Kong Disneyland expansion financing approved [Electronic Version]. *Los Angeles Times Business.* Retrieved October 3, 2010.

Christie, R. and Geis, F. L. (1970). *Studies in Machiavellianism.* New York: Academic Press.

Chua, R. Y. J., Morris, M. W., and Ingram, P. (2009). Guanxi vs. networking: Distinctive configurations of affect- and cognition-based trust in the networks of Chinese vs. American managers. *Journal of International Business Studies, 40*(3), 490–508.

Chua, R. Y. J., Morris, M. W., and Mor, S. (2010). Collaborating across cultures: The role of cultural metacognition and affect-based trust in creative collaboration. Working paper. Harvard Business School.

Chung, S. A., Singh, H., and Lee, K. (2000). Complementarity, status similarity, and social capital as drivers of alliance formation. *Strategic Management Journal, 21*, 1–22.

Cialdini, R. B. (1993). *Influence: Science and Practice*, 3rd Edition. Boston: Scott, Foresman and Company.

Cialdini, R. B. (2001). *Influence: Science and Practice*, 4th Edition. Boston: Allyn and Bacon.

Cialdini, R. B. (2007). Podcast: Secrets from the science of persuasion by Robert Cialdin. http://www.timesonline.co.uk/tol/tools_and_services/podcasts/article2792158.ece. Retrived Oct. 22, 2010.

Cimilluca, D. and Carolan, M. (2009, September 14). Corporate news: Cadbury lays out Kraft rejection. *Wall Street Journal.* Retrieved from http://www.wsj.com

Cimilluca, D. and Rohwedder, C. (2010, January 20). Kraft wins a reluctant Cadbury with help of clock, hedge funds. *Wall Street Journal.* Retrieved from http://www.wsj.com

Cimilluca, D., Brat, I., and Jargon, J. (2009, September 8). Cadbury sour on Kraft Bid: British firm rebuffs $16.73 billion offer; sweetened proposal, rival Hershey loom. *Wall Street Journal.* Retrieved from http://www.wsj.com

Cimilluca, D., Rohwedder, C., and McCracken, J. (2009, November 10). Cadbury sneers at Kraft's hostile bid: U.S. food giant takes unsweetened, $16 billion offer to confectioner's holders. *Wall Street Journal.* Retrieved from http://www.wsj.com

Citera, M., Beauregard, R., and Mitsuya, T. (2005). An experimental study of credibility in e-negotiations. *Psychology and Marketing, 22*, 163–179.

Clark, H. and Brennan, S. (1991). Grounding in communication. In L. Resnick, J. Levine, and S. Teasley (eds.), *Perspectives on Socially*

Shared Cognition, 127–149. Washington, DC: American Psychological Association.

Clark, M., Ouenette, R., Powell, M., and Milberg, S. (1987). Recipient's mood, relationship type, and helping. *Journal of Personality and Social Psychology, 53*, 94–103.

Cleary, T. (1992). *The book of Leadership and Strategy: Lessons of the Chinese Masters*. Shambhala.

Cohen, R. (1991). *Negotiating Across Cultures: Communication Obstacles in International Diplomacy*. Washington, DC: United States Institute of Peace Press.

Coleman, J. S. (1988). Social capital in the creation of human capital. *American Journal of Sociology, 94*, S95–S120.

Coleman, J. S. (1990). *Foundations of Social Theory*. Cambridge, MA: Harvard University Press.

Collier, M. J. (2009). Negotiating intercommunity and community group identity positions: summary discourses from two Northern Ireland intercommunity groups. *Negotiation and Conflict Management Research, 2*(3), 285–306.

Compte, O. and Postlewaite, A. (2004). Confidence-enhanced performance. *The American Economic Review, 94*, 1536–1557.

Cooper, A. and Sportolari, L. (1997). Romance in Cyberspace: Understanding online attraction. *Journal of Sex Education and Therapy, 22*, 7–14.

Costa, P. T., Jr. and McCrae, R. R. (1992). Four ways five factors are basic. *Personality and Individual Differences, 13*, 653–665.

Costa, P. T., Jr. and McCrae, R. R. (1995). Domains and facets: Hierarchical personality assessment using the revised NEO personality inventory. *Journal of Personality Assessment, 64*, 21–50.

Cousins, P. D., Lawson, B., and Squire, B. (2008). Performance measurement in strategic buyer-supplier relationships: The mediating role of socialization mechanisms. *International Journal of Operations and Production Management, 28*(3), 238–258.

Craver, C. (2002). *The Intelligent Negotiator*. Roseville, CA: Prima.

Croson, R. (1999). Look at me when you say that: An electronic negotiation simulation. *Simulation and Gaming, 30*, 23–27.

Croson, R. T. A. (1991). Look at me when you say that: An electronic negotiation simulation. *Simulating and Gaming, 30*, 23–37.

Crott, H., Kayser, E., and Lamm, H. (1980). The effects of information exchange and communication in an asymmetrical negotiation situation. *European Journal of Social Psychology, 10*, 149–163.

Crusco, A. and Wetzel, C. G. (1984). The Midas touch: The effects of interpersonal touch on restaurant tipping. *Personality and Social Psychology Bulletin, 10*, 512–517.

Culnan, M. J. and Markus, M. L. (1987). Information technologies. In F. M. Jablin, L. L. Putnam, K. H. Roberts, and L. W. Porter (eds.), *Handbook of organizational communication: An interdisciplinary perspective*, pp. 420–443. Newbury Park, CA: Sage Publications.

Curhan, J. R., Neale, M. A., Ross, L., and Rosencranz-Engelmann, J. (2008). Relational accommodation in negotiation: Effects of egalitarianism and gender on economic efficiency and relational capital. *Organizational Behavior and Human Decision Processes, 107*, 192–205.

Curhan, J., Elfenbein, H., and Xu, H. (2006). What do people value when they negotiate? Mapping the domain of subjective value in negotiation. *Journal of Personality and Social Psychology, 91*, 493–512.

Curtin, M. (2009, September 8). Krafty timing in bid for Cadbury. *Wall Street Journal.* Retrieved from http://www.wsj.com

Dabbs, Jr., J. M., Ruback, R. B., Frady, R. L., Hopper, C. H., and Sgoutas, D. S. (1988). Saliva testosterone and criminal violence among women. *Personality and Individual Differences, 9*, 269–275.

Daft, R. L. and Lengel, R. H. (1984). Information richness: A new approach to managerial behavior and organizational design. *Research in Organizational Behavior, 6*, 191–233.

Dahl, R. A. (1957). The concept of power. *Behavioral Science, 2*, 201–215. Reprinted in J. Scott (ed.) (1994) *Power: Critical Concepts.* London: Routledge.

Daimler and Renault-Nissan join forces. (2010, April 8). *The Economist*, 66–67.

Dalton, D. R. and Dalton, C. M. (2009). On the many limitations of threat in negotiation, as well as other contexts. *Business Horizons, 52*, 109–115.

Daly, J. (1991). The effects of anger on negotiations over mergers and acquisitions. *Negotiation Journal, 7*, 31–39.

DeCallieres, F. (1716/1983). The art of negotiating with sovereign princes. In H. M. A. Keens-Soper and K. W. Schweizer (eds.), *The Art of Diplomacy* (pp. 55–185). New York, NY: Leicester.

DeCallieres, Francois. (1716). *On the Manners of Negotiating with Princes*. Houghton Mifflin Company. Printed in (2000). Translation by A. F. Whyte.

DeDreu, C. K. W. (1995). Coercive power and concession making in bilateral negotiation. *The Journal of Conflict Resolution, 39*(4), 646–670.

DeDreu, C. K. W. (2004). Motivation in negotiation: A social psychological analysis. In M. J. Gelfand and J. M. Brett (eds.), *The Handbook of Negotiation and Culture* (pp. 114–135). Stanford, CA: Stanford University Press.

DeDreu, C. K. W., Beersma, B., Stroebe, K., and Euwema, M. C. (2006). Motivated information processing, strategic choice, and the quality of negotiated agreement. *Journal of Personality and Social Psychology, 90,* 927–943.

DeDreu, C. K. W., Carnevale, P. J. D., Emans, B. J. M., and Van de Vliert, E. (1994). Effects of gain-loss frames in negotiation: Loss aversion, mismatching, and frame adoption. *Organizational Behavior and Human Decision Processes, 60,* 90–107.

DeDreu, C. K. W., Nijstad, B. A., and Van Knippenberg, D. (2008). Motivated information processing in group judgment and decision making. *Personality and Social Psychology Review, 12,* 22–49.

DeDreu, C. K. W., Weingart, L. R., and Kwon, S. (2000). Influence of social motives on integrative negotiation: A meta-analytic review and test of two theories. *Journal of Personality and Social Psychology, 78,* 889–905.

DeDreu, C. K. W., Weingart, L. R., and Kwon, S. (2000). Influence of social motives on integrative negotiation: A meta-analytic review and test of two theories. *Journal of Personality and Social Psychology, 78,* 889–905.

DeCremer, D. (2002). Respect and cooperation in social dilemmas: The importance of feeling included. *Personality and Social Psychology Bulletin, 28,* 1335–1341.

DeDreu, C. (2006). When too little or too much hurts: Evidence for a curvilinear relationship between task conflict and innovation in teams. *Journal of Management, 32*(1), 83–107.

Dennis, A. R. and Valacich, J. S. Rethinking media richness: Towards a theory of media. *Information Systems Research, 10*, 375–377.

DePaulo, B. M. and Friedman, H. S. (1998). Nonverbal communication. In D. T. Gilber, S. T. Fiske and G. Lidzey (eds.), *The Handbook of Social Psychology*, 4ᵗʰ Edition, 3–40. Boston, MA: McGraw Hill.

DeSanctis, G. and Monge, P. (1999). Introduction to the special issues: Communication processes for virtual organizations. *Organization Science, 10*, 693–703.

Desivilya Syna, H. and Yassour-Borochowitz, D. (2010). Israelis' moral judgments of government aggression and violations of human rights: Is democracy under siege of protracted conflict? *Beliefs and Values, 2*(1), 38–48.

Desivilya, H. (2008). Conflict management in work teams. In Charles Wankel (ed.), *Handbook of 21ˢᵗ Management*. Sage.

Dunlop, J. T. (1984). *Dispute Resolution: Negotiation and Consensus Building*. Greenwood Press.

Deutsch, M. (1949). A theory of co-operation and competition. *Human Relations, 2*, 129–152.

Deutsch, M. (1962). Cooperation and trust: Some theoretical notes. *Nebraska Symposium on Motivation*: 275–320. Lincoln: Nebraska University Press.

Deutsch, M. (1973). *The Resolution of Conflict: Constructive and Destructive Processes*. New Haven, CT: Yale University Press.

DeYoung, C. G. and Gray, J. R. (2009). Personality neuroscience: Explaining individual differences in affect, behavior, and cognition. In P. J. Corr and G. Matthews (eds.), *Cambridge Handbook of Personality* (pp. 323–346). New York: Cambridge University Press.

DeYoung, C. G., Hirsh, J. B., Shane, M. S., Papademetris, X., Rajeevan, N., and Gray, J. R. (2010). Testing predictions from personality neuroscience: Brain structure and the Big Five. *Psychological Science, 21*, 820–828.

Dickerson, C., Thibodeau, R., Aronson, E., and Miller, D. (1992). Using cognitive dissonance to encourage water conservation. *Journal of Applied Social Psychology, 22*, 841–854.

Diehl, M. and Stroebe, W. (1987). Productivity loss in brainstorming groups: Toward the solution of a riddle. *Journal of Personality and Social Psychology, 53*, 497–509.

Diekmann, K. A, Tenbrunsel, A. E., and Galinsky, A. D. (2003). From self-prediction to self-defeat: Behavioral forecasting, self-fulfilling prophecies, and the effect of competitive expectations. *Journal of Personality and Social Psychology, 85*, 672–683.

Diem, W. (1999, May). The Renault-Nissan deal: The view from Paris. *Ward's Auto World, 35*(5), 59–60.

Digman, J. M. (1990). Personality structure: Emergence of the Five Factor Model. *Annual Review of Psychology, 41*, 417–440.

Dirks, K. T. and Ferrin, D. L. (2001). The role of trust in organizational settings. *Organization Science, 12*, 450–467.

Dirks, K. T. and Skarlicki, D. P. (2009). The relationship between being perceived as trustworthy by coworkers and individual performance. *Journal of Management, 35*, 136–157.

Dirks, K. T., Kim, P. H., Cooper, C. D., and Ferrin, D. L. (2007). Understanding the effects of substantive responses on trust following a transgression. Paper presented at the European Institute for Advanced Studies in Management (EIASM) Workshop on Trust Within and Between Organisations, Vrije Universiteit (Free University) Amsterdam, Netherlands.

Douin, G. (2002, November-December). Behind the scenes of the Renault-Nissan alliance (R. Martin, Trans.). *Les amis de l'École de Paris, 38* (Association des Amis de l'École de Paris du management).

Drahos, P. (2003). When the weak bargain with the strong: Negotiations in the World Trade Organization. *International Negotiation, 8*, 79–109.

Drolet, A. L. and Morris, M. W. (2000). Rapport in conflict resolution: Accounting for how face-to-face contact fosters mutual cooperation in mixed-motive conflicts. *Journal of Experimental Social Psychology, 36*, 26–5.

Drolet, A. L. and Morris, M. W. (2000). Rapport in conflict resolution: Accounting for how face-to-face contact fosters mutual cooperation in mixed-motive conflicts. *Journal of Experimental Social Psychology, 36*(1), 26–50.

Duval, T. S. and Wicklund, R. A. (1972). *A Theory of Objective Self-awareness*. New York: Academic Press.

Dyer, J. H. and Chu, W. (2003). The role of trustworthiness in reducing transaction costs and improving performance: Empirical evidence from the United States, Japan, and Korea. *Organization Science, 14*(1), 57–68.

Eagley, A. H. and Johnson, B. T. (1990). Gender and leadership style: A meta-analysis. *Psychological Bulletin, 108*, 233–256.

Earley, C. and Ang, S. (2003). *Cultural Intelligence: Individual Interactions across Cultures*. Stanford Business Press.

Earley, P. C. and Mosakowski, E. (2004). Cultural intelligence. *Harvard Business Review, 82*, 139–146.

Ebner, N. (2007). Trust-building in e-negotiation. In L. Brennan and V. Johnson (eds.), *Computer-mediated Relationships and Trust: Managerial and Organizational Effects*, pp. 139–157. Hershey, PA: Information Science Publishing.

Ebner, N., Bhappu, A., Brown, J. G., Kovach, K. K., and Kupfer Schneider, A. (2009). "You've got agreement: Negoti@ing via email." In C. Honeyman, J. Coben and G. DiPalo (eds.), *Rethinking Negotiation Teaching: Innovations for Context and Culture*, pp. 89–114. St Paul, MN: DRI Press.

Eccles, G. R., Lanes, L. K., and Wilson, C. T. (1999). Are you paying too much for that acquisition? *Harvard Business Review, 77*(4), 136–146.

Eden, C., Jones, S., Sims, D., and Smithin, T. (1981). The intersubjectivity of issues and issues of intersubjectivity. *Journal of Management Studies, 18*(1), 37–47.

Eek, D., Loukopoulos, P., Fujii, S., and Garling, T. (2002). Spill-over effects of intermittent costs for defection in social dilemmas. *European Journal of Social Psychology, 32*, 801–813.

Eisemann, J. W. (1978). Reconciling "incompatible" positions. *Journal of Applied Behavioral Science, 14*, 133–150.

Eisenberger, R., Armeli, S., Rexwinkel, B., Lynch, P. D., and Rhoades, L. (2001). Reciprocation of perceived organizational support. *Journal of Applied Psychology, 86*, 42–51.

Eisenstein, P. (1999). Why marriage makes sense. *Professional Engineering, 12*(7), 35.

Ellison, N., Heino, R., and Gibbs, J. (2006). Managing impressions online: Self-presentation processes in the online dating environment. *Journal of Computer-Mediated Communication, 11,* 415–441.

Emerson, R. M. (1962). Power-dependence relations. *American Sociological Review, 27,* 31–41.

Engelmann, J. B. (2006). Personality predicts responsivity of the brain reward system. *The Journal of Neuroscience, 26,* 7775–7776.

Epley, N. and Gilovich, T. (2001). Putting adjustment back in the anchoring and adjustment heuristic: Self generated versus experimenter provided anchors. *Psychological Science, 12,* 391–396.

Epley, N. and Kruger, J. (2005). When what you type isn't what they read: The perseverance of stereotype and expectancies over e-mail. *Journal of Experimental Social Psychology, 41,* 414–422.

Epstein, S., Pacini, R., Denes-Raj, V., and Heier, H. (1996). Individual differences in intuitive-experimental and analytical-rational thinking styles. *Journal of Personality and Social Psychology, 71*(2), 390–405.

Erez, M. and Early, P. C. (1993). *Culture, Self-identity, and Work.* New York, Oxford University Press.

Ertel, D. (1999). Turning negotiation into a corporate capability. *Harvard Business Review, 77,* 3–12.

Fan, M. (November 22, 2006). Disney culture shock [Electronic Version]. *The Standard.* Retrieved September 28, 2010.

Farrell, G. (2010, January 20). Hershey still has time to counter-bid. *Financial Times.* Retrieved from http://www.ft.com

Fehr, E. and Gachter, S. (2002). Altruistic punishment in humans. *Nature, 415,* 137–140.

Feng, J., Lazar, J., and Preece, J. (2004). Empathy and online interpersonal trust: A fragile relationship. *Behavior and Information Technology, 23*(2), 97–106.

Ferguson, T. (June 1, 2009). Google and BBC in talks to deepen ties [Electronic Version]. *Bloomberg Businessweek.* Retrieved October 7, 2010.

Ferrin, D. L. and Dirks, K. T. (2003). The use of rewards to increase and decrease trust: Mediating processes and differential effects. *Organization Science, 14,* 18–31.

Ferrin, D. L., Dirks, K. T., and Shah, P. P. (2006). Direct and indirect effects of third-party relationships on interpersonal trust. *Journal of Applied Psychology, 91,* 870–883.

Fisher, J. D., Rytting, M., and Heslin, R. (1976). Hands touching hands: Affective and evaluative effects of interpersonal touch. *Sociometry, 39,* 416–421.

Fisher, R. (2008). *Oil Pricing Exercise.* Cambridge, MA: The President and Fellows of Harvard College.

Fisher, R. and Shapiro, D. L. (2005). *Beyond Reason: Using Emotions as You Negotiate.* New York: Viking.

Fisher, R. and Ury, W. (1991). *Getting to Yes: Negotiating without Giving.* New York: Penguin Books.

Fisher, R., Ury, W. L., and Patton, B. (1991). *Getting to Yes: Negotiating Agreement Without Giving In,* 2nd Edition. New York, NY: Penguin Books.

Flynn, F. J. and Ames, D. R. (2006). What's good for the goose may not be as good for the gander: The benefits of self-monitoring for men and women in task groups and dyadic conflicts. *Journal of Applied Psychology, 91,* 272–281.

Follett, M. (1926). Constructive conflict. In Metcalfe H. C. (ed.), *Scientific Foundations of Business Administration.* Baltimore MD: Williams and Wilkins.

Foucault, M. (1994). The Subject and Power. In Rubinow P. and Rose N. (eds.) *The Essential Foucault,* New York: New Press.

Frank, R., Lattman, P., Searcey, D., and Lucchetti, A. (December 13, 2008). Fund fraud hits big names [Electronic Version]. *The Wall Street Journal.* Retrieved October 4, 2010.

French, J. and Raven, B. H. (1959). The basis of social power. In D. Cartwright (ed.), *Studies in Social Power,* 150–167. Ann Arbor, MI: Institute for Social Research.

French, J. P. R. and Raven, B. (1959). The bases of social power. In D. Cartwright (ed.), *Studies in Social Power* (150–167). Ann Arbor, MI: Institute for Social Research.

Friedman, R. (1992). The culture of mediation: Private understandings in the context of public conflict. In D. Kolb and J. Bartunek (eds.), *Hidden Conflict: Uncovering Behind-the-scenes Disputes* (pp. 143–164). Beverly Hills, CA: Sage.

Friedman, R. A. and Currall, S. C. (2003). E-mail escalation: Dispute exacerbating elements of electronic communication. *Human Relations, 56,* 1325–1357.

Friedman, V. and Berthoin Antal, A. (2004). Negotiating reality: An action science approach to intercultural competence. *Management Learning, 36*(1), 67–84.

Friedman, V. and Desivilya Syna, H. (forthcoming). Integrating social entrepreneurship and conflict engagement for regional development in divided societies. *Entrepreneurship and Regional Development.*

Froman, L. A. and Cohen, M. D. (1970). Compromise and logroll: Comparing the efficiency of two bargaining processes. *Behavioral Science, 30,* 180–183.

Fromkin, D. (1992). *A Peace to End All Peace.* New York: Basic Books.

Fry, W. R. (1985). The effect of dyad Machiavellianism and visual access on integrative bargaining outcomes. *Personality and Social Psychology Bulletin, 11,* 51–62.

Fryer, R. and Jackson, M. O. (2008). A categorical model of cognition and biased decision making. *The B. E. Journal of Theoretical Economics, 8,* 6.

Fu, P. P. and Yukl, G. (2000). Perceived effectiveness of influence tactics in the United States and China. *Leadership Quarterly, 11*(2), 251–266.

Fu, P. P., Kennedy, J., Tata J., Yukl, G., Bond, M. H., Peng, T. K., Srinivas, E., S., Howell, J. P., Prieto, L., Koopman, P., Boonstra, J. J., Pasa, S., Lacassagne, M. F., Higashide, H., and Cheosakul, A. (2004). The impact of societal cultural values and individual social beliefs on the perceived effectiveness of managerial influence strategies: A meso approach. *Journal of International Business Studies, 35,* 284–305.

Fulk, J. (1993). Social construction of communication technology. *Academy of Management Journal, 36,* 921–950.

Fulk, J., Schmitz, J., and Steinfield, C. W. (1990). A social influence model of technology use. In Fulk J., and Steinfield C., (eds.), *Organizations and Communication Technology,* pp. 117–140. Newbury Park, CA: Sage.

Galin, A., Gross, M., and Gosalker, G. (2007). E-negotiation versus face-to-face negotiation: What has changed — if anything? *Computers in Human Behavior, 23,* 787–797.

Galinsky, A. and Mussweiler, T. (2001). First offers as anchors: The role of perspective-taking and negotiator focus. *Journal of Personality and Social Psychology, 81*(4), 657–669.

Galinsky, A. D. and Moskowitz, G. B. (2000). Perspective-taking: Decreasing stereotype expression, stereotype accessibility, and in-group favoritism. *Journal of Personality and Social Psychology, 78*, 708–724.

Galinsky, A. D. and Mussweiler, T. (2001). First offers as anchors: The role of perspective-taking and negotiator focus. *Journal of Personality and Social Psychology, 81*, 657–669.

Galinsky, A. D., Maddux, W. W., Gilin, D., and White, J. B. (2008). Why it pays to get inside the head of your opponent: The differential effects of perspective taking and empathy in negotiations. *Psychological Science, 19*, 378–384.

Galinsky, A. D., Mussweiler, T., and Medvec, V. H. (2002). Disconnecting outcomes and evaluations: The role of negotiator focus. *Journal of Personality and Social Psychology, 83*, 1131–1140.

Gallagher, H. L. and Frith, C. D. (2003). Functional imaging of 'theory of mind'. *Trends in Cognitive Sciences, 7*, 77–83.

Gallic charm. (1999, March 13). *The Economist*, 72.

Geis, F. L. and Moon, T. H. (1981). Machiavellianism and deception. *Journal of Personality and Social Psychology, 41*, 766–775.

Gelfand, M. J. and Dyer, N. (2000). A cultural perspective on negotiation: Progress, pitfalls, and prospects. *Applied Psychology: An International Review, 49*, 62–69.

Gelfand, M. J., Major, V. S., Raver, J. L., Nishii, L. H., and O'Brien, K. (2006). Negotiating relationally: The dynamics of the relational self in negotiations. *Academy of Management Review, 31*, 427–451.

Gelnar, M. (2010, January 6). Corporate news: Nestle buys U.S. pizza lines: Company pays $3.7 billion for Kraft unit, rules out bid for U.K. candy maker. *Wall Street Journal*. Retrieved from http://www.wsj.com

Gesteland, R. (1999). Cross-cultural business behavior: Marketing, negotiating and managing across cultures. Copenhagen: Copenhagen Business School Press.

Ghosn, C. (2002). Saving the business without losing the company. *Harvard Business Review*, January: 37–45.

Ghosn, C. and Riès, P. (2003). *Citoyen du Monde.* Paris: Grasset.

Gibson, C. B. (1998). Do you hear what I hear: A framework for reconciling intercultural communication difficulties arising from cognitive styles and cultural values. In Earley P. C. and Erez M. (eds.), *New Perspectives on International Industrial/Organizational Psychology*, pp. 335–362. San Francisco: The New Lexington Press.

Giebels, E., De Dreu, C. K. W., and Van de Vliert, E. (2003). No way out or swallow the bait of two-tided exit options in negotiation: The influence of iocial motives and interpersonal trust. *Group Processes and Intergroup Relations*, 6(4), 369–386.

Gilbert, D. T. (1998). Ordinary personology. In Gilbert, D. T., Fiske, S. T., and Lindzey, G. (eds.), *The Handbook of Social Psychology*, 4th Edition. New York: McGraw Hill.

Gist, M. E., Stevens, C. K., and Bavetta, A. G. (1991). Effects of self-efficacy and post-training intervention on the acquisition and maintenance of complex interpersonal skills. *Personnel Psychology*, 44, 837–861.

Glass, G. (2007). The East-West divide: Cultural differences affecting deals. *Asia Law*, 5(5), 13–17.

Glick, P. and Fiske, S. T. (1996). The ambivalent sexism inventory: Differentiating hostile and benevolent sexism. *Journal of Personality and Social Psychology*, 70, 491–512.

Global Investment Technology. (2003). Harborside offers a large-block trading facility but building awareness is the paramount challenge. http://www. globalinv.com/Harborside-RHall-GIT%204-28-03.pdf). Retrieved Oct. 26, 2010.

Goldberg, L. R. (1992). The development of markers for the Big-Five factor structure. *Psychological Assessment*, 4, 26–42.

Goleman, D. (1995). *Emotional intelligence.* New York: Bantam Books.

Graham, J. L. and Lam, N. M. (2003). 'The Chinese negotiation'. *Harvard Business Review*, 81, 82–91.

Graham, J. L. and Requejo, W. H. (2009). Managing face-to-face international negotiations. *Organizational Dynamics*, 38(2), 167–177.

Granovetter, M. S. (1973). The strength of weak ties. *American Journal of Sociology*, 78, 1360–1380.

Grant, V. J. and France, J. T. (2001). Dominance and testosterone in women. *Biological Psychology*, 58, 41–47.

Graziano, W., Jensen-Campbell, L., and Hair, E. (1996). Perceiving inter-personal conflict and reacting to it: The case for agreeableness. *Journal of Personality and Social Psychology, 70,* 820–835.

Greenberg, J. (1983). Overcoming egocentric bias in perceived fairness through self-awareness. *Social Psychology Quarterly, 46,* 152–156.

Greenberg, J. and Baron, R. (2008). *Behavior in Organizations,* 9th Edition. Upple Saddle River, N. J.: Pearson Prentice Hall.

Greenhalgh, L. and Gilkey, R. (1993). The effect of relationship orienta-tion on negotiators' cognitions and tactics. *Group Decision and Negotiation, 2,* 167–183.

Greenhalgh, L., Neslin, S. A., and Gilkey, R. W. (1985). The effects of negotiator preferences, situational power, and negotiator personal-ity on outcomes of business negotiation. *Academy of Management Journal, 28,* 9–33.

Greenwald, A. G., McGhee, D. E., and Schwartz, J. K. L. (1998). Measuring individual differences in implicit cognition: The implicit association test. *Journal of Personality and Social Psychology, 74,* 1464–1480.

Griffith, T. L. and Northcraft, G. B. (1994). Distinguishing between the forest and the trees: Media, features, and methodology in electronic communication research. *Organization Science, 5,* 272–285.

Guastella, A. J., Mitchell, P. B., and Dadds, M. R. (2008). Oxytocin increases gaze to the eye region of human faces. *Biological Psychiatry, 63,* 3–5.

Gudykunst, W. B. and Ting-Toomey, S. (1988). *Culture and Interpersonal Communication.* Newbury Park, CA: Sage.

Gudykunst, W. B., Matsumoto, Y., Ting-Toomey, S., Nishida, T. Kim, K., and Heyman, S. (1996). The influence of cultural individualism-collectivism, self construals, and individual values on communica-tion styles across cultures. *Human Communication Research, 22*(4), 510–543.

Hachman, M. (September 17, 2010). Google hires Netflix exec to bolster video [Electronic Version]. *PC Magazine.* Retrived October 10, 2010.

Hackley, S. (2005). Balancing act: How to manage negotiation tensions. *Negotiation,* February, 3–5.

Hall, E. T. and Hall, M. R. (2002). Key concepts: Underlying structures of culture. In J. M. Martin, T. K. Nakayama, and L. A. Flores (eds.),

Readings in Cultural Communication: Experiences and Contexts. Boston, MA: McGraw Hill.

Hall, E. T. (1959). *The Silent Language.* New York, NY: Random House.

Hall, E. T. (1960). The silent language in overseas business. *Harvard Business Review, 38*(3), 87–96.

Hall, E. T. (1966). *The Hidden Dimension.* New York, NY: Doubleday.

Hall, E. T. (1976). *Beyond Culture.* New York, NY: Random House.

Hall, E. T. (1989). *Beyond culture.* New York: Anchor Books.

Halpert, J. A., Stuhlmacher, A. F., Crenshaw, J. L., Litcher, C. D., and Bortel, R. (2010). Paths to negotiation success. *Negotiation and Conflict Management Research, 3,* 91–116.

Hancock, T. J. and Dunham, J. T. (2001). Impression formation in computer-mediated communication revisited, *Communication Research, 28,* 325–347.

Handgraaf, M. J., Van Dijk, E., Vermunt, R. C., Wilke, H. A., and De Dreu, C. K. (2008). Less power or powerless: Egocentric empathy gaps and the irony of having little versus no power in social decision making. *Journal of Personality and Social Psychology, 95*(5), 1136–1149.

Hansen, T. (2008). Critical conflict resolution theory and practice. *Conflict Resolution Quarterly, 25,* 403–427.

Harasim, L. M. (1993). Networlds: Networks as a social space. In L. M. Harasim (ed.), *Global Networks: Computers and International Communication,* pp. 15–34. Cambridge, MA: MIT Press.

Harding, D. and Rovit, S. (2004). *Mastering the Merger.* Boston, MA: Harvard Business School Press.

Harding, D. and Yale, P. (2002). Discipline and the dilutive deal. *Harvard Business Review, 80*(7), 18–20.

Harr, J. (1996). *A Civil Action.* New York: Vintage.

Harris, M. (1968). *The Rise of Cultural Theory.* New York: Crowell.

Harsanyi, J. C. (1962). Bargaining in ignorance of the opponent's utility function. *Journal of Conflict Resolution, 6,* 29–38.

Hayes, R. H. (1981). Why Japanese factories work. *Harvard Business Review, 59*(4), 56–66.

Hayward, M. and Hambrick, D. (1997). Explaining the premiums paid for large acquisitions: Evidence of CEO hubris. *Administrative Science Quarterly, 42,* 103–127.

Heath, C., Larrick, R. P., and Klayman, J. (1998). Cognitive repairs: How organizational practices can compensate for individual shortcomings. *Research in Organizational Behavior, 20,* 1–37.

Heilman, M. E. and Wallen, A. S. (2010). Wimpy and undeserving of respect: Penalties for men's gender-inconsistent success. *Journal of Experimental Social Psychology, 4,* 664–667.

Heilman, M. E., Wallen, A. S., Fuchs, D., and Tamkins, M. M. (2004). Penalties for success: Reactions to women who succeed at male gender-typed tasks. *Journal of Applied Psychology, 89,* 416–427.

Heinrichs, M., Baumgartner, T., Kirschbaum, C., and Ehlert., U. (2003). Social support and oxytocin interact to suppress cortisol and subjective responses to psychosocial stress. *Biological Psychiatry, 54,* 1389–1398.

Hendrick, C. and Hendrick, S. (1983). *Liking, Loving and relating.* Monterey: Brooks/Cole.

Hermans, E. J., Putman, P., Baas, J. M., Koppeschaar, H. P., and vanHonka, J. (2006). A single administration of testosterone reduces fear-potentiated startle in humans. *Biological Psychiatry, 59,* 872–874.

Hilton, J. L. and Hippel, W. (1996). Stereotypes. In J. T. Spence, J. M. Darley, and D. J. Foss (eds.), *Annual Review of Psychology, 47,* 237–271.

Hiltz, S. R., Johnson, K., Turoff, M. (1986). Experiments in group decision making: Communication process and outcome in face-to-face versus computerized conferences. *Human Communication Research, 13,* 225–252.

Hinds, P. J. and Mortenson, M. (2005). Understanding conflict in geographically distributed teams: The moderating effects of shared indentity, shared context, and spontaneous communication. *Organization Science, 16*(3), 290–307.

Hodgson, J. (2010, February, 10). Cadbury's Carr fault U.K.s takeover rules. *Wall Street Journal.* Retrieved from http://www.wsj.com

Hodgson, J. D., Sano Y., and Graham, J. L. (2008). *Doing Business in the New Japan.* Lanham, Maryland: Rowman and Littlefield Publishers, Inc.

Hollander-Blumoff, R. and Tyler, T. R. (2008). Procedural justice in negotiation: Procedural fairness, outcome acceptance, and integrative potential. *Law and Social Inquiry, 33,* 473–500.

Howard, E. S., Gardner, W. L., and Thompson, L. (2007). The role of the self-concept and the social context in determining the behavior of power holders: Self-construal in intergroup versus dyadic dispute resolution negotiations. *Journal of Personality and Social Psychology, 93*(4), 614–631.

Howard, R. A. and Matheson, J. E. (1984). *Readings on the Principles and Applications of Decision Analysis.* Menlo Park, CA: Strategic Decisions Group.

Hsee, C. and Weber, E. U. (1999). Cross-national differences in risk preference and lay predictions. *Journal of Behavioral Decision Making, 12*, 165–179.

Huber, V. L. and Neale, M. A. (1986). Effects of cognitive heuristics and goals on negotiator performance and subsequent goal setting. *Organizational Behavior and Human Decision Processes, 38*, 342–365.

Hurley, R. F. (2006). The decision to trust. *Harvard Business Review.*

Hurtz, G. and Donovan, J. (2000). Personality and job performance: The Big Five revisited. *Journal of Applied Psychology, 85*, 869–879.

Imai, L. and Gelfand, M. J. (2010). The culturally intelligent negotiator: The impact of cultural intelligence (CQ) on negotiation sequences and outcomes. *Organizational Behavior and Human Decision Processes, 112*(2), 83–98.

Jacobs, J. (1965). *The Death and Life of Great American Cities.* London: Penguin Books.

Jargon, J. and Ball, D. (2009, September 9). Kraft's pursuit of Cadbury: Nestle, Hershey, face risk of fresh perils. *Wall Street Journal.* Retrieved from http://www.wsj.com

Jarvenpaa, S. L., Knoll, K., and Leidner, D. E. (1998). Is anybody out there? The implications of trust in global virtual teams. *Journal of Management Information Systems, 14*, 29–44.

Jasperson, J., Carte, T. A., Saunders, C. S., Butler, B. S., Croes, H. J. P., and Zheng, W. (2002). Review: Power and information technology research: A metatriangulation review. *MIS Quarterly, 26*(4), 397–459.

Jensen-Campbell, L. and Graziano, W. (2001). Agreeableness as a moderator of interpersonal conflict. *Journal of Personality, 69*, 323–362.

Jervis, R. (1970). *The Logic of Images in International Relations.* Princeton, NJ: Princeton University Press.

Jessup, L. M. and Tansik, D. A. (1991). Decision making in an automated environment: The effects of anonymity and proximity with a group decision support system. *Decision Sciences, 22,* 266–279.

Johnson, N. A. and Cooper, R. B. (2009). Power and concession in computer-mediated negotiation: An examination of first offers. *MIS Quarterly, 33*(1), 147–170.

Johnston, D. A. and Kristal, M. M. (2008). The climate for co-operation: Buyer-supplier beliefs and behavior. *International Journal of Operations and Production Management, 28*(9), 875–898.

Kahneman, D. (1992). Reference points, anchors, norms, and mixed feelings. *Organizational Behavior and Human Decision Processes, 51,* 296–312.

Kahneman, D. (2003). Maps of bounded rationality: Psychology for behavioral economics. *American Economic Review, 93,* 1449–1475.

Kahneman, D. and Tversky, A. (1979). Prospect theory: An analysis of decision under risk. *Econometrica, 47,* 263–291.

Kahneman, D., Slovic, P., and Tversky, A. (1982*). Judgement under Uncertainty. Heuristics and Biases.* Cambridge: Cambridge University Press.

Kahnemann, D. and Tversky, A. (2004). The power of random numbers. *Negotiation, 7*(9), 10.

Kakabadse, A. and Kakabadse, N. (1999). *The Essence of Leadership.* London: Thomson.

Kakabadse, A., Bank, J., and Vinnicombe, S. (2005). *Working in Organisations: The Essential Guide for Managers in Today's Workplace,* 2nd Edition, London: Penguin.

Katz, D. and Braly, K. (1933). Racial stereotypes of one hundred college students. *Journal of Abnormal and Social Psychology, 28*(3), 280–290.

Katzenbach, J. R. and Smith, D. K. (1993). *The Wisdom of Teams: Creating the High-performance Organization.* Boston: Harvard Business School.

Keesing, R. (1974). Theories of culture. *Annual Review of Anthropology, 3,* 73–97.

Kelley, H. H. (1966). A classroom study of the dilemmas in interpersonal negotiation. In K. Archibald (ed.), *Strategic Interaction and Conflict: Original Papers and Discussion*, pp. 49–73. Berkeley, CA: Institute of International Studies.

Kemp, N. J. and Rutter D. R. (1982). Duelessness and the content and style of conversation. *British Journal of Social Psychology, 21*, 43–9.

Kenneth S. Courtis: Having a (crystal) ball. (2000, January). *The Journal.*

Kesmodel, D. and Rohwedder, C. (2009, September 8). Kraft's pursuit of Cadbury: Sugar and spice: A clash of two change agents: CEOs of both companies have sought to turn operations around, on though adding revenue, on by cutting costs. *Wall Street Journal.* Retrieved from http://www.wsj.com

Kiesler, S. and Sproull, L. (1992). Group-decision making and communication technology. *Organizational Behavior and Human Decision Processes, 52*, 96–123.

Kilgour, M. and Koslow, S. (2009). Why and how do creative thinking techniques work? Trading off originality and appropriateness to make more creative advertising. *Journal of the Academy of Marketing Science, 37*, 298–309.

Kilmann, R. H. and Thomas, K. W. (1977). Developing a forced-choice measure of conflict-handling behavior: The "Mode" instrument. *Educational and Psychological Measurement, 37*(2), 309–325.

Kim, P. and Fragale, A. (2005), Choosing the path to bargaining power: An empirical comparison of BATNA and contributions in negotiation. *Journal of Applied Psychology, 90*(2), 373–381.

Kim, P. H., Ferrin, D. L., Cooper, C. D., and Dirks, K. T. (2004). Removing the shadow of suspicion: The effects of apology versus denial for repairing competence- versus integrity-based trust violations. *Journal of Applied Psychology, 89*, 104–118.

Kimmel, M. J., Pruitt, D. G., Magenau, J. M., Konar-Goldband, E., and Carnevale, P. J. D. (1980). Effects of trust, aspiration, and gender on negotiation tactics. *Journal of Personality and Social Psychology, 38*, 9–22.

Kolb, D. and McGinn, K. (2009) Beyond gender and negotiation to gendered negotiations. *Negotiation and Conflict Management Research, 2*(1), 1–16.

Kolb, D. M. and Williams, J. (2000) *The Shadow Negotiation: How Women Can Master the Hidden Agendas that Determine Bargaining Success.* New York: Simon and Schuster.

Kollock, P. (1993). An eye for eye leaves everyone blind: Cooperation and accounting systems. *American Sociological Review, 58,* 768–86.

Kolo, A. and Walde, T. (2000). Renegotiation and contract adaption in international investment projects. *The Journal of World Investment, 1,* 5–28.

Kong, D. T. (2010). *Emotions and Contingent Contracting Decisions in Negotiation.* Working dissertation, Olin Business School, Washington University in St. Louis.

Kong, D. T. and Bottom, W. P. (2010). *Emotional intelligence, negotiation outcome, and negotiation behavior.* Paper presented at the Annual Meeting of the Academy of Management, Montreal, Canada.

Korine, H., Asakawa, K., and Gomez, P-Y. (2002). Partnering with the unfamiliar: Lessons from the case of Renault and Nissan. *Business Strategy Review, 13*(2), 41–50.

Kosfeld, M., Heinrichs, M., Zak, P., Fischbacher, U., and Fehr, E. (2005). Oxytocin increases trust in humans. *Nature, 435,* 673–676.

Kovick, D. and Harvey, K. (2009). *Ellis v. MacroB.* Cambridge, MA: Program of Negotiation, Harvard Law School.

Kramer, R. M. (1999). Trust and distrust in organizations: Emerging perspectives, enduring questions. In J. T. Spence (ed.), *Annual Review of Psychology.* Palo Alto, CA: Annual Reviews.

Kraut, R., Galegher, J., Fish, R. and Chalfonte, B. (1992). Task requirements and media choice in collaborative writing. *Human Computer Interactions, 7,* 375–408.

Kray, L. J. (2007). Leading through negotiating: Harnessing the power of gender stereotypes. *California Management Review, 50,* 159–173.

Kray, L. J. (2010). Gender discrimination in negotiators' ethical decision making. *Under Review.*

Kray, L. J. and Babcock, L. (2006). Gender in negotiations: A motivated social cognitive analysis. In L. Thompson (ed.), *Negotiation Theory and Research* pp. 203–224. New York: Psychology Press.

Kray, L. J. and Gelfand, M. J. (2009). Relief versus regret: The effect of gender and negotiation norm ambiguity on reactions to having one's first offer accepted. *Social Cognition, 27,* 418–436.

Kray, L. J. and Thompson, L. (2005). Gender stereotypes and negotiation performance: An examination of theory and research. *Research in Organizational Behavior, 26,* 103–182.

Kray, L. J., Galinsky, A. D., and Thompson, L. (2002). Reversing the gender gap in negotiations: An exploration of stereotype regeneration. *Organizational Behavior and Human Decision Processes, 87,* 386–409.

Kray, L. J., Galinsky, A. D., and Thompson, L. (2002). Reversing the gender gap in negotiations: An exploration of stereotype regeneration. *Organizational Behavior and Human Decision Processes, 87,* 386–409.

Kray, L. J., Haselhuhn, M. P., and Schweitzer, M. (2010). Male pragmatism in ethical decision making in negotiations. Unpublished manuscript. Haas School of Business, University of California, Berkeley.

Kray, L. J., Reb, J., Galinksy, A., and Thompson, L. (2004). Stereotype reactance at the bargaining table: The effect of stereotype activation and power on claiming and creating value. *Personality and Social Psychology Bulletin, 30,* 399–411.

Kray, L. J., Thompson, L., and Galinsky, A. D. (2001). Battle of the sexes: Gender stereotype confirmation and reaction in negotiations. *Journal of Personality and Social Psychology, 80,* 942–958.

Kray, L. J., Thompson, L., and Lind, E. A. (2005). It's a bet! A problem solving approach promotes the construction of contingent agreements. *Personality and Social Psychology Bulletin, 31,* 1039–1051.

Kronzon, S. and Darley, J. (1999). Is this tactic ethical? Biased judgments of ethics in negotiation. *Basic and Applied Social Psychology, 21:* 49–60.

Kruger, J., Epley, N., Parker, J., and Ng, Z. (2005). Egocentrism over e-mail: Can we communicate as well as we think? *Journal of Personality and Social Psychology, 89,* 925–936.

Kumar, R. (1999). A script theoretical analysis of international negotiating behavior. In R. J. Bies, R. J. Lewicki and B. H. Sheppard (eds.), *Research in Negotiation in Organizations,* pp. 285–311. Stamford, CT: JAI Press.

Kunda, Z. and Spencer, S. J. (2003). When do stereotypes come to mind and when do they color judgment? A goal-based theoretical framework for stereotype activation and application. *Psychological Bulletin, 129,* 522–544.

Kurtzberg, T. R. (1998). Creative thinking, cognitive aptitude, and integrative joint gain: A study of negotiator creativity. *Creativity Research Journal, 11,* 283–293.

Kurtzberg, T. R., Naquin, C. E. and Belkin, L. T. (2009). Humor as a relationship-building tool in online negotiations. *International Journal of Conflict Management, 20*(4), 377–397.

Kwok, V. W. (September 18, 2009). Airline alliances battle over JAL [Electronic Version]. Forbes. Retrieved October 8, 2010.

Larrick, R. P. and Blount, S. (1997). The claiming effect: Why players are more generous in social dilemmas than in ultimatum games. *Journal of Personality and Social Psychology, 72,* 810–825.

Larrick, R. P. and Wu, G. (2007). Claiming a large slice of a small pie: Asymmetric disconfirmation in negotiation. *Journal of Personality and Social Psychology, 92,* 212–233.

Lauer, S. (1999a, April 9). Neuf mois de négociations discrètes, de doutes ... et de certitudes. *Le Monde,* 25.

Lauer, S. (1999b, March 28). Les salariés de Nissan ont envie de s'en sortir. *Le Monde,* 14.

Lawless, D. J. (1979). Organisational *Behavior: The Psychology of Effective Management,* 2nd Edition. Englewood Cliffs: Prentice-Hall.

Lax, D. A. and Sebenius, J. K. (1986). *The Manager as Negotiator.* New York: Free Press.

Lax, D. A. and Sebenius, J. K. (2006). *3D Negotiation: Powerful Tools to Change the Game in Your Most Important Deals.* Boston, MA: Harvard Business School Press.

Leana, C. R. and Van Buren, H. J. III. (1999). Organizational social capital and employment practices. *Academy of Management Review, 24,* 538–555.

Lebra, T. S. (1987). The cultural significance of silence in Japanese conversation. *Multilingua, 6*(4), 343–357.

Ledyaev, V. (1997). *Power: A Conceptual Analysis.* Commack, NY: Nova Science.

Lee, B. K., Glass, T. A., McAtee, M. J., Wand, G. S., Bandeen-Roche, K., Bolla, K. I., and Schwartz, B. S. (2007). Associations of salivary cortisol with cognitive function in the Baltimore memory study. *Archives of General Psychiatry, 64,* 810–818.

Lerner, J. S. and Tiedens, L. Z. (2006). Portrait of the angry decision maker: How appraisal tendencies shape anger's influence on cognition. *Journal of Behavioral Decision Making, 19,* 115–137.

Levav, J. and Argo, J. J. (2010). Physical contact and financial risk taking. *Psychological Science, 21,* 804–810.

Lewicki, R. (1983). Lying and deception: A behavioral model. In M. H. Bazerman and R. J. Lewicki (eds.), *Negotiating in Organizations.* Sage: Beverly Hills.

Lewicki, R. (1992). Negotiating Strategically. In A. Cohen (ed.). *The Portable MBA in Management,* pp. 147–189, New York, NY: John Wiley and Sons.

Lewicki, R. and Litterer, J. (1985). *Negotiation.* Homewood, IL: Irwin.

Lewicki, R. J. and Litterer, J. (1985). *Negotiation: Readings, Exercises and Cases.* Boston, MA: Irwin.

Lewicki, R. J. and Robinson, R. J. (1998). Ethical and unethical bargaining tactics: An empirical study. *Journal of Business Ethics, 17,* 665–682.

Lewicki, R. J., Barry, B., and Saunders, D. M. (2010). *Negotiation,* 6th Edition. New York: McGraw Hill/Irwin.

Lewicki, R. J., Saunders, D. M., and Barry, B. (2003). *Essentials of Negotiation.* Irwin Professional Pub.

Lewicki, R. J., Saunders, D. M., and Barry, B. (2006). *Negotiation,* 5th Edition. New York: McGraw-Hill.

Lewicki, R., J., Saunders, D. M., and Litterer, J. A. (1999). *Negotiation.* Homewood, IL: Richard D. Irwin.

Lewin K. (1951). *Field Theory in Social Science: Selected Theoretical Papers.* New York, NY: Harper and Row.

Lewis, R. D. (2006). *When Cultures Collide: Managing Successfully across Cultures,* 3rd Edition. London: Nicholas Brealey Publishing.

Li, M., Tost, L., and Wade-Benzoni, K. (2007). The dynamic interaction of context and negotiator effects: A review and commentary on current and emerging areas in negotiation. *International Journal of Conflict Management, 18*(3), 222–259.

Liebert, R. M., Smith, W. P., Hill, J. H., and Kieffer, M. (1968). The effects of information and magnitude of initial offer on interpersonal negotiation. *Journal of Experimental Social Psychology, 4*, 431–441.

Lim, J. (2000). An experimental investigation of NSS and proximity on negotiation outcomes. *Behaviour and Information Technology, 19*, 329–338.

Lim, R. G. (1993). Overconfidence in negotiation revisited. *International Journal of Conflict Management, 8*, 52–79.

Liman, A. L. (1998). *Lawyer: A Life of Counsel and Controversy.* New York: PublicAffairs.

Lippmann, W. (1992). *Public Opinion.* New York: Macmillan.

Lituchy, T. R. (1997). Negotiations between Japanese and Americans: The effects of collectivism on integrative outcomes. *Canadian Journal of Administrative Sciences, 14*(4), 386–395.

Liu, M. and Wang, C. (2010). Explaining the influence of anger and compassion on negotiators' interaction goals: An assessment of trust and distrust as two distinct mediators. *Communication Research, 37*, 443–472.

Liu, Y. and Ginther, D, (1999). A Comparison of Task-Oriented Model and Social-Emotion-Oriented Model. In *Computer-Mediated Communication; Commerce, Texas* (ERIC Document Reproduction Service Number ED 437 924).

Liu, Y., Ginther, D., and Zelhart, P. (2001). How do frequency and duration of messaging affect impression development in computer-mediated communication? *Journal of Universal Computer Science, 7*, 893–913.

Locke, E. A., Shaw, K. N., Saari, L. M., and Latham, G. P. (1981). Goal setting and task performance. *Psychological Bulletin, 90*, 125–152.

Loewenstein, G., Issacharoff, S., Camerer, C., and Babcock, L. (1993). Self-serving assessments of fairness and pretrial bar-gaining. *Journal of Legal Studies, 22*, 135–59.

Loewenstein, G., Thompson, L., and Bazerman, M. (1989). Social utility and decision making in interpersonal context. *Journal of Personality and Social Psychology, 57*, 426–441.

Lowenstein, J., Morris, M. W., Chakravarti, A., Thompson, L., and Kopelman, S. (2005). At a loss for words: Dominating the conversation and the outcome in negotiation as a function of intricate arguments and communication media. *Organizational Behavior and Human Decision Processes, 98*, 28–38.

Lukes, S. (2005). *Power: A Radical View*, 2nd Edition. New York: Palgrave Macmillion.

Lurigio, A. J. and Carroll, J. S. (1985). Probation officers' schemata of offenders: Content, development and impact on treatment decisions. *Journal of Personality and Social Psychology, 48*, 1112–1126.

Lys, T. and Vincent, L. (1995). An analysis of value destruction in ATT's acquisition of NCR. *Journal of Financial Economics, 39*, 353–378.

Ma, Z. and Jaeger, A. (2005). Getting to yes in China: Exploring personality effects in Chinese negotiation styles. *Group Decision and Negotiation, 14*, 415–437.

Macduff, I. (2006), 'Your pace or mine? Culture, time and negotiation'. *Negotiation Journal, 22*, 31–45.

Maddux, W. W., Mullen, E., and Galinsky, A. D. (2008). Chameleons bake bigger pies and take bigger pieces: Strategic behavioral mimicry facilitates negotiation outcomes. *Journal of Experimental Social Psychology, 44*, 461–468.

Magee, J. C. and Galinsky, A. D. (2008). Social hierarchy: The self-reinforcing nature of power and status. *Academy of Management Annals, 2*, 351–398.

Malholtra, D. and Bazerman, M. (2007). *Negotiation Genius*. New York, NY: Bantom Dell.

Malhotra, D. M. (2004). Six Ways to Build Trust in Negotiations. *Harvard Business School Working Knowledge: A First Look at Faculty Research.*

Mannix, E. A. and Neale, M. (1993). Power imbalance and the pattern of exchange in dyadic negotiation. *Group Decision and Negotiation, 2*, 2, 119–133.

Mantoux, P. (1992). *Deliberations of the Council of Four*. Princeton NJ: Princeton University Press.

Markey, P. M. and Wells, S. M. (2002). Interpersonal perception in Internet chat rooms. *Journal of Research in Personality, 36*, 134–146.

Markus, H. R. and Kitayama, S. (1991). Culture and the self: Implications for cognition, emotion, and motivation. *Psychological Review*, *98*(2), 224–253.

Martell, R. F., Lane, D. M., and Emrich, C. (1996). Male-female differences: A computer simulation. *American Psychologist*, *51*, 157–158.

Matherson, K. and Zanna, M. P. (1989). Persuasion as a function of self-awareness in computer-mediated communication. *Social Behavior*, *4*, 99–111.

Mayer, B. (2000). *The Dynamics of Conflict Resolution*. San Francisco: Jossey Bass.

Mayer, J. D. and Salovey, P. (1997). What is emotional intelligence? In P. Salovey and D. Sluyter (eds.), *Emotional Development and Emotional Intelligence: Educational Implications*, pp. 3–31. New York: Basic Books.

Mayer, R. C., Davis, J. H., and Schoorman, F. D. (1995). An integrative model of organizational trust. *Academy of Management Review*, *20*, 709–734.

Maznevski, M. L., Chudoba, K. M. (2000). Bridging space over time: Global virtual team dynamics and effectiveness. *Organization Science*, *11*, 473–492.

Mazur, A. and Booth, A. (1998). Testosterone and dominance in men. *Behavioral and Brain Sciences*, *21*, 353–363.

McAfee. (2009). *The Carbon Impact of Spam Report*. http://resources.mcafee.com/content/NACarbonFootprintSpamConfirm. Last acessed Sept 6th, (2010).

McAlister, L., M., Bazerman, M. H., and Fader, P. (1986). Power and goal setting in Channel negotiations. *Journal of Marketing Research*, *23*, 228–236.

McAllister, D. J. (1995). Affect- and cognition-based trust as foundations for interpersonal cooperation in organizations. *Academy of Management Journal*, *38*(1), 24–59.

McCracken, J., Cimilluca, D., and Brat, I. (2010, January 10). Cadbury, Hershey directors hold talks. *Wall Street Journal*. Retrieved from http://www.wsj.com

McCracken, J., Cimilluca, D., and Brat, I. (2010, January 16). Hershey drafting Cadbury bid: Chocolate maker would top Kraft Foods offer,

setting stage for shootout. *Wall Street Journal.* Retrieved from
http://www.wsj.com

McCraty, R. and Childre, D. (2004). The grateful heart: The psychophys-
iology of appreciation. In R. A. Emmons, M. E. McCullough, (eds.)
The Psychology of Gratitude, pp. 230–255. New York: Oxford
University Press.

McCusker, C. and Carnevale, P. J. (1995). Framing in resource dilemmas:
Loss aversion and the moderating effects of sanctions. *Organizational Behavior and Human Decision Processes, 61,* 190–201.

McGinn, K. L. and Keros, A. (2002). Improvisation and the logic of
exchange in embedded negotiations. *Administrative Science
Quarterly, 47,* 442–473.

McGrath, J. E. and Hollingshead, A. B. (1993). Putting the "group" back
into group support systems: Some theoretical issues about dynamic
processes in groups with technological enhancements. In L. M.
Jessup and J. S. Valacich (eds.), *Group Support Systems: New
Perspectives,* pp. 78–79. New York, NYU: Macmillan.

McMillan, J. and Woodruff, C. (1999). Interfirm relationships and informal
credit in Vietnam. *Quarterly Journal of Economics, 114*(4), 1285–320.

Mehta, P. H. and Josephs, R. A. (2006). Testosterone change after losing
predicts the decision to compete again. *Hormones and Behavior, 50,*
684–692.

Meichtry, S. (2009, November 19). Entering Cadbury fray would put
Ferrero outside its comfort zone. *Wall Street Journal.* Retrieved from
http://www.wsj.com

Miles, E. W. and Clenney, E. F. (2010). Gender differences in negotiation:
A status characteristics theory view. *Negotiation and Conflict
Management Research, 3*(2), 130–144.

Miles, E. W. and LaSalle, M. M. (2008). Asymmetrical contextual ambiguity, engotiation self-efficacy, and negotiaiton performance.
International Journal of Conflict Management, 19, 36–56.

Miller, S. and Zaun, T. (2002, April 5–7). Rescued by Renault, Nissan now
works to return the favor. *Wall Street Journal Europe,* B1.

Mintu-Wimsatt, A. and Gassenheimer, J. B. (1996). Negotiation differences between two diverse cultures: An industrial seller's
perspective. *European Journal of Marketing, 30*(4), 20–39.

Mischel, W. (1977). The interaction of person and situation. In D. Magnusson and N. Endler (eds.), *Personality at the Crossroads: Current Issues in Interactional Psychology.* Hillsdale, NJ: Erlbaum.

Mnookin, R. H., Peppet, S. R. and Tulumello, A. S. (2000). *Beyond Winning: Negotiating to Create Value in Deals and Disputes.* Cambridge, MA: The Belknap Press of Harvard University Press.

Molm, Linda D. (1988). The structure and use of power: A comparison of reward and punishment power. *Social Psychology Quarterly, 51,* 108–22.

Moore, C. (2003). *The Mediation Process,* 3rd edition. San Francisco: Jossey Bass.

Moore, D. A. (2004a). Myopic prediction, self-destructive secrecy, and the unexpected benefits of revealing final deadlines in negotiation. *Organizational Behavior and Human Decision Processes, 94*(2), 125–139.

Moore, D. A. (2004b). The unexpected benefits of final deadlines in negotiation. *Organizational Behavior and Human Decision Processes, 40*(1), 121–127.

Moran, S., Bereby-Meyer, Y., and Bazerman, M. H. (2008). Stretching the effectiveness of analogical training in negotiations: Teaching diverse principles for creating value. *Negotiation and Conflict Management Research, 1,* 99–134.

Morck, R., Shleifer, A., and Vishny, R. W. (1990). Do managerial objectives drive bad acquisitions? *Journal of Finance, 45,* 31–48.

Morhenn, V. B., Park, J. W., Piper, E., and Zak, P. J. (2008). Monetary sacrifice among strangers is mediated by endogenous oxytocin release after physical contact. *Evolution and Human Behavior, 29,* 375–383.

Morley, I. E. and Stephenson, G. M. (1977). *The Social Psychology of Bargaining.* London: Allen and Unwin.

Morosini, P. (2005). *Renault-Nissan: The paradoxical alliance* (ESMT-305-0047-1). European Case Clearinghouse, Cranfield University, United Kingdom.

Morris, M. W. and Keltner, D. (2000). How emotions work: The social functions of emotional expression in negotiations. *Research in Organizational Behavior, 22,* 1–50.

Morris, M. W., Nadler, J., Kurtzberg, T. R., and Thompson, L. (2002). Schmooze or loose: Social friction and lubrication in e-mail negotiations. *Group Dynamics: Theory, Research, and Practice, 6*, 89–100.

Morris, M., Larrick, R., and Su, S. (1999). Misperceiving negotiation counterparts: When situationally determined bargaining behaviors are attributed to personality traits. *Journal of Personality and Social Psychology, 77*, 52–67.

Morris, M., Nadler, J., Kurtzberg, T. R., and Thompson, L. (2002). Schmooze or lose: Social friction and lubrication in e-mail negotiations. *Group Dynamics, 6*(1), 89–100.

Mortenson, G. (2009) *Stones into Schools.* New York, NY: Penguin Books.

Mortenson, G. and Relin, D. O. (2006). *Three Cups of Tea.* New York, NY: Penguin Books.

Morton, D. (1920). A theory of cooperation and competition. *Human Relations, 2*, 129–151.

Movius, H. and Susskind, L. (2009). *Built to Win: Creating a World-Class Negotiating Organization.* Boston, MA: Harvard Business Press.

Mulder, L. B., Dijk, E., De Cremer, D., and Wilke, H. A. M. (2006). Undermining trust and cooperation: The paradox of sanctioning systems in social dilemmas. *Journal of Experimental Social Psychology, 42*, 147–162.

Munk, Nina. (2004). Fools rush in. Harper Business.

Murtoaro, J. and Kujala, J. (2007). Project negotiation analysis. *International Journal of Project Management, 25*, 722–733.

Nadler, J. and Shestowsky, D. (2006). Negotiation, information technology and the problem of the faceless other. In L. Thompson (ed.), *Negotiation Theory and Research*, pp. 145–172. New York, NY: Psychology Press.

Nahapiet, J. and Ghoshal, S. (1998). Social capital, intellectual capital and the organizational advantage. *Academy of Management Review, 23*, 242–266.

Naquin, C. E. (2003). The agony of opportunity in negotiation: Number of negotiable issues, counterfactual thinking, and feelings of satisfaction. *Organizational Behavior and Human Decision Processes, 91*, 97–107.

Naquin, C. E. and Paulson, G. D. (2003). Online bargaining and interpersonal trust. *Journal of Applied Psychology, 88*(1), 113–120.

Naquin, C. E., Kurtzberg, T. R., and Belkin, L. T. (2008). E-mail communication and group cooperation in mixed motive contexts. *Social
Justice Research, 21*(4), 470–489.

Naquin, C. E., Kurtzberg, T. R., and Belkin, L. T. (2010). The finer points
of lying online: E-mail versus pen and paper. *Journal of Applied
Psychology, 95*(2), 387–394.

Neale, M. A. and Bazerman, M. H. (1985). The effects of framing and
negotiation overconfidence on bargaining behaviors and outcomes.
Academy of Management Journal, 28, 34–49.

Neale, M. A. and Bazerman, M. H. (1991). *Cognition and Rationality in
Negotiation*. New York: The Free Press.

Neale, M. A. and Northcraft, G. B. (1991). Behavioral negotiation theory:
A framework for conceptualizing dyadic bargaining. In Cummings,
L. L. and Staw, B. M. (eds.), *Research in Organizational Behavior*,
pp. 147–190. Greenwich, CT: JAI Press.

Nelson, R. E. (1989). The strength of strong ties: Social networks and
inter-group conflict in organizations. *Academy of Management
Journal, 32*, 377–401.

Nemeth, C. J., Personnaz, B., Personnaz, M., and Goncalo, J. A. (2004).
The liberating role of conflict in group creativity: A study in two
countries. *European Journal of Social Psychology, 34*, 365–374.

Neslin, S. and Greenhalgh, L. (1983). Nash's theory of co-operative
games as a predictor of the outcomes of buyer-seller negotiations:
An experiment in media purchasing. *Journal of Marketing Research,
20*, 368–379.

Ng, K. Y. and Chua, R. Y. J. (2006). Do I contribute more when I trust
more? Differential effects of cognition- and affect-based trust.
Management and Organization Review, 2(1), 43–66.

Nisbett, R. E. (2003). *The Geography of Thought: How Asians and
Westerners Think Differently... and Why*. New York: The Free Press.

Noelle-Neumann, E. (1984). *The Spiral of Silence: Public Opinion — Our
Social Skin*. Chicago: University of Chicago.

Northcraft, G. B. and Neale, M. A. (1987). Experts, amateurs, and real
estate: An anchoring-and-adjustment perspective on property pricing decisions. *Organizational Behavior and Human Decision
Processes, 39*, 84–97.

Nunamaker, J. F., Dennis, A. R., Valancich, J. S., and Vogel, D. R. (1991). Information technology for negotiating groups: Generating options for mutual gain. *Management Science, 37*(10), 1325–1346.

O'Connaill, B., Whittaker, S., and Wilbur, S. (1993). Conversations over video conferences: An evaluation of the spoken aspects of video-mediated communication. *Human Computer Interaction, 8,* 389–428.

O'Connor, K. M. and Arnold, J. A. (2000). Distributive spirals: Negotiation impasses and the moderating role of disputant self-efficacy. *Organizational Behavior and Human Decision Processes, 84,* 18–176.

O'Connor, K. M., Arnold, J. A., and Burris, E. R. (2005). Negotiators' bargaining histories and their effects on future negotiation performance. *Journal of Applied Psychology, 90,* 350–362.

Ocker, R. J. and Yaverbaum, G. J. (1999). Asynchronous computer-mediated communication versus face-to-face collaboration: Results on student learning, quality and satisfaction. *Group Decision and Negotiations, 8*(5), 427–40.

Odendaal, J. S. J. and Meintjes, R. A. (2003). Neurophysiological correlates of affiliative behaviour between humans and dogs. *Veterinary Journal, 165,* 296–301.

Ofir, E., Nass, C., and Wagner, A. D. (2009). Cognitive control in media multitaskers. *Proceedings of the National Academy of Sciences, 106*(37), 15583–87.

Ogilvie, D. T. and Simms, S. (2009). The impact of creativity training on an accounting negotiation. *Group Decision and Negotiation, 18,* 75–87.

Osborne, A. F. (1953). *Applied Imagination.* New York: Scribners.

Paese, P. W. and Yonker, R. D. (1993). Toward a better understanding of egocentric fairness judgments in negotiation. *International Journal of Conflict Management, 12,* 114–131.

Patton, C. and Balakrishnan, P. V. (2010), The impact of expectation of future negotiation interaction on bargaining processes and outcomes. *Journal of Business Research, 63*(8), 809–816.

Paulus, P. B., Dzindolet, M. T., Poletes, G., and Camacho, L. M. (1993). Perception of performance in group brainstorming: The illusion of group productivity. *Personality and Social Psychology Bulletin, 19,* 78–89.

PBS Frontline, November 24, (2009). The Card Game.

Peterson, R. L. (2005). The neuroscience of investing: fMRI of the reward system. *Brain Research Bulletin, 67*, 391–397.

Pfeffer, J. (1992). *Managing with Power: Politics and Influence in Organizations*. Harvard Business School Press.

Philips, M. (September 27, 2008). The monster that ate Wall Street: How 'credit default swaps' — an insurance against bad loans — turned from a smart bet into a killer. [Electronic Version]. *Newsweek*. Retrieved October 5, 2010.

Pietroni, D., Van Kleef, G. A., De Dreu, C. K. W., and Pagliaro, S. (2008). Emotions as strategic information: Effects of other's emotional expressions on fixed-pie perception, demands, and integrative behavior in negotiation. *Journal of Experimental Social Psychology, 44*, 1444–1454.

Pinkley, R. L. (1995). Impact of knowledge regarding alternatives to settlement in dyadic negotiations: Whose knowledge counts? *Journal of Applied Psychology, 80*(3), 403–417.

Pinkley, R. L., Griffith, T. L., and Northcraft, G. (1995). "Fixed pie" a la mode: Information availability, information processing, and the negotiation of suboptimal agreements. *Organizational Behavior and Human Decision Processes, 62*, 101–112.

Pinkley, R. L., Neale, M. A., and Bennett, R. J., (1994). The impact of alternatives to settlement in dyadic negotiation. *Organizational Behavior and Human Decision Processes, 57*, 97–116.

Podsakoff, P. M. and Schriesheim, C. A. (1985). Field studies of French and Raven's bases of power: Critique, reanalysis, and suggestions for future research. *Psychological Bulletin, 97*(3), 387–411.

Polzer, J. T. (1996). Intergroup negotiations: The effect of negotiating teams. *Journal of Conflict Resolution, 40*, 678–698.

Porter, M. E. (1980). *Competitive Strategy: Techniques for Analyzing Industries and Competitors*. New York, Free Press.

Portes, A. (1998). Social capital: Its origins and applications in modern sociology. *Annual Review of Sociology, 24*, 1–24.

Postmes, T., Spears, R., and Cihangir, S. (2001). Quality of decision making and group norms. *Journal of Personality and Social Psychology, 80*, 918–930.

Prentice, D. A. and Carranza, E. (2002). What women and men should be, shouldn't be, are allowed to be, and don't have to be: The contents of prescriptive gender stereotypes. *Psychology of Women Quarterly, 26,* 269–281.

Program on Negotiation, Harvard Law School (2004). Great negotiator case study series 2004: Richard Holbrooke.

Pruitt, D. G. (1981). *Negotiation Behavior.* New York: Academic Press.

Pruitt, D. G. (1983). Strategic choice in negotiation. *American Behavioral Scientist, 27,* 167–194.

Pruitt, D. G. and Carnevale, P. G. (1993). *Negotiation and Social Conflict.* Buckingham: Open University Press.

Pruitt, D. G. and Carnevale, P. J. (1993). *Negotiation in Social Conflict.* Buckingham: Open University Press.

Pruitt, D. G. and Lewis, S. A. (1975). Development of integrative solutions in bilateral negotiation. *Journal of Personality and Social Psychology, 31,* 621–633.

Pruitt, D. G. and Rubin, J. Z. (1986). *Social Conflict: Escalation, Stalemate, and settlement.* New York: Random House.

Purdy, J. M., Nye, P., and Balakrishnan, P. V. (2000). The impact of media richness on negotiation outcomes. *International Journal of Conflict Management, 11,* 163–188.

Putnam, L. L. (2003). Dialectical tensions and rhetorical tropes in negotiations. *Organization Studies, 25*(1), 35–53.

Putnam, R. D. (1993). The prosperous community: Social capital and public life. *American Prospect, 13,* 35–42.

Putz, D. A., Gaulin, S. J. C., Sporter, R. J., and McBurney, D. H., (2004). Sex hormones and finger length: What does 2D:4D indicate? *Evolution and Human Behaviour, 25,* 182–199.

Rabin, M. (1993). Incorporating fairness into game theory and economics. *American Economic Review, 83,* 1281–1302.

Raiffa, H. (1981). *The Art and Science of Negotiation.* Cambridge: Harvard University Press.

Raiffa, H. (1985). Post-settlement settlements. *Negotiation Journal, 1,* 9–12.

Rapoport, A., Erev, I., and Zwick, R. (1995). An experimental study of buyer-seller negotiation with one-sided incomplete information and time discounting. *Management Science, 41*(3), 377–394.

Raven, B. (1993). The bases of power: Origins and recent developments. *Journal of Social Issues, 49,* 227–251.

Raven, B. H (1990). Political applications of the psychology of interpersonal influence and social power. *Political Psychology, 11,* 493–520.

Raven, B., Schwartzwalk, J., and Koslowski, M. (1998). Conceptualizing and measuring a power/interaction model of interpersonal influence. *Journal of Applied Social Psychology, 28,* 297–332.

Reis, H. T. and Burns, L. B. (1982). The salience of the self in responses to inequity. *Journal of Experimental Social Psychology, 18,* 464–475.

Renault Communication. (1999, March 27). *Accord entre Renault et Nissan: Annexe-Chronologie des négociations et de l'accord entre Renault et Nissan.* Paris: Renault (Agence Information Interne).

Renault, S. A. (n.d.) *Renault/Nissan: Une ambition globale.* Lettre de Renault B ses actionnaires, numéro exceptionnel.

Requejo, W. H. and Graham, J. L. (2008). *Global Negotiation: The New Rules.* New York, NY: Palgrave MacMillan.

Rice, S. A. (1926). "Stereotypes": A source of error in judging human character. *Journal of Personnel Research, 5,* 267–276.

Richter, A., W., West, M. A., van Dick, R., and Dawson, J. F. (2006). Boundary spanners' identification, intergroup contact, and effective intergroup relations. *The Academy of Management Journal, 49,* 1252–1269.

Riddell, G. (1986). *The Riddell Diaries: 1908–1923.* London: Athlone Press.

Ridgeway, C. (2001). Gender, status, and leadership. *Journal of Social Issues, 57,* 637–655.

Ritov, I. (1996). Anchoring in simulated competitive market negotiation. *Organizational Behavior and Human Decision Processes, 67,* 16–25.

Roberson, L., Deitch, E. A., Brief, A. P., and Block, C. J. (2003). Stereotype threat and feedback seeking in the workplace. *Journal of Vocational Behavior, 62,* 176–188.

Robinson, R. J., Lewicki, R. J., and Donahue, E. M. (2000). Extending and testing a five factor model of ethical and unethical bargaining tactics: Introducing the SINS scale. *Journal of Organizational Behavior, 21,* 649–664.

Rocco, E. (1998). Trust breaks down in electronic contexts but can be repaired by some initial face-to-face contact. In *Proceedings of the*

1998 SIGCHI *Conference on Human Factors in Computing Systems,* (pp. 496–502). Los Angeles: ACM Press.

Rohweeder, C. and Brat, I. (2009, September 22). Cadbury CEO eases tone about bid from Kraft. *Wall Street Journal.* Retrieved from http://www.wsj.com

Roman, S. and Iacobucci, D., (2010). Antecedents and consequences of adaptive selling confidence and behavior: A dyadic analysis of salespeople and their customers. *Journal of the Academy of Marketing Science, 38,* 363–382.

Rosette, A. S., Brett, J. M., Barsness, Z., and Lytle, A. (2001). The influence of e-mail on Hong Kong and U.S. intra-cultural negotiations. Paper delivered at the Annual Meeting of the International Association for Conflict Management, Paris, France, June 23–27, (2001).

Ross, L. and Ward, A. (1995). Psychological barriers to dispute resolution. *Advances in Experimental Social Psychology, 27,* 255–304.

Rothman, J. (1997*). Resolving Identity-Based Conflict: In Nations, Organizations and Communities.* San Francisco, Ca.: Jossey-Bass.

Rotter, J. B. (1967). A new scale for the measurement of interpersonal trust. *Journal of Personality, 35,* 651–665.

Rousseau, D. M., Sitkin, S. B., Burt, R. S., and Camerer, C. (1998). Not so different after all: A cross-discipline view of trust. *Academy of Management Review, 23,* 393–404.

Rubin, J. and Brown, B. (1975). *The Social Psychology of Bargaining and Negotiation.* Academic Press, New York, NY.

Rubin, J. Z. and Brown, B. R. (1975). *The Social Psychology of Bargaining and Negotiation.* New York: Academic Press.

Rubin, J. Z., Pruitt, D. G., and Kim, S. H. (1994). *Social Conflict: Escalation, Stalemate, and Settlement,* 2nd Edition. New York, NY: McGraw-Hill.

Ruble, T. L. and Thomas, K. W. (1976). Support for a two-dimensional model of conflict behavior. *Organizational Behavior and Human Performance, 16,* 143–155.

Rudman, L. A. (1998). Self-promotion as a risk factor for women: The costs and benefits of counterstereotypical impression management. *Journal of Personality and Social Psychology, 74,* 629–645.

Russ, G. S., Galang, M. C., and Ferris, G. R. (1998). Power and influence of the human resources function through boundary spanning and information management. *Human Resource Management Review,* *8*(2), 125–148.

Salacuse, J. W. (2001). Renegotiating existing agreements: How to deal with "life struggling against form". *Negotiation Journal,* Oct, 311–331.

Salovey, P. and Mayer, J. D. (1990). Emotional intelligence. *Imagination, Cognition and Personality, 9,* 185–211.

Sanchez-Burks, J., Bartel, C., and Blount, S. (2009). Fluidity and performance in intercultural workplace interactions: The role of behavioral mirroring and social sensitivity. *Journal of Applied Psychology, 94*(1), 216–223.

Sanchez-Burks, J., Lee, F., Choi, I., Nisbett, R., Zhao, S., and Koo, J. (2003). Conversing across cultures: East-West communication styles in work and nonwork contexts. *Journal of Personality and Social Psychology, 85,* 363–372.

Sapienza, P., Zingales, L., Maestripieri, D. (2009). Gender differences in financial risk aversion and career choices are affected by testosterone. *Proceedings of the National Academy of Sciences, 106,* 15268–15273.

Sapolsky, R. (1990). Stress in the wild. *Scientific American, 262,* 106–113.

Schneider, A. K. (2002). Shattering negotiation myths: Empirical evidence on the effectiveness of negotiation style. *Harvard Negotiation Law Review, 7,* 143–233.

Schneider, A. K., Tinsley, C. H., Cheldelin, S., and Amanatullah, E. T. (2010). Likeability v. competence: The impossible choice faced by female politicians, attenuated by lawyers. *Duke Journal of Gender Law and Policy, 17,* 363–384.

Schneider, W. (2007). *The Psychology of Stereotyping.* New York: Guilford Press.

Schriesheim, C. and Hinkin, T. (1990). Influence tactics used by subordinates: A theoretical and empirical analysis and refinement of the Kipnis, Schmidt, and Wilkinson Subscales. *Journal of Applied Psychology, 75*(3), 246–257.

Schultz, C. J. (1993). Situational and dispositional predictors of performance: A test of the hypothesized Machiavellianism × structure interaction among sales persons. *Journal of Applied Social Psychology, 23,* 478–498.

Schulz-Hardt, S., Brodbeck, F. C., Mojzisch, A., Kerschreiter, R., and Frey, D. (2006). Group decision making in hidden profile situations: Dissent as a facilitator for decision quality. *Journal of Personality and Social Psychology, 91*, 1080–1093.

Schurr, P. H. and Ozanne, J. L. (1985). Influences on exchange processes: Buyers' preconceptions of a seller's trustworthiness and bargaining toughness. *Journal of Consumer Research, 11*, 939–953.

Schweitzer, M. E., Ordonez, L., and Douma, B. (2004). Goal setting as a motivator of unethical behavior. *Academy of Management Journal, 47*, 422–432.

Sebenius, J. K. (1992). Negotiation analysis: A characterization and review. *Management Science, 38*, 18–38.

Sebenius, J. K. (1998). Negotiating cross-border acquisitions. *Sloan Management Review, 9*(2), 27–41.

Seidel, M. L., Polzer, J. T., and Stewart, K. J. (2000). Friends in high places: The effects of social networks on discrimination in salary negotiations. *Administrative Science Quarterly, 45*, 1–24.

Shamay-Tsoory, S. G., Fischer, M., Dvash, J., Harari, H., Perach-Bloom, N. and Levkovitz, Y. (2009). Intranasal administration of oxytocin increases envy and schadenfreude. *Biological Psychiatry, 66*, 864–70.

Shapiro, D. L. (2002). Negotiating emotions. *Conflict Resolution Quarterly, 20*(1), 67–82.

Shapiro, D. L. (2010a). From signal to semantic: Uncovering the emotional dimension of negotiation. *Nevada Law Journal*, 2010.

Shapiro, D. L. (2010b). Relational identity theory: A systematic approach for transforming the emotional dimension of conflict. *American Psychologist, 65*(7), 634–645.

Shell, R. G. (2006). *Bargaining for Advantage.* New York, NY: Penguin Books.

Shemer, O. and Schmid, H. (2007). Toward a new definition of community partnership: A three-dimensional approach. *Journal of Rural Cooperation* (accepted for publication).

Shipley, D. and Schwalbe, W. (2007). *Send: The Essential Guide to Email for Office and Home.* New York: Alfred A. Knopf.

Short, J., Williams, E., and Christie, B. (1976). *The Social Psychology of Telecommunications.* Chichester, England: John Wiley and Sons Ltd.

Simon, H. A. (1985). Human nature and politics: The dialogue of psychology with political science. *American Political Science Review, 79*, 293–304.

Sims, J. (2005). The ideal location for negotiation: An alternative view. Retrieved online on October 1, 2010 at http://www.negotiator-magazine.com/article290_1.html

Singer, T., Seymour, B., O'Doherty, J., Kaube, H., Dolan, R. J., and Frith, C. D. (2004). Empathy for pain involves the affective but not sensory components of pain. *Science, 303,* 1157–1162.

Singer, T., Snozzi, R., Bird, G., Petrovic, P., Silani, G., Heinrichs, M., and Dolan, R. J. (2008). Effects of oxytocin and prosocial behavior on brain responses to direct and vicariously experienced pain. *Emotion, 8,* 781–791.

Slovic, P. and Lichtenstein, S. (1971). A comparison of Bayesian and regression approaches to the study of information processing in judgment. *Organizational Behavior and Human Performance, 6,* 649–744.

Small, D. A., Gelfand, M., Babcock, L., and Gettman, H. (2007). Who goes to the bargaining table? The influence of gender and framing on the initiation of negotiation. *Journal of Personality and Social Psychology, 93*(4), 600–613.

Smith, D. H. (1969). Communication and negotiation outcome. *The Journal of Communication, 19,* 248–25.

Smith, T. W. (1992). Hostility and health: Current status of a psychosomatic hypothesis. *Health Psychology, 11,* 139–150.

Snyder, M. (1987). *Public Appearances, Private Realities: The Psychology of Self-monitoring.* New York, NY: W H Freeman/Times Books/ Henry Holt and Co.

Snyder, M. and Swann, W. (1978). Hypothesis-testing proceses in social interaction. *Journal of Personality and Social Psychology, 36,* 1202–1212.

Spears, R., Postmes, T., Lea, M., and Wolbert, A. (2002). The power of influence and the influence of power in virtual groups: A SIDE look at CMC and the Internet. *The Journal of Social Issues, 58,* 91–108.

Spekman, R. E., Kamauff, J. W. Jr, and Myhr, N. (1998). An empirical investigation into supply chain management: A perspective on partnerships. *International Journal of Physical Distribution and Logistics Management, 28*(8), 630–650.

Sproull, L. and Keisler, S. (1991). *Connections: New Ways of Working in the Networked Organization.* Cambridge, MA: MIT Press.

Sproull, L. and Kiesler, S. (1986). Reducing social context cues: Electronic mail in organizational communication. *Management Science, 32*(11), 1492–513.

Standifer, R. and Bluedorn, A. (2006). Alliance management teams and entrainment: Sharing temporal mental models. *Human Relations, 59*(7), 903–927.

Steele, C. M. (1997). A threat in the air: How stereotypes shape intellectual identity and performance. *American Psychologist, 52,* 613–629.

Stern, L. W. and Reve, T. (1980). Distribution channels as political economies: A framework for comparative analysis. *Journal of Marketing, 44*(3), 52–64.

Stevens, C. K., Bavetta, A. G., and Gist, M. E. (1993). Gender differences in the acquisition of salary negotiation skills: The role of goals, self-efficacy, and perceived control. *Journal of Applied Psychology, 78,* 723–735.

Strack, F. and Mussweiler, T. (1997). Explaining the enigmatic anchoring effect: Mechanisms of selective accessibility. *Journal of Personality and Social Psychology, 73,* 437–446.

Stuhlmacher, A. F. and Walters, A. E. (1999). Gender differences in negotiation outcome: A meta-analysis. *Personnel Psychology, 52,* 653–677.

Stuhlmacher, A. F., Gillespie, T. L., and Champagne, M. V. (1998). The impact of time pressure in negotiation: A meta-analysis. *International Journal of Conflict Management, 9*(2), 97–115.

Subramaniam, M. and Youndt, M. A. (2005). The influence of intellectual capital on the types of innovative capabilities. *Academy of Management Journal, 48,* 450–463.

Subramanian, G. (2010). *Negotiauctions: New Dealmaking Strategies for a Competitive Marketplace.* New York: W. W. Norton and Company.

Swaab, R. I. and Swaab, D. F (2009). Sex differences in the effects of visual contact and eye contact in negotiations. *Journal of Experimental Social Psychology, 45,* 129–136.

Swan, J. and Scarbrough, H. (2005). The politics of networked innovation. *Human Relations, 58*(7), 913–943.

Tagliabue, J. (2000, July 2). Renault pins its survival on a global gamble. *The New York Times,* Section 3, p. 1.

Tajfel, H. and Turner, J. (1986). The social identity theory of intergroup behavior. In S. Worchel and W. G. Austin (eds.), *The Social Psychology of Intergroup Relations*, pp. 7–24. Chicago: Nelson-Hall.

Takahashi, T. (2005). Social memory, social stress, and economic behaviours. *Brain Research Bulletin, 67*, 398–402.

Taylor, S. E., Klein, L. C., Lewis, B. P., Gruenewald, T. R., Gurung, R. A. R., and Updegraff, J. A. (2000). Biobehavioral responses to stress in females: Tend-and-befriend, not fight-or-flight. *Psychological Review, 3*, 411–429.

Tenbrunsel, A. E. (1998). Misrepresentation and expectations of misrepresentation in an ethical dilemma: The role of incentives and temptation. *Academy of Management Journal, 41*, 330–339.

Thaler, R. H. and Sunstein, C. R. (2008). *Nudge: Improving Decisions about Health, Wealth, and Happiness.* New Haven, CT: Yale University Press.

The shuttle diplomacy of a car deal. (1999, March 29). *Business Week*, 22.

The Sydney Morning Herald, October 31, (2007). BHP after open iron ore market.

Thompson, L. (1990). Negotiation behavior and outcomes: Empirical evidence and theoretical issues. *Psychological Bulletin, 108*(3), 515–532.

Thompson, L. (2004). *The mind and heart of the negotiator*, 3rd Edition. Upper Saddle River, NJ: Prentice Hall.

Thompson, L. (2006). *Negotiation Theory and Research.* New York: Psychology Press.

Thompson, L. and DeHarpport, T. (1998). Relationships, goal incompatibility, and communal orientation in negotiations. *Basic and Applied Social Psychology, 20*, 33–44.

Thompson, L. and Loewenstein, G. (1992). Egocentric interpretations of fairness in interpersonal conflict. *Organizational Behavior and Human Decision Processes, 51*, 176–197.

Thompson, L. and Nadler, J. (2002). Negotiating via information technology: Theory and application. *Journal of Social Issues, 58*(1), 109–24.

Thompson, L. L. (1991). Information exchange in negotiation. *Journal of Experimental Social Psychology, 27*, 161–179.

Thompson, L. L. (2008). *The mind and heart of the negotiator*, 4th Edition. New Jersey: Pearson Prentice Hall.

Thompson, L. L. and Hastie, R. (1990). Social perception in negotiation. *Organizational Behavior and Human Decision Processes, 47*, 98–123.

Thompson, L. L. and Hrebec, D. (1996). Lose-lose agreements in interdependent decision making. *Psychological Bulletin, 120*, 396–409.

Thompson, L. L., Peterson, E., and Brodt, S. (1996). Team negotiation: An examination of integrative and distributive bargaining. *Journal of Personality and Social Psychology, 70*, 66–78.

Thompson, L. T., Wang, J., and Gunia, B. C. (2010). Negotiation. *Annual Review of Psychology, 61*, 491–515.

Thornton, E. *et al.* (1999, October 11). A new order at Nissan. *Business Week*, 54.

Tiedens, L. Z. (2001). Anger and advancement versus sadness and subjugation: The effects of negative emotion expressions on social status conferral. *Journal of Personality and Social Psychology, 80*, 86–94.

Tinsley, C. H., O'Connor, K. M., and Sullivan, B. A. (2002). Tough guys finish last: The perils of a distributive reputation. *Organizational Behavior and Human Decision Processes, 88*, 621–642.

Tjosvold, D. (1994). Team organization: An enduring competitive advantage. New York: John Wiley and Sons.

Tjosvold, D. (2006). Defining conflict and making choices about its management: Lighting the dark side of organizational life. *International Journal of Conflict Management, 17*(2), 87–96.

Tomlinson, F. (2005). Idealistic and pragmativc versions of the discourse of partnership. *Organization Studies, 26*(8), 1169–1188.

Tooby, J. and Cosmides, L. (1992). The psychological foundations of culture. In J. H. Barkow, L. Cosmides, and J. Tooby (eds.), *The Adapted Mind: Evolutionary Psychology and The Generation of Culture*, pp. 19–136. Oxford, England: Oxford University Press.

Torrance, E. P. (1972). Can we teach children to think creatively? *Journal of Creative Behaviour*, 114–143.

Tost, L. P., Hernandez, M., and Wade-Benzoni, K. A. (2008). Pushing the boundaries: A review and extension of the psychological dynamics of intergenerational conflict in organizational contexts. In J. Martocchio, H. Liao, and A. Joshi (eds.), *Research in Personnel and Human Resources Management, 27*, 93–147.

Triandis, H. C. (1980). Values, attitudes, and interpersonal behavior. In H. E. Howe and H. M. Page (eds.), *Nebraska Symposium on Motivation*. Lincoln: University of Nebraska Press.

Triandis, H. C. (1989). The self and social behavior in differing cultural contexts. *Psychological Review*, *96*(3), 506–520.

Triandis, H. C. (1994). *Culture and Social Behavior*. New York, NY: McGraw Hill.

Tse, D. K., Francis, J., and Walls, J. (1994). Cultural differences in conducting intra- and inter-cultural negotiations: A Sino-Canadian comparison. *Journal of International Business Studies*, *25*, 537–555.

Turnbull, A. A., Strickland, L. H., and Shaver, K. G. (1976). Medium of communication, differential power, and phasing of concessions: Negotiating success and attributions to the opponent. *Human Communication Research*, 2, 262–270.

Tversky, A. and Kahneman, D. (1981). The framing of decisions and the psychology of choice. *Science*, *211*, 453–458.

Ueda, K. (1974). Sixteen ways to avoid saying no in Japan. In J. C. Condon and M. Saito (eds.), *International Encounters with Japan*, pp. 185–192. Tokyo: Simul Press.

Ury, W. (1991). *Getting Past No*. New York, NY: Bantam Books.

Ury, W. L., Brett, J. M., and Goldberg, S. B. (1988). *Getting Disputes Resolved*. San Francisco, CA: Jossey-Bass.

Uzzi, B. and Dunlap, S. (2005). How to build your network. *Harvard Business Review*, *83*, 53–60.

Uzzi, B. and Lancaster, R. (2003). Relational embeddedness and learning: The case of bank loan managers and their clients. *Management Science*, *49*, 383–399.

Vallacher, R. R. and Solodky, M. (1979). Objective self-awareness, standards of evaluation, and moral behavior. *Journal of Experimental Social Psychology*, *15*, 254–262.

Valley, K. L., Moag, J., and Bazerman, M. H. (1998). A matter of trust: Effects of communication on the efficiency and distribution of outcomes. *Journal of Economic Behavior and Organization*, *34*, 11–238.

Valley, K. L., Moage, J. and Bazerman, M. H. (1998). 'A matter of trust': Effects of communication on the efficiency and distribution of outcomes. *Journal of Economic Behavior and Organization*, *34*, 211–38.

Van Vugt, M. and De Cremer, D. (1999). Leadership in social dilemmas: The effects of group identification on collective actions to provide public goods. *Journal of Personality and Social Psychology, 76,* 587–599.

Vazire, S. and Gosling, S. D. (2004). E-perceptions: Personality impressions based on personal websites. *Journal of Personality and Social Psychology, 87,* 123–132.

Wade, M. E. (2001). Women and salary negotiation: The costs of self-advocacy. *Psychology of Women Quarterly, 25,* 65–76.

Wallace, P. (1999). *The Psychology of the Internet.* New York: Cambridge University Press.

WalmartWatch.com, Research Team, May 29, 2008. Issues–Supplier Relationships.

Walters, A., Stuhlmacher, A., and Meyer, L. (1998). Gender and negotiator competitiveness: A meta-analysis. *Organizational Behavior and Human Decision Processes, 76,* 1–29.

Walther, J. B. (1992). Interpersonal effects in computer mediated interaction. *Communication Research, 19,* 52–90.

Walther, J. B. (1996). Computer-mediated communication: Impersonal, interpersonal, and hyperpersonal interaction. *Communication Research, 23,* 3–43.

Walther, J. B. and Bunz, U. (2005). The rules of virtual groups: Trust, liking and performance in computer-mediated communication. *Journal of Communication, 55*(4), 828–46.

Walther, J. B., Anderson, J. F., and Park, D. W. (1994). Interpersonal effects in computer-mediated interaction: A meta-analysis of social and antisocial communication. *Communication Research, 21,* 460–487.

Walther, J. B. and Tidwell, L. C. (1995). Nonverbal cues in computer-mediated communication, and the effect of chronemics on relational communication. *Journal of Organizational Computing, 5,* 355–378.

Walton, R. E. and McKersie, R. B. (1965). *A Behavioral Theory of Labor Negotiations: An Analysis of Social Interaction Systems.* New York: McGraw-Hill.

Wang, C. S. and Leung, A. K-y (in press). Cross-cultural reactions to honesty and deception. *Personality and Social Psychology Bulletin.*

Watkins, M. (2000). *Negotiation Analysis: A Synthesis.* Boston, MA: Harvard Business School.

Watkins, M. (2002). *Breakthrough Business Negotiation.* San Francisco: Jossey-Bass.

Watson, J. B. (1913). Psychology as the behaviorist views it. *Psychological Review, 20,* 158–177.

Weber, J. M. and Murnighan, J. K. (2008). Suckers or saviors? Consistent contributors in social dilemmas. *Journal of Personality and Social Psychology, 95,* 1340–1353.

Weech-Maldonado, R. and Merrill, S. (2000). Building partnership with the community: Lessons from the camden health improvement learning collaborative. *Journal of Health Care Management, 45*(3), 189–205.

Weingart, L. R., Hyder, E. B., and Prietula, M. J. (1996). Knowledge matters: The effect of tactical descriptions on negotiation behavior and out-comes. *Journal of Personality and Social Psychology, 70,* 1205–1217.

Weingart, L. R., Thompson, L. L., Bazerman, M. H., and Carroll, J. S. (1990). Tactical behavior and negotiation outcomes. *International Journal of Conflict Management, 1*(1), 7–31.

Weisband, S. and Atwater, L. (1999). Evaluating self and others in elec-tronic and face-to-face groups. *Journal of Applied Psychology, 84*(4), 632–639.

Weiss, S. E. (1987). Creating the GM-Toyota joint venture. *Columbia Journal of World Business, 22*(2), 23–37.

Weiss, S. E. (1997). Explaining outcomes of negotiation: Toward a grounded model for negotiations between organizations. In R. J. Lewicki, R. J. Bies, and B. H. Sheppard (eds.), *Research on Negotiation in Organizations,* pp. 247–333. Greenwich, CN: JAI Press.

White, R. K. (1984). *Fearful Warriors: A Psychological Profile of U.S.-Soviet Relations.* New York: Free Press.

Whyte, G. and Sebenius, J. K. (1997). The effect of multiple anchors on anchoring in individual and group judgment. *Organizational Behavior and Human Decision Processes, 69,* 75–85.

Wiesenfeld, B. M., Raghuram, S., and Garud, R. (1999). Managers in a vir-tual context: The experience of self-threat and its effects on virtual work organizations. In Trends in Organizational Behavior, (ed.) C. L. Cooper and D. Rousseau, *6,* 31–34.

Wiggins, J. (2009, September 10). Cadbury rejection is just for starters. *Financial Times.* Retrieved from http://www.ft.com

Wilkinson, C., Browne, M., and Dweyer, P. (2002). Partnerships: Imperative or illusion in work-force development. *Drug and Alcohol Review, 21,* 209–214.

Williams, J. E. and Best, D. L. (1982). *Measuring Sex Stereotypes: A Thirty Nation Study.* Beverly Hills, CA: Sage.

Wilson, P. A. (1997). Building social capital: A learning agenda for the twenty-first century. *Urban Studies, 34,* 745–760.

Wit, A. and Wilke, H. (1990). The presentation of rewards and punishments in a simulated social dilemma. *Social Behavior, 5,* 231–245.

Wolfe, R. J. and McGinn, K. L. (2005). Perceived relative power and its influence on negotiations. *Group Decision and Negotiation, 14*(1), 3–20.

Wong, E. and Maynard, M. (April 27, 2003). A taut, last-minute stretch to save an airline [Electronic Version]. *The New York Times.* Retrieved December 28, 2009.

Woodruff, D. (1999, March 31). Renault bets Ghosn can drive Nissan. *Wall Street Journal,* p. 1.

Woolcock, M. and Narayan, D. (2000). Social capital: Implications for development theory, research and policy. *The World Bank Research Observer, 15,* 225–249.

Yamagishi, T. (1986). The provision of a sanctioning system as a public good. *Journal of Personality and Social Psychology, 51,* 110–116.

Yates, J. F., Lee, J. W., Shinotsuka, H., Patalano, A. L., and Sieck, W. R. (1998). Cross cultural variations in probability judgment accuracy: Beyond general knowledge overconfidence. *Organizational Behavior and Human Decision Processes, 74,* 89–117.

Young, R. (1976). Invention: A topographical survey. In Tate, G. (ed.), *Teaching Composition: 10 Bibliographical Essays,* pp. 1–43. Fort Worth, TX: Texas Christian University.

Yukl, G. (1994). *Leadership in Organizations.* Englewood Cliffs, NJ: Prentice Hall.

Yukl, G. and Falbe, C. (1990). Influence tactics and objectives in upward, downward, and lateral influence attempts. *Journal of Applied Psychology, 75,* 132–140.

Yukl, G. and Tracey, B. (1992). Consequences of influence tactics used with subordinates, peers, and the boss. *Journal of Applied Psychology, 77*, 525–535.

Yukl, G., Kim, H., and Falbe, C. (1996). Antecedents of influence outcomes. *Journal of Applied Psychology, 81*, 309–317.

Yukl, G., Chavez, C., and Seifert, C. (2005). Assessing the construct validity and utility of two new influence tactics. *Journal of Organizational Behavior, 26*, 705–725.

Zaheer, A., McEvily, B., and Perrone, V. (1998). Does trust matter? Exploring the effects of interorganizational and interpersonal trust on performance. *Organization Science, 9*, 141–159.

Zajonc, R. B. (1965). Social facilitation. *Science, 149*, 269–74.

Zak, P. J., Kurzban, R., and Matzner, W. T. (2005). Oxytocin is associated with human trustworthiness. *Hormones and Behavior, 48*, 522–527.

Zartman, W. I. and Rubin, J. Z. (2000). *Power and Negotiation.* Ann Arbor: University of Michigan Press.

Zetik, D. C. and Stuhlmacher, A. F. (2002). Goal setting and negotiation performance: A meta-analysis. *Group Processes and Interpersonal Relations, 5*, 35–52.

Zhang, D., Foo, N., Meyer, T., and Kwok, R. (2004). Negotiation as mutual belief revision. *Knowledge Representation and Reasoning*, 317–322.

Zheng, J., Veinott, E., Bos, N., Olson, J. S., and Olson, G. M. (2002). Trust without touch: Jumpstarting long-distance trust with initial social activities. In *Proceedings of the SIGCHI 2002 Conference on Human Factors in Computing Systems*, pp. 141–6. New York, NY: ACM Press.

Zyphur, M. J., Narayanan, J., Koh, G., and Koh, D. (2009). Testosterone–status mismatch lowers collective efficacy in groups: Evidence from a slope-as-predictor multilevel structural equation model. *Organizational Behavior and Human Decision Processes, 110*, 70–79.

Index